D0082837

"Through Sunshine and Shadow"

McGILL-QUEEN'S STUDIES IN THE HISTORY OF RELIGION
G.A. Rawlyk, Editor

Volumes in this series have been supported by the Jackman Foundation of Toronto.

1 Small Differences
Irish Catholics and Irish Protestants, 1815–1922
An International Perspective
Donald Harman Akenson

2 Two Worlds
The Protestant Culture of Nineteenth-Century Ontario
William Westfall

3 An Evangelical Mind
Nathanael Burwash and the Methodist Tradition in Canada, 1839–1918
Marguerite Van Die

4 The Dévotes
Women and Church in Seventeenth-Century France
Elizabeth Rapley

5 The Evangelical Century
College and Creed in English Canada from the Great Revival to the Great Depression
Michael Gauvreau

6 The German Peasants' War and Anabaptist Community of Goods
James M. Stayer

7 A World Mission
Canadian Protestantism and the Quest for a New International Order, 1918–1939
Robert Wright

8 Serving the Present Age Revivalism, Progressivism, and the Methodist Tradition in Canada
Phyllis D. Airhart

9 A Sensitive Independence
Canadian Methodist Women Missionaries in Canada and the Orient, 1881–1925
Rosemary R. Gagan

10 God's Peoples
Covenant and Land in South Africa, Israel, and Ulster
Donald Harman Akenson

11 Creed and Culture
The Place of English-Speaking Catholics in Canadian Society, 1750–1930
Terrence Murphy and Gerald Stortz, editors

12 Piety and Nationalism
Lay Voluntary Associations and the Creation of an Irish-Catholic Community in Toronto, 1850–1895
Brian P. Clarke

13 Amazing Grace
Studies in Evangelicalism in the United States, Canada, Britain, Australia, and Beyond
George Rawlyk and Mark A. Noll, editors

14 Children of Peace
W. John McIntyre

15 A Solitary Pillar
Montreal's Anglican Church and the Quiet Revolution
Joan Marshall

16 Padres in No Man's Land
Canadian Chaplains and the Great War
Duff Crerar

17 Christian Ethics and Political Economy in North America
A Critical Analysis of U.S. and Canadian Approaches
P. Travis Kroeker

18 Pilgrims in Lotus Land
Conservative Protestantism in British Columbia, 1917–1981
Robert K. Burkinshaw

19 "Through Sunshine and Shadow"
The Woman's Christian Temperance Union, Evangelicalism, and Reform in Ontario, 1874–1930
Sharon Anne Cook

"Through Sunshine and Shadow"

The Woman's Christian Temperance Union, Evangelicalism, and Reform in Ontario, 1874–1930

SHARON ANNE COOK

McGill-Queen's University Press
Montreal & Kingston • London • Buffalo

ISBN 0-7735-1305-1

Legal deposit third quarter 1995
Bibliothèque nationale du Québec

Printed in Canada on acid-free paper

This book has been published with the help of a grant from the Canadian Federation for the Humanities, using funds provided by the Social Sciences and Humanities Research Council of Canada.

McGill-Queen's University Press is grateful to the Canada Council for support of its publishing program.

Canadian Cataloguing in Publication Data

Cook, Sharon A. (Sharon Anne), 1947–
"Through sunshine and shadow": the Woman's Christian Temperance Union, evangelicalism, and reform in Ontario, 1874–1930
(McGill-Queen's studies in the history of religion ; 19)
Includes bibliographical references and index.
ISBN 0-7735-1305-1
1. Woman's Christian Temperance Union – History.
2. Women's rights – Ontario – History. 3. Women's rights – Ontario – Religious aspects – History.
4. Evangelicism – Ontario – History. 5. Temperance – Ontario – History. I. Title. II. Series.
HV5239.06C66 1995 305.42'09713 C95-900207-3

Typeset in Palatino 10/12
by Chris McDonell, Hawkline Graphics

Contents

Acknowledgments

The completion of this book has been assisted by the generosity of several research institutions. The project is supported by the Aid to Scholarly Publications branch of the Social Science Federation of Canada. I am indebted to the staff at the National Archives of Canada, the National Library of Canada, and the Archives of Ontario, where Bennett McCardle, manager of public services, and Leon Warmski and Carolyn Heald, reference archivists, were particularly kind and helpful. Ed Phelps, then chief of the Regional Collection at the University of Western Ontario, was extremely cooperative in my search for the London District documents. The Ottawa YWCA permitted me to make use of its records while they were being catalogued.

Other individuals have contributed to the successful completion of this work. As copy editor, Elizabeth Hulse has improved this manuscript in many ways. I am appreciative of her sharp eye, patience, and intelligent questions. Grant Carr-Harris, son of Bertha Wright (Carr-Harris), gave me full access to his personal archives and genealogies. His and Mrs Carr-Harris's gracious hospitality while I worked through the papers made the research a very pleasant experience. I have been astonished at the knowledge and commitment of the Rev. Jim Collins, especially as it relates to Bertha Wright. He has been a great source of inspiration for me.

Throughout the period of research and writing, I have been on the Faculty of Education at the University of Ottawa. I am grateful for the support accorded me by my colleagues, most particularly by Cheryll Duquette. Special gratitude is reserved for Jeff Lanther and Louis Lattion, computer technologists in the Faculty of Education, who were able to unlock the many mysteries of WordPerfect for me.

The ideas of several members of the History Department at Carleton University have been beneficial and stimulating in my work. I am especially indebted to Marilyn Barber, John Taylor, and Brian McKillop. My doctoral thesis supervisor, Deborah Gorham, was encouraging throughout the process of researching and writing the dissertation, on which this work is based. She was incisive in her questions, and a continual source of wonder through the force of her academic and personal example. George Rawlyk and Marguerite Van Die of Queen's University have provided important insights into the religious thought of the women of the Ontario WCTU.

Through both Carleton and the University of Ottawa History Departments, I have been a member of two women's history reading groups. Both have been invigorating and helpful in clarifying many of the ideas contained in this book. Several members of these groups deserve note: as mentioned, Deborah Gorham and Marilyn Barber, as well as Beverly Boutilier, Naomi Griffiths, Ruby Heap, Lorna MacLean, and particularly Dianne Dodds and Diana Pederson, who have made very valuable suggestions for parts of this work. Reading groups are especially important for those of us who teach outside our field of research. But they also serve an important function as support groups. Many members of the third reading group of which I am a proud member – SWIVEL, the meaning of whose name has been lost in the mists of the last decade – have also been instrumental in the refining of many notions associated with the WCTU, not the least of which concerns the significance of enduring friendships that result in distinct local culture. Hélène Beauparlant, Heather Blackburn, Kerry Callan-Jones, Eileen Fairbairn, Beth Handley, Kerry Houlihan, Elizabeth McCullough, Heather MacDonald, Lorna Miller, Bob Pierce, Jane Reid, and Joyce Thompson have carved a collective identity very different from that characterizing the local WCTUs but quite as satisfying.

This research topic has been a part of my extended family's interests for many years. My great-aunt, Annie R. Fry, was an "independent woman," a teacher, and dominion superintendent of the WCTU medal contests during the 1920s and 1930s. When I was a child, she was a source of admiration for me. Both her example and that of my parents, Ethel and Harold Killins, staunch temperance advocates, Christian humanitarians, and challenging intellectuals, have fed my interest in this topic for many years. My research necessitated lengthy periods at the Archives of Ontario in Toronto. During this time I was fortunate to be cared for – in sickness and in health – by my remarkable sister-in-law, Suzanne Killins, and my brother, David. In the finest tradition of the WCTU, Suzanne took charge of my physical and emotional needs and, with David, welcomed me into their warm family life. Their kindness will never be forgotten.

It is difficult to imagine that anyone could have a more supportive and interesting family than I enjoy. My sons, Timothy and Graham, have buoyed me with their patience, interest, and unfailing good humour. I have become convinced that the WCTU prescriptive literature on mother-son relationships would have been improved if a few lads like my sons had served as models. My husband, Terry, has read and heard more about the WCTU than he would otherwise have chosen, I am certain. My gratitude for his generosity in editing this manuscript, questioning me closely about problems, and providing unwavering support is beyond my ability to express. One of his numerous talents is the production of creative titles, many of which he suggested for this book. I will always regret that I could not see my way to entitling this work *Through a Bottle Brightly*. Sadly, that will stand as one of life's lost opportunities.

With all this help and consideration, I acknowledge any deficiencies in this work as, of course, my responsibility alone.

The Home for Friendless Women, Wellington Street, Ottawa, ca. 1885 (National Archives of Canada [NAC], PA-26742)

Bertha Wright's residence and YWCTU house, 98 Albert Street, Ottawa, 1890 (NAC, PA-027203)

The Ottawa YMCA, June 1930 (NAC, PA–27414)

The folding room at the Home for Friendless Women, Ottawa, ca. 1885 (NAC, PA–27434)

Bertha Wright, ca. 1890 (Photograph by Topley; NAC, PA–167608)

Letitia Youmans, president of the Ontario WCTU (Archives of Ontario [AO], MU 8471–13)

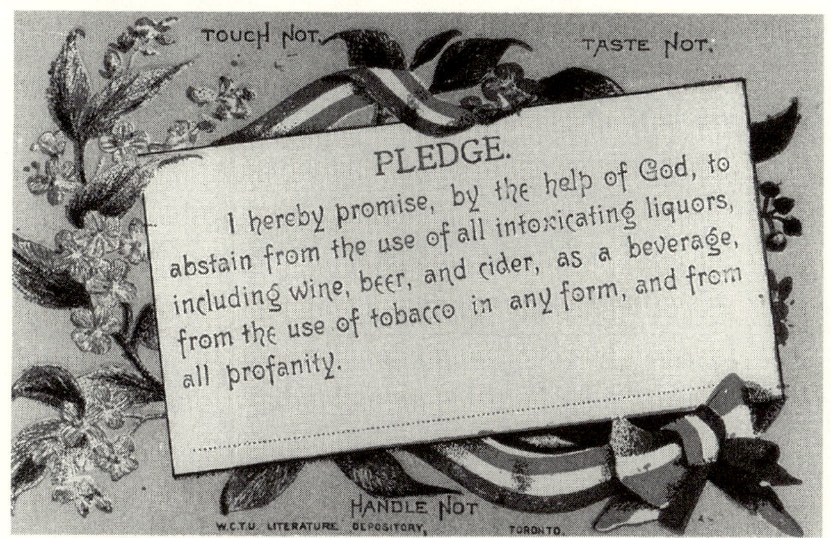

A "triple pledge" card issued by the WCTU (AO, MU 8397–3)

DEATH CARS

The drinking driver is the greatest single hazard on our highways.

"At least fifty percent of all fatal accidents are caused by drinking."

Dr. J. M. Russel,
Teacher's Manual for Alcohol Education,
Toronto.

Canadian W. C. T. U., 11 Prince Arthur Avenue, Toronto

A card handed out by WCTU members during their temperance drives (AO, MU 8397–3)

The Templar Quarterly.

A SOCIAL REFORM MAGAZINE.

VOL. 3. HAMILTON, CANADA, AUGUST, 1897. NO. II.

WCTU

TEMPLAR

WELCOME TO THE WORLD'S WOMEN.

PRESIDENT RUTHERFORD (Miss Canada):

The cover of the *Templar Quarterly,* August 1897 (AO, MU 8471)

The WCTU headquarters in Toronto in 1897 (AO, MU 8471–13)

The Dominion W.C.T.U. RECITER

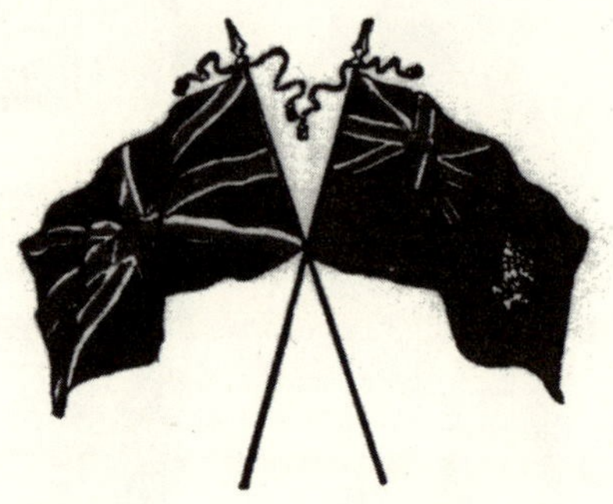

Senior No. 2

FOR SALE AT

Canadian National W.C.T.U. Literature Depository
76 Byron Avenue, London, Ont.

PRICE 25 CTS.

One of several "reciters" used by WCTU medal contestants (AO, MU 8472–19)

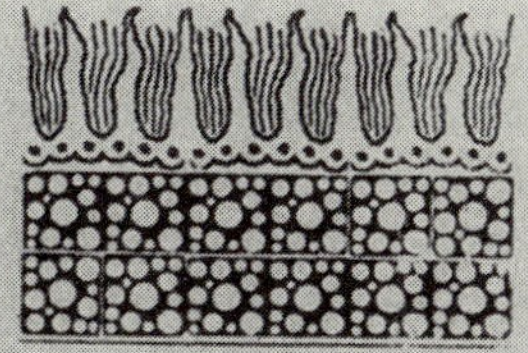

White Life Truths ....

A Schoolroom Story

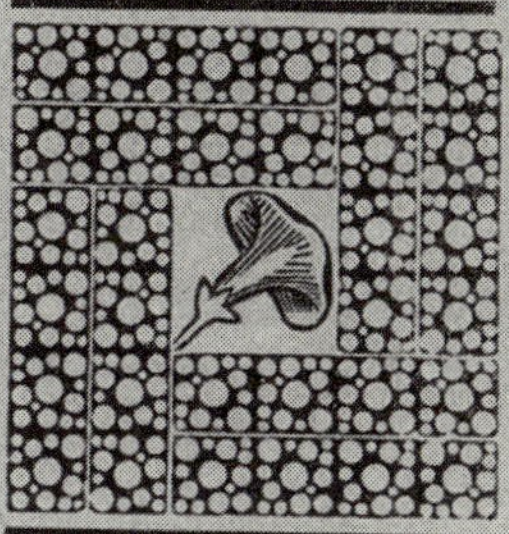

By MISS F. A. DANARD, B.A., with a Word to Parents by SAMUEL FARMER and Prefatory Note by J. W. L. FORSTER

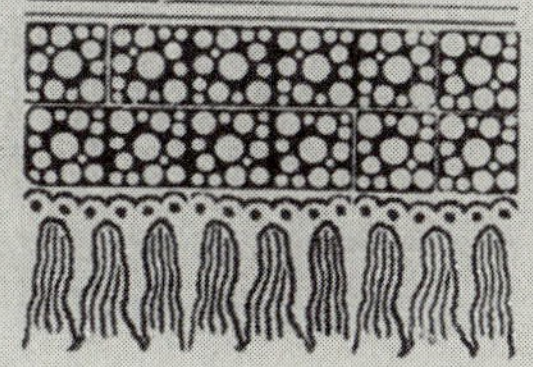

Sweet childish days that were as long
As twenty days are now.
—*Wordsworth*

The cover of one of the social purity pamphlets produced by the Canadian WCTU (AO, MU 8288–1)

PLEDGE

"I promise, by God's help. to abstain from all intoxicating drinks, and to try to induce others to do the same."

Name ....

Date ....

The man who indulges in Alcohol lays himself open to chances of tubercular infection. His children are born with a diminished power of resisting this disease.—SIR VICTOR HORSLEY.

Mothers! Taking of Alcoholic drink such as beer or wine

Before Birth, it Starves! After Birth, It Stunts!

Orders for Requisites for the working of this Department to be obtained of

CANADIAN NATIONAL W.C.T.U. LITERATURE DEPOSITORY

97 Askin Street - London, Ontario

Price of this Leaflet—2c each, 50c per 100.

The Mother's Promise Leaflets

"The Little White Ribboners"

●

A Department of Work of the

CANADIAN NATIONAL WOMAN'S CHRISTIAN TEMPERANCE UNION

●

NATIONS

are gathered out of

NURSERIES

The cover and back of a leaflet in the Mother's Promise series (AO, MU 8288–3)

LITTLE WHITE RIBBONERS

BADGE—A Band of White Ribbon tied in a Bow on Left Wrist.

Dear Friend:

Thousands of little ones (from babies up to 7 years of age) are already enrolled among the

"LITTLE WHITE RIBBONERS"

by mothers who wish to bring up their children with a record of Total Abstinence, and to dedicate them at the very beginning of life to this great cause.

We hope you may wish to add the name of your little one to our Roll by signing the promise given on the next page and handing it in with TEN CENTS* to your Local Superintendent. We will then give you a Card to certify enrollment, and on which to keep a yearly record, which we trust will keep us in touch with you both.

"The Hope of the Race is in the Child," and we invite your hearty co-operation in our effort to train up a race that shall not know the taste of alcohol.

Yours very truly,

THE SUPERINTENDENT

of the Little White Ribboners.

Adopted by the Canadian National Woman's Christian Temperance Union.

THE MOTHER'S PROMISE

"I hereby place my child's name among the Little White Ribboners, promising not to give or allow him (or her) to take any intoxicating Drink."

[No Mother who takes alcohol during the period of nursing can enroll her baby until it is weaned.]‡

Child's Name ....

....

Age .... Date of Enrollment ....19.......

Mother's Name and Address } ....

....

....

Is Mother herself a Total Abstainer? ....

***The only expense in connection with this Enrollment is TEN CENTS, to be paid before name is entered on the Roll.**

Date of Payment:	Name of Receiver:
....	....
	....

‡For Pledge See Over

A pledge card for the Little White Ribboners (AO, MU 8288–3)

LAYING OF THE CORNER STONE

OF THE HEADQUARTERS BUILDING AND WILLARD HALL OF THE DISTRICT UNION OF TORONTO OF THE WOMAN'S CHRISTIAN TEMPERANCE UNION, 16 TO 22 GERRARD STREET EAST NOV. 30, 1911, AT 3.30 P.M.

Announcement of the laying of the cornerstone for the WCTU building in Toronto in 1911 (AO, MU 8289–5)

Frances Willard, president of the National (American) WCTU and the World's WCTU, ca. 1897 (AO, MU 8471–13)

"LET'S EXHIBIT"

W. C. T. U.

FAIRS AND EXHIBITS DEPARTMENT

PROVINCE OF ONTARIO

W.C.T.U. — at the Kitchener-Waterloo Industrial Exhibition, September, 1949.

Approximately 20,000 leaflets and blotters were distributed by the various Church groups, of the W.C.T.U., during the five days.

A three-tiered revolving table was used for display of free literature. A small bookcase was used for books suitable for teachers and church workers. The "Stop and Go" Sign drew attention to the booth. Fresh flowers were brought in every day.

INSTRUCTION FOR WORKERS

Before fair time have literature made into bundles, perhaps two leaflets and a blotter for each one. Carefully sort literature, suitable for distribution to children or adults.

Be sure and have your name on your booth. We are proud of the W.C.T.U.

Young people love to do something worthwhile. Ask them to help you with the literature.

Make your booth, or Exhibition project a matter of prayer for guidance and strength.

Study available literature so that you may give a reason for your faith. Many people do not know the simplest facts about alcohol or what it does.

Be kindly, courteous and **please** do not argue with anyone.

SUGGESTIONS FOR EXHIBITS

A large placard on the wall above a table:

"What this country amounts to depends on what happens to its homes."

Flier sent to exhibitors by the WCTU Fairs and Exhibits Department (AO, MU 8406 F885)

CHAPTER ONE

Introduction

On a wintry night in Hull of 1890, Bertha Wright and a "brave little band" of female temperance workers caused a riot that reverberated through Ottawa society, eventually reaching the floor of the House of Commons. The *Ottawa Daily Citizen* described this religious upheaval as follows:

A Band of evangelistic workers announced a few days ago by handbills distributed throughout Hull, that meetings would be held every Tuesday evening in that city in a hall at the corner of Duke and Queen streets ... It seems that preparations were made by a gang of roughs, headed by an unlicensed saloon keeper, to give the new-comers a warm reception; in fact, the intention was more or less openly expressed to 'clean them out.' The band of evangelists was composed of Miss Bertha Wright, accompanied by a considerable number of young ladies ... On opening the doors of the Hall a crowd of about TWO HUNDRED MEN well primed with liquor rushed in and filled the place. For a time, their interruptions were confined to noises, etc., but on being remonstrated with they made an attack on the speaker and singers. For a time everything was in confusion, and there was reason to fear the worst, missiles being thrown and blows freely given, but not returned. The young women who were present joined hands and formed a circle around the speakers, and the roughs refrained from striking them but confined their efforts to separating the little band ... Finally the police managed to clear the hall and took the Ottawa people to the station, fighting off the crowd with their batons all the way. At this time some of the young women were badly hurt by the missiles that were thrown.[1]

The young women were members of Ottawa's Young Woman's Christian Temperance Union. The Hull mission had been established by Bertha Wright and the YWCTU to accomplish several objectives. As with their similar mission in Ottawa, these zealous young women hoped to lure men and women from local bars to the mission hall, where temperance leaflets and evangelical addresses would encourage listeners to begin the long process of moral reform. In addition, intemperate mothers with children would be invited to the YWCTU-supported Home for Friendless Women. But the first meeting in Hull had gone very badly, and judging from the *Citizen*'s account, the women and their male supporters were lucky to make it back to Ottawa alive. The popular image of the Victorian woman would strongly suggest that young women exposed to such rough treatment would retreat to the safety of home and family, resolving never again to jeopardize their security and virtue by a public display of this sort. This is not how the story ends, however, perhaps calling into question too easy assessments of the typical Victorian woman's behaviour.

Ottawans were strongly supportive of Bertha Wright and "her gallant little band of workers."[2] Editorials defended her right to freedom of speech and action, and deplored the "supremacy of ruffianism"[3] and Hull's apparent disinclination to "assert the supremacy of the law."[4] Both Sir John A. Macdonald and Wilfrid Laurier in the House of Commons denounced the "brutal and cowardly" violence.[5] Even the Hull press was embarrassed by the "bagarre sanglante." Like the *Citizen*, *Le Spectateur* applauded the attempts of Bertha Wright and the other women evangelists to present a brave front to the mob. "Voyant leurs directeurs de conscience menacés, elles formèrent un cercle, une espèce de garde protectrice autour d'eux dans l'espoir de les sauver des coups de la foule amentée." The Hull paper did find it amusing, however, that one of the male evangelists had promised to "treat" his attacker if he would agree to stop beating him, commenting that "il etait comique, même au milieu du carnage, d'entendre les plaintes des Reverends qui pensaient en être quitte en offrant du whiskey aux ameutés."[6]

But the battle did not end here, for Bertha Wright fully intended to carry on with her evangelistic meetings, and apparently the ruffians of Hull were just as determined to run the young women out of town. By 11 February, *Le Spectateur*'s embarrassment had turned to irritation. On that evening a second riot occurred, this time involving a hostile crowd estimated by the *Citizen* at four hundred. While Hull's press granted the evangelists the technical right to exercise the freedom of their religion, "ils devraient comprendre que quand l'exercise d'un droit est une insulte à une population on ne l'exerce pas." The paper supported the Hull police chief's recommendation that the "Reverends protestants" stay at home unless they "veulent éviter un conflit comme celui dont ils ont été la cause."[7]

In Ottawa, much criticism was levelled against the inadequate protection provided by Hull police. A sympathetic Citizen reporter noted: "It was said that special constables were to be sworn in, that the Hull police would be out in force, and that everything would be conducted decently and in order. If any of these special protectors were present, it was impossible to observe their efforts. Practically, as it appeared to the onlookers, the mob did just as it pleased."[8] The *Evening Journal* was even more condemnatory of Hull's police, the police chief, and even the entire citizenry. "That the police authorities of Hull are either Bigots, who have no desire to protect Protestants from mob violence, or are imbeciles who don't know how, does not relieve the people of Hull from the onus of allowing murderous fanaticism to run riot in their streets."[9] Where, indeed, were the Hull police during the mêlée? Did their noticeable absence signal their discomfort with Bertha Wright and her "gallant little band's" intention to bring spiritual light to their shadowed lives?

In this second and more serious riot, the women evangelists were themselves attacked and knocked down. The *Evening Journal* described the scene as one "of the wildest excitement and disorder compared with which last Tuesday's proceedings were mild."[10] The *Citizen* suggested that the offending "toughs and sluggers" be "tied to a whipping post and lashed by the people of that city, a vast majority of whom, are law abiding, God-fearing and generous spirited."[11] One report made to the House of Commons suggested that the "fact that murder was not committed was more accident than intention on the part of the rioters."[12] Not surprisingly, the Hull press, while defending the right to religious freedom in its city, clearly resented the women's presence there. In response to a charge in the *Free Press* that personalized the issue by reminding Hull of the many services provided to that city by Bertha Wright's revered ancestors (her great-grandfather Philemon Wright had founded Hull), *Le Spectateur* replied huffily, "Mlle Wright, faisant valoir tous les bienfaits accordés à la ville par ses parents, oublie de dire que ces derniers n'ont jamais fait don à Hull de sermons insensés comme ceux qu'elle delivre ici."[13]

Although Bertha Wright insisted in an interview with The *Citizen* that "the meetings must be continued,"[14] she was convinced that they should be held by her Hull associates "till order and quiet are secured."[15] Plans were also made to move the mission to a less vulnerable location on one of the front streets. Not to be edged out of the furore she had created, she remained very much in charge behind the scenes, writing letters – including one to Quebec's premier, Honoré Mercier, in which she demanded to know how he proposed to "vindicate the law" – lobbying civic and religious authorities, and developing her network with such groups as the Dominion Evangelical Alliance. Nevertheless, her active patronage of the Hull mission was on the wane, and she seems to have fairly gracefully given up any hope of reforming the Roman Catholics of Ottawa's twin city. Several weeks later, in an address to the Evangelical Alliance, Wright surveyed the wreckage of "the unfortunate Hull mission," noting that the

> people of Hull have not had the gospel preached to them by force, on the contrary every effort had been made to avoid the appearance of endeavor to compel them by earthly power to allow the meetings to be held. Unfortunately for themselves and the honor of the city, their church and their province, they had attacked and damaged the hall, herself and her workers, and worse than all stirred up an intense feeling on the part of the Protestant community which it would be exceedingly difficult to allay ... Hull needed the Gospel and by His Grace they would endeavor to carry it thither week by week.[16]

Just who were these fearless young women? They belonged to a dynamic youth group within the Woman's Christian Temperance Union, one of the most productive, yet today forgotten, evangelical temperance organizations in nineteenth-century Ontario. Its central evangelical task was to reform society around the concept of a reconstituted family committed to Christian values. These women not only had a major impact on Canadian society, but reflected a leading religious and intellectual current of their age. This book is their story.

The last quarter of the nineteenth century in Canada was a period of profound social change and uncertainty. The dislocating effects of industrialization, immigration, urbanization, apparent heightened continentalism, imperial decline, and secularization in public life were mirrored in a deep concern about the survival of the family unit as it had been idealized in nineteenth-century literature. Worries about the family centred on changing patterns of sexual morality, the appropriate role of women and children, and the "intemperate" behaviour of men. The latter included men's tendency to enjoy violence in sports, a double standard of sexual morality, resulting in a "white slave trade," their indulgence in personally destructive pastimes, such as gambling and tobacco use, and very important, their violent behaviour towards wives and children, often as a result of drunkenness.

One of the organizations founded in this period to ameliorate the many dangers faced by the family unit was the Woman's Christian Temperance Union. The National (American) WCTU was founded in

1874 at an international Sunday school conference in Chautauqua, New York. One of the participants at this meeting was Letitia Youmans from Picton, Ontario. An evangelical temperance youth worker, Sunday school teacher, and stepmother of eight, she established a Canadian WCTU branch in her home town later the same year, an Ontario WCTU convention in 1877, and a Canadian organization in 1888.

The Woman's Christian Temperance Union was one of the largest non-denominational women's organizations of the nineteenth century in Canada.[17] By 1914 the dominion level maintained a membership of just over 16,000, while the Ontario branch's total exceeded 8,000. In Ontario it retained a strong appeal far into the twentieth century for middle-class women, particularly those in small towns and rural areas. But the WCTU represented much more than a temperance organization: it became the nucleus for the development of a distinct women's middle-class culture which included, but also transcended, temperance. Its appeal was thus more fundamental than issues of temperance or the desire for class respectability.

This book argues that the culture characterizing the women of the Ontario WCTU in the late nineteenth and early twentieth centuries was based on an evangelical vision for society, which in turn created a liberated climate for women that some scholars have termed "evangelical feminism." It was evangelicalism's emancipating theology that originally empowered women and caused them to approach temperance as a moral and religious issue, not simply a social one. It was evangelicalism's campaigns that taught women the power of effective collective action and provided them with a rationale to take progressive action against male vices. And it was evangelicalism's support for the ideology of the central place of home and family that continued to validate the progressive behaviour of these conservative women. Without evangelicalism's strengthening influence, the many disappointments faced by Ontario's WCTU would likely have dulled the edge of their anger, their optimism, and their resolve much more than was the case. Between 1874 and 1930 the women of the Ontario WCTU developed an evangelical feminist ideology with a distinct code of personal and public behaviour, a broad program of social activism, and a legislative strategy. While there were differences between unions, the tenets of evangelical feminism are clearly visible in the women's thoughts and actions in the nineteenth century. As conservative evangelicalism was supplanted for many Ontario WCTU women during the 1920s by a more limiting fundamentalism, the movement described in this book consequently lost its momentum and its influence.

The second half of the nineteenth century was also characterized by the construction of a definable Canadian middle class. In this period,

> the focus of evangelicalism began to shift from that of a specific religious disposition centred in the Christian revelation to a more general (and ultimately more secular) moralism concerned with ethical conduct, with "culture." Gradually the evangelical need for personal conversion waned, but it left an important attitudinal residue: the "high seriousness" embodied in the word "earnestness," itself a reflection of the larger phenomenon of an emergent middle class that was attempting to define its mission.[18]

The WCTU mission was central to this process of middle-class construction, for the moral virtues of "work, sobriety, thrift, duty, and the sanctity of family life" underlying this awakening class consciousness were the special purview of women as they sustained and reinforced family life through an evangelical code. These virtues underlined the "complementarity of evangelical and middle-class values [which] served implicitly to discount those of other groups."[19] An analysis of the origins, structures, strategies, and ideas of the Ontario WCTU also helps, therefore, to illuminate the process of middle-class construction.

The WCTU organizational structure will be discussed at length in chapter 3, but some brief comments about how the levels interacted are appropriate here. The WCTU operated through local unions, which had an executive and a series of departments of work headed by a superintendent. The local union's president and departmental superintendents reported to the provincial executive and relevant departmental superintendents. Once a year, representatives of the local unions met with the provincial executive at a convention, where reports were received and resolutions debated. The provincial executive and superintendents reported to the dominion body, which in turn reported to the secretariate of the World's WCTU (with its departmental superintendents) and conventions. The American organization, called the National WCTU, acted as a mentor in the Ontario WCTU's earliest days, but no formal reporting arrangements existed between either the Ontario or dominion and the National WCTU.

Previous studies of women's groups have relied almost exclusively on the national records, which represent a narrow élite in urban centres.[20] Such records naturally reflect the ideas and actions of relatively homogenous groups that evinced a common mind-set, including a resigned acceptance of the gradual erosion of conservative evangelical ideals after 1900. Yet this resignation is not reflected in the organization's local records. While the present inquiry is grounded in provincial and dominion documents, it also reflects extensive use of the minute books of individual rural, town, and urban WCTU unions from the 1870s to the 1940s. These local records provide a detailed account of WCTU activities and views throughout the province. Admittedly "official" in orientation, the minute books tell a great deal about the ideas of women at the meetings, their reactions to directives from "headquarters," and frictions within the union and the community. All of these ideas and activities were filtered through the pen of the union's corresponding or recording secretary. There is no doubt that as a group the remarkably literate and energetic union secretaries spoke in a different voice than the organization's provincial or dominion leaders and that local secretaries interpreted events differently from their leaders – distinctions that widened over time. The secretaries, many of whom served in their positions for decades, were important vehicles for the creation and expression of local women's culture; along with other key members of the local unions, they monitored community and members' behaviour, recorded and often critiqued presentations and entertainments, and translated provincial and dominion events for local consumption. In short, they served as participant historians for the twenty-five unions across Ontario for which records from this period survive.

Women involved at the local level tended to occupy less affluent and influential positions within the middle class than did those at the dominion level and to exercise their authority in different ways.[21] As the twentieth century progressed, the motivation, work, and rhetoric of the local organizations became increasingly dissimilar to those of their provincial and dominion counterparts. During the nineteenth century, WCTU women at all levels held to a fairly common understanding of society and their role within it. However, as conservative evangelicalism altered to meet the challenges of biblical criticism, and secularism, industrialization, and immigration, the local unions and provincial leadership reacted differently. At the provincial and dominion executive levels, the records show a gradual rejection of evangelical ideas from the early 1890s. Many local unions held to traditional evangelicalism far longer. In the early twentieth century, local women gradually came to accept many of the ideas of the new fundamentalism. In a number of ways, this fundamentalism resembled the evangelical position common in nineteenth-century Ontario. In one respect, however – the public role of women – the two differed dramatically. Where evangelicalism had acted as a liberating force for women, fundamentalism constricted their lives. The ragged acquisition of new ideas and the shedding of old also demonstrates that class development assumes different forms in urban, small-town, and rural districts. The intersection of gender, class, and religion in specific town and urban sites helps to uncover patterns of change and continuity in women's lives.

The widening gap between women's ideas at the organization's various levels was undoubtedly also due to the bureaucratization and evolving notions of professionalization amongst women occupying leadership positions in the provincial and national WCTU.[22] However, as the WCTU became ever more marginalized at all levels – a process well advanced by the 1920s – the provincial and dominion executives also adopted fundamentalist rhetoric at their conventions and in publicity leaflets.

From the middle of the nineteenth century until the beginning of the twentieth, the dominant form of religious expression in most Protestant denominations in Britain, the United States, and Canada had been evangelicalism.[23] Nineteenth-century evangelicals believed that the world was sunk in original sin and that each individual faced eternal death and damnation unless he or she invited God's saving grace to enter the soul, to become "born again." This personal salvation could be transformed into love for others. William Westfall has noted that "the divine method of human improvement begins in human hearts through evangelical truth, and it spreads from within outwardly till all is renewed."[24] Unlike the "personal morality" espoused by Dwight L. Moody in his urban revivals of the late nineteenth century,[25] Ontario evangelicalism assumed the existence of a community of believers. John Webster Grant describes the process through which a community that had experienced salvation could induce conversion in the sinful by disseminating literature (including Bibles, manuals of devotion, and tracts) and staging prayer meetings and rallies to awaken the sinner's hunger for salvation.[26] "Within evangelicalism there was no clear-cut dichotomy between one's personal relation with God and the commitment to building a social order based on Christian principles; they were integrally related,"[27] notes David Marshall.

As part of this spiritual renewal, evangelicals sought to create nurturant communities by upholding the primacy of the family and sanctity of the home while at the same time condemning all frivolous pastimes, particularly dancing, gambling, and alcohol consumption. Canadian and American evangelicalism also included a strong tradition of female piety,[28] which had its roots in American women's earlier activity in revivalism, abolitionism, and the Women's Crusades against the liquor trade in 1873 and 1874.[29]

Many scholars argue that in the late nineteenth century, the evangelical consensus was shattered, splitting into "liberal" and "conservative" camps.[30] In general, the latter held a view of salvation as being personal and experiential, rather than societal, and an analysis of society as being composed, ideally, of sanctified, Christian family units in which moral leadership was exercised by the "angel in the house" – the mother.[31] Liberal evangelicalism reflected the view that individual salvation depended on the collective cleansing of society as a whole, and it eventually became a constituent element of social gospelism. During the nineteenth century, the women of the Ontario WCTU, as well as many leaders at the dominion level, who combined their evangelical religiosity with temperance reform and voluntarist social activism, reflected conservative evangelicalism. But with the changes wrought within the religious community by such factors as biblical criticism, WCTU members who held official posts within the provincial and dominion organization moved away from conservative evangelicalism towards a more liberal stance. At the same time, some accepted the elements of fundamentalism, with its fears of modernism, consumerism, and the breakdown of the family unit.[32] Most local union members were drawn to the apocalyptic principles of fundamentalism. Sectors of the Ontario WCTU executive and rank and file were thus more ideologically reconciled than they had been in twenty years.

The notion of evangelical feminism has been developed by American historians, who argue that in the nineteenth century, women used their base of power in evangelical religion to serve their own ends in fashioning an ideology of the importance of home, with women as the primary vehicles of redemptive power, as "embodiments of a pure community of feeling."[33] The long-range result of women's association with evangelical revivalism, argues Nancy Hardesty, was to prepare the nation for nineteenth-century feminism. Revivalism's "theology and practice motivated and equipped women and men to adopt a feminist ideology, to reject stereotyped sex roles, and to work for positive changes in marriage, church, society, and politics."[34] This interpretation, also shared by Nancy Cott,[35] Anne Boylan,[36] Sandra Sizer,[37] and Kathryn Sklar,[38] is in opposition to the earlier work of Barbara Welter, which argued that the idealized view of womanhood exemplified by the "cult of true womanhood"[39] was created by men to marginalize nineteenth-century middle-class women. Welter asserts that women's continuing involvement in evangelical religion added credence to the cult of true womanhood by threatening neither republican ideals nor male authority and by validating such behaviours as submissiveness, domesticity, and purity.[40] Martha Blauvelt supports this view: "Victorian America insisted that the 'true woman's' very nature was pious: religiosity, it was declared, was synonymous with femininity."[41]

Research into Canadian women's involvement with religion generally, not to mention the specific effect of Protestant evangelical ideals on women, is much more recent. Ruth Compton Brouwer finds a "persistent pattern of avoidance" in Canadian historical writing relating to women's experience with religion, which reflects the trend in England, if not that in the United States.[42] Her own work has explored the importance of the foreign missions movement to Canadian Presbyterian Church women in India, the "siren call to a vocation and to a larger life," and the institutional and social services accomplished by this zealous group.[43] Rosemary Gagan has examined the work and the personnel of the Woman's Missionary Society of the Methodist Church between 1881 and 1925, particularly the expanded opportunities for leadership by single women who served as its representatives in Canada, Japan, and China.[44] In tracing the transformation of the Canadian revivalist tradition and the reconstruction of the Methodist identity, Phyllis Airhart examines the Methodist mandate for religious activism, which sparked the growth of voluntary associations and created a public function for women. "Daily life was invested with religious significance as men and women aspired to conform their personal behaviour, homes, and communities to evangelical ideals."[45] The egalitarianism implicit in revivalist movements created a special role for women's leadership in religious and philanthropic projects. This and other aspects of the evangelical tradition have been examined by George Rawlyk.[46] Diana Pedersen has surveyed the evangelical roots and social ethic of the national Young Woman's Christian Association.[47] Marguerite Van Die's study of Nathaniel Burwash emphasizes the importance of family worship, under the steady guidance of his mother, Anne Taylor, in shaping his evangelical faith.[48] Katherine McKenna has considered the importance of evangelical ideals in the life of Harriet Dobbs Cartwright,[49] while the links between evangelical notions and militant moral-reform movements in late-nineteenth- and early-twentieth-century Canada are examined by Mariana Valverde.[50]

As in several of the aforementioned studies of Canadian evangelical women, the history of the Ontario WCTU demonstrates that the tradition of feminine piety imbued women, not with an unquestioning acceptance of clerical and male authority, but with a sense of moral superiority and righteousness that bred discontent with a society apparently rejecting the primacy of the family and the sanctity of the home. In the case of the Ontario WCTU, this evangelical piety also provided self-identity, collective consciousness, and organizational strategies for women themselves.

The importance of conservative evangelical religion (with its affinity to temperance) to Ontario women – and their considerable contribution to the development of a distinctive Protestant culture in the last half of the nineteenth century – has been under-recognized by mainline Canadian historians. The role of male or female conservative evangelicals is unexamined by either Richard Allen in his celebrated study of the social gospel or by Ramsay Cook in his award-winning *The Regenerators*. While this omission is partially corrected in the fine work of John Webster Grant[51] and William Westfall,[52] who carefully trace the evangelical tradition in Ontario, neither examines in any detail the particular role of women in that tradition or the shaping by conservative evangelicalism of non-denominational organizations such as the WCTU.[53]

The Ontario WCTU provided a forum for middle-class women to become active participants in their own communities long before they were accorded the prerequisites of full citizenship through the right to vote. Their involvement was initiated through religious duty and temperance reform. Yet temperance was for them a "constellation" issue, which involved not only temperance *per se*, but also several associated – and ultimately more important – concerns, through which women expressed their outrage at male violence and irresponsibility, their fears for the survival of the family unit, and, eventually, their collective demands for legislative solutions to these problems. Evangelicalism asserted that "the enemy is the spirit of the world, silently blotting out any true awareness of the Christian destiny of man and the life of moral earnestness it demanded."[54] The spirit of the world could only be denied, in evangelical thought, within the fortress of the home:

> The home was a source of virtues which were nowhere else to be found, least of all in business and society. And that in turn made it a place radically different from the surrounding world ... it was a place apart, a walled garden, in which certain virtues too easily crushed by modern life could be preserved, and certain desires of the heart too much thwarted be fulfilled ... a sacred place, a temple.[55]

It is not difficult to appreciate the power of the romanticizing of home and of the woman who ruled in that private sphere. "Evangelicalism was never really a theological system so much as a way of life," writes Ian Bradley. "It did not present itself to its adherents as a logical set of beliefs but rather as a series of vivid and compelling personal experiences."[56] In A.B. McKillop's recent analysis, it was "a temper, a disposition ... Its appeal to the individual conscience broadened in the nineteenth century into a general moral seriousness that gave religious sanction to secular self-improvement."[57] As a malleable and improving disposition, it was also open to individual interpretation, particularly to the shaping influences of women placed in powerful positions.[58] So too, proponents of evangelical feminism emphasized the critical importance of the home in providing a refuge from an evil world and a base for this self- and societal improvement. As "mother" in this sanctified space, women "could tame, and ultimately save, the rest of the world."[59] As one local WCTU recording secretary put it, "No nation rises higher than its Motherhood."[60]

The WCTU continues with a much reduced program to this day. Still, it must be admitted that when taken in perspective, the groundbreaking ideas and work of the Ontario WCTU were in decline by about 1900. After that date, it was edged out of the public eye by a range of temperance organizations which were more adept at using, and more committed to forcing, legislative change. Nevertheless, in its heyday before 1900, the WCTU in Ontario succeeded in legitimizing a number of controversial causes, including the provision of a wide range of social services for isolated men and poor women and children, the placing of a compulsory course on "scientific temperance" in the public school curriculum, the passage of several pieces of legislation to protect young women, the provision of education for working- and middle-class children, and the validation of a public role for women distinguished by neither class prerogative nor formal education. In so doing, the WCTU reflected the experience, concerns, and talents of many Ontario women.

CHAPTER TWO

Origins: "Not to Buy, Sell or Give Alcoholic Liquors While I Live"

The first local Ontario Woman's Christian Temperance Union was organized by Letitia Youmans in Picton, Prince Edward County, in December 1874. The organization had been founded in Fredonia, New York, almost a year earlier, but the National WCTU was not constituted until its convention, held in Cleveland in November 1874. Fired by the evangelical enthusiasm of the Cleveland convention, Youmans resolved to plant the WCTU in Ontario soil. That the first local union arose in a small town rather than in an urban setting is indicative of the profile which the WCTU would maintain in the province. That it was founded by the evangelical Letitia Youmans also set the Ontario WCTU apart from its mother organization in the United States.

LETITIA YOUMANS: FOUNDER OF THE ONTARIO WCTU

From her childhood, Youmans had held to an evangelically inspired critique of social ills and solutions. Born in 1827 on a farm near Cobourg, Letitia Creighton was raised in an intensely evangelical Methodist household, in which she had experienced the excitement of revivalism. As a young girl, she presented herself for prayers at a revival meeting, but to her distress, although supported by her family, she was turned away because of her youth. Long after the event, she recalled: "This seems to me to have been a mistake. Christians instead of bringing the children to Jesus, too often allow them to grow up in sin, until their hearts are so hardened as to be almost impervious to the Spirit's influence. Never, at any subsequent period, have I had keener consciousness of sin, nor a higher sense of my responsibility to God than I had at this time."[1]

Youmans's childhood had also been indelibly marked by the almost gothic sufferings of townspeople sacrificed to alcoholism. In later years, she made effective use of these shocking portraits in her discussions with young people and in her speeches and writings. She was well aware of the powerful impact of the bizarre and grotesque contrasted with sentimentalized innocence. For example, in her recollections of her youth, she describes coming upon the rotting body of the local drunkard, "swarming with worms" after he had lain unattended and unmissed for days. "This was my first impressive temperance lesson and I still look back to it with horror."[2] In another story, Youmans tells of the next-door neighbour, a "heart-broken wife and mother" who sewed to support herself and her children, "while the man who had promised at God's altar to support and protect her until death, and who might have had a first-class salary as an accountant, was spending what little he did earn in a bar-room and sharing the pittance of his wife's earnings with the children." One day his children discovered his liquor hidden in the long grass and ran to tell their mother. She had them lead her to it, whereupon she announced:

> "Children, I want you to kneel down," and then, holding up the bottle, said, "Here is the cause of all our trouble, and the reason I have to work so hard, and why you cannot get books to go to school, and sometimes we have not even enough food or fire to keep us warm. Now, there is one thing that would make me suffer still more than I have yet, that is, if one of my children should ever get to be a drunkard, it would break my heart. Raise your right hands to heaven" (they raised those little hands, with streaming eyes fixed on their mother). "Now," said she, "I want you to promise – and God will hear the vow – that you will never taste anything that would make you a drunkard." They made the solemn promise while she broke the bottle.[3]

There is no way of knowing how true to time or place this story was. Without any doubt, however, stories such as this one struck a chord with Youmans's audiences, and most particularly with women who harboured many fears: of their economic dependence on morally compromised husbands; of the beguiling, catastrophic effects of alcohol; of innocent children being led astray by their fathers' poor examples. Of course, Youmans was not alone in recognizing the value of a good story: much temperance literature was developed on the same model.[4] The difference lay in her use of this narrative tradition to develop a critique of intemperance which privileged the plight of women and children. From this position, she developed a structure for temperance education with a specific focus on women and children.

Youmans's belief that education and evangelicalism were inextricably linked was representative of prevailing thought in Ontario Methodism and North American evangelicalism.[5] The connection was further developed by her attendance at Professor Van Norman's Ladies' Seminary at Cobourg, where Friday evenings were devoted to religious services involving all the denominations represented in the school. These too were strongly revivalist in tone. As she was to describe one later, "[I] rose and from that moment I felt that I was committed to the service of God, and in a little prayer-meeting a few evenings afterwards, with a few of my schoolmates, who, like myself, were seeking to realize the pardoning love of God, we were enabled to venture upon the sin-atoning sacrifice, and claim Jesus as our Saviour, and take Him as our guide."[6] Her developing sense of piety and duty pointed her towards a life-view that Sandra Sizer has called "evangelical domesticity." This ideology placed women as the sacred centre of domestic life, in contrast to the masculine and intensely competitive world of business and politics.[7]

After graduation the young Letitia taught at Van Norman's Cobourg Ladies' Seminary (later to be relocated in Burlington); at another women's seminary in Picton, and at the common school in that same community. Her life long interest in evangelical education attests to her belief in its value to achieve personal and societal reform. Letitia Creighton's teaching career at the Picton Ladies' Academy was cut short when she decided to marry a widower with eight children. In 1850, at the age of twenty-three, she gave up schoolteaching to care for her merchant husband and his young family. Nevertheless, her marriage by no means ended her efforts to achieve a society imbued with evangelical principles through education. In fact, Youmans's new role as wife and mother seems to have given her greater confidence to undertake her most outstanding public achievements.

With her supportive husband, she became deeply involved throughout the 1850s and 1860s with the Grand Lodge of the Order of Templars, the only one of the temperance lodges to accord women full equality in membership, office holding, and speaking rights.[8] Youmans was representative of many temperance women in this period who had held executive positions with the Templars, serving a kind of apprenticeship in temperance work, before re-routing their allegiance and energies to the WCTU. She served as lodge superintendent of juvenile work and was also an editorial member of the Templars' *Temperance Union*.

Youmans was the main proponent in Ontario of the successful juvenile Bands of Hope organization. Active too in Sunday school temperance work, she travelled with her husband to a Sabbath School

Convention at Lake Chautauqua in 1874. Later that same year, she began the WCTU in her town. In 1875 she established the first urban union in Toronto, and became the inaugural Ontario WCTU president in 1877 and Dominion WCTU president at the organization's initial Ottawa meeting in 1885.[9] She went on to have a prominent role at the World's level and with the American National WCTU.

Letitia Youmans was widely recognized as a "woman of brains and power" and as an outstanding orator.[10] Her fervour could cause trepidation in those against whom it was directed. An early historian of the Ontario WCTU credits Youmans's demands for a scientific temperance course in the public schools as the source for the government's nick name for the WCTU: "Women Constantly Troubling Us." When the education minister provided an inadequate response to the Ontario WCTU's request for a course in temperance, "Mrs. Youmans, metaphorically, took her slipper to Hon. Geo. Foster ... Mr. Foster's critic certainly left her mark, if not on his body, at least on his spirit."[11] A Canadian Frances Willard, she was the Ontario WCTU's strongest personality. However, as the organization's pioneer organizer, Youmans drafted a different blueprint for the Ontario and Canadian organizations than Willard used for the American. More decentralized in structure, more consciously evangelical in ethic, and less inclined to fight legislative battles, the Ontario WCTU developed a separate identity almost from the start.[12]

THE CANADIAN STRUCTURE

No Ontario structure was set up until 1877, and even then, and for several years thereafter, the focus of provincial work was the convening of annual conferences. Because of the personal friendship of Letitia Youmans and Frances Willard, president after 1879 of the National (American) WCTU, the Ontario and American organizations kept in close communication throughout much of the nineteenth century.

By the 1880s the WCTU had been organized in several other provinces, and by 1883 a Dominion WCTU was established in Montreal by representatives of the Ontario and Quebec provincial unions. The primary function of the dominion level was to hold conventions and to speak for the WCTU on national matters. The Dominion WCTU was a pioneer association in being the first non-denominational woman's group in Canada to organize on the national level.[13] Wendy Mitchinson credits the Dominion WCTU with providing a national podium for women, a chance for such women to broaden their perspective on public issues, and the confidence to speak out on such issues.[14] While this is undoubtedly true, the Dominion WCTU was a "late starter" in comparison with the provincial and local unions, where far more substantial work was accomplished. The Dominion level's work was not representative of the typical WCTU activities during this era. Increasingly, the national group saw itself as a rather august political forum where florid sentiments were expressed, resolutions passed, and high-profile guests honoured.[15] Neither the provincial nor the county level devoted as much time to posturing in this way. Thus, because she based her comments almost exclusively on the dominion level of the WCTU and very heavily on the leadership at that level, Mitchinson's analysis of the motivation, work, and impact of the WCTU in Canada is somewhat distorted.

THE WORLD STRUCTURE

Founded in 1885, the World's Woman's Christian Temperance Union first met in Boston six years later. It drew almost 3,000 delegates and visitors. At the centre of the meetings, rallies, and social activities was Frances Willard of the National WCTU, the new president, and her British friend and champion, Lady Henry Somerset.[16] Willard and Somerset's close personal relationship was reflected in the American and British dominance in this organization. While Canadian representatives regularly attended its conventions, the World's WCTU was an even later starter than the Canadian dominion organization had been. It did not reach its peak in membership and influence until 1927.[17] Thus, with the notable exception of the dispute over Lady Henry Somerset's stand on social purity in 1896–98, in which a Canadian contingent led a revolt against the World's WCTU vice-president, the world organization's concerns and influence was generally remote from that of the Ontario WCTU.[18]

THE ONTARIO ORIGINS

The Ontario WCTU had its origins in several types of American and British temperance organizations: the temperance society and lodge, the Women's Crusades and the resulting National Woman's Christian Temperance Union, the Sunday school movement, and the Bands of Hope. The American influence through male temperance groups, evangelical women's initiatives, and the original WCTU was undoubtedly stronger than the British in the early and mid nineteenth century. American male temperance groups established a tradition in Ontario that further informed the early Ontario WCTU efforts. Non-evangelical and male-directed, these temperance lodges and societies had different motivations and used different tactics in their campaign to rid the province of "demon rum." As Ontario women had learned to cooperate with male temperance groups, the models set by the Women's Crusades and the American WCTU were also adapted to the Ontario setting. The British influence was felt mainly in the Ontario WCTU's work with children. Techniques pioneered by the Sunday school movement and the Bands of Hope provided the Ontario organization with an enduring focus for this work. Even though the Sunday schools and Bands of Hope had predated the WCTU, the Ontario union pioneered strategies to disseminate the temperance cause through Sunday schools, and it took over control of most Bands of Hope from temperance societies. Its multi-pronged program to educate youth shaped the WCTU in Ontario. The result was an organization that differed from both its mentors and from Canadian male-dominated temperance groups as well.

AMERICAN INFLUENCES

The first American temperance reformer was Dr Benjamin Rush, whose major concern was the effect of alcohol on health. His 1785 pamphlet *An Enquiry into the Effects of Ardent Spirits on the Human Body and Mind*[19] became a model for the medical temperance lecture. The cause in Ontario was pioneered by Peter Scholefield, who delivered a similar message in his lecture in June 1828. In arguing the medical implications of alcohol, Scholefield cited "an instance where a whole family, a woman and several children, died the last winter entirely from the effects of ardent spirits. I have been credibly informed that the coroner of the District of Bathhurst has held about twenty inquests over dead bodies, and that every one, without exception, had been produced by ardent spirits."[20] Temperance societies from the United States appeared soon afterward in British North America.[21] By the early 1830s, it has been estimated there were about one hundred with around 10,000 members.[22]

The American temperance societies had developed along two lines. The Massachusetts Society for the Suppression of Intemperance had tried to unite the social élite in enforcing standards of morality on an intemperate lower class. Much of the early temperance literature, produced between 1839 and 1859, reinforced this approach by pitching its stories to the working class and intemperate poor and emphasizing the contemptible lives of those who imbibed.[23] By contrast, the American Temperance Society sought self-reform by emphasizing the qualities of respectability and encouraging intemperate individuals to gain regeneration through total abstinence. It was this second model that was generally adopted by temperance societies in Canada.

However, in the case of the temperance lodges, one finds also a modification of the first model. Here members of the upper stratum of the working class, bent on self-improvement, attempted to turn themselves into an élite group within the community by enforcing moral standards in an often intemperate community. Similarly, the WCTU used a mixture of the two approaches. Its evangelicalism placed the onus on the alcohol imbiber, while its program of social and political activism tried to establish a community standard through law and custom. In so doing, it attempted to have its group defined as the moral élite in each community and to create a special space for itself in the jockeying for position that inevitably accompanied the development of a middle class.

The leaders of the American Temperance Society were mainly evangelical clergy.[24] American preachers of the Methodist, Presbyterian, and Quaker denominations had long spoken out against intemperance, but until the early nineteenth century the afflicted were encouraged to take a personal pledge of temperance. The temperance society as transplanted to Canada was sometimes associated with a specific congregation and sometimes not. But one common element held: the society made this pledge a social contract with others who were like-minded. The societies also introduced the issue of the morality of intemperance in both societal and spiritual terms.

Typical of the temperance society of this period was that created by the community of Beaver River:

> We, the undersigned, firmly believing and most assuredly gathering that the use of spirituous liquor is prejudicial to the body and soul of mankind in general, both spiritual and temporal, and to remedy this great and spreading evil. We, therefore, whose names are hereunto annexed, do forever renounce the use of ardent or distilled spirituous liquors of any kind except what may be taken as a medicine in case of sickness. And we pray Almighty God to establish our hearts and strengthen our serious resolutions.[25]

Thus by mid century, intemperance by male groups was condemned on medical, social, and moral grounds. Nevertheless, in spite of the grand language and ardent appeal to the deity, there was as yet no widespread acceptance of either total abstinence or involvement of Canadian denominations in the movement. The concept of total abstinence is credited to Joseph Livesay, a merchant and social reformer of Preston, England, who formulated the teetotal pledge in 1832.[26] This hardening of the position of abstinence in temperance circles was encouraged by evangelical moral principles. It, in turn, was reflected in evangelicals taking tougher positions on other issues of the day, for example, on animal cruelty and sabbath breaking.[27] Thereafter, however, total abstinence was quickly adopted by the Canadian movement, and in line with the more rigid stance on leisure, rejection of alcohol was often grouped with strictures against profanity and the use of tobacco. The churches in Canada did not formally support the temperance movement until very late in the century. For most of the nineteenth century, then, Canadian temperance was a secular, though morally grounded, program of abstinence from alcohol and usually tobacco as well.

TEMPERANCE LODGES

The temperance lodge or fraternal society reached what is now Canada through New Brunswick from the United States in 1848.[28] A year later, temperance lodges were established in Upper Canada.[29] The lodge provided sickness insurance and funeral benefits for male members and their wives, as well as alcohol-free recreation in exchange for a pledge of total abstinence. Benefits were paid only to members in good standing, which meant adherence to the pledge of total abstinence from all intoxicants.[30] These self-help groups, such as the Sons of Temperance, the Independent Order of Good Templars, and the Royal Templars of Temperance, grew rapidly throughout the century, peaking and declining just as dramatically near the century's close.[31] The minute books for the Sons of Temperance in Orono, Ontario, provide us with a full account of the process of acquiring members, the mutual monitoring, the substance of the meetings, and the ideas that appear to have motivated the lodge. Espousing a vague Christianity, the lodges' non-evangelical motives set them apart from the later Ontario WCTU, while at the same time influencing the WCTU's approach to intemperance.

The Sons of Temperance at Orono attempted to interest members of the community in their lodge by staging "programs" or entertainments. Generally a program evening would begin with a speech from the chairman, followed by other impromptu addresses or songs. On 3 April 1878, for example,

> Bro Dean from Kirby Division on being called on made a speech, which was followed by one from Bro Dean of Orono after which Bro Dean (Kirby) gave another speech. he [*sic*] was then called on for a song which he gave. he [*sic*] then said he would sing song about with any or all members of the Division. Sisters Pierce & Vinson then favored the Div. with a song after – according to promise – Bro Dean sang another but as there were no more who accepted Bro Dean's challenge the amusement stopped.[32]

On another occasion a program included a covenant reading, a chapter reading, a musical selection followed by one unspecified reading and one entitled "Downey's Slaughter," a recitation, another chapter reading, and a final musical number. Sometimes skits were offered, at other times debates.[33] Paid lecturers worked their way through the province,[34] and prohibition literature was studied and distributed.[35] Thus new members were solicited by presenting programs that would appeal to those bent on self-improvement and within an oral tradition where one could hope to improve one's expository skills.

Individuals indicating a desire to join the lodge were sponsored by members in good standing. An investigation committee was then named to look into the suitability of the candidate. It appears from the Orono example that the committee was required to be of the same sex as the candidate. Following a favourable report from the committee, the members voted for or against the candidate's admission. Typically, five negative votes from the existing membership meant refusal of a candidate.[36] Sometimes an unsuccessful candidate could present himself or herself for re-election, as in the case of the persistent Mr Best. After having received a positive assessment from the committee, the candidates "were then balloted for and with the exception of A. Best declared elected ... Moved and Seconded that we reconsider the case of Mr. Best. Carried. He [Mr Best] was then balloted for and again rejected."[37] Acceptance was followed by an initiation ceremony and the conferring of an "order" or position in the lodge.

Had Mr Best been accepted, however, there is no guarantee that his association with the Sons of Temperance would have been a long one. The first minute book opens with the expulsion of a Brother Heney and the curt admonition that "his name be entered on the black book."[38] Thereafter, charges are hurled back and forth amongst the company: Brother Copeland charged brothers Watson, McDonald, and Hunter with "violating article 2 of the constitution by drinking spirituous liquors."[39] Brother Lang, having been similarly accused and convicted, forfeited "all honors previously carried by this bro ... Ballots was [*sic*] then taken & Bro Lang was declaired [*sic*] expelled ... instructed to erase his name from the books."[40] Sometimes, however, a member known to have transgressed could still retain his membership. "Bro. C.T. Mallon acknowledged having violated Article II of our constitution. The Division then proceeded to ballot on the question of expulsion and Bro Malon's [*sic*] membership was declared retained."[41] He was far luckier than most; given the expulsion rates, it is amazing that any members dared to attend meetings. Perhaps one reason why prospective and accepted members continued to brave their peers' suspicion and criticism was their need for a personal support group to remain temperate, a sort of nineteenth-century Alcoholics Anonymous. The records are strongly suggestive of a lodge membership which frequently strayed from sobriety. Operating under the guise of reforming others, the lodges clearly had as a prime motive to reform themselves. Certainly, their custom of exposing members to regular examination of behaviour, and implicitly of character, is reminiscent of the early Ontario Methodist practice of requiring that prospective itinerant ministers join a weekly class where the candidate "would be examined on his or her spiritual progress and encouraged to seek further growth in grace."[42] Intense self-examination of motive and act was a common theme of most early-nineteenth-century Ontario religious groups. It remains a staple of support groups such as Alcoholics Anonymous.

Perhaps people came also for the energetic discussions. These seem often to have gotten out of hand: "The W.P. then gave a few remarks asking the members to aid him in the discharge of his duties and saying that he wanted to have Good Order and was going to have it, and that he hoped the members would in future conduct the discussions in the Division in a more Brotherly manner than he had seen several times of late, and concluded by thanking the Division for electing him to the office of head of the Division."[43] In addition to accusations of backsliding and defence or capitulation by the member, meetings discussed the arrangements for visiting lecturers,[44] the generally critical state of their finances,[45] the lodge's funeral benefits,[46] the provision of pledge cards,[47] the possibility of organizing a youth corps (called "cadets"[48]), and attendance at temperance conventions.[49] But the business of a meeting held in October 1879 deserves to be quoted at length because of its presentation of ideas held by and about a typical temperance lodge. A visiting Sons of Temperance official made a visit and brought greetings. He also

> made reference to a report, which he heard from some person on the street. That our Dramatic Company while practising the Drama "The Little Brown Jug" had on Monday evening left the "Brown Jug" partly full of whiskey. Bros. J. Allen and F. Squair replied to last part of Bro. Walkley's speech saying that they did not have any "Brown" Jug at their practice on Monday evening. Bro. Callahan thought the report was groundless, and that it had been started by some person to injure the Division. he [*sic*] said that those who buy Whiskey do not often leave it for others to drink and therefore those who drank the Whiskey out of the Brown Jug were the same who put it in. Bros Smith and Morrison though [*sic*] the story was not worthy of our notice. Bro. Daniel Allen said he thought the main fault was the way in

which the doors of the hall is secured, that had they been properly fastened that story could not have been started. Bro Walkley agreed with Bro Allen that the evil lay in the carelessness of the Division, he said he did not credit the report when he heard it but that he thought if it could be talked about outside it could be in this Hall.[50]

The tendency to wild and hurtful accusation, even by an outside official, is clear in this instance, as in others. That the lodge had generated some hostility in the community is also apparent: Brother Callahan assumes that the story has been created by someone wishing to "injure" the division, and Brother Allen opines that the problem is an ill-fitting door, thus eloquently conveying a garrison mentality. The secrecy of lodge proceedings to reduce the liability of public exposure is also apparent.[51] The self-righteousness of the lodge shines. One wonders at the wisdom of presenting a play clumsily satirizing demon whisky in a community that seems to be devoted to its consumption. Even the imagery is informative: sly metaphors are used abundantly, suggesting a group given to colourful language and speech making. Perhaps most interesting, however, is the discussion's conclusion as to where to lay the blame: not with the visiting dignitary who spreads malicious stories, not with a community that ridicules the lodge's efforts to dramatize the alcohol problem, but with the "carelessness of the Division." In the firm tradition of self-help groups, the error is seen to be interior to the lodge and to lie with lodge members.

The lodge was not alone in detecting hostility from the community. The women of the Newmarket WCTU complained plaintively that "roughs congregate in front of the Temp Hall during Lodge hours making outsiders believe the disturbance is caused by the members. Where are our constables?"[52] This was a embattled collection of characters, attempting, it seems, to improve the moral tone of the town or at least themselves.

Undoubtedly, the WCTU learned from the lodges' acrimonious relationships with their communities. There is no evidence from the Ontario WCTU records of similar vandalism of union quarters or meetings. This was largely because the tactics used by the women in the WCTU were non-confrontational and generally indirect. There is also no indication in the organization's records that the members were themselves drawn to alcohol, as was the case with lodge members. This too must have provided greater credibility and less hostility from the community for the WCTU.

One element of temperance lodge life that obviously was attractive to its participants was the highly ritualized meeting, including positions with elegant titles.[53] Since the drama of lodge life was played out in secret, members could act their parts to outrageous excess without fear of outsiders' ridicule.[54] For instance, the Royal Templars of Temperance were fond of medieval militaristic imagery: the officers included the select councillor, who opened the meeting with the Royal Decree, the herald, the guard and sentinel, and members of varying grades, including the Select and Royal Degrees.[55] Minutes note the appropriate drapery for the chairperson's table and the use of impressive gavels.[56] Again, the Sons of Temperance adopted elaborate regalia, decorating both the meeting rooms and the officers and members of the order.[57] But how were the costumes used? Were ritual handshakes and greetings exchanged as in the Masonic Order? Did the temperance lodges, like the Orange Order, stage marches as well as entertainments?[58]

The rituals cannot be discerned from the available literature. It does seem safe to conclude, however, that the pomp and ceremony of the temperance lodge satisfied a need to feel important and experience a sense of community in small-town Ontario. This conclusion is supported by Canadian research carried out by Lynne Marks on Thorold, Campbellford, and Ingersoll, Ontario, where she discovered that lodge members tended to be male, working class, and less likely than their female working-class counterparts to be church members.[59] American findings about the profile of members in the Sons of Temperance in Beverly and Salem, Massachusetts, are similar: the majority were found to be younger, poorer, and less likely to hold church membership or town office than were prohibitionists in their communities.[60] These findings present another point of contrast with the WCTU, which depended very little on ritual and ceremony, particularly in the early years. The Ontario WCTU's evangelicalism, it will be argued, endowed the members with an ardent sense of personal importance and group identification, based, not on ritual and ceremony, but on service to others.

The Ontario temperance lodges admitted both men and women to membership. This practice broke with the model of many American temperance lodges, which until 1867 established women's auxiliaries or separate women's organizations, such as the Daughters of Temperance, instead of permitting women full membership.[61] In one acrimonious convention of the American Sons of Temperance in 1852, the Daughters of Temperance were not permitted to speak. Sustained male opposition to women's full participation in the lodge convinced many women to transfer their energies to the women's rights movement.[62]

After its founding in 1852, the Good Templars lodge provided a training ground for women interested in temperance activism, as was the case with Letitia Youmans. The Templars were the first of the lodges to accord women full equality. Women's enthusiasm for the temperance cause through lodge activities is reflected in surviving records of Ontario's lodges. The records of the Wardsville Royal Templars of Temperance and the Orono Sons of Temperance indicate that women represented a significant proportion of the membership roll in both. In 1899, for example, thirty-eight of one hundred and five members in the Wardsville Royal Templars of Temperance were women.[63] Particularly in the Templars lodge, there is ample evidence of women participating in programs, helping to arrange entertainments, and acting as officers.[64] The records also suggest that many of the members, particularly the female members, were young and single; Marks's analysis of lodge members in Thorold and Campbellford supports this pattern.[65] There is in the sources consulted no mention of married women holding office or participating in any way in the lodge's activities, while there is much mention of single women doing so. In April 1898 this tantalizing note appears in the Royal Templars minutes: "Report from Miss Bryan of North Ekford – Struck with matrimonial fever having a somewhat bad effect but nevertheless Council flourishing with increased membership." One is tempted to speculate that the temperance lodge served as a type of nineteenth-century singles club where one could expect to find an appropriate marriage partner.

Despite the role played by women in the lodges, however, it is apparent also that in policy-making sessions where political or financial issues were discussed, the ascendant voices were male.[66] Thus, it can be said that while women had an important stake in lodge activities, even where they technically possessed equal standing as with the Templars, their roles were strictly circumscribed. This may have been one reason why the WCTU was able to lure female members away from the lodge.[67]

Another reason may have been the perceived lower status of the lodges in comparison with such a middle-class organization as the WCTU. The lodges' sensitivity to community ridicule has already been noted. The minute books demonstrate an awe and fear of those glib-tongued detractors of temperance who were better educated than lodge members. One finds the West Middlesex Council of the Royal Templars deeply concerned about the following that could be commanded by such well-educated individuals as Principal George Grant of Queen's University in his campaign against prohibition, and their fear that they were powerless to oppose such august persons.[68] The lodges appear to have had an "image problem" in the community, and one can well understand some women moving to a more respectable group such as the WCTU. In Lynne Marks's detailed analysis of the class position of lodge officers in three Ontario small towns, her evidence is persuasive of the working-class profile of many Ontario lodge members in this period in contrast to the middle-class status of local WCTU members. She finds, for example, that almost half of the Templars executive in Thorold and Campbellford were working class, while fewer than one-quarter of the WCTU executive members in Campbellford could be thus classified. A similar pattern prevailed in Thorold, where more than two-thirds of the executive of the WCTU were middle class. While she found little overlap in membership between the WCTU and lodges in these towns, she did find some instances where husbands of WCTU members attended local temperance lodges.[69]

A different culture characterized the temperance lodges and the WCTU. Where the lodges engaged freely in raucous oratorical contests and sustained criticism as a social-control device, the WCTU typically adopted a courteous, mutually supportive approach that avoided internal dissension and personal slights at all costs.[70] The WCTU took careful note of its members' family crises and deaths, and faithfully extended gratitude, sympathy, and prayers to members in times of need or retirement,[71] while the temperance lodge records consulted show only one resolution of "sympathy and condolence." This was extended to no one in particular but to record the lodge's "deep sense of loss in the death of Rev. A.M. Phillips, B.D. of Montreal, the father of Royal Templarism in Canada, a hero in the Prohibition Ranks, and a fellow worker in the Truth in every department of the Kingdom of Christ."[72] Where the WCTU ran "medal contests" to encourage children to give temperance lectures and thus train the next generation of workers, the lodges ran "gold medal contests" for their own members' stirring speeches about temperance. There is no evidence from these records that women participated in these lodge contests.

Other differences that may not be attributable to male or female patterns of behaviour are also evident. The lodges were more inclined to attempt to control local unions from a centralized authority.[73] In 1897, for example, the Middlesex Templars agreed that the District Council would bear half the cost of resuscitating the moribund Middlemiss Council, and someone was delegated to meet monthly with the members to assist them. Again, in 1899 a committee was struck to "work up the fallen councils of the District."[74] Once founded (often by the provincial organizer), the WCTU local unions supervised their own activities and membership almost entirely. The provincial or dominion associations existed primarily to register the number of members and activities and to lobby for changes in attitude and legislation, not to "work up" flagging unions. In fact, the local minute books show that the unions were sufficiently independent that the provincial executive had difficulty even gathering specific information about them.[75] Local unions would certainly not have been amenable to the heavy-handed control exercised by the temperance lodges.

Finally, the lodges demonstrated far more interest in ritualized behaviour than did the WCTU. Aside from the white ribbon and the varied trappings provided for youth groups, the WCTU depended little on rituals, especially at the local level, with the exception of course, of the essential evangelical ceremony that underlay every meeting. In this case, however, religious ceremony defined the group's *raison d'etre;* it was not an artificial means to group glorification. As the century wore on, the provincial, dominion, and world levels developed more ceremonies of a non-evangelical nature, but in the local unions where most of the work was completed, there is little evidence of this change.

At the same time, there was a good deal of similarity between the tactics used by the WCTU and the temperance lodges in the battle to gain prohibition. Both organizations attempted to maintain interest in temperance amongst the community by sponsoring itinerant lecturers. Petitions were sent to legislatures,[76] local papers were encouraged to print temperance pieces,[77] plebiscite campaigns were fought,[78] and conventions were held.[79] Women participating in the activities of the temperance lodges would have learned a good deal about the political process from their male associates.

The Women's Crusade

Although American temperance societies in the nineteenth century often admitted women, their role, as with the temperance lodges, was usually subsidiary.[80] Women had, however, taken on leadership during periods of religious revival in the United States, particularly during the periods of the First and Second Great Awakenings.[81] In 1874, fear of intemperance was combined with revivalist techniques in a Women's Crusade in Ohio. In Clarkesville and Hillsboro the towns' saloons were closed by women holding prayer meetings outside and in, by their occupying the premises of uncooperative bar-keeps, through embarrassment of the clientele by the recording of the names of men who entered drinking establishments, and by bell-ringing. Within a few months, the Women's Crusade had spread to 130 towns, villages, and cities in Ohio, 36 in Michigan, and 34 in

Indiana.[82] Independent women's temperance societies developed from the crusades, with state-level organizations in ten states.[83] Beyond the organizational level, the crusade profoundly influenced what would become the National WCTU.

The Women's Crusade contributed to the model for WCTU activity by showing women the results that were possible with effective organization and powerful leadership. Barbara Epstein contends that the crusades "expanded the horizons of the ... women who participated in them. They began to feel their collective power, and what had been a rather amorphous, if widely shared, set of moral values began to take shape as a social outlook and a guide to women's action."[84] Ruth Bordin concurs: "The Crusade had an emotional impact equivalent to a conversion experience and moved these women to feminist principles, whether they recognized them or not."[85] Although Jack Blocker remains unconvinced of the ultimate attitudinal change effected in crusade participants, he does accept that the creation of new women's institutions represented a genuine change in behaviour. Pioneering temperance reformer Frances Willard described her attendance at a crusade meeting at which the participants "spoke, they sang, they prayed with the fervor of a Methodist camp." The effect on her was galvanizing: "What I said I do not know except that I was with the women heart, hand and soul, in this wonderful new 'Everybody's War.'[86] There is no doubt that for most crusaders, the exhilaration of the campaign acted as a tonic; as one participant exclaimed, "The Crusade was a daily dissipation from which it seemed impossible to tear myself. In the intervals at home I felt, as I can fancy the drinker does at the breaking down of a long spree."[87]

The Women's Crusade helped crystallize the methodology and organizational structure to be adopted, especially in Ontario: a strong communication network between "locals" would be maintained, while the formal political dimension would be largely ignored and effort expended instead on changing public attitudes towards alcohol, as in the Women's Crusade. It has been suggested that the education gained by women in the crusade permitted the Cleveland convention to create "from the top down."[88] Lacking this experiential base, the Ontario WCTU formed a far more decentralized structure than its American cousin. The apolitical networking approach to societal change characterized the American WCTU in its first decade, until Willard increasingly involved the union in direct political action; in Ontario the apolitical approach remained the pattern through the organization's long history.

Finally, the Women's Crusade contributed to the evolution of a workable ideology for a women's temperance organization operating in an era of declining per capita consumption of hard liquor. The temperance societies and lodges of the 1820s had arisen in a period of increasing hard liquor consumption in the United States, which exceeded 5 gallons per capita per annum,[89] and the ideological positions had been fashioned to meet this challenge. By the 1870s, consumption had declined in the United States to about 2 gallons per capita,[90] and in Canada to 1.1 gallons a year.[91] The replacement of whisky by beer, however, especially in urban areas, alarmed many. In the United States the 1865 per-capita consumption of beer totalled a little over 3 gallons, which doubled the level of 1850. By 1900, however, per-capita beer consumption reached 16 gallons. This represented a major shift in drinking habits, with a likely increase in the drinking population.[92] But the pattern of consumption had changed as well. More solitary drinking was believed to be occurring,[93] more binge drinking which resulted in family violence and financial pressure, and more drinking took place in male-segregated locations.[94] The crusade's credo, it has been argued, was a response to the injuries suffered by women, who had become victims in an alien landscape. But while the beliefs remained, the tactics changed. Where the crusaders had utilized confrontational strategies, the WCTU opted instead for manipulative ones.[95] Jack Blocker observes, "The WCTU not only institutionalized the Crusade, it also domesticated the Crusade."[96]

The National WCTU and Frances Willard

As the last crusades were subsiding, churchwomen and men were drawn from the northeast and midwest to the National Sunday School Assembly in New York State. This group enthusiastically endorsed the establishment of a women's temperance organization. The first president of the National WCTU was Annie Wittenmyer, a proponent of strong central authority with veto power over local and state unions. She was wary of the implications of a rapidly expanding membership, and her diffidence contributed to the WCTU's slow growth during the first few years. Wittenmyer also held to a strict temperance program, with involvement only in education through evangelical persuasion, on the model of the crusades. In the late 1870s, however, her leadership was challenged by Frances Willard, who foresaw a far wider and politicized role for the WCTU. While it may be too facile to suggest that under Wittenmyer's presidency the organization had "slowly begun to grow into a stiff and stilted body of automatic workers, whose chief aim was uniformity, whose local unions were held with too tight a hand, and whose business was done by the most official of committees,"[97] as Willard's loyal biographer has done, Willard certainly did bring a new set of objectives to the organization.

She had come to temperance work at the age of thirty-five, with a family heritage rich in academic excellence and evangelical commitment. Her father had been a revival leader as a young man.[98] When she was still a schoolgirl, Willard and her family migrated to Charles Finney's fledgling school, the Oberlin Collegiate Institute, where her parents took classes. Firm abolitionists, the family made their cellar a haven for travellers on the Underground Railway. After a short schoolteaching career and two years' travel in Europe, Willard was chosen to be the initial president of Evanston College for Ladies, the first institution headed by a woman to confer degrees.[99] The Chicago fire impoverished the struggling college, and it was merged with Northwestern University, where Willard became dean of the Women's College and professor of aesthetics in the liberal arts faculty in 1873. Resigning this post a year later after an argument with the university president, she became corresponding secretary of the National WCTU and president in 1879.

A supporter of female suffrage (or the "home protection ballot," as she termed it), birth control, "social purity," and fair treatment of prostitutes and women in the courts, Willard became known for her "do everything" policy and her aggressive membership drives. Political involvement extended from formally supporting the National Prohibition Party, which included a plank for female suffrage in its platform, and later the Progressive Party, to the creation of a separate political organization, the Home Protection Party. The American WCTU also identified closely with the American labour movement, stressing the oppression of women and children in factories. For many years it was associated with the Knights of Labour.[100] While the organization had fewer than 27,000 members when Willard became president in 1879, it boasted 73,000 names on the rolls just four years later, and by 1900 there were 168,000 members in 7,000 locals.[101]

Willard's early evangelicalism and feminism are undisputed. In a letter to the revivalist D.L. Moody, with whom she worked for a year, she emphasized her commitment to women's equality in evangelical religious organizations and practice:

> All my life I have been devoted to the advancement of women in education and opportunity. I firmly believe God has a work for them to do as evangelists, as bearers of Christ's message to the ungospeled, to the prayer-meeting, to the church generally and the world at large, such as most people have

not dreamed. It is therefore my dearest wish to help break down the barriers of prejudice that keep them silent. I cannot think that meetings in which "the brethren" only are called upon, are one half as effective as those where all are freely invited.[102]

Even unsympathetic historians credit Willard with exceptional ability. Jack Blocker allows, for example, that she "had a subtle and sometimes devious mind and an extraordinarily graceful pen, and consequently, was able to make revelations and express opinions upon subjects which her more straightforward contemporaries dared not touch."[103] Barbara Epstein suggests that Willard's leadership permitted the American WCTU to rise above its religious base and focus the opinions of middle-class women on broader issues of social reform. "While avoiding the language of feminism, she initiated discussion within the WCTU about female equality in the home and outside it. She outlined what she regarded as a feminine vision of social order."[104] Ruth Bordin argues that precisely because Willard accepted the precepts of the cult of domesticity, she became, more than any other woman of her age, the embodiment of the ideal of female moral superiority. This firm foundation of acceptance by men and women in her society equipped her to nurture a massive following in the wider community. Nancy Hardesty takes a different perspective, contending that, while Willard used the rhetoric of domesticity, separate spheres, home, and motherhood, she articulated more forcefully an egalitarian vision rooted in the evangelical tradition of Finney.[105] Most remarkable, however, was Willard's success in taking a male-controlled temperance movement and making it the centrepiece for a wide-ranging program of female social reform, including women's suffrage, improved working conditions, and the more general evangelization of American society.[106] It seems unfair to assume that the cult of domesticity ruled out a concept of equal rights, at least within the home. Increasingly, women's historians see the dichotomy of maternal feminism versus equal rights as an artificial one.[107] Quite obviously, Frances Willard accepted both, as did many of the women of the Ontario WCTU.

In terms of personal style, Willard adopted a charismatic, though never strident, approach in her leadership, characterized by energetic travel, writing, and speech making.[108] As the "uncrowned Queen of America,"[109] she elicited passionate responses from both male and female admirers and opponents. One of her classmates wrote that as a student she "came to be something of a 'beau'" and that as a teacher she "attracted love letters from her girl students written in passionate terms that hardly seem appropriate even for heterosexual correspondence."[110] Willard had been engaged to marry after a whirlwind romance and had several other suitors, but she broke the engagement after a month. However, Ruth Bordin indicates that she never relinquished the idea of marriage.[111] While Willard spent most of her adult life with her secretary, friend, and confidante, Anna Gordon, she refused to accept the "loves of women for each other." "The friendships of women are beautiful and blessed; the loves of women ought not to be."[112]

As part of her membership campaigns, Willard took a personal interest in the Canadian organization and herself organized a number of urban unions in Ontario, for example, Ottawa's in 1881.[113] Her visits were frequent and emotionally charged. She took an active part in the proceedings; at the 1890 meeting she took the chair and gave the members a "parliamentary drill."[114] Still, the adulation accorded Willard by the American sisterhood was not duplicated in Canada.[115]

The bond with the American organization extended beyond Willard's personal role, however. The Canadian WCTU regularly sponsored American speakers, as in 1891 when the Ontario provincial convention heard Rev. Dr Anna Shaw of Boston speaking on the enfranchisement of women as a weapon for home defence. "The next day the Convention endorsed woman's franchise without any attached tags."[116] Local unions also supported American speakers sponsored by others. In 1893 the London WCTU "announced that Rev. Dr. Aurora H. [*sic*] Shaw of Washington will lecture in the Talbot St. Baptist Church on Thursday evening, March 16th, Subject Woman's Enfranchisement. At the close of the lecture Miss Shaw will answer questions from the audience. The President urged all present to attend, especially those not in favor of Woman's Enfranchisement as it would at least be fair to hear what the eloquent advocate had to say before condemning her."[117]

Beyond speakers, the American WCTU provided much of the literature for the Ontario organization, both for distribution and to train members in their duties. Some of the tracts were written by Frances Willard herself. Short courses initiated by the American organization were adopted as well in Canada. In 1912 the Ontario WCTU used the seven-week temperance course offered at the Chicago Training School as a model and decided "to look for a bright young woman who would do the same in Ontario," finally settling on Miss Bertha McLeod of Cainsville, who became their young peoples' temperance worker.[118] The powerful influence of Frances Willard, a similar structure, and common speakers and literature created many similarities between the American and Canadian WCTU organizations. They were by no means, however, indistinguishable from one another. As will be discussed in chapter 3, the Ontario WCTU differed from its American model in its principal interests, tactics, demography, and leadership.

Chautauqua

A final American influence on the Ontario WCTU was the chautauqua movement, a system of adult education started in Chautauqua, New York. Chautauqua meetings were held annually, often in association with Sunday school conventions. At one of these in Chautauqua in 1874, the news of the recent Women's Crusade was broadcast. As has been mentioned, Letitia Youmans attended the women's temperance meetings held at the Sabbath School Convention at Lake Chautauqua in 1874. She and her husband had also been drawn there by Palestine Park, a kind of nineteenth-century religious theme park where costumed guides took the faithful on guided tours of the Bible and acted out biblical stories.[119] But it was Mrs Youmans who attended the Sabbath School Convention, not her husband, and there were enough other women from Canada and the northern American states to organize women's temperance meetings daily. Here she was surprised to meet women "of mental culture, good social position and deep piety, not by any means belonging to the class I had supposed."[120] While men were invited to attend the temperance meetings, women organized and ran the sessions. One speaker was Jennie Fowler Wiling.[121] "This was the first lecture I had ever heard delivered by a woman,"[122] reports Letitia Youmans. Women who became active in the chautauqua movement developed essential organizational and speaking skills that would be required in the women's temperance movement.

BRITISH INFLUENCES

The British contribution to the women's temperance movement in Canada is closely associated with efforts by the middle class in the early nineteenth century to provide "rational recreation" for itself and for the working classes, who were thought to be vulnerable to corrupt appeals of an alcohol-oriented leisure industry. The campaign for rational recreation was part of a front pushing for temperance and educational reform: "Abstinence and edification were common prescriptions of rational recreation."[123]

The Sunday School

One of the primary vehicles to be developed by which rational principles could be instilled in children was the Sunday school.

Although originally the effort of middle-class evangelicals to replace the defunct charity-school movement, by the early nineteenth century, Sunday schools were largely controlled by the upper working class as institutions of self-help and self-improvement. Thomas Laqueur notes that by 1810, some 60 per cent of all English Sunday school teachers had once been students themselves.[124] Furthermore, a good number of these teachers were women, supported also by the British tradition of dame-schools.[125] Teachers were usually unpaid and would leave if unhappy. Thus, out of necessity, operations in Sunday schools were often governed by consensus.[126] This was the tradition adopted for the Canadian Sunday school movement. It was a distinctly different approach to education than was accepted by the American Sunday school, where mainly male instructors taught a clientele of children from both the middle and lower classes, and increasingly identified the school with a single denomination and congregation.[127]

As with so many other features of Canadian culture, Sunday schools in Ontario adopted a blend of the British and American practice. Like those in Britain, early Sunday schools in the province were non-denominational, but as the population grew, most churches saw the value of sponsoring individual schools.[128] The Sunday school's function was to inculcate Christian morality (and behaviour consistent with this) and such work-related attitudes as punctuality and diligence, as well as fundamental arithmetic and reading skills. As in England, many of these schools were staffed by women and some male laity.[129] And following its American counterpart, after about 1832 the Sunday school in Upper Canada used American evangelical literature, including appeals for temperance.[130] Increasingly, too, the children attending Ontario schools came from the middle, as well as the labouring, classes. And like both precedents, the province's Sunday schools flourished after their introduction to Upper Canada around 1820.[131]

Allan Greer estimates that by 1832 about 10,000 children were attending 350 to 400 Sunday schools in the province.[132] Clearly, however, the influence of the private-venture school waned as the century progressed. Gidney and Millar point out that while the private-venture school was the dominant form available in Upper Canada until the expansion of the grant-aided common schools after 1841, by mid-century about one-third of all educational enrolments in the cities and urban areas of the province were in the voluntary sector; by the 1870s the proportion had shrunk to between 5 and 10 per cent, increasingly catering to those families who could afford tuition fees.[133] Nevertheless, for significant numbers of children from poor, non-urban families, the Sunday school continued to play an important role in literacy and moral instruction. Houston and Prentice note that the press occasionally acknowledged society's debt to the Sunday school; as late as 1867 the *Globe* recognized that there were "'a surprising number in Toronto alone' who if not instructed in the Sabbath school 'will not be instructed at all.'"[134] Thus the impact of the Sunday school curriculum, including temperance education, would have been considerable, particularly with non-middle-class children in Ontario's rural areas and towns who attended the common school only sporadically and who might also have come from intemperate homes.

During the revivals of the American Second Great Awakening of 1795 to 1840, the belief in infant damnation had waned,[135] and with it the age of child baptism and conversion declined. One result was that the North American Sunday school took on the task of providing young people with enough knowledge to seek conversion on their own. With the resultant flourishing of the concept of Christian nurture, an even higher profile was given to the Sunday school as the institution which would teach Christian values and ideals to children.[136] Therefore it is not surprising that the Sunday school has been called "one of the most under-studied major undertakings in ... education."[137]

Revised teaching strategies that moved away from memorization to stress understanding reflected the younger clientele.[138] Teachers were encouraged to present lessons thematically, interspersing the didactic sections with songs, choral readings, and personalized anecdotes. These expectations of a more sophisticated program and varied format placed a heavier burden on Sunday school teachers and created a new mass market for inexpensive tracts, Bible study guides,[139] and gospel songbooks, such as the volume produced by Sankey and Bliss in 1875.[140] At the same time, there was a call for greater standardization in Sunday school lessons. Daily plans and suggestions of motivating strategies were distributed to many American denominational Sunday schools by the 1860s. A Sunday school magazine was produced for continental distribution, and a Sunday school teacher training institute was established in Chicago in the same decade.[141]

By 1875 the informal local and state conventions of American Sunday school workers were moulded into the International Sunday School Association – international because of Canada's participation. More training institutes were founded, such as the one at Lake Chautauqua. It was this varied summer program that drew Letitia Youmans, Sunday school teacher and temperance advocate from Picton, Ontario, in 1874. She attended a series of daily women's temperance meetings with between two and three hundred participants, together with many of the organizers fresh from the Women's Crusade in Ohio. From these meetings the American and Canadian WCTU organizations were born. Hence, the Sunday schools of the 1870s were strongly influenced by, and in turn further affected, the focus of women's temperance organizations. From the founding of the Ontario WCTU in 1877, the fortunes of the organization were intertwined with the province's Sunday school movement. Women's leadership in the Canadian Sunday schools provided them with oratorical skills and a forum for practising those skills; teaching materials and strategies intended to standardize the Sunday school lessons were readily adapted by the WCTU to further the temperance cause.

The Band of Hope

Children who were drawn to the rational recreation of the Sunday school were prime candidates for another British group that greatly influenced the work of the WCTU, the Band of Hope. Inaugurated by the Leeds Temperance Society in 1847 to inculcate the respectable values of honesty, cleanliness, punctuality, and delayed gratification with children in the working class, the movement soon gave its name to any children's temperance group.[142] In Britain, Bands of Hope were non-denominational, although several denominations set up their own groups, usually quite separate from church-controlled Sunday schools. As in the Sunday schools, a large proportion of the workers were of working-class background, having successfully made the transition into middle-class life, "absorbing and then generating without condescension the 'respectable' values sought by the members."[143] This was the first English organization to work with children in a general recreational, as well as educational way. The message was conventionally anti-drink, but the recreationally oriented methodology was comprehensive and highly successful. A strong *esprit de corps* was fostered through temperance concerts, where children recited and put on musical entertainments, and temperance parades, complete with banners and costumes. Mass choirs were organized: in 1886, for example, fifteen thousand children were divided into three choirs appearing in one day on the stage of the Crystal Palace.[144] Beyond these extravagant productions, organizers attempted to maintain interest in temperance issues by sponsoring lectures, especially by medical doctors. Didactic biographies of self-made abstainers were published and distributed nationally; journals with items written for children were published, and temperance novels, such as *Danesbury House*, were printed in cheap editions.[145]

The Band of Hope Blue Book, A Manual of Instruction and Training was published to aid in organizing and running a band. The manual included outlines for local lectures against drinking and gambling. It was one of these publications that Letitia Youmans consulted when organizing her Band of Hope in Picton.[146]

There is some evidence of organized temperance work with children in the United States before the Civil War.[147] The Sons of Temperance formed the first Boys' Temperance Association in 1846 in Pennsylvania; by the 1850s the association had become known as the Cadets of Temperance. In 1853 there were cadets in every state, although the numbers were small in some areas.[148] The National WCTU Bands of Hope or juvenile unions must have drawn members from the cadets, as in Ontario, where the WCTU lured children from the temperance societies' Bands of Hope. In the mid 1870s, the National WCTU formally initiated its Band of Hope organization, the locals of which were usually affiliated with Sunday schools. These Bands of Hope held much more closely than the Canadian to martial themes, frequently providing demonstrations of marching and song. For example, Bands of Hope in Kansas adopted a military motif in which the children were divided into companies headed by captains, identified as cadets in the temperance "army."[149] American Band of Hope children often provided entertainments at WCTU conventions.[150] This was not the approach taken in Canada, where the Bands of Hope operated through a network of local groups, rarely massing with other bands. The American Bands of Hope were most often middle-class organizations of WCTU members' children, but occasionally, as in the large Ontario cities, working-class children were conscripted into special units. American membership numbers remained much smaller than the British.[151]

While the Canadian Band of Hope movement could not claim the spectacular success of its British counterpart – by 1900 three million children were members across the United Kingdom[152] – its close identification with the WCTU helped to shape the enduring focus of work with children and to remind the temperance women, as the Ottawa WCTU reported in its minute book, "that work among the young insures [*sic*] ultimate triumph."[153] In Ontario the Band of Hope was sometimes associated with the Sunday school and at other times it was consciously removed from Sunday school quarters to emphasize the interdenominational nature of the sponsorship. For example, Youmans feared that the Band of Hope in Picton would be too closely identified with the Methodist Church if the children used its quarters, and therefore she moved them to a rented hall.[154] For the same reason, the Ottawa WCTU held its Band of Hope at the

Orphans' Home[155] and thereafter free of charge in the Orange Hall.[156] The Dunnville union ran the Band of Hope alternately in the Presbyterian and Methodist churches to dispel any suspicion of denominationalism.[157] The Newmarket union acquired as its Band of Hope worker a woman "who is quite a capable Teacher in the Model School." Soon thereafter, the band was held in the schoolrooms after hours.[158] A close association with the local school was not atypical. Even when the classes were held on other sites, the same texts were often used as the public schools employed in their scientific temperance courses, when the schools presented the subject at all.[159] Thus the Ontario Bands of Hope remained non-denominational. Moreover, one suspects that Bands of Hope were sometimes created in the province to spur on a flagging public school temperance program.[160]

Through the combined influences, therefore, of several temperance and evangelical organizations, the Ontario WCTU was moulded. The male-dominated temperance societies and lodges identified the central evil to be attacked and continued to work in league with the Ontario WCTU throughout most of the period examined. The American Women's Crusade and WCTU provided direction in ideology and strategies for change, as well as a feminization and evangelicalization of the whole process. The Sunday schools and Bands of Hope permitted women to exercise leadership and organizational skills in their work with children. The Ontario organization would now need to translate these influences into formal structures.

CHAPTER THREE

The Ontario Structure: "A Mint of Wealth for Us Somewhere"

This chapter will examine the WCTU within the context of the campaign to achieve prohibition in Ontario. However, it should be emphasized that although prohibition represented an early and primary aim of the Ontario WCTU, it was by no means the organization's only objective. Within a few years of its founding, efforts to obtain prohibition were supplemented with a wide range of other causes, including crusades for social purity, female suffrage, and temperance education. The Ontario WCTU argued that most social evils were rooted in intemperate behaviour. Alcohol intemperance was a visible expression of this failing and a causal force in the acquisition of other social vices. Thus, while the WCTU began by viewing prohibition as the chief panacea for a multitude of social ills, it soon accepted the challenge of fighting this multifaceted sin on more than one front. It continued to support the prohibition contests, but not to the exclusion of its other evangelical efforts to eradicate evil. In this respect it differed from male temperance groups in its approach to the alcohol problem, with the result that it was virtually ignored by the coalition of forces which eventually secured the Ontario Temperance Act in 1916. Its different approach also helps to explain why every WCTU local union for which records exist neglected to mention the passage of the 1916 act. By this date the organization, especially at the local level, gauged its success less by legislative measuring sticks and more by behavioural change.

THE CAMPAIGN FOR PROHIBITION

The nineteenth century was paradoxically an era of reduced alcohol consumption and increased acceptance of the temperance organization. Within this climate of public concern about the dangers posed by alcohol, both the federal and provincial governments found themselves under sustained pressure to introduce legislation in order to further curb drinking. The approach taken by all levels of government was to defer action as long as possible, thus estranging as few interest groups and voters as it could in this period of changing public mores.

The first piece of legislation to encourage temperance groups such as the WCTU was the provincial Crooks Act of 1876. It placed the granting of a locally determined number of licences for taverns under the control of a government-appointed board in each riding. The result was that the board, usually the nominees of the local member of the legislature, could be petitioned by concerned citizens to further limit the number of licences granted.[1] If, from the point of view of those same citizens, a board did not act responsibly, pressure could and was applied for a new slate to be named. Take for example, the Richmond Hill WCTU, which decided at its second meeting in 1884 that its major work would be "the better enforcement of the Crooks Act."[2] This union, like many others across the province, monitored the decisions of its local board carefully and on occasion demanded that members be replaced. Thus the Crooks Act kept temperance forces active through providing a mechanism by which the licensing system could be observed and significantly amended if consistent pressure were maintained. It provided a first and consistent political focus for temperance activities.[3]

The first federal initiative to affect the WCTU in Ontario was the Canada Temperance Act, often called the Scott Act, of 1878. Like the Dunkin Act of 1864, which it superseded, the Scott Act provided for local option in the retail sale of liquor. This provision effectively gave counties, cities, towns, and townships the authority to prohibit the sale of liquor by popular vote.[4] A poll could be forced by petition of one-quarter of the electors of any city or county, and a simple majority of votes cast was considered to be decisive. Hence, from 1878 members of local WCTU unions busied themselves with circulating petitions and fighting local-option campaigns, even though they themselves could not vote. A second political front had been opened. Local-option votes increased membership in the combat zone and won support for their other activities from sympathetic soldiers-in-arms. In fact, the Crooks and Scott acts were contiguous with the founding of many WCTU local unions and together probably help to account for the earlier and faster growth of the local unions as compared with the provincial or dominion organizations.

A federal prohibition act passed in 1884 was almost wholly worthless in controlling the liquor trade,[5] but seems to have helped to coerce the provincial government to declare its support for temperance. In 1887 the Ontario government, in response to a WCTU-initiated petition from 30,000 temperance sympathizers, introduced a course in scientific temperance into the public schools.[6] This provided a new rallying point for the WCTU and a focus for the organization's increasing emphasis on education. In turn, it spurred WCTU efforts to influence teachers and principals, teachers' associations, and curriculum leaders in the Department of Education. It also led to demands for women to be given the right to vote and hold office, particularly as school trustees.

A federal Royal Commission into the Liquor Traffic was named in 1891, and while it resulted in no new legislation, its deliberations provided the WCTU with more fodder for the struggle against the "liquor interests." It also undoubtedly forced a provincial plebiscite in 1894, in which the Mowat government gave women who already held the municipal franchise – widows and spinsters who owned real property – the right to vote. The plebiscite campaign is credited with having forced the Dominion Alliance, a coalition of male temperance groups created in 1876, to develop an effective political structure,[7] and obviously it had a similar effect on the WCTU in Ontario. After winning the plebiscite by a majority of 81,769 votes,[8] the Mowat government promised to refer the issue of provincial jurisdiction to the Privy Council and bring in "all the provincial Prohibition the Privy Council decision would permit." S.G.E. McKee, president of the Ontario WCTU, reported that the "Convention fairly sizzled with indignation" at the weak government response.[9] After the Privy Council cleared the way for provincial legislation in 1896, the Ontario government passed a new law reducing liquor licences by 130 and raising the age limit for drinking from eighteen to twenty-one years, with a ten-dollar fine attached to each infraction. "The mountain had labored and brought forth a mouse!" sniffed Mrs McKee.[10] Another plebiscite, this time by the federal government, was taken in 1898 and won by the temperance forces, but still no legislation resulted. An embittered President McKee reported that the plebiscite had been carried in spite of "every trick that was known to politicians."[11]

By 1899 the provincial organization saw that "the year's work ended in gloom and depression of spirit. Three years of heart-breaking toil had resulted in nothing tangible, because of the casuistry of political double dealers."[12] Nevertheless, by 1900 the referenda and local-option campaigns had drawn more than 5,000 committed members to the organization, so that it was healthier than it had ever been. The same applied at the local level. For example, in 1900 the London WCTU had the strongest membership list in its history, with

240 members,[13] and the Dunnville union had 55 members but gathered 221 names on a petition demanding prohibition.[14] Still, the impact was felt, and by 1905 it was apparent that membership figures were not growing (see table 2 in the appendix).

Most of the unions' energies were taken up with local-option campaigns between 1906 and 1910. The declaration of war in 1914 further distracted potential members. Even so, by that year there were over 9,000 members in Ontario, and the organization remained one of the strongest in the field of temperance groups.[15] When a "committee of one hundred" used the patriotic fervour of war to pry legislation from the provincial government in 1916, the Ontario WCTU had over 10,000 members. Women across the province were well practised in the techniques of plebiscite, referenda and petition. Over 850,000 names were collected, many by WCTU members, and in September 1916 the Ontario Temperance Act was unanimously passed. It closed all bars, clubs, and liquor shops for the duration of the war, banished liquor from hotels, boarding-houses, offices, and places of business, and permitted legal sale only for "medicinal, mechanical, scientific and sacramental purposes."[16]

Although the WCTU had been one of the most powerful and longstanding players in this drama, contributing almost one-third of the expenses to the successful campaign, it was not included in the final plans or celebrations. The legislative success was jealously guarded by the male temperance societies.[17] This slight disappointed the Dominion WCTU, and as has been noted, not one local union made mention of the passage of the act in its minute books. The only conclusion to be drawn from this dazzling omission is that local unions had long since abandoned political solutions to social problems. The women of WCTU unions across Ontario were too busy reforming society to notice the passage of a prohibition act that had formed the major objective of male temperance groups for almost seventy years.

THE ORGANIZATIONAL STRUCTURE OF THE ONTARIO WCTU

The basic structure of the Ontario WCTU was modelled on the American National WCTU under the leadership of Frances Willard. However, in Ontario the organization began at the local level, later adding a provincial and dominion executive and convention. Mitchinson argues that it was this network of local unions which made it the first truly national organization, rather than just another Toronto-centred women's group.[18] Where local unions were established in rural areas or small towns, a county executive was occasionally created. In all but the local unions, and in the larger unions even here, the association operated with the same structure. The executive consisted of a president, sometimes an ex-president, vice-presidents, recording and corresponding secretaries, and a treasurer. The executive officers were usually chosen by election at all levels. These officers met separately at the provincial, dominion, national, and world levels to maintain contact with other groups and arrange conferences. As a general rule, the executive did not set policy. Representatives to annual conventions delivered reports and considered resolutions drafted by the executive to determine official policies. It was then the task of the executive to implement these decisions, reporting any difficulties that arose in the course of their work to the unions through written reports or convention statements.

The organizational structure pioneered by the WCTU – locally, provincially, nationally, and internationally – has been credited with creating a more sophisticated bureaucratic design to promote temperance and with applying new ideas of large corporate models to those involved in moral reform.[19] Its organizational blueprint has been dubbed by one historian "moral 'bureaucratization.'"[20] Its creation can also be seen as a further manifestation of purposeful political action by a sector intent on self-promotion through class creation.

The local unions replicated this structure whenever they had sufficient numbers, but often no ex-president sat on the executive since the same woman carried the presidency for years at a time. Whenever possible, the local unions named representatives from the community's denominations as vice-presidents, thus expanding the executive group disproportionately to the membership. However, this had the positive effect in some local unions of garnering sustained support for the organization from a number of congregations and clergy in one area. The tasks of the local union executive were to arrange and run interesting meetings, recruit membership, represent the local WCTU to the public, and supervise the departmental superintendents.

The labour of the WCTU at all levels was carried out by the "departments of work," committees headed by a superintendent which concentrated on promoting temperance with one interest group or through a particular strategy. The departmental structure was adopted from the National WCTU and represented the type of work encouraged by the mother organization. There was no suggestion that all levels, or all unions at the same level, should attempt to engage in every department of work. The range was far too broad for any but the National or Dominion levels to be able to contemplate such activity. At the same time, local concerns could be addressed by the creation of new departments of work that appeared at none of the other levels. As interests or conditions changed, old departments could be phased out and new ones introduced. The departmental arrangement was intended to provide for maximum flexibility within an internationally recognized structure. Thus the Dominion WCTU supported departments of work that had no provincial or local counterparts (for example, the department of foreign work federally), and local unions created departments that did not exist provincially or federally (such as the Band of Hope).

While it was the responsibility of WCTU unions lower in the hierarchy to report to those above them, there is no indication that the higher levels controlled the local unions by monitoring their adherence to official policy or disciplining infractions. The local groups operated in a loose confederation to form the next level of the hierarchy, deciding the degree to which they would support the provincial or dominion structures financially and ideologically. This virtual autonomy may account for the longevity and vitality of the local unions in otherwise difficult circumstances.

Women were chosen for superintendencies in the dominion and provincial WCTUs through election by the annual convention; in the local unions, superintendents generally volunteered, and often for several departments where numbers were limited. At the provincial or dominion levels, the superintendent had a different mandate than at the local, however. The role of the provincial and dominion departmental superintendents was to gather information about actual work completed from the next level down. Reports were then compiled and sent up to the next level in the hierarchy. In the local union the superintendent had the roles of working with the women on her committee to set goals, supervise their implementation, maintain morale when disappointments intervened, and report all this activity to the provincial, dominion, or world superintendent of the appropriate department. The local records indicate that where a superintendent was inactive, the department normally lapsed. The breadth of departmental work and the vigour of individual departmental effort was a reliable indicator of the union's general health.

For example, during the provincial convention of 1887, 119 delegates met in Napanee to elect a new slate of executive officers and departmental superintendents. The president in this year was Addie Davis Chisholm, a divorced woman, who would lead the Ontario WCTU until she bid an emotional and permanent departure in 1889.[21] Each superintendent from the previous year gave a verbal report of all work undertaken and completed in her department, as well as editorial comments on the significance of its success or failure, both spiritual and temporal. In the style of evangelical ministers, Letitia

Youmans as president felt free to comment on reports, providing a nudge to greater effort here, morale building there, and congratulations where they seemed due. After Mrs Inkster of Kingston, provincial superintendent of prisons, delivered her report, President Youmans "followed with earnest words, showing how much drink has to do with the first fall."[22] To encourage the involvement of all women at the meeting, a "question drawer" was opened, with a plenary discussion of "troublesome issues" that had been suggested by the convention delegates. Letters were read to inform the convention of actions taken on their behalf by the executive. Eleven resolutions proposed by the executive were debated, amended, and approved. In addition to the superintendents' reports, each union gave an accounting of its triumphs over the course of the previous year. For example, the Hamilton union set the pattern for the many types of childhood education to which it devoted years of dedication. It reported that its 152 members were instructing 1,525 children, while 86 young ladies in the Young Woman's Christian Temperance Union were involved in teaching in some way. In addition, the union sponsored a sewing school, a night school for boys, five Bands of Hope, a pledge committee, and a committee to distribute literature and temperance ribbons. Finally, the president gave her address, which was structured very much like an evangelical sermon, punctuated by single verses of hymns sung by the assembled delegates.[23]

Local unions of the WCTU were organized in a variety of ways. During the 1880s and early 1890s, several women acted as official organizers. For example, the Peterborough Union was founded by Miss Bowes and the Toronto group by Letitia Youmans on behalf of the provincial union. The Picnic Grove WCTU in rural Lancaster was organized by the county president, Mrs McDougall.[24] Several Ontario unions were established through the personal intercession of Frances Willard, sometimes on the ashes of defunct philanthropic organizations such as Ottawa's Woman's Christian Association.[25] Once set up, unions were encouraged to scatter the seed for new growth. In the Ottawa case, letters were dispatched to women in the surrounding communities, and while the women in Fitzroy Harbour, Merivale, and Richmond neglected to set up unions,[26] those in New Edinburgh and Hintonburg eventually created their own organizations.

To sustain the new unions, the Ontario WCTU provided pamphlets to instruct officers and members in their duties. In the earliest years, these were ordered from the National WCTU repository, but by the 1890s the Ontario group was producing its own "methods booklets," as they were called. For a small sum, local unions could purchase *The Local Recording Secretary* by Ella Cosford, Jennie Macarthur's *The*

Local Treasurer and Her Books, or a selection of three booklets by May Thornley (like Cosford from London, Ontario): *The Local President: Her Duties and Responsibilities*, *Programs*, and *The Local Corresponding Secretary*.[27]

Provincial Departments of Work in the Nineteenth Century

In order to gain a sense of the range and type of work tackled at the provincial level, the 1887 departmental list might be surveyed. In retrospect, the departments were of four general types: educational, social, religious, and political, with an emphasis on the first two of these. From the beginning, the Ontario WCTU devoted the bulk of its energies to educational and social projects.

The most popular category involved education. The social purity department made literature on personal purity available to members and schools, and urged ministers to preach sermons on the theme. The message emphasized the dangers of overindulgence in food and social pastimes, the connection between alcohol and irresponsible behaviour, impurity in language, and thought, and most particularly, the perils of masturbation for young men. In general, the greater the threat, the more obliquely it was expressed. Occasional travelling lecturers were engaged to help disseminate the news.

The scientific temperance instruction department pressured the Department of Education to introduce a mandatory textbook, compulsory courses, and an examination on temperance as part of the high school entrance competitions. It also tried to convince principals, teachers, and their professional associations to support them in the introduction of scientific temperance instruction to the public schools.

The temperance literature department coordinated and supplied a wide variety of materials to local unions. The materials included pamphlets for members' use and a separate series for young men and women, which attempted to fashion the temperance argument in language and imagery that would appeal to youths. Instructional guides were offered to local unions to educate the women in officers' responsibilities and to improve the quality of programs.

The organization and lecture bureau attempted to provide support for new unions through advice and literature. It also coordinated occasional speakers' tours on topics of interest to develop informed support for the WCTU's causes. The hygiene and heredity department provided instruction on eugenics and health issues through printed materials and speakers. These it made available to unions, schools, and civic authorities.

The departments of young woman's work and of juvenile work instructed the next generation of temperance workers. At the 1887 convention, the superintendent of the Young Woman's Christian Temperance Union, Mary Scott, asked, "What hope then for the army if bands of new recruits have not been trained to fill the gaps and continue the warfare, and what hope for us, beloved sisters, and the cause we hold so dear, if others are not being made ready to fill our places ... What is all this doing for our young women? It is teaching them lessons of forbearance, patience and love, which is rounding out the character and making them grander, Christian women." To accomplish their goals, the young women were encouraged to teach younger children in temperance and home-making skills. One of the prime vehicles for this instruction to working-class girls was the kitchen garden program, a kind of homemakers' club.

Members were kept abreast of national, provincial, international (particularly American), and local activities, crises, and ideas through the *Woman's Journal* and later the *Canadian White Ribbon Tidings* and the *Canadian White Ribbon Bulletin*. The press department was charged with the task of providing informative articles to newspapers and periodicals and with urging authorities to print and support temperance ideals.[28]

The department of Sunday school work made available "pledge cards," Sunday school temperance quarterlies, Sunday school teachers' lesson plans, and quantities of inexpensive temperance leaflets for scholars of various ages. It also prodded local superintendents to lobby for quarterly "temperance Sundays" in all churches in their districts.

A second area of work might be called social issues. In 1887 all provincial departments in this category were focused on groups outside the WCTU fold. Four departments concentrated on temperance and charity work with men perceived to be in high-risk vocations: the departments of work among lumbermen, work among railroad men, work among soldiers, and work among sailors. In each case, temperance literature was tucked in with "comfort bags" containing such items as needles, thread, buttons, quilts and a Bible. Men attending county fairs or provincial exhibitions were considered highly vulnerable to the blandishments of gambling and drink; hence a department was set up to disseminate information concerning tea tents and other healthy refreshments that might be provided by local unions.

A department of prisons and police sought to maintain links with law-enforcement agents so that temperance aid could be provided. It also placed pressure on government to classify prisoners. The 1892 Ontario convention went even further in recommending that unregenerate prisoners be reminded of the consequences of evil acts: it called for the introduction of enforced labour at county and local jails.

The final socially inspired department dealt with flower missions, the provision of flowers, fruit, and other delicacies to the poor and ill, particularly women in straightened circumstances. Thus it is clear that only a portion of the educationally and socially oriented departments of work were concerned directly with alcohol. The multifaceted nature of social problems was addressed by the Ontario WCTU through a wide variety of channels.

A third category of departmental work dealt with matters of religion, attesting to the organization's evangelical agenda. In 1887 three departments were identified of this type. An evangelistic department issued inexpensive tracts, made suggestions for meetings and prayer services, and outlined a variety of worthy causes, from helping the indigent aged to providing refuge for reforming prostitutes. The department of unfermented wine provided printed materials for local unions and assiduously compiled statistics of victories and near victories in denominational use of non-alcoholic sacramental beverage.

The sabbath observance department offered guidelines for local monitoring of sabbath observance and attempted to place pressure on provincial authorities whenever contraventions were uncovered. For example, in 1889 the Ontario convention passed the following resolution: "That as Christians we should be careful not only to keep the Sabbath ourselves but to see that there is no infringement of its hours in the family; to watch our music that it be wholly sacred and that our children be early trained to meet with God's people in public worship. To neither purchase or patronize any trade carried on on the Sabbath. To avoid as much as possible Sunday funerals. To use our influence for the early closing of stores on Saturday night, and by making the Sabbath work at home as light as possible, let all enjoy the day of rest." On the basis of such resolutions, one can well appreciate the depth of feeling on typical sabbatarian issues as the running of streetcars on Sunday in Toronto.

The fourth and final area of interest supported by the 1887 convention was in the effective use of the political process. Only two provincial departments served to promote a myriad of causes: the legislation, franchise, and petitions department and the conference with influential bodies department. Both sought to influence policy makers at the provincial level on a number of issues. While the emphasis in these early years by the provincial departments of work was on evangelically inspired educational and social service in the community, interest in political issues was also expressed.

There was a good deal of duplication of effort in this structure, but the departmental design permitted a broad range of topics to be dealt with by relatively few women. These areas of interest were represented as well at the dominion level after its constitution was adopted in 1885, with some interesting additions. The same four categories of work are represented in the 1889 dominion convention, for example, but with the addition of a department of "foreign work." The Dominion WCTU was more aware of the negative implications for temperance of the increased immigration to Canada by such groups as Germans who were thought to be especially inclined to use alcohol. There were also twice as many politically oriented departments, suggesting a greater interest and confidence in direct political action.[29]

At the level of the local union, the range of departments in 1887 generally mirrored the provincial and dominion structures. The growing community of North Toronto might be taken as an example. There the union was able to support twelve departments. One of its most important, the evangelistic Band of Hope with four hundred members, did not appear on the departmental roster for either the provincial or dominion WCTU until several years later. This attests to the autonomous initiative of local unions and to the high value placed on youth work in many areas. In later years, the Bands of Hope would figure prominently in both the higher levels. In this union, attendance at each meeting during 1887 ranged between six and eighteen women.[30] As a final comparison, the six regular members of the Dunnville union managed during 1887 to run vigorous departments in temperance literature, juvenile work, evangelistic work, and heredity and hygiene and to maintain contact with the press.[31]

This is not to suggest, however, that it was a simple matter for so few women to complete work in so many departments. For example, in 1887 the North Toronto WCTU corresponding secretary did not arrive for the meeting with the union's other five active members. She sent word that due to overwork, she had not prepared the report of the union for the provincial and county conventions. She had, however, written forty-one letters and a hundred postcards on behalf of the union, and she wished to be reimbursed. Furthermore, she tendered her resignation, which the union wisely refused.[32] Miss Rose was not alone in feeling pressured by the demands of her temperance work.

Although the Young Woman's Christian Temperance Union will be discussed in a later chapter, it is important to note that where the YWCTU thrived, it often took on responsibility for the WCTU's evangelistic work with working-class children. One WCTU member called the Ys the "power plant" of the whole organization.[33] In fact, strong Y unions often extended the range of their activities far beyond work with children. The Ottawa Y evangelists who precipitated the Hull riots are a prime example. Another case in point was the Toronto Central YWCTU, with about thirty members in 1905. Operating with a fairly small active membership, the union involved itself in a number of social projects. The Y evangelistic department distributed large numbers of tracts, often through door-to-door canvassing. A flower mission provided bouquets and delicacies for the infirm, elderly, and poor: "afternoon tea was served to 20 of our old and lonely ones at headquarters, little birthday parties were given for the shut-in ones, also take them out in invalid chairs; take our tea with us in a basket and share it with some lone one, in fact do all we can to brighten and uplift their lives." A kitchen garden program for working-class girls was offered, and materials were distributed to their brothers on the topic of social purity, specifically to discourage "self-abuse." The Ys arranged lectures and provided pamphlets for the same group under their White Cross Society. A Y heredity and hygiene department gathered publications and prepared programs on the importance of physical purity. The WCTU refreshment booth, directed primarily at working-class men, was supported by the YWCTU at the fairs. The Ys contributed to the Willard Home for working girls, an inexpensive residence and dining-room for young women newly arrived to Toronto. Finally, the Ys prepared "comfort bags" for men in lumber camps.[34]

Provincial Departments of Work in the Twentieth Century

In order to assess the Ontario WCTU and its changes over time, the same levels of the organization can be contrasted twenty-two years later, in 1909–10. By this date, the WCTU had a much expanded departmental structure at the provincial and dominion levels, while the local unions in most cases had pared down their activities. The primary focus now differed between the provincial and dominion organizations on the one hand and the local unions on the other. While the largest number of departments continued to fall into the educational category for the dominion and provincial groups, the Dominion WCTU in particular remained active in its attempts to influence the political process. Women involved at the provincial level had less confidence in this strategy for change after 1900. The local unions, however, tended to emphasize the widespread social mission of the organization, maintaining only a limited direct temperance program.

Most had long since abandoned much of a directly political agenda.

In this second period, the Dominion WCTU created fourteen departments directly concerned with education and several additional departments for which education was a secondary, but important, issue.[35] A number of these departments had existed in 1888, although often not at the dominion level. For example, scientific temperance instruction, health and heredity (formerly the hygiene and heredity department), Sunday school work, and the press were familiar areas. Such departments as work among soldiers and militia, sailors, fishermen and lighthouse keepers, raftsmen and lumbermen, and railway employees were new definitions of old target groups and combined a social and educational focus. New target groups were added, such as work among coloured people, to be approached using the same model of distributing uplifting literature and conducting judicious visits.

The department concerned with work among coloured people seems to have been largely inactive in 1909–10 (although it would be active again during the First World War), but the new young peoples' societies department had much attention lavished upon it. The introduction of the YPS groups meant that young men were vigorously recruited as members, where the nineteenth-century organization had emphasized the enlisting of young women.

By 1909 scientific temperance instruction was supported by a new department of medical temperance, which provided printed materials and speakers dealing with the medical implications of alcohol use. In 1893 the Ontario WCTU had succeeded in having William Nattress's *Public School Physiology and Temperance* authorized as the recommended textbook for use in Ontario public schools by the provincial Department of Education. In a survey of the medical effects of alcohol, children were invited to inspect every major organ in the human body. To take one instance, the danger of alcohol to the stomach was profound, it was argued. The child reader was warned that "further action of the persistent use of alcohol is shown in its extension to all the coats, thickening and hardening them, until the stomach is of little use as a digestive organ. Think of the condition of the poor unfortunate drunkard; appetite gone, nausea, vomiting, intense thirst, pain in the head, red eyes, bloated face, coated and red tongue, frequent pulse, and often fever."[36] In an age when medical doctors were revered, "medical temperance" work sought to add credibility to a traditional educational program.

The public school temperance curriculum was further supported by two new structures by 1908: first, the school saving banks department, which encouraged children to delay economic gratification in the hope that they would mature into abstemious adults. It was also hoped that these childrens' parents would be positively influenced by the good example of their offspring. Secondly, and much more successful, a department of medal contests was introduced to reward children's essays and speeches on temperance. Originally sponsored by a New York City editor, publisher, and early member of the Sons of Temperance, W. Jennings DeMorest, the medal contests were adopted by the Canadian WCTU around the turn of the century, and by 1909 they occupied a central place in its education program. Although the medal contests were primarily directed to children's temperance instruction, some Dominion WCTU members also saw potential in the contests for women to sharpen their elocution skills. As illustration, the 1903 dominion convention passed a resolution that "we encourage in every way the training of our women and especially the younger women, in the art of speaking concisely, to the point, and loud [*sic*] enough to be heard in every part of the audience room, and, to this end, we recommend that all local unions be asked to take up medal contests." The dominion superintendent of medal contests provided prizes to provincial unions and suggested essay topics and appropriate selections for recitation. By this date, the medal contests seem to have replaced the public, "improving" entertainments provided throughout the late nineteenth century by the Bands of Hope. While the Dominion WCTU maintained its commitment to childhood education, it was dependent on the provincial and local levels to attract and hold children in its various groups. Nevertheless, the 1909 convention reported with satisfaction that "our Loyal Temperance Legion army outnumbers both the W's and Y's, having increased 3,500 the past year, making an army of over 8,000 strong."

Tobacco users were thought to be particularly vulnerable to the alcohol menace since nicotine, like alcohol, is a narcotic and has a similar impact on the nervous system. Many temperance advocates, including the WCTU, believed that tobacco users (and consumers of spicy foods and stimulating beverages) acquired an appetite for stimulants, which would drive the victim into alcohol and ultimately to opium use.[37] The new department of anti-narcotics waged war against the many threats of "cheap thrills" and aimed its efforts primarily at boys and young men.

For an organization as dependent on the printed word as the WCTU, stocking, revising, and disseminating literature became a major task. The objective of the Dominion Literature Depository was to serve Canadian WCTU members and the interested public. At the 1891 dominion convention a resolution had been passed that barber shops be supplied with the "proper kind of literature." A further resolution proposed that literature concerning scientific temperance instruction be distributed at the International Teachers' Association, to be convened that year in Toronto. In return, members would seek an expression of support "in favour of the educational methods of the Dominion and National WCTU." Mothers were the main objects for the new department of moral instruction and mothers' meetings. Here the topics were exceedingly far-ranging, from dangers of the theatre and "self-abuse" to improved diet.

Finally, by 1909 the Dominion WCTU sought to educate provincial and local unions in parliamentary procedure and effective organizational techniques. By raising women's awareness of political procedures and sharpening their skills in efficient and appropriate goal setting, the Dominion WCTU hoped to retain more women within the movement and to increase the organization's success rate in its various campaigns. This school of methods program involved making available printed materials, speakers, and workshop suggestions. Refresher courses were also offered periodically.

The dominion organization continued to lend its support to social programs among groups likely to be exposed to and victimized by alcohol. While the provision of educational materials remained the primary thrust of this work, by 1909 the Dominion WCTU encouraged other procedures to remove individuals in special danger from the polluting evil. This was the rationale behind the prison reform and police stations department, which visited inebriates in jail and sought a declaration of their intention to reform. When this had been received, measures were often taken to relocate the victim to a healthier setting. As a political measure, pressure was placed on prison authorities to separate hardened criminals from neophytes and to provide female matrons for women prisoners. The same strategy of removing temptation motivated the work of the dominion curfew bell department. It encouraged local unions to pressure town and city councils for the invocation of a curfew, usually at 9 P.M., so that young men would be safely in the family's care rather than frequenting public houses. A second strategy of providing alternative, non-alcoholic refreshments for thirsty men and women was the objective of the dominion department of exhibitions and fairs. This department also reminded local unions that such work could add to the membership roll.

Departments that sanctioned the serving of members' social needs were more obvious in the 1909 records of the Dominion WCTU than had been the case earlier. Two departments fall directly into this category, with a third also being concerned with members' socializing. The department of parlour meetings gave official recognition and support for union "socials" of various types. Tea parties, luncheons, prayer meetings, membership drives, and "at homes" were all suggested by the Dominion WCTU to weld together present members and to facilitate new members' acceptance into the local unions. This formal acceptance of the importance of members' socializing suggests that even the dominion organizers recognized the potential value in nurturing a middle-class women's culture at all levels. That this nurturant women's culture was regarded as a strength and not a distraction to the achievement of the organization's goals is further explanation for the receding importance of temperance *per se* and the increasing significance accorded to social interaction amongst the members.

The department of evangelistic work was most directly a reflection of the religious foundation of the organization. However, as with the evangelistic department in Ottawa in 1888, many of its activities had a social element that unified the women working in aid of religious conversion. The other religiously oriented departments – the Lord's Day observance and unfermented wine departments – were, along with the evangelistic department, reflective of the earliest objectives of the WCTU. A new concern had been added since 1887. This was the coordination of temperance missionary work on a world scale through the World's WCTU. To help sustain this huge structure by 1909, the department of systematic giving was created to encourage members to support local, provincial, and dominion initiatives financially on a regular basis.

A significant difference between the dominion structure of 1887 and that of 1909 was the markedly wider range of activity and political involvement by the later date. In 1909 four dominion departments (conference with influential bodies, legislation and petitions, equal franchise, and Christian citizenship) and the internationally directed peace and arbitration department demonstrated a new interest in waging political battles.[38] Unfortunately, there was more sound than substance; very little was achieved at this level in political terms.[39] It is apparent also that the Dominion was the level of the WCTU where these political issues were debated most energetically. Increasingly, the provincial and local levels of the organization worked in the cause of educational and social reform, rather than political change. For example, the provincial WCTU in 1909 established only two politically directed departments: one devoted to winning the franchise and the other concerned with law enforcement. Similarly, only two departments of religious work remained at the provincial level: a relatively inactive unfermented wine group – since most denominations amenable to removing fermented wines from the Communion table had long since done so, that is to say, all but the Anglicans – and the consistently active evangelistic department.

In 1909 the Provincial WCTU continued to maintain its prime interest in the education of children. Departments functioned in Sunday school temperance work, juvenile unions, hygiene and heredity, medal contests, and scientific temperance instruction. The provincial campaign to have a course in scientific temperance mandated in the public schools with a compulsory textbook and examination had peaked in the mid 1890s, and by 1909 the organization was fighting a rearguard action against an increasingly disaffected teachers' association. A resolution from its 1909 convention made the perennial request of "examinations and asking to have books placed in each public library." The WCTU's position on the critical role of morally upright teachers in this process is captured by a resolution dating from the 1899 convention:

> Whereas, We believe that teachers throughout our land wield a powerful and life-long influence over their pupils, Resolved, That we urge them to endeavor more earnestly to inspire those under their charge with exalted ideals of purity, nobility and integrity of character, and Further, That in teaching of physiology and hygiene we ask them to lay special stress upon the evil effects of alcohol and tobacco upon the human system, also their debasing power over mind and soul. And that still further, We would emphasize our belief that no person addicted to the use of any of these narcotics should ever enter the schoolroom as a teacher.

The provincial body also became increasingly concerned with the nature of teacher training: "we urge the necessity of our Model and Normal schools giving to the teachers in training, as thorough a preparation for teaching Scientific Temperance as any other subject; and we believe no teacher should receive his or her certificate who has not passed a satisfactory examination upon it and the best method of teaching it."[40]

Mothers were addressed through the departments of purity and mothers' meetings, the *Canadian White Ribbon Tidings*, the White Cross Society, and the press. By 1909, however, that message was less concerned with pure food and (young men's) unsullied thought, and more with the personal danger to women presented by impurity in its many guises. The 1909 provincial convention passed several resolutions in this vein, all characterized by overblown and catastrophic language. One represents the convention as being "thoroughly alarmed" at the white slave trade, placing on record "its abhorrence of this debasing and diabolical evil"; another warns women against impure literature, calling on them to be "watchful of this evil"; a third registers its amazement at learning "that adultery and lewd cohabitation are not unlawful in the present criminal code, and whereas divorce cases are on the increase in Canada," moves that the dominion government be requested to pass laws "that will protect Canadian society and morals against this evil." So many evils, so few causes for celebration.

Of continuing concern, too, in 1909 were those groups requiring both educational materials and support to help shield them from the alcohol peril: the departments which worked among prisoners, soldiers, sailors, Indians, blacks and lumbermen in the Muskoka area all remained active during this period. Similarly, the flower mission and work at county fairs continued. Finally, those internally supportive departments such as the school of methods and parlour meetings were well supported across the province.

However, the list of provincial departments to have been dropped by 1909 is as instructive as those that remained. The department of young woman's work had disappeared, and with it went the provincial recognition of the special role of the single young woman. With the eclipse of the YWCTU, the kitchen garden program, as well as many activities subsumed under the evangelistic department, disappeared as well. Gone too were the legislation, parliamentary practice, and sabbath observance departments, suggesting a deep frustration with the legislative route to gain control of the liquor traffic.[41] This movement away from efforts to influence law making and towards informal pressure tactics and small-group activism was reflected even more strongly in the local unions.

The minute books of selected local unions in 1909 and 1910 reveal not only the types of work favoured by small women's groups, but also the relative amount of time spent on each activity, as well as the recording secretary's views of these endeavours. In this period the Newmarket union operated with between five and thirteen members. They chose to set up no political departments at all and explicitly refused a community request to mobilize in favour of early shop closings. "One of the local Merchants requested the WCTU to get signers to a petition for early closing of the stores Sat. nights. the plan was not taken up. after former experience it was decided to 'tell the Merchants to let sleeping dogs lie.'"[42]

Most Newmarket WCTU efforts were directed to social matters and not primarily to temperance. Help was given to "the foreign women up the canal to clothing"[43] to "a family we heard was in need. there are some coats still at Mrs. Mairs ready for any who are in need also some pieces for another quilt and other clothing";[44] to another "family whose mother lies very ill and weak; decide to finish a quilt for them, and to provide a washerwoman to clean up at a cost of $1.00 to the treasury";[45] to the people of Muskoka and to cases "where one or other of the parents were dead and the poor innocent children suffering for clothing. 2 quilts were donated immediately another offered her Home for the WCTU to make clothing and send to the poor unfortunates. all hearts were touched and longed to help."[46] On 1 February 1910 "Mrs. C.E. Cane asks to have a box filled with clothing suitable for a family of children whose mother was taken from them by death. At the next meeting of the WCTU sewing circle the box is to be filled and sent." The women were tireless in ministering to the needs within and beyond their community. In addition, they organized a social to raise money for the Muskoka missionary cause. It featured the Rev. Mr Cornell's magic lantern views and a short musical program. Later in 1910 a tea was organized and realized $10.00 for the Lumbermen.

But the WCTU women did more than pack clothing and give parties. They sought to educate both the young people and themselves about a number of troubling problems. Arthur Beall, the WCTU purity lecturer, was engaged for $3.50 to speak to the boys about their personal "purity" habits.[47] After the president read a resolution on "the Evil of the Tobacco habit," the recording secretary noted, "oh! what can be accomplished when men of high degree in prominent positions indulge in the habit setting a bad example for young boys even women and girls are taking to the habit in some places not far distant."[48] In addition to confirming their own worst fears about tobacco, the members had educational meetings dealing with "Social Purity in the Home" and the "White Slave Trade which is being carried on in our own fair Canada. How can we stop it? our hearts ache for the Mothers whose innocent Daughters have been captured & carried away by vile women in sheep's clothing. several cases have been reported in the various papers. oh! that we might send a warning into every home to beware of such creatures."[49] The recording secretary's comments are most revealing of righteous anger and fear, and are directed against men of influence and women who are seen as turncoats. Papers were also read on the pest of flies and on the morality of the stage.

Although in general, the young woman's movement within the WCTU had undergone a decline, the Newmarket union still had a YWCTU connected with it during this period. The Ys' main responsibility seems to have been to run mothers' meetings, and the minute books recount their ongoing problems in locating appropriate quarters for the working-class women attending. "Prayers are being offered by them [YWCTU] to have the Mothers Meetings continued hoping good may be done for their Eternal welfare as these women meet with mothers who never go to any church and who may be persuaded to attend these meetings occasionally where they may get both physical and spiritual good."[50]

The list of departments for the Newmarket WCTU and YWCTU indicates that work was done in the department areas of evangelistic, flower, fruit, and delicacy, parlour, systematic giving, sabbath schools, narcotics, purity and mothers' meetings, press, and lumbermen. This list, however, is inadequate to fairly assess the amount of effort consistently and conscientiously expended by this small group of women for the welfare of their families and community, and all in the name of their Saviour. Their favoured work was educational, mainly among young men and themselves in this later period. The shift in educational focus away from young women towards young men is representative of the WCTU's general movement away from perceiving women to be a motive force and towards men as the protector of women and the family, and the primary agent of change in society. The Newmarket union's second major interest was in social reform to lighten the burden of women and families in the immediate area and beyond.

Wendy Mitchinson argues that the departmental organization handicapped the WCTU's efforts by spreading members' energies too thinly, so that little effective work resulted.[51] The record of WCTU accomplishments at all levels, but especially at the local, casts doubt on this conclusion. Mitchinson also suggests that "once formed, [departments] became a permanent feature," with the result that the field of work expanded beyond reasonable limits.[52] This has been shown not to have been so. As issues were resolved satisfactorily or as unions became discouraged with the reaction to their efforts to improve society, departments were dropped. When new issues arose, such as war work, departments were added. The records of the Newmarket WCTU demonstrate that the women of that local union chose areas of work within departments that interested them and that were concerned with issues where they believed they could make a difference in the community. The departments of work which they chose were different from those undertaken by, for example, the women of the Ottawa WCTU and YWCTU. However, in both instances the members devoted enormous energies to the tasks which they deemed important. Furthermore, and contrary to Mitchinson's contention, neither group seems to have felt that it had overextended itself. Had it done so, the overambitious departmental range likely would have been cut back in the next year. The structure of the Ontario WCTU encouraged this type of flexibility. In summary, it has been shown that the departmental organization did not handicap the WCTU or the YWCTU, but rather added to their effectiveness in communities where the organization's goals varied with local needs.[53]

MEMBERSHIP FIGURES

The membership figures for the Dominion WCTU are impressive: by 1891 almost 10,000 women were reported as active members,[54] but eighteen years later, the figure had grown to just under 12,000.[55] By 1914 the Dominion listed 16,838 members,[56] making it one of the the largest non-denominational organizations in Canada[57] (see tables 4 and 5 in the appendix).

The largest and most active of the provincial unions was the Ontario WCTU.[58] Yet even here, the membership figures demonstrate slowed growth after its enthusiastic and well-supported start in the 1880s, with no real recovery until after 1910. Just five years after its creation, the Ontario union in 1882 could boast of having 96 unions with 2,500 members.[59] By 1891 there were 175 unions with 4,318 members.[60] In 1895, 205 unions had almost 5,000 members,[61] but by 1900 the membership had risen to only 5,521 in 222 unions.[62] The number of unions remained steady; by 1911 there were 215, but individual unions were stronger, with a total membership of 7,128.[63] In 1913 a modest expansion occurred, with 479 unions and 8,179 active members[64] (see tables 1 and 2 in the appendix). Yet these figures represent only the active members and give little sense of the general support for specific issues, such as temperance. For example, during the "petition campaign" in 1916, when the WCTU worked with a coalition of prohibition forces in enlisting support for temperance legislation, 850,000 names were collected on a petition and submitted to the Hearst government.[65] This effort resulted in the Ontario Temperance Act of the same year.

For most organizations membership figures are deceptive. Official reports usually provide inflated totals, even though they purport to list only "active members." So it is with the WCTU. Blurring occurs in two directions. Although the stated membership of a union might be 66, as in the case of Ottawa in 1886, the actual attendance on a representative date was 11 (see table 3 in the appendix). The disparity appears to have been more pronounced in city unions than in town or village ones. At the same time, unions with modest memberships were able to attract large numbers of sympathetic adherents for special presentations. Such was the case, for example, with the Meaford union, which struggled for years with a small attendance at its regular meetings. Nevertheless, in a three-month period in 1902 it was able to sponsor three highly successful temperance revival lectures in the town hall.[66] This plumping of the membership rolls was partly negated by a counter process through which membership was under-reported. It is important to note that official WCTU membership figures were based entirely on those submitted by the local unions. Virtually every annual report of the Ontario WCTU contains complaints that some local secretaries or presidents had neglected to submit these figures, in which case, membership totals omitted such unions, even if the union had shown a strong membership in the preceding year. Hence it is certain that the membership as recorded each year excluded whole unions and sometimes a good number of unions. Clearly, membership figures do not begin to tell the story of a group's real support or influence in a community.

Several factors affected the membership of unions at the dominion, provincial, and local levels. Of primary importance at the dominion and provincial levels was the status of temperance reform in the wider community: with the growth of temperance societies of various types throughout Canada, the WCTU grew apace. As support for temperance, or suffrage or purity legislation, waned internationally and nationally, the popularity of the WCTU diminished, although its membership had greater stability than most other temperance groups. This fluctuating support for temperance was both influenced and demonstrated by provincial and federal plebiscites, petitions, referenda, local-option campaigns, and statutes. All of these had an enormous effect on WCTU membership. At the local level, these larger movements also had an impact, but a less critical one. Here the health of the membership rolls was most closely linked to the number and strength of other women's groups of all types and men's temperance groups in that locale. While much more research needs to be carried out into competing societies for women at every level, the annual reports and minute books do provide some sense of the competitors and cooperators at each level of operation. A third determinant of a union's success or failure proved to be the strength of social relations between members. Where unions nurtured friendships and social gatherings, membership was more consistently buoyant than in unions where the only link was service to the community or a shared sense of religion.

THE WCTU AND OTHER ORGANIZATIONS

The Temperance Lodges

Throughout most of the nineteenth century the relationship with the individual temperance lodges had been warm. Official greetings were extended at the annual meetings of the provincial and dominion WCTU,[67] and high-ranking officers of the WCTU and various temperance lodges paid visits to each others' meetings. Letitia Youmans tells how a deputation of the Right Grand Lodge of Good Templars was to meet in Napanee, and being in the area, she decided to attend and bring greetings. She was called upon to prepare and deliver an address, but when the time came for her to mount the platform, she was too frightened to move. "I had never stood on a public platform in my life. I could not do it, but did venture to read the address from the aisle."[68]

On occasion, too, delegations met with the dominion or provincial executive, as in 1890, when a delegation from the Royal Templars of Temperance proposed the establishment of a "Home for Intemperate Men." While the WCTU executive supported the idea, it insisted that to receive any financial support, the home would have to be open also to inebriated women.[69] Positions such as this are indicative of the Ontario WCTU's sympathy with women's plight beyond their own direct experience. It is suggestive too of the difference in outlook between the male-dominated lodge and the female-run WCTU on social problems.

Local WCTU unions often teamed with their temperance lodge counterparts to effect political change, as in London when the union resolved in 1894, "That the Executive be appointed a deputation who will confer with the London and Western Ontario Prohibition Union and Royal Templars and who will go with them to interview the License [*sic*] Commissioners in regard to whatever requests are thought advisable to make." In the same vein, the Woodstock union decided that to wage the local-option campaign effectively in 1913, it would send a delegation to work with the Temperance Citizens' League.[70] The Toronto union worked with the local Good Templars, Royal Templars, and Young Men's Prohibition Club to demand scientific temperance instruction in the schools[71] and to protest the availability of liquor in military camps and police forces.[72] Some unions held Sunday afternoon gospel meetings to promote the cause of temperance and shared the duties with local temperance lodges.[73] Inexpensive temperance literature was procured from the lodges,[74] and quarters were shared for temperance meetings.[75] Where the latter arrangements were made, the WCTU generally owned the rooms and charged the lodges rent. There is little evidence from the minute books that the offer was reciprocated by the lodges when they owned quarters. When conferences were held, the lodges even requested billets from the local union.[76]

In fact, where cooperation did not occur, the WCTU was not always the loser. For example, the Newbury town report to the district council of the Royal Templars of Temperance noted that there were "too many other meetings in the village, a WCTU had been started there and some of the Sisters had joined it."[77] Generally, however, the temperance lodges and local WCTU unions worked amicably together in the period before 1900 when the lodges were thriving.

Attendance figures for the lodges were impressive. In 1882, for instance, when the WCTU in Ontario had about 2,500 active members, the Ontario division of the Sons of Temperance boasted of over 5,000 members, while the Independent Order of Good Templars six years earlier had signed memberships from 25,000 Ontario residents![78] If the growth in the lodges was phenomenal, so was their decline. In 1891, when the Ontario WCTU membership had climbed to almost 5,000, only 12,000 members remained of the Independent Order of Good Templars.[79] Their numbers further declined to 2,268 in 1899, while the WCTU membership remained well above 5,000.[80] By 1904 the Royal Templars of Temperance membership had slipped to 6,000 from 15,000 eleven years earlier.[81] In the same year, the Ontario WCTU had almost 5,400 members.

Thus, while D.C. Masters contends that the temperance movement was at flood-tide in Toronto by 1850[82] and Graeme Decarie surveys temperance lodges and organizations and concludes that most were in serious decline by the 1890s,[83] these conclusions appear to be accurate only for the male temperance lodges, where minute books speak of the sliding membership and apathy in formerly vibrant divisions.[84] WCTU membership, by contrast, grew more slowly, but maintained its numbers in the face of bitter disappointments over slow-to-react governments.

The Dominion Alliance

In the early days of the WCTU's existence, the relationship with the lodges' federation, the Dominion Alliance, had also been cordial. The Dominion Alliance for the Total Suppression of the Liquor Traffic had been established in 1876, very soon after the WCTU's founding,by the many temperance societies operating across Canada. Similar to the

American Anti-Saloon League, it took a very different approach to prohibition from the WCTU. Whereas the Woman's Christian Temperance Union sought to unite supporters behind a multifaceted reform program, the Dominion Alliance was a single-issue organization that emphasized the lowest common denominator upon which temperance supporters could agree. This approach brought it, like the Anti-Saloon League, "the greatest political triumphs in the history of temperance reform and contributed as well to the reform's most resounding political defeat."[85] Membership was also open to churches, the YMCA, the League of the Cross, Societies of Christian Endeavour, Epworth Leagues, and the St Andrew's Brotherhood.[86] The dominion and provincial levels of the WCTU regularly stated their support for the Dominion Alliance,[87] and there is evidence that, particularly before 1890, the Alliance was regarded as the mouthpiece for the WCTU in political matters. For example, Mrs Chisholm, president of the Ontario County union, in speaking to the Ottawa WCTU in 1884, noted that "while the WCTU would like to have the liquor trade law amended, the Dominion Alliance has asked them to delay until the time is right."[88] The WCTU complied. WCTU representatives were regularly entertained and courted by the Dominion Alliance.[89]

After 1890 the relationship appears to have cooled at the dominion and provincial levels, although the *Woman's Journal* continued to advertise Dominion Alliance conventions and legislative initiatives.[90] Most of the Alliance's efforts, however, seem to have been directed to the local unions which were often contacted directly, many opting to support the Alliance in a variety of ways. The Ottawa union accepted a Dominion Alliance lecturer on the condition that two-thirds of the proceeds be given to the WCTU.[91] Similarly, the Dunnville union extended an invitation to the Alliance lecturer to visit for a modest fee.[92] A good deal of evidence exists that the Dominion Alliance regularly sent appeals to the local unions for financial support and that they were often successful.[93] In fact, the women of the Dunnville union generously presented five dollars to the Dominion Alliance convention meeting at their Baptist Church, which so depleted the union's financial resources that three months later the contribution was noted as the reason that the WCTU's missionary could not be entertained for a visit.[94]

Periodically the Alliance requested that union members and their sympathetic friends write directly to their member of Parliament, for example, "asking him to use his influence to secure legislation in fulfillment of the promises made."[95] Nevertheless, by 1916 the association between the Dominion Alliance and the WCTU was strained. The most plausible explanation related to the WCTU's waning interest in political action of any type after the many discouragements over plebiscites in the 1890s. The Alliance's reasons cannot be ascertained from the records consulted for this study. For some reason, however, it appears to have found the WCTU official involvement embarrassing or an obstacle to political success.

The YMCA

Another male organization that worked warmly and productively with the WCTU was the YMCA. As with the temperance lodges, rooms were often shared, although in this case the owners were generally the YMCA and not the WCTU.[96] In several instances at the local level the two organizations were able to carry out their temperance programs by cooperating closely. Temperance literature was purchased jointly,[97] and in the case of the Ottawa union, the rough work with lumbermen was taken over by the YWCA, "as most of our honorary [male] members and church workers are connected with the association."[98]

Protestant Ministers

The final men's group to work cooperatively with the WCTU at all levels were the ministers of individual Protestant congregations, primarily the Methodists, Presbyterians, and Baptists. Ministers and stewards often provided the church basement or manse parlour as a meeting place for the union,[99] and ministers regularly preached temperance sermons and gave public encouragement to the local unions.[100] By far the strongest support came from the Methodist Church, which had been fully committed to total abstinence and legal prohibition since the early 1880s.[101] A good deal of sympathy also came from the Presbyterian Church, although it was not as unified in its support as were the Methodists.[102] Nevertheless, it should not be assumed, as Wendy Mitchinson has done, that the WCTU was a child of the Methodist Church. In her examination of the leadership of the Dominion WCTU, she finds that almost 44 per cent of the women were Methodist and 21 per cent of their husbands were clergy.[103] Given that her sample only comprised thirty-two women, all at the dominion level which, it has been argued, was hardly representative of local union membership, this assumption of a close identification of the WCTU with the Methodist Church at all levels must be questioned. In fact, most of the local unions examined for this study attempted to maintain their non-denominational status by appointing vice-presidents from each of the town's denominations.[104]

Protestant Churchwomen

Beyond the male-controlled church organizations, the WCTU worked very closely with churchwomen of many Protestant denominations, including Baptists, Anglicans, and Congregationalists, as well as Methodists and Presbyterians. It was especially in youth work and in the missionary societies that the churchwomen and WCTU women were drawn together. The temperance Sunday school quarterlies were generally distributed in every sympathetic denomination's Sunday school. At the very least, this involved interviewing all Sunday school superintendents or teachers in the community's churches.[105] Sometimes the cooperation was extended to the public schools, as in the case of the London union which authorized the "Superintendents of Juvenile Work and Narcotics to ask for the co-operation of the Societies of Christian Endeavour and Epworth League in the different churches be called to meet with the Superintendents of Juvenile Work [of the WCTU] for the purpose of devising plans for more energetic and Systematic effort in introducing Scientific [Temperance] Instruction in our schools."[106] Cooperation was also evident in arranging for temperance Sunday school lessons.[107] Greetings were often extended to meetings of denominational missionary societies held nearby.[108]

The local unions' minute books provide a sense of the WCTU women working effectively with women in many other organizations and possibly sharing members. This generalization applies particularly to the village and town unions, where little evidence is provided that the WCTU women were in hot competition with any other group. Aside from the women's missionary societies, one might expect that some competition in the rural and small-town unions would be provided by the Women's Institute, a popular organization for rural and town women in the late nineteenth and early twentieth centuries. Not a single instance of this emerged from the primary research. Clearly, the WCTU worked hard to be considered a respectable women's group, and at least in the small towns and rural districts, that designation was beyond doubt.

It is in the cities and on the provincial and national stage that one can detect some evidence of competition between certain women's organizations. The city provided many more options for middle-class women in the last quarter of the nineteenth century and the first two decades of the twentieth. In addition to the WCTU, a city such as Ottawa in 1895 had a variety of missionary societies, the Orphans' Home and Refuge for Aged Women, the Lady Stanley Institute for the training of nurses, a Local Council of Women, the

Ottawa Maternity Hospital, the Home for Friendless Women, the Associated Charities, a YMCA, a YWCA, and a number of literary and cultural societies. It was in this rich milieu that the WCTU was thrown into some competition with other groups. Most challenging to its position was the new National Council of Women, headed by the indomitable wife of the governor-general, Lady Aberdeen.

The National Council of Women of Canada

An outgrowth of the Women's Congress held in Chicago in 1893, the National Council of Women of Canada took as its vague aim the promotion of international sympathy and the conservation of "the highest good of the Family and the State."[109] The NCWC was not only non-sectarian, it was non-religious and happily accepted into its federation all women's groups, including those not "acknowledging God and Christ."[110] This position, as well as the use of silent prayer and an unwillingness by the NCWC to formally support prohibition, caused the Dominion WCTU to not affiliate with the NCWC until 1919. In addition to the substantive differences between the two organizations at the national level, there were less tangible differences that nevertheless resulted in the NCWC assuming a more élitist image. Undoubtedly, Lady Aberdeen's spirited leadership helped to elevate the NCWC in the public's perception, and the group conducted its conventions with this image firmly in mind. Wayne Roberts has criticized the NCWC for its "aristocratic pretensions," describing it as a group "of the bland leading the bland. Their conventions bristled with ceremonies lacking only in content."[111] The social cachet of the NCWC was difficult for the WCTU to compete with, and nationally and possibly in the cities, the organization seems to have garnered less status than did the NCWC.

The YWCA

In the same year that the NCWC was formed, Adelaide Hoodless called the inaugural meeting of the Dominion YWCA in Toronto. The principal address was given by Bertha Wright, president of the Ottawa YWCA, who was also an active member in the Ottawa WCTU and YWCTU.[112] As evangelically inspired and sustained organizations, the YWCA and the WCTU coexisted reasonably well and even shared several characteristics and approaches. While the YWCA was particularly concerned about the plight of the young working woman in an urban setting, it shared the WCTU's horror at the dangers posed by alcohol, particularly among the young. The London

YWCTU, for example, ran the YWCA as one of its departments, providing an "attractive suite of rooms open daily with a paid secretary in charge" and a library of three hundred volumes for mutual use.[113] The YWCA also participated energetically in the social purity campaign with the WCTU, the two organizations joining forces to engage Arthur Beall as their itinerant purity speaker in 1901.[114] Delegates were dispatched as representatives to each other's conventions.[115] As the WCTU had not affiliated with the NCWC until after the First World War, so too the YWCA declined to join until 1914.[116]

Nevertheless, the YWCA was perceived by some WCTU women as a threat to its own organization for young women, the YWCTU. At the World's conference of the WCTU in 1906, a Mrs Clara Parrish-Wright made the YWCA challenge explicit. "Now, I believe in the work of the YWCA," she insisted,

> but we all know that it does not "broaden the horizon" of young women, and "drive self from the throne" as does the work of the YWCTU. Can we not do something to meet this? I do not mean can we not push them out – no indeed. I rejoice in all the good they are doing, but can we not formulate some plan whereby we may "hold our own" too? Without a *single* exception, I believe we were on all those grounds first. Oh, if we *only* might unlock the "storehouses" of gold and send our young women forth! There *must* be a mint of wealth for *us* somewhere. Let us pray, and *let us ask* that its "hiding place" may be revealed.[117]

This statement transparently anxious of losing a foothold that once had been so firm indicates that a young woman's life devoted to self-betterment, in order to "broaden the horizon," and to selfless labour, in order to "drive self from the throne," was no longer held in such high esteem. By 1906 the YWCTU in the international, national, and provincial arenas felt its appeal slipping. By 1918 the anxiety had deepened. As one provincial convention delegate noted, "There is a decided decrease in the number of Unions, owing to the difficulty of securing officers, and also to the ever-increasing demands on the young womanhood of our land."[118]

At the city union level, some competition was also apparent, but far less than in the provincial or dominion associations. For instance, the year after the president of the Dominion WCTU was treated shabbily by the council of the NCWC in not being allowed to bring greetings from her organization,[119] the London WCTU cheerfully decided to send a delegation to the NCWC conference, to be addressed by Lady Aberdeen,[120] and two months later the London union federated with the Local Council of Women. Similarly in Ottawa, a network of women worked together during the 1890s in the Methodist and Presbyterian missionary societies, the Orphans' Home and Refuge for Aged Women, the Local Council of Women, the Woman's Christian Temperance Union, and the Young Woman's Christian Association.[121] Cooperation was more evident than ever in twentieth-century local union work. For instance, on 26 March 1928 the women of the Peterborough WCTU listened to an address given by Miss Amy Wood of the Salvation Army. "She said a woman appointed in each church to mother lonely and troubled girls would be a great help." The union agreed. In September of 1929 it affiliated with the Local Council of Women and worked with it in establishing a well-baby clinic.[122] It is reasonable to conclude that at the local level, women's organizations cooperated far more than they competed.[123]

The erosion of inter-organizational cooperation seems to have been extended during the 1920s. At the 1922 provincial convention, the Ontario president reported worriedly, "Some of our members and many true-hearted temperance women outside our ranks really think our society has finished its work and are turning to other organizations. Some that still believe in our work give from union funds to maintain other societies."[124] It is apparent that by this time the WCTU's relevance was being questioned by many former supporters.

RELATIONS BETWEEN LEVELS OF THE WCTU

Through much of the period under examination, the relationship between the local, provincial, dominion, and world WCTU organizations was uneasy. With the exception of the local unions, a small corps of workers maintained operations throughout the year. Tremendous exertion was necessary to stage the annual or semi-annual conventions, which began provincially in 1877, dominion wide in 1888, and on a world scale in 1885.[125] The convention became the most ritualized of the WCTU undertakings. It was also an opportunity to report on the year's achievements and to formulate resolutions of future action. The debates were occasionally heated, with local interests and personalities clashing. Doctrinal changes, based on the evolving relationship between evangelicalism and empiricism, created strains in the association, a topic that will be explored more fully in the next chapter.

The uneasiness was also due in part to the fact that the WCTU had originally been organized in Ontario and had much of its strength at the local level. The other tiers of the organization were in search of causes and constituencies not currently served by the local unions.

This did not leave a great deal of territory. Funding such a sizeable organization presented a continual worry, even though much of the work was carried on through volunteer action. In 1884 the Richmond Hill union noted one of the many calls for funds from the provincial level, and later the minutes noted wearily a further campaign by the dominion and world executive: five cents per member to be sent to each level.[126] The area of jurisdiction was an additional source of irritation. After local unions complained that they were being bombarded with appeals, the provincial executive reached an agreement with the dominion level that local unions would be approached only through the provincial organization and with its consent.[127] The pact was usually observed, but the general question of jurisdiction was not settled until 1911, when representatives' credentials to dominion conventions were agreed to be provincially determined.[128]

The other matter to cause hard feelings between the dominion and Ontario levels was the status and financial support of the WCTU journal, at various times called the *Woman's Journal*, the *Canadian White Ribbon Tidings*, and *Canada's White Ribbon Bulletin*. The *Woman's Journal* was first published in 1885 in Ottawa. While it attempted to represent the WCTU and its youth groups across Canada, it was from the start more representative of the Ontario group than any other. The periodical was chronically short of money, and repeated appeals for financial aid to the dominion conventions were often ignored. At the 1896 provincial convention, for example, delegates suggested that the dominion WCTU salvage the *Journal* by levying a ten-cent fee on every member.[129] There is no evidence that the suggestion was pursued. By 1903 the *Journal* had been reduced to providing spotty coverage of even Ontario's activities. It carried a sizable debt and had an inexperienced editor after the retirement of Mary McKay Scott, who had ably headed the magazine for thirteen years. The dominion organization found itself unable to provide better financial terms, and, in 1903 the publication ceased.[130] When the magazine was resuscitated in 1904, its banner identified it as the "Official Organ of the Woman's Christian Temperance Union in Canada" even though Ontario continued to pay most of the bills. Also, the name had been changed to the *Canadian White Ribbon Tidings*. The Dominion WCTU demanded control of the editorial policy and writing; Ontario resisted and suggested a revised mandate for a paper partly devoted to dominion matters and partly to Ontario's. The power struggle continued until 1906, when the relationship between the dominion and provincial levels in supporting the *Canadian White Ribbon Tidings* was terminated,[131] and the paper became the organ of the Ontario WCTU.

In 1910 the Dominion WCTU initiated publication of *Canada's White Ribbon Bulletin*, the "Official Organ of the WCTU of Canada," and the dominion level again had a vehicle for the discussion of pan-Canadian issues.[132] The *Canadian White Ribbon Tidings* continued to be published by the Ontario WCTU.[133] But even within the same level, the policies of the WCTU's journal could cause acrimony. In 1916 the *Bulletin* published an editorial that was critical of the British Woman's Temperance Union. On receiving a protest from the BWTU, the dominion convention promptly passed a resolution avowing its support for the British organization and dissociating itself from the editorial. The BWTU was applauded as a group "who have been an example to us in their self-sacrificing devotion to the highest ideals for which our World's WCTU stands."[134] The confusion of role and responsibility between the provincial and dominion levels, and between individuals at the same level, is amply demonstrated in the chequered history of the WCTU's beleaguered journal.

The relationship between the dominion and world levels of the WCTU was uneven as well. The World's WCTU first became a high-profile organization with the accession to the presidency of Frances Willard at its meeting in Boston in 1891. Willard's efforts to promote international temperance through the World's WCTU during these years were strongly supported by her deputy, Lady Henry Somerset, then one of the wealthiest women in England. In 1893 alone, Lady Somerset personally contributed as much to the World's WCTU as did the entire American organization.[135] From Willard's death in 1898 until 1906, the World's WCTU was directly controlled by Lady Somerset, long the president of the British Woman's Temperance Union. One historian of the world organization, Ian Tyrrell, grants that it created tensions with national WCTU groups. "The lofty preoccupations of a small coterie of internationally oriented leaders would at times threaten to erode their support within their own national constituencies."[136]

The deepest division between the World's and Canadian levels of the WCTU occurred over the organization's response to the social purity terror of the 1890s. Ian Tyrrell sets the stage for this dispute by averring that "temperance women were not systematic thinkers, and they responded to the needs and opportunities of the moment."[137] But the differing views were also related to national experience: the purity campaigns in North America were quite unlike those in Europe and the British Empire; as a result, reaction to such policies as the state regulation of prostitution differed widely and generated divisions within the international women's temperance movement. In response to a proposed British policy to control the spread of venereal disease, Lady Somerset, as vice-president of the World's WCTU, publicly sanctioned state regulation of prostitution.[138] Predictably, she created a furore in the organization, particularly amongst national WCTU groups committed to single-standard morality, such as the Canadian.

Lady Somerset compounded this distress by declaring herself unconvinced that total prohibition, rather than temperance, was the best policy for the WCTU.[139] Her views were made clear to the World's, including the Canadian, WCTU when the world convention was held in Toronto in 1897. In that year's report of the Ontario convention, it was noted that the delegates felt deeply agitated over Lady Somerset's position, but that they would defer action for the present. The Ontario executive had agreed at a closed meeting to discuss the matter in "Christ-like and harmonious spirit," but still to express concern for Lady Somerset's sliding position on prohibition.[140] However, Dr Amelia Youmans, vice-president of the Dominion WCTU and Letitia Youmans's daughter, was not prepared to support errant policies being framed for the world organization. She accused Lady Somerset of taking an inappropriate view of prohibition and purity regulation, and professed to back the "time-honoured principles of absolute abolition and prohibition of all and every kind of licensed sin."[141] She addressed the convention, questioning Lady Somerset's "faithfulness."

> I see as I speak a mental picture, a vast circle. In the centre the legalized liquor traffic, staunch and sturdy; by it united by a fleshy bond its twin, fed by alcohol ... [T]he circle is bounded by great guns, which represent the departments of work of the WCTU, and the mouth of every gun is turned upon these monsters ... One of these guns is our department of social purity. Oh, let it not be spiked or charged with nourishment for the monster impurity through any unfaithfulness on our part with regard to our chosen officers, for it is by our actions, not our resolutions, that we shall be judged.[142]

Although Tyrrell credits Youmans as leading a "Canadian revolt" against Somerset,[143] he misses the fact that, surprisingly, the Dominion WCTU backed, not Dr Youmans, but Lady Somerset. There was, however, a good deal of disapproving discussion before the final decision. Dr Youmans resigned.[144]

The Somerset-Youmans conflict demonstrates much about the working nature of the various levels of the WCTU. The organization championed many causes, a number of which were in contrast. Tyrrell notes that "the WCTU's work was overdetermined in a set of interlocking contradictions expressed in the various issues the WCTU championed."[145] This comment might be extended to locating the "interlocking contradictions" in the organization's many levels as well. National experience, strong personalities, intense friendships (between Willard and Somerset, for example), and just as intense rivalries (between Somerset and Josephine Butler, for example), as well as extended distances between the upper levels of the organization, created problems of unity.

Organizationally, the WCTU was made more effective by its varied departments of work. They permitted much flexibility in the choice of issues to which unions could devote their labour. It might be conjectured that because of this choice and, as will be seen, the evangelical motivation for social action, the WCTU was more successful in holding its membership than were male temperance groups, which were limited to the single issue of alcohol reform. At the local level, relations between the WCTU and other male and female societies was generally mutually supportive. Nevertheless, the WCTU maintained its independence; it affiliated with none, while cooperating with many.[146] Unfortunately, the same spirit of cooperation did not mark the deliberations of the provincial, dominion, and world levels. The WCTU found its strength, energy, and endurance in its local unions; it was from this base that the middle-class women of Ontario carried out their mission of social reform within their communities.

CHAPTER FOUR

Ideas: "For Time and Eternity"

The ideas of the Ontario WCTU were representative of those which scholars have identified as maternal and evangelical feminist. As nurturant and morally superior mothers and daughters, the women of the WCTU accepted as their task the clarifying of evangelical family roles, thus shoring up the family as a bulwark against the dangers presented by a dissolute society. Ultimately, the purified and reconstituted family held the promise of a reformed society, with the ascending middle class and its cardinal values of sobriety, diligence, and civic and domestic responsibility occupying a favoured position. It would accomplish this by providing physical and spiritual shelter for its members, by imbuing them with the evangelical ethic, which demanded service to others as an expression of personal salvation, and by introducing and reinforcing responsible behaviours by each individual. Infused with the principles of conservative evangelicalism, the women of the WCTU developed a vision of this ideal social order, grounded as it was in an idealized family structure and attendant social relationships. Women, married and single, took a central role in the private and public expressions of this societal vision.

Such an exemplary society would place Christ's saving grace as the central experience, with the family unit the chief embodiment of evangelical Christian ethics. The WCTU held that equality of expression, opportunity, and behaviour for men and women was grounded in Christian teachings, even if life tasks were different. It envisioned a society that would shun growing secularism and materialism by rejecting both self-destructive behaviour arising from overindulgence in food, use of drugs, alcohol, and tobacco, sexually explicit clothing and entertainment, and the "secret vice," and the socially injurious behaviour arising from alcohol and impurity. The original WCTU target had been alcohol. Although the organization remained steadfast in its condemnation of drink and its associated vices, this came to represent just one of its designated causes. From the mid 1880s the Ontario WCTU viewed alcohol as a primary, but not isolated, social evil. In the same vein, the solution to societal problems was no longer seen by the Ontario WCTU to be simply prohibition, but a wide array of social programs, including prohibition.

Individuals had a responsibility to Christ, to themselves, to their families and (middle-class) friends, and to the extended society. The WCTU never espoused an evangelicalism bent solely on personal salvation: the social imperative was clear from its inception as an organization. Nevertheless, it based this social imperative and its vision of the ideal society firmly on the ethics of personal salvation, on the relationship of each human being with God. As each person was part of a wider community – family, locality, nation, empire – the broader social dimension automatically entered the equation of the individual's spiritual relationship with, and salvation through, God.

WCTU IDEAS ABOUT THE FAMILY

A major component of the WCTU ideology involved clarifying the obligations of all members of the human family. Children and youth were regarded as having rights and responsibilities in the promotion of temperance and clean living. As youths moved towards adulthood, the responsibilities for young men and women were shaped by societal needs and expectations, including the cult of domesticity for women. To adult males the Ontario WCTU ascribed the primary role in any direct political action, while women were expected to be most prominent in indirect lobbying through the promotion of ethical solutions to domestic and public problems.

Children

Temperance organizations had long recognized the value of involving children in their activities. Not only could children be convinced of personal abstinence far more easily than their seniors, but a purehearted cherub could act as a powerful force in convincing adults to accept temperance. The WCTU's view of children contained, then, both of these elements. First, children were thought to be naturally inclined to goodness and therefore especially amenable to moral education. Secondly, the WCTU believed that children had a responsibility to hold to the truth, to make themselves useful, and to proselytize others. This view applied to children of all classes, although working-class children would require more education before they could effectively participate in disseminating the truth.

The WCTU approach to children was consistent with the emerging concept of "childhood" during the nineteenth century. During the latter half of the century, "the child became, in fact, the primary focus of family life and, thus, a central commitment of society."[1] Using a paradigm to locate the beginning of the concept of "childhood," Rooke and Schnell identify four elements in the treatment of children, including the provision of protection, segregation, dependence, and delayed responsibilities.[2]

The WCTU's ideas of children generally reflected this analytical framework. Its only departure from these ideas would occur in the issue of personal responsibility. As an evangelical institution, the WCTU advocated personal duty at a very early age in spiritual and temperance matters. Youth was no excuse for inactivity in improving self and society. In fact, children could bring about reformation where adults would often fail.

Frances Willard's experience as a child informed her view of how other children reasoned and should be treated. In her autobiography she describes the close supervision provided by her parents. "We never went anywhere except with our parents until I was sixteen, and almost never, after that, until fully fledged and flown ... We were literally never left alone with children or work people."[3] Children were innocent and impressionable. Such decisions as sending a child to the corner saloon to obtain liquor for intemperate parents could cause lasting damage.[4] Children must be protected from irresponsible adults and removed from homes where neglect or abuse was present. The family was not an indivisible unit, but if children were to be placed with other than relatives, the WCTU preferred family-like settings to provide the necessary care.

Lavishing attention on the blameless and innocent child became the focus of the WCTU's Little White Ribboners, a department catering to the instruction of children under seven years of age. Never very popular in Ontario, the groups seemed to operate as play groups for very small children and as opportunities for mothers to meet. The extensive network of youth organizations established by the WCTU for older children under sixteen, including the Bands of Hope, Loyal Temperance Legions, and kitchen garden groups, was intended both to convince children to lead a temperate life and to allow them to minister to intemperate acquaintances, young or old. In Ontario the Bands of Hope and Loyal Temperance Legions were largely directed to middle-class children, although working-class boys in the major cities and in some towns were often included also. In spite of class differences, however, the expectations were the same, and these were firmly rooted in developing middle-class notions of childhood. Children were first to pledge themselves to abstinence from liquor, tobacco, and foul language. The temperate child would provide a testimonial of his or her determination to hold to a high moral standard before peers and adults.[5] These testimonials would be furnished through public entertainments and personal conduct. The WCTU never doubted the persuasive power of a winsome child in convincing others to reform. "We have the whole future of the liquor traffic in our power if we will only take up this children's work with a will. Be sure and save the children, and the fathers and mothers will follow."[6]

Wives and Mothers

Unfortunately, the WCTU spent far less energy discussing and refining the ideas of its own prescribed role. Most often this role was obliquely discussed in the treatment of other issues, such as social purity, where the ideal relationship between mothers and sons was carefully traced. The WCTU accepted the essential elements of the cult of domesticity and separate spheres. The centrality of the woman's place in the home, and her responsibilities for creating a supportive, moral environment in that private sphere, was a cardinal idea about women held by the WCTU throughout the period. The recording secretary of the Newmarket union, in a summary of the 1915 president's speech to the union, noted: "Then another bit of advice to try to be cheerful in the Home yes, everywhere, especially now when so many hearts are sad ... let us remember her especial thought that 'Home is the center,' not the boundry [*sic*] and let all good go out from that."[7]

The responsible woman undertook her domestic duties with energy and commitment, providing nourishing, varied, and safe food and medicinal remedies and tonics that contained no alcohol or narcotics[8] and displaying modesty of speech and comportment.[9] She took care to venture outside alone only during daylight. The Meaford union reported that "some particular subjects spoken of was [*sic*] being out In the Twilight, In the Evening. In the Dark hours of the night and dressing in Gay attire. Contrast last Chap. of Prov. Describing the virtuous woman and the busy woman."[10]

The WCTU woman was generally portrayed as keeping no servants, so the burden of housekeeping was presented as one she should expect to shoulder personally. In fact, WCTU members often described themselves as having only modest means: "Then, again, you and I are not wealthy. We can see just what 'our town' needs, but we can not hire eloquent speakers, one after another, to come and arouse the people. We can not furnish a single drunkard's family with food or clothing; perchance we can not even afford to purchase tracts for free distribution!"[11] This portrayal of the WCTU woman managing without servants is validated by the many profiles that emerge from the local minute books. The membership in urban unions would have been most likely to keep servants. Yet scant mention is made of this in the minute books for the Ottawa, London, or Toronto groups.[12] In addition, no town or rural unions mention domestic servants. This finding calls into question the contention of historians Wendy Mitchinson[13] and Veronica Strong-Boag[14] that an important ulterior motive for middle-class women's involvement in social reform was to train domestic servants for their own homes.

Nevertheless, when a woman was faced with the choice of keeping a clean home,[15] monetary gain, or developing her mothering skills, the last must surely win. "No woman ought to be allowed to take upon herself the possibilities of motherhood without first passing an examination proving her fitness for the same,"[16] asserted a correspondent to the *Canadian White Ribbon Tidings*. A story in an 1886 issue of the *Woman's Journal* points out the danger of mothers placing cleanliness before spiritual succour in the home.

"There are those banisters all fingers marks again," said Mrs. Curry, as she made haste with a soft linen cloth to polish down the shining oak again. "George," she said as she gave a decided wrench out of the basin of suds, "If you go up those stairs again before bed-time you shall be punished." "I should like to know where I am to go," said George, "I cannot stay in the kitchen I am so much in the way, and I can't go into the parlor for fear I'll muss that up; and now you say I can't go up to my room. I know of a grand place I can go," he added to himself, "boys are never told they are in the way there, and we can have lots of fun. I'll go down to Neil's corner. I can smoke a cigar as well as any boy, if it did make me sick the first time. They shall not laugh at me again about." And so the careful housekeeper virtually drove her son from the door to hang about the steps and sit under the broad, inviting portico of the village grog-shop.[17]

Since motherhood was regarded as a sacred trust, the WCTU reserved the deepest scorn for alcoholic mothers. Generally, such women were presented in WCTU literature as working class, but a few references are made to upper-class women who desecrated the motherhood role. Where mothers were found to drink, the assumption was made that husbands also used liquor. In 1913 the editor of the *Canadian White Ribbon Tidings* carried a number of items linking child mortality to alcoholic mothers. It reported that in families regularly using alcohol, thirty of fifty-five live births resulted in death during infancy, while the rate of survival in abstemious, although poor families was sixty-eight of seventy.[18] Stories were run of obese and drunk mothers mistreating their starving, wretched children. Mothers were shown taking their children's wages to buy drink; work was hard for such children to find, it was suggested, because of the children's ragged clothing and lack of shoes. "Oh, how I cried, ragged and cold, turned out at 15 years old, to the dangers of the midnight streets, while my mother raved and raged, a drink maniac, in our room! A good doctor, going home late from a patient, found me, crouched in a doorway, sobbing with terror. He took me to his wife. She was one of the 'strong women'; strong to defend the weak and insist on the right ... Oh! the tender mercies of drunken mothers are cruel!"[19] It should not be considered accidental that the strong woman to rescue the victimized fifteen-year-old male was a middle-class paragon of womanly virtue.

The pinnacle of every woman's life and her supreme task was thought by the WCTU to be mothering. "If a mother failed in the task of raising healthy, seriously minded and well trained children, she sent forth 'damaged material,'" note Davidoff and Hall of the English middle-class mother.[20] The same could well be said for the ideas of the Ontario WCTU on woman's central role.

Daughters

The WCTU's views of the appropriate roles for men and women can be understood most easily from the mountain of literature it directed towards youths. The point of much of this prescription was to mould youthful behaviour into morally acceptable, middle-class habits for life. Because of the creation in the Young Woman's Christian Temperance Union of a separate and powerful group for single and usually young women over the age of sixteen, the WCTU was forced to distinguish the role prescription for the young single woman as opposed to that for the mature married woman. This special role will be outlined fully in chapter 6, but it included the concepts of the sanctity of the home and the prominent role of women in that setting, the necessity of acting as a witness to Christ's salvation, and temperance to self, elders, male and female friends, and, most importantly, children within an educational setting. That the YWCTU chose to expand this prescribed role to include such things as evangelical work with dissolute and fallen women caused some of the older women, as will be seen, to feel threatened. Nevertheless, it must surely be regarded as a success in the inculcation of ideas when such a subsidiary group so thoroughly imbibes the ideology of its parent and even embellishes and expands it.

Daughters were to be trained, lovingly but firmly, to help their mothers and retain all virtues essential to Christian womanhood. Certain impediments stood in the way of young women attempting to emulate this role, and to these the WCTU devoted some discussion in its pamphlet series and journals. Occasionally, there was worried mention about young women within the temperance fold taking on the "hideous habit of sneak drinking,"[21] but this was not regarded as a form of rebellion that would be adopted by many young women. Of much greater concern were presumably innocent pleasures such as Coca-Cola, about which mothers were enjoined to warn their daughters. The WCTU demonstrated its acceptance of prevailing beliefs in the "closed system" of the human body, with the resulting requirement for a balanced diet and careful life-force expenditure. The *Canadian White Ribbon Tidings* reported to mothers that "Coca-Cola is a dangerous medical compound which will originate, engender, cultivate and inflame the desire for stimulants, opiates and narcotics."[22] Similarly, the drinking of cider was thought to be dangerous "because it will create an appetite for stronger drink."[23] Even such stimulating drinks as coffee and tea held terrors for mothers of budding young daughters.[24] Feasting was dangerous: too much food "deranged bodily functions," causing the mind to suffer through sympathy of the brain with the stomach. This produced irritable feelings and peculiar temptations. The moral powers, especially those of young women, could not maintain equanimity under these circumstances, with the dreadful result that "many are held captive by their animal passions."[25]

The exciting of passion in young women appears to have been the greatest fear of mothers for their daughters. It was most vividly illustrated in a YWCTU leaflet entitled *A Girl's Influence*. An orphan of unimpeachable character, Mabel, meets a shady young man, Ed, at a temperance revival. He confesses past transgressions with liquor and a new-found desire to rebuild his life. Mabel, trusting, sweet-tempered, and intelligent, resolves to help Ed "come to Christ." "Mabel was enlisted heart and soul in his rescue; she thought of and prayed for little else; she believed herself entrusted with a sacred mission; she grew a little pale and large-eyed in the intensity of the struggle." To Mabel's astonishment, Ed proposes a romantic attachment, and she recognizes the error in her efforts. Ed backslides; Mabel mourns. A friend explains consolingly that while her intentions were the best, the mistake was in making Ed's redemption "a personal matter."[26]

Strong emotions, such as Mabel's, are misleading and dangerous and can be devastating to an inexperienced young woman. Should these pitfalls be avoided, however, the nineteenth-century prescriptive literature demonstrated considerable confidence in young women and their capability to carry on the movement.

Sons

More problematic, however, was the relationship of mother and son. Mothers must act as a model for all womanhood and must inculcate in their sons a respect for women generally and a commitment to translate this respect into action.[27] Mothers must actively guide their sons, listening to their concerns and worries. Doing so could require a mother, unblemished of spirit and behaviour, to witness the distressing crudity of the male world. Frances Willard recounted the story of a young minister who had been taught at home by his widowed mother until he was ten.

> On the first day in public school he heard such language at recess as outraged his sense of purity, and rushing home he poured out his heart to the dear mother whose name stood first on his calendar of saints. But to his astonishment she turned away from him with indignation, saying: "Charlie, never come to me again repeating what the boys have said, for I won't hear it." As she thus spoke it seemed to him that the hand he trusted most was roughly snatched from the helm of his life barque, and he was thrust out to sea without a guide, nor did he regain the port of purity until after a storm of sin that lasted many years.[28]

In another story, a young man turns to selling tobacco and a sinful life because his mother was unwilling to pray for him.[29] It seems, then, that the son was less answerable for his years of sin than was his mother.

To provide this level of ethical direction, mothers must know virtually everything about their sons. To young men indulging in "the secret pleasure" of masturbation, a writer warns: "But you are told that mother must not, under any condition, know of it. O boys, the first effort Satan makes toward your ruin is to interpose himself between you and your mother!"[30] An article in the *Canadian White Ribbon Tidings* has a "noble" young lad assert, "'You may laugh if you want to ... but I've made up my mind never, as long as I live, to do anything I would be ashamed to tell my mother.' We need a thousand boys to talk like that."[31] However, the WCTU goal for the young man went beyond simply informing mother of one's most private thoughts and actions to empowering him to reject societal evil on his own. "I have been told by many a fortunate mother that her son indignantly repelled the degradation of the common school-boy talk upon subjects he had learned to regard as sacred by reason of confidences exchanged between himself and her who bore him,"[32] wrote Frances Willard.

Did this role description indicate an elevated or reduced position for the mother in an ideal society? While in the short term the mother's position was raised almost to the status of a confessor, if she properly carried through her responsibilities this power was only transitory. The young man was expected to develop independence and self-reliance, thus ending the need for his mother to act as a moral guardian.

The assumption of young men's growing personal authority differed dramatically from the WCTU view of young women's ideal development, as will be discussed in chapter 6. Young women were expected to serve with their mothers in reaching the organization's evangelical goals. This service was not foreseen to result in increasing authority or independence, however. When it did just this, the WCTU felt threatened and uneasy.

As difficult as it would be for mothers to carry out this systematic surveillance of their sons' lives, none should doubt its importance. If the sons were properly and thoroughly influenced, mothers could assume that "when they grow up they shall be ours in sympathy, ours in pure habits, and ours as the coming leaders of the future in State and philanthropic work."[33] But the greater bonus of this intrusive mothering style, WCTU women were assured, was that their sons would be grateful. The portrayal of the emotionally charged, almost sexually reverential mother-son relationship was common in WCTU literature. "'Oh mother, mother,' he sobbed, 'I wish I had never left you! ... I'll keep as near to you in heart as I can. I wish I hadn't grown away from you so; but I'll get back again if I can!'"[34] Another woman enthused: "One of the beautiful sights I have seen is a lady and her son walking, arm in arm, from church, Sabbath after Sabbath. He was like a lover in his tenderness. It made no difference who saw him, he was just as considerate as he could have been if she had been radiant with youth and beauty."[35] This romanticized characterization reached its height during the First World War, when the enforced separation caused women pain and worry. In the WCTU journals, mothers and sons spend long hours together, "walking to take communion when she had noted the consecrated expression on his young face,"[36] sharing the same opinions, glorying in each other.

Allowance must be made, of course, for the Victorian and Edwardian tendency to describe all relationships in an overblown manner. Even so, the idealized mother-son relationship was both unrealistic and unhealthy in its implications for the mother. In his analysis of Victorian "boy culture" in America, Anthony Rotundo points out that by about age six, middle-class boys "cut loose from these social and physical restraints" of mother's world by creating an oppositional play culture in backyards, streets, parks, playgrounds, and vacant lots characterized by free movement, casual hostility, and social sadism.[37] Lynne Marks has also argued that young, single (and sometimes married) men were easily enticed into a "convivial masculine culture" that thrived in the hotels and on street corners of Ontario's small towns in this period. The middle-class women of the Ontario WCTU were more strongly motivated, she believes, by fears for their sons' unspeakable fates than by hopes in their developing strength to control their future.[38] Nevertheless, WCTU mothers were presented with an impossible model to emulate.

If a mother received anything more than a polite hearing from her son as a youth, she would have been fortunate. But to achieve the level of intimacy propounded in the literature would require a complete rejection of masculine culture by her son. Further, if a mother succeeded in forging this intensely emotional relationship with her son, she risked the attendant pain of inevitable separation when her son struck off on his independent path. If the bond were never broken, the mother would be criticized for blunting her son's growth as a Christian, middle-class man. If a mother did not build this ardent alliance with her son, forcing independence too early, she stood as an object of unfit motherhood. A superficially powerful mothering role was actually an unreachable goal for most WCTU women.

Husbands and Fathers

Where middle-class husbands make any appearance at all in WCTU literature, they are depicted as kind but weak, inept at any domestic skill, and with an almost complete lack of facility in meaningful conversation or in facing the power of human emotions. The second prize winner of the *Woman's Journal* fiction contest told the story of two men, wise Grandmother Brandon's father-in-law and her husband. The young Mrs Brandon is first encountered defying the foolish medical doctor who suggests that cognac be used to revive her father-in-law, who had almost drowned. To the doctor's surprise, Mrs Brandon brings the patient around through the ministrations of scalded milk. Unfortunately, however, this would not have been the first time that Mr Brandon Sr had tasted alcohol, and in the eugenist's worst fear, the taste for liquor had been inherited by Mrs Brandon's husband. While drunk one evening, the husband gives baby Frank the wrong medicine and almost kills him. The doctor's reputation is salvaged when he saves child and father, causing Mr Brandon Jr to vow never again to touch liquor.[39] These men are morally weak through lack of will, miscalculation, and misdeed. Their only redeeming quality is that having seen the error of their behaviour, they determine to reform by disciplining their selfish nature. The reader's hopes are not brought too high, however, by their pathetic histories of failure. The subtext in this story of a ridiculous and self-important doctor whose "knowledge" placed the family in danger would not be lost on the Victorian woman reader witnessing the professionalization of a medical community which sought women's exclusion.[40]

Husbands are occasionally criticized, if obliquely, as in an article entitled "Undervalued Work of Wives": "almost all wives engaged in domestic duties work harder, longer hours, and more productively than any other class of laborers, yet receive, instead of wages, only food, clothing and medicine."[41] It does not require a great leap to assume that the article's author meant that wives work harder than their husbands and without the respect due to them. Sixteen years later, in 1926, this proto-feminist statement has been hardened considerably. A report on temperance in the Sunday schools to the Ontario WCTU convention asks:

> Who does the work in Sunday Schools? The women. But the women do the hard work and put the men into the higher offices. In a book entitled "Women," this statement is found: "Women have always had the unchallenged right to do the world's dirty work, for a pittance so small that a man would not stoop to pick it up, so he waited until she had earned it, and then took it away from her." Perhaps this may seem far fetched and harsh, but it has been very close to the truth in the past, and women must see to it that they put women in office in the Sunday schools and stand by each other, for only then will this subject of Temperance in Sunday schools get the opportunity which is due it.[42]

Such stark feminism is startlingly in contrast to the submissive pose taken by these same women in their role as mothers of sons. The negative portraits of husbands betray frustration and bitterness at the social inequities of men and women, while the hopeful discussions of radiant mothers and fair-minded, disciplined sons points to a future of reformed social roles.[43]

Working-class men appear much more frequently in the WCTU journals and pamphlets. That they do might relate to WCTU Women's anxiety concerning their own position in a developing middle class. By identifying a target group that exhibited a triple inferiority – class, gender, and intemperance – the WCTU solidified its moral control. The profiles of working-class males were stereotyped and unflattering. Working-class husbands were represented as weak, selfish, irresponsible, and violent. These men are described as struggling "under a power with which they could not cope,"[44] of being "lured into the barroom for company ... where despair and ruin alike, two expectant vultures, hover around their dissolute, self-sacrificed prey,"[45] as squandering slim family finances on tobacco and alcohol rather than providing the necessities for their families,[46] as making poor use of the little money they managed to earn,[47] as drunkenly striking out against defenceless women and children "in the hubbub of unmeaning laughter and howls and curses."[48] The Mizpah union program on 4 April 1916 featured a presentation by Mrs Henderson, a local member. In her address on "the drink problem," she noted that she did "not fear immoral women as much as men – there are 20 such men to 1 woman – they ruin the minds of little boys."[49] The cure for men's irresponsibility and violence towards their families was, in the view of the WCTU, twofold. They must be reminded of their Christian duty to their dependents; at the same time, women must become more assertive in pointing out injustice in their own family units and in those dysfunctional families within their ken. Behind much of this family distress lay the combined evils of alcohol use, impurity – which included visiting prostitutes and engaging in masturbation – and the silencing of women's moral voice by a male-controlled government.

THE NATIONAL AND ONTARIO WCTU IDEAS ON ALCOHOL

Frances Willard's "do everything" policy, it has been argued, may have been grounded in domestic feminism,[50] with its emphasis on temperance and protection of the home, a conservative analysis of appropriate roles, and evangelicalism. But before the end of the 1880s, the American organization under her leadership had adopted pragmatic or social feminism, through which it aimed to solve specific societal problems, many of which were not directly associated with temperance. "Of all major women's organizations, the nineteenth-century WCTU came closest to advocating sweeping societal reform."[51] While this pragmatic approach of "do everything" was reflected in the broadly based Ontario WCTU program, it remained more restricted in scope than its model, Willard's National WCTU. The "do everything" policy implicitly de-emphasized temperance by placing it in a wider program of social action. But the major difference between Willard's and the Ontario program was not its scope, but the motivation for the program itself. The Ontario WCTU action was grounded, not in pragmatism, but in evangelicalism.

The evangelical obligation to engage in social reform was sustained across the province until the turn of the century. It operated in unions of all sizes, in rural, small-town, and urban settings, and amongst married and single women. In this way, the Ontario WCTU impetus appears to differ from that described in some American analyses of the WCTU, where evangelicalism has not been identified as important.[52] However, it has been seen as central to understanding the World's WCTU.[53] During the nineteenth century, single young women in the Ontario YWCTU generally evinced a more militant evangelicalism and developed their skills with different groups, but the basic ideological blueprint did not greatly differ.

The WCTU, like many organizations of the period, blamed alcohol for individuals' and society's ills. Early in its existence, however, it tried to show the devastating effect of alcohol when combined with a variety of other abuses. Although the organization came to accept that alcohol was both cause and effect, it never retreated from its ideas of the evil of alcohol combined with other substances and with other patterns of behaviour. This relationship was clearly outlined in the earliest of the National Leaflets. The leaflets' evangelical argument concentrated on the relationship between individual character and physical health: "physical being is the firm base of the whole pyramid of character." But one's health is undermined by several threats: poor ventilation; dress which is too light, too heavy, constricting, or dirty; "unbalanced exercise"; over-spicy food, including pork; and strong tea or coffee; alcohol, or narcotics, such as nicotine, which first excite the body, then depress it, and finally derange it, leading to compulsive excess.[54] Alcohol is especially dangerous to the balanced body, since it consumes water, "precisely as fire acts upon water, lapping it up with a fierce and insatiable thirst. This affinity of alcohol for moisture is like a feverish and consuming passion, and the blistered nose, burnt brain, and parboiled stomach of the drinking man are nature's perpetual object lessons to illustrate the fact that alcohol must be the redoubtable enemy of an organization made up as the human being is, of seven in every eight parts of water."[55] After the balance has been destroyed and will remain destroyed because of alcohol's addictive qualities, the individual's character is permanently crippled, possibly for several generations.[56] "Character," then, is comprised of sobriety, integrity, industry, and gentleness, all of which are upstanding middle-class values. "But these cardinal points are all determined by the the first, sobriety."[57] Largely because of the organization's stress on temperance in the nineteenth century, the WCTU accepted eugenics in this period. However, this determinist approach had eroded by the 1890s. With the impact of environmentalism, along with the organization's growing endorsement of the redeeming effects of education, eugenics and the primacy of temperance were reduced in significance.

The WCTU knew that sometimes individuals were unknowingly exposed to alcohol in their own homes by mothers or doctors seeking medicinal agents. To correct this misguided home use by mothers and to further buttress its anti-alcohol arguments with medical support, the WCTU devoted much effort to denigrating alcohol's curative powers and to suggesting healthful alternatives. For example, one of its National Leaflets, entitled *Spirituous Liquors Not Needed in Medicine or the Arts*, hopefully complimented housewives on their rejection of alcohol-based medicines: "Since it became known that alcoholic solutions of camphor, paregoric, cordials, tincture of peppermint etc., – articles once found in every household – are remedial agents of doubtful efficacy, or positively hurtful under indiscriminate use, they have been to a large extent banished from dwellings." Doctors were encouraged to replace alcohol-based products with glycerine, naphtha, bisulphide of carbon, pyroligneous products, carbolic acid, "and a hundred other agents which are capable of taking the place of alcohol in a very large number of appliances and processes." The entire argument is grounded in respect for the new scientism and modern, laboratory-proven methodology. Alcohol is portrayed, then, as not so much as immoral as pathetically out of date. "This view of the chemical and therapeutical needs and uses of alcohol, as related to the human family, is not presented from the standpoint of the temperance orator, but from that of the scientific investigator."[58]

Women in America, Britain, and Canada had long been regarded as guardians of the home by the time the WCTU was formed in the last quarter of the nineteenth century. Denied a public role, women had been encouraged to set a good example and exercise moral suasion on their menfolk in a domestic setting, and thus influence public life indirectly. The early temperance movement assumed individual agency, as contrasted to legislative fiat, to be the means of redemption from alcohol. This concept fit neatly with woman's role as domestic helpmeet and with the non-intrusive role of government. Individual women gave spiritual and physical support to their individual male kin. For the most part, this remained the approach counselled by Annie Wittenmyer, president of the American WCTU from 1874 to 1879. But this view was rejected by Frances Willard, who saw defeat of alcohol, or any other evil in society, being accomplished only through the united action of a group, as had been illustrated with the successes of the Women's Crusade. Willard argued further that change could only occur with direct legislative action, rather than moral suasion. While it took some time for Willard's strategies to be condoned, by the 1880s it had become accepted that if temperance were to be realized, women must unite in their efforts, since the attack on the family affected the entire society, including themselves. An additional incentive to initiate a public struggle in defence of the family unit came with the recognition that women and children suffered grievously from the effects of alcohol even though they were not the offenders.

By the last quarter of the nineteenth century, then, the "drink problem" came to be seen as a male problem, with its most destructive impact on the home and the often defenceless family. It did not require a huge mental leap from seeing some men as the embodiment of iniquity to seeing all men as prone to engaging in the destructive behaviour. By the 1870s this view was called by Frances Willard the "home protection" movement. Such a conclusion might logically lead a group of women to feel powerless and victimized, but in the case of the WCTU this was not the result. It reasoned that if women and children were the victims of this widespread abuse, women must correct the wrongs by protecting the helpless. Therefore, in terms of their ideas about patriarchal controls in the family and society, the WCTU presented a fairly radical interpretation of the problem and its solutions. Their ideas of female moral superiority and male weakness propelled them to demand a more equitable power balance within the family unit. It must be granted that a reconstituted family unit would ultimately look to its young men to right the wrongs which had been pointed out in the WCTU analysis, but this outcome would be accomplished through women's moral training. Thus conservative ideas of family relationships could, and did, result in progressive demands.

How widespread was support for this set of ideas around the concept of "home protection"? Norman Clark attests that in this period the American family was more threatened than that in any other society because of westward movement which interfered with continuity of place, by mass immigration of non-English-speaking peoples, and by the dangers posed by urbanization and industrialization.[59] Anxiety for the future of the family was pronounced in both the

United States and Canada. "Home protection" ideas would, therefore, likely strike a responsive chord in many a listener and adherent.

The early WCTU in both the United States and Canada viewed drink as the primary cause of poverty.[60] The poor were enjoined to reject alcohol so that society's bounty, available to all temperate citizens, could be theirs as well. By the late 1880s, national leaders and local members were beginning to accept that drunkenness was a result, as well as a cause, of poverty. Since an unjust division of society's wealth made alcohol the inevitable escape to ameliorate suffering, the solution came to be seen in fundamental changes in the environment. This also resulted in a reduced stress on temperance as a panacea for the many interrelated social ills. Hence the Ontario WCTU by the 1890s supported temperance, as well as prison reform, separate facilities for women, improved arrangements for neglected and dependent children, the kindergarten movement, social and reading rooms for the working poor, refuges for abandoned and fallen women, mother's education, and vocational training, among other initiatives.

IDEAS ON SOCIAL PURITY

The social purity, or White Shield–White Cross, program was regarded as an important means to achieving home protection. The movement is also intimately associated with evangelical ideas of womanhood. In Frances Willard's opinion, social purity was linked with intemperance; she classified them as "iniquity's Siamese Twins."[61] In fact, Ian Tyrrell asserts that of the twin iniquities, social purity was the more important to the WCTU.[62] In her analysis of the Canadian moral-reform movement, Mariana Valverde argues that social purity, "along with temperance and Sunday observance, helped to constitute a powerful if informal coalition for the moral regeneration of the state, civil society, the family, and the individual."[63] Its connection to temperance was close. "In some respects, temperance and social purity acted as a single movement," she suggests.[64]

What came to be called "social purity" was really an uneven aggregate of issues championed in Britain (and most of the colonies) from the 1860s, and in the United States and Canada by the mid 1870s. Topics of public concern ranged from opposition to regulated prostitution in Britain or prostitution in any form in North America, to censorship of popular culture such as explicit literature, moving pictures, and revealing clothing, the elimination of masturbation, and the ideal of a "white life for two," – a single standard for men's and women's sexual behaviour.

David Pivar suggests that social purity was "multidimensional, yet apparently unified" and that as it "pressed in different directions and possessed various possibilities for potential development ... [it] underwent many changes as it was communicated through the women's movement and applied locally."[65] The involvement of, first, the American WCTU and thereafter the Canadian, Ontario, and local unions demonstrates the truth of this assessment.

The American WCTU joined with moral reformers first in 1876 through its rescue work with prostitutes.[66] In 1877 the committee for work with fallen women was established, and by 1883 it had become the department for the suppression of the social evil, signalling a new confidence in social, rather than exclusively personal, reform. The (American) national department of social purity, as it became in 1885, worked towards the joint elimination of prostitution and liquor: "every house of ill-repute is a secret saloon and nearly every inmate an inebriate."[67] It sought to achieve this by several routes. "Houses of refuge" to reform poor prostitutes, such as Ottawa's Home for Friendless Women, was one means attempted. Travellers' aid, in Ontario most notably at Toronto's Union Station, was introduced to intercept young women coming to the city and to provide them with decent shelter before they "fell" into iniquity.

At the dominion level, a department of "purity in literature, art and fashion" was created in 1890,[68] and provincially, a department of social purity existed from 1886 to counter the work of "wicked, designing men, subtle, treacherous women ... used daily in the unclean hands of our Lord's enemy."[69] Many local unions, such as West Toronto, Richmond Hill, Brampton, and Port Credit also supported social purity departments.[70] By the 1890s "purity" also covered Ontario WCTU opposition to the regulation and existence of prostitution, its support for legislation to raise the age of consent, and censorship of "obscene" literature and theatre.

One example of an early and important purity issue in Ontario was the plight of the prostitute. Within the broader social purity movement, two distinct positions developed to combat prostitution. The "new abolitionists" concentrated on remedial strategies, such as rescuing the "fallen woman" and closing brothels, while the moral education wing, heavily dominated by women, sought to eliminate prostitution through appropriate childhood education.[71] In its earliest years, the WCTU in both Canada and the United States favoured the conservative solutions of the new abolitionists, but increasingly it carved out a role for itself in providing moral education for mothers, youths, and children. In the nineteenth century, the ideological position of the Ontario WCTU on the fallen woman was highly ambiguous. The organization blamed men for forcing themselves on young women who were previously sexually innocent: "Young girls are decoyed by all manner of subtleties and deception ... he is liable to five years penal servitude. And this is the penalty for the offenders, if captured and convicted for entrapping a guileless young girl and plunging her, against her will or wish into a life – the horrors of which one's pen dare not write or depict."[72] At the same time, the women of the WCTU across North America showed disappointment that women's allegedly superior moral qualities were inadequate to protect them in this time of need. Clearly, the pivotal ethical issue was whether or not women found their debased behaviour agreeable. In the early years of the WCTU, the assumption was generally made that no woman would ever willingly comply with a man requesting sexual favours because of her feminine lack of sexual desire. The popularization of the "white slave trade" as a middle-class issue encouraged a bifurcation in the WCTU-approved view of the unchaste woman. The concept of the asexual and pure, but naïve young woman as victim could coexist with an acknowledgment that some degraded women consciously chose such a lifestyle. The former view permitted an outpouring of anger against men, but the latter was much more resistant to solution. In most cases, the strategy taken was to force unchaste women to face the depth of their sinfulness and take stock of the errant choice they had made. Hence the evangelical approach of challenging one's sinfulness through guided introspection was the one favoured in treating the fallen woman.

By the 1890s the Canadian WCTU had all but abandoned the "new abolitionism" in its emphasis on moral and health education, both in the schools through scientific temperance instruction and in extracurricular youth groups. Angus MacLaren argues that the intrusiveness of moral-reform education, in which women "positively exulted," effected a revolution in the "science" of eugenics by providing children with "mystifying accounts of sexual matters by purported experts who implicitly or explicitly attacked the competency of parents and friends to deal with such subjects."[73] But as has been discussed, purity education was seen by the WCTU as carried out most effectively in the home by mothers. They were to act as a model for all womanhood, educating and purifying themselves, husbands, daughters, and most especially, sons.

The message of mothers' special role in social purity became a mainstay of the lectures given by Arthur W. Beall, the Ontario WCTU's "purity agent" between 1905 and 1911 and thereafter a purity lecturer employed by the Ontario Department of Education. Beall's position on purity education had been shaped by his early association with the WCTU, and it stands in contrast to that of other social purity groups, such as the White Cross Society. His remarks to the women of the Richmond Hill WCTU in 1927 were interpreted in this way by the local union's recording secretary:

In introducing the subject of social hygiene, Mr. Baele [*sic*] said that the name often antagonized people who thought that it was merely combatting social diseases, but means the best methods of giving to the community moral and mental health ... as mothers we should safe guard our families against it by knowledge of the care of the body ... the duty of every mother is to teach obedience, truth and self respect which is the basic principle of good citizenship.[74]

Beall expanded on this theme in his 1933 handbook on social purity, a set of ten "lessons" that closely followed the lectures provided to thousands of Ontario schoolchildren. For example, in lesson 8, delivered to boys after the girls had been dismissed, Beall proclaims that "on the day that you were born your mother went down into the Valley of the Shadow of Death so that you might live ... Your mother A-L-M-O-S-T went."[75] Of both boys and girls, Beall asks: "Look here, girls and boys, if such a picture is not fit for your mother to look at, is it fit for you to look at? No, indeed! And you won't dream of doing so."[76]

A second area of concern in social purity for both the American and Canadian WCTU was women's dress reform. The decline in the simplicity and modesty of women's dress was seen by social purists within the WCTU and without as emblematic of societal demoralization, symbolizing a loss of female moral purpose and social function.[77] The campaign for modest dress was taken up by several purity advocates, including Anthony Comstock and Josiah and Deborah Leeds, as a route to redefining acceptable social behaviour. The campaign for modest dress was intimately associated with the suppression of impure advertising and the identification of objectionable theatrical performances, ballet, social dancing, and especially "pornographic magazines" and "indecent art."[78] Although men were involved in all of these, the campaign was peculiarly directed to woman and the crucial purity that she symbolized.

Leeds's pamphlet on *Simplicity of Attire in Relation to Social Purity* so impressed Frances Willard that she published it as an official WCTU tract. And she herself wrote on the issue, possibly in response to Leeds's publication. One of her pamphlets, produced before 1885 and intended for group study, was entitled *Society and Society Women*.

Banish wine from the dinner, dancing from the "evening entertainment" and "society" with its bare arms and exposed busts, its late hours and indigestions, would collapse. Nothing is surer than that wine is to be banished, and that with the growing uplift and dignity of womanhood, dancing, and the outrageous mode of dress that goes along with it, will one day be held as a mere relic of barbarism.[79]

In 1890 the convention of the Dominion WCTU passed a resolution discountenancing "the objectionable style of evening dress which obtains in society gatherings throughout the Dominion."[80] As late as 1913 the annual convention of the Ontario WCTU resolved to "do all in our power to raise the whole question of dress to a higher plane, training our daughters to desire only beauty of line and color – the visible sign of the soul which is 'all glorious within.'"[81] A number of articles in the *Woman's Journal* adapted the main precepts of the American WCTU literature on modest dress to the Canadian setting. Wool was endorsed as the best possible fabric since it permitted the skin to perspire and thus keep cool in summer and warm in winter. The *Journal* recommended that underclothing be kept scrupulously clean since "when it becomes clogged with perspiration, it becomes unwholesome as well as becoming less capable of keeping the body warm." Tight lacing and garters were criticized, the latter tending to produce varicose veins. A final, spirited condemnation was reserved for women who neglected to bundle their babies properly and who "can lay aside their flannels for an evening, bare the upper part of their chests and the greater part of their arms, leave their own warm apartments and promenade in cold banqueting rooms, disregard the dictates of common sense altogether in the bitterest weather, and yet survive."[82]

Local unions also made dress reform a favourite topic, "a subject which is every day receiving increased attention."[83] It is apparent that modest-dress reform was closely associated in the minds of the women in the Ontario and Dominion WCTU with health, safety, and class concerns. The prescriptive behaviour code connected to modest-dress reform did not convince WCTU women of their fragility and vulnerability. In all of the Canadian literature generated around modest-dress reform, women's initiative and authority is apparent. Rather than paralysing women through fear, the literature assumes that they can control their own destiny, provided that they take reasonable precautions. It also helps to define the new middle-class woman in physical terms. Here too the WCTU woman could speed her ascent into middle-class status by "looking the part."

This view of female agency contrasts dramatically with WCTU-supported White Cross literature directed to young men.[84] "Fallen" male youths became the focus of the Ontario WCTU's social purity education activities from the mid 1880s. The American WCTU adopted the British White Cross series For Men Only and distributed it across North America. These pamphlets, sponsored by a male-dominated society and directed to young men, stand in direct and startling contrast to the Canadian WCTU-produced social purity series White Life Truths.

The Church of England initiated the White Cross Society in 1883 "to promote social purity and to assist young men in their resistance to illicit sexual relations."[85] The society soon gained status as a church organization and was extended throughout the British Empire. Two years later a White Cross Army was established in New York, with Frances Willard taking a major propagandist role in the organization. She became a White Cross speaker, endorsed (and authored one of) the White Cross pamphlets, and created a comparable girls' association, the White Shield Society, under the auspices of the American WCTU. "White Cross work contemplates a direct appeal to the chivalry of men; that they shall join this holy crusade by a personal pledge of purity and helpfulness; that boys shall early learn the sacred meaning of the White Cross and that the generous Knights of this newest and most noble chivalry shall lead Humanity's sweet and solemn song."[86] In the United States, meetings of the White Cross and White Shield societies were held, but the more common practice in Canada was to use White Cross–White Shield literature at WCTU, YWCTU, or youth temperance meetings.

Beginning in 1885, the American WCTU journal, the *Union Signal,* began reprinting the works of Ellice Hopkins, the English purity reformer,[87] and soon thereafter, the entire White Cross Series was made available to North American readers. Willard's championing of the White Cross Series is surprising when the fundamental tenets of the White Cross Society are considered. The series utilized paternalistic ideas and stark and violent imagery that emphasized good (white) and bad (black). It presented the problem of impurity as one largely created by women's intellectual and physical weakness, with the concomitant solution resting entirely with the strengthened male. The imagery tended to be medieval or militaristic, with archaic language used to give an extra flourish.

For example, in Ellice Hopkins's pamphlet *My Little Sister*, young men are told that "if you look at the best and highest men, the men who are touched to fine issues, you will find them knightly men, thoroughly chivalrous in their conduct towards women."[88] Women are weak and dependent on men to correct injustice: "Young men, I write unto you because you are strong; use your strength to protect our dear girls from the devils in human form that lie everywhere in wait for them. Never was knight of old more needed than you are to take up the cause of the wronged, the helpless, the unprotected."[89] Impurity was like other historical evils, such as witch burning, duelling, and drunkenness: "each in turn has been conquered by brave Christian men daring to resist them."[90] It must have been disconcerting for WCTU members to read that brave Christian men had conquered drunkenness, presumably obviating their efforts in this arena![91] Women are naïve and childish, "having none to care for them; some flung out by the hand of the very man they loved and trusted, some drugged and trapped; some leaping down of their own free will on that fatal stage of death in pursuit of some childish bauble, unknowing of the bitter end till it is too late to escape."[92] Women had significance only in the private sphere; men had significance in both the private and the public: "impurity in the woman destroys the family, but impurity in the man destroys the wider family of the nation."[93]

To convince young men to take up this noble work, the White Cross Series endeavoured to frighten recalcitrant youths into compliance. This message was consistent with literature produced by most social purity authorities, including the Self and Sex Series[94] and A.W. Beall's lectures on behalf of the Ontario WCTU. Young men were told that self-abuse took hold gradually but steadily, with the inevitable end being the ruin of one's constitution. Physical and mental powers atrophied, and the victim suffered from weakness and disease, a failing memory, and a loss of interest in nature, athletics, society, and "good" books; "unless he controls himself and breaks the spell of the temptation *at once and forever*, he becomes a mere wreck, possibly idiotic or insane."[95] Should a young man feel that he might succumb to temptation, it is suggested that he engage in vigorous outdoor sports, choose companions "of cheerful, hopeful natures," and avoid rich or spicy food, tobacco, alcohol, or "exciting novels."[96] It might be noted that women – portrayed as intellectually dull, naïve, and confused – were seen to have no role in saving the vulnerable young man from a hideous fate. Pity the overburdened male youth: he was charged with saving frail womankind and himself!

Contrast this approach to the Canadian WCTU purity literature series White Life Truths. It probably dated from the early 1920s, and the message and connotations were very different from the White Cross Series. The WCTU series is carefully situated within a fundamentalist Christian context and highly respectful of parental authority and consistent motherly teaching of all of life's moral issues.[97] *A Schoolroom Story* tells of the problems faced by a Sunday school teacher when reading with her class about Christ's conception. A shamefaced grin makes the rounds of her coeducational class. The female teacher protests, "'We never treat other verses in this way. When from other passages you have taken a low thought it was never allowed to pass until a higher thought had been given to crowd out the lower.'" The teacher is offended. "'All God's works are beautiful and good. Yet some of us are so separated from God by sin that in our ignorance and folly we think meanly of that which in itself is good.'" She proceeds with the class through an object lesson of ways that "mother"(!) beans or mother birds protect and nurture their young; the class is encouraged to discuss the natural hierarchy of life, with a bean worth less than a bird, a bird less than a child. "The shame-faced look was gone and now thirty pairs of bright, frank, sympathetic eyes were looking straight into mine." The teacher follows this breakthrough with the notion that God has ensured that none of us come into this world without two strong, loving parents to guide and protect us. But her clinching argument is reminiscent of Beall's lectures about the special nature of mother love: "'There is just this about it all, boys, whenever I think of your mother and mine I think of Christ. He gave His life for us. Mother has gone to the very border of the grave to give us life ...' The eyes that looked into mine were dimmed with tears. Heads were slowly bowed. After a short silence some mothers' hearts would have bounded with joy *could* they have heard the tone in which one boy said, 'My, we ought to be good for our mothers!'"[98]

The Sunday school teacher's position should be noted in this fundamentalist text: working in concert with a sanctified home, she is the conduit to bring youths "separated from God by sin" to a Christian vision for society. The teacher's assurance that we are all endowed with "two strong, loving parents to guide and protect us" is so patently false that it cannot be viewed as a realistic text, but as one tracing the outline of an idealized society in an increasingly dissolute age. Where the British White Cross Series glorified man's pugilistic and moral might, the Canadian White Life Truths – in a period when much of the WCTU's confidence had been sapped – honoured a mother's purity and sturdiness, selfless love, and Christly example as the signposts for young men seeking the path to social purity.

But if the WCTU hoped to gain members through its support of social purity, it was to be disappointed. Few mature women were drawn into the organization directly through social purity work. The "mother's meetings" were one attempt to popularize the issue with women. Here women were provided with materials and strategies to impart sex education to their children, although the meetings obviously served other purposes as well. In many Ontario unions, for example, the mother's meetings became a forum for the discussion of infant and child care, nutrition, and pure food preparation.[99]

To further broaden the appeal of this message, American purity reformers such as Anthony Comstock argued that many more "germs of licentiousness"[100] than prostitution or the white slave trade needed to be identified and rooted out in order to prevent them from contaminating public morality. To this end, undesirable billboard advertising, "impure theatrical placards," objectionable theatrical performances, ballet, social dancing, "pornographic magazines," suggestive and binding clothing, peep-shows, fair midways, and "indecent art" were all condemned.[101]

But even though the social purity movement was broadened and personalized through the dress reform issue, it failed to attract large-scale support in the American or Canadian community. This was certainly not for lack of effort. In 1887 the American WCTU uncovered an example of the white slave trade and energetically publicized it in the tradition of William T. Stead. A young woman, searching for employment, had answered a sly advertisement for work at a lumber camp in Michigan. Her employers-cum-captors imprisoned her with other prostitutes in a compound guarded by vicious dogs. Determined to escape this life of evil, she fled into the surrounding swamps in an unsuccessful bid for freedom. Like the slaves before her, she was, inevitably, recaptured and returned to her degraded life, where she was punished horribly. To the WCTU's surprise and dismay, the exposé failed to spark public indignation. Dr Kate Bushnell, a WCTU missionary, conducted an investigation into the "Michigan dens" in 1888, documenting sixty "stockades" in which women were forced to remain in prostitution, "abused and often murdered."[102] Disappointingly, an incredulous public was not even swayed when Frances Willard verified Dr Bushnell's findings, published as "Another Maiden Tribute," and averred that her name ought to be placed among the "Grace Darlings of moral rescue work"[103] for the service she had rendered. The chief result of this investigative reporting was that some states raised the age of consent[104] and the National WCTU came to be identified with the exposé, moral outrage backed by documented facts.[105]

Indeed, a major campaign was waged internationally to raise the age of majority. The English social purity leadership, including Josephine Butler and William T. Stead, was credited with starting the public outcry against abuses of the "daughters of the people" and with maintaining pressure until the Criminal Law Amendment Act of 1885 raised the age of consent to sixteen.[106] By 1894 twenty American states had raised the age to sixteen, an accomplishment for which the WCTU could take substantial credit.[107] In Canada the legislative changes dating from 1892 sprang from a belief that "positive social goals could be achieved by negative means, that is, by prohibiting certain kinds of behaviour."[108] The age of consent was raised from sixteen to eighteen in 1900. At the same time, the crime of seduction no longer applied only to females "of previously chaste character." Now the onus was placed on the accused male to prove the previous loss of the seduced female's chastity.[109]

But this legislative change was just one of many for which the Canadian WCTU and other social purity groups pressed. In 1892 there had been demands that legislation protect young girls and immigrant women from seduction and abduction, that brothels be crushed, and that the procuring of underaged females be stopped. As a result, "Canada's Criminal Code of 1892 had and retains the most comprehensive system of offences for protecting young women and girls from sexual predators."[110] In the same year, a new section declared it a criminal offence for an employer or manager in a factory, mill, or workshop to seduce or have "illicit connection with" any female under age twenty-one. In 1896 women in shops and stores were similarly protected.[111] Two years earlier the Ontario WCTU had demanded that the names of prostitutes and their clients be published, insisting that by withholding men's names, "unjust discrimination ... brands the one sinner and shields the other."[112] In 1904 the WCTU, in association with the YWCA, the police magistrate of Winnipeg, the Moral and Social Reform Council of Canada, and the plenary council of the Roman Catholic Church, demanded stiffer punishment of adultery and extra-legal marriage. Although legislation did not result, adultery was attacked through a variety of indirect measures.[113] In 1909 the Ontario WCTU requested the establishment of juvenile courts, "being thoroughly alarmed at the white slave trade."[114] This broad campaign to regulate sexual behaviour and marriage had clear connections to the drive for middle-class status. By lobbying as strenuously as it did for legislative changes associated with family life, the WCTU ensured that it would help to define the moral standards underlying middle-class behaviour, especially as these related to the shoring up of the family unit. The American and Canadian WCTU fought the battle for social purity on the basis of both individual conscience and legislative intervention, and in the latter case, enjoyed considerable success.

IDEAS ON WOMAN'S SUFFRAGE

The women of the WCTU regarded themselves as dutiful citizens of their society even though, throughout much of this period, they lacked the right to vote. Their involvement in the political process was generally indirect, but they prided themselves on understanding that process sufficiently to exercise great authority as a pressure group. Furthermore, they accepted the critical role of government in regulating social evils such as the liquor trade, and in Canada they even came eventually to accept the wisdom of a government-licensed monitoring system.[115] In fact, when the government was perceived to be lazy in its surveillance system, the WCTU demanded vociferously and repeatedly that it carry out its leadership duties. To support their involvement in the political system, the women of the WCTU long agitated for the right to vote.

Frances Willard describes her "conversion" to the ballot for women in her autobiography. In 1876, during a visit to Ohio, while she was praying alone, "there was borne in upon my mind ... the declaration, 'You are to speak for woman's ballot as a weapon of protection to her home and tempted loved ones from the tyranny of drink.'"[116] Later that year, the National WCTU passed a resolution in support of the "home-protection ballot," the name having been lifted from an address given by Letitia Youmans.[117] Ruth Bordin calls the phrase "a masterstroke of public relations, which made suffrage palatable to many, both men and women, who would not otherwise have been able to swallow it."[118]

In Canada, acceptance of woman's franchise gained endorsement somewhat more slowly. Contrary to the arguments presented by Carol Bacchi about the leadership role played by urban women in promoting woman's franchise,[119] there is some evidence that small-town WCTU members supported the vote for women before it became fashionable at the provincial and dominion levels. In any case, as Daniel Malleck's work has shown, some local unions were much more enthusiastic in their support of the vote for women than were others.[120] The records indicate that the first local union to formally champion the cause of woman's suffrage was London in 1893.[121] It directed a resolution to its member of the provincial legislature to vote in favour of the current bill. The Richmond Hill and Newmarket unions were also early and consistent supporters. However, the Dunnville union recorded that in 1903 the question was discussed, "but was not favorably received as an unqualified and universal vote for women,"[122] and the Ottawa WCTU was only lukewarm in its advocacy as well.

On occasion, unions' support for the franchise pitted them against their natural allies. For instance, the women of Richmond Hill in early 1887 discussed an opinion expressed by Dr Gilmour, their MPP

To his assertion that "woman's influence could be more beneficially felt in the home than at the polls," the recording secretary noted that "the opinions of the ladies did not on the whole harmonize with that of Dr. Gilmour."[123] Later the same year, the Ontario convention created a "legislation, franchise and petitions" department, and the following year it passed a resolution calling for "the still further extention [*sic*] of the Franchise to women in any and every possible way."[124]

A similar department was created by the Dominion Convention in 1889. In that year, Dr Stowe-Gullen addressed the convention on the franchise. The Ontario president, Letitia Youmans, repeatedly emphasized the duty of women duly qualified to vote in municipal elections and to serve as school board trustees.[125] It would be several years before the demand for woman's franchise in provincial or federal elections would be made, however. The Canadian WCTU continued to have confidence that indirect influence would result in women's political ideas being accepted by male parliamentarians. In 1896 the Dominion WCTU issued a statement redolent with evangelical fervour and confidence:

> That as God's intentions concerning woman must be measured by the capabilities with which He has endowed her, as we have no right to let any of His gracious gifts to us lie unused, and as he has provided us with all the qualifications which make intelligent and helpful voters, and added to them, that tender and vital interest in the human race which inheres in womanhood and maternity, we will never rest until we can fight Christ's battles armed with ballots, and we demand from our Dominion government the speedy enactment of an Act which will give equal franchise with men, to the women of our vast Dominion.[126]

Three years later, a similar resolution was formally passed by the Ontario WCTU.[127] After 1905 there is evidence that female suffrage became a more significant issue for the Ontario organization. Children engaging in the medal contests (as discussed in detail in chapter 5) were encouraged to give speeches on set topics, including after 1909 in Ontario, woman's franchise. In 1910 the columns of the *Canadian White Ribbon Tidings* were bursting with acerbic comments on disenfranchised womanhood:

> The contemptuous reference in regard to the signatures of women on the anti-gambling petitions is enough to raise an army of belligerent suffragettes on Canadian soil ... If the majority of signatures were those of women, it goes to show that women as a class are against gambling and furthermore

that their home influence is counteracted, in a large degree, by outside forces. This gives the ancient lie: "The hand that rocks the cradle is the hand that moves the world" a denial. The hand that holds the ballot is the hand that moves the political world.[128]

By 1916 the WCTU's support for woman's franchise was so engrained and well publicized that when the Regina mayor sent his greetings to the dominion convention meeting in his city, he presented his credentials as "a total abstainer and prohibitionist, but also a believer in woman suffrage."[129]

The war years saw the culmination of the Ontario WCTU's campaign for woman's suffrage, gained provincially in 1917 and federally in 1918 with the Women's Franchise Act. The achievement was recognized through warm resolutions and speeches at the Annual Conventions. It is important to note, however, that like the passing of the Ontario Temperance Act in 1916, enfranchisement did not receive even passing comment in the minutes of local unions. How can such a glaring omission be explained? The Dominion WCTU had continued to agitate for woman's suffrage, but the issue was supported much more quietly at the Ontario level and in the local unions, with the notable exception of the London WCTU. When the franchise victory was announced, the provincial convention reacted quickly and enthusiastically, but the organization could not claim to have been a powerful pressure group at either the provincial or the federal level. The local unions of the Ontario WCTU had redirected their efforts almost exclusively into social and educational projects by this time. These undertakings, with their short-range and concrete achievements, validated the women's considerable efforts and their evangelical principles. By 1917 woman's suffrage was not irrelevant, but like prohibition, it no longer dominated the members' thoughts or actions.

IDEAS ON NATIONALISM, IMPERIALISM, PEACE, RACE, AND ETHNICITY

The average Ontario resident of the late nineteenth century was proud of Canada's place in the British Empire and of the latter's "civilizing" tradition throughout the world. Most women of the Ontario WCTU would have agreed with James Cappon from Queen's University, although they would have been unlikely to have travelled in circles where their sentiments would have been expressed so grandly. "The Empire represents an ideal of high importance for the future of civilization, the attempt to assemble in a higher unity than even that of nationality the forces which maintain and advance the white man's ideals of civilization, his sense of justice, his constitutional freedom, his respect for law and order, his humanity. It is an attempt to transcend the evils of nationality ... without impairing the vigour which the national consciousness gives to a people."[130] Seen from our vantage point nine decades later, in an age which has a heightened sensitivity to racial, ethnic, and gender inequity, these views are without doubt racist. But the women of the Ontario WCTU in the period under examination did not live in our age or hold to our notions of equity, and it seems unfair to judge them by criteria which they would have found decontextualized and lacking in pride.

It has been posited that the Ontario WCTU was a racist organization.[131] Mariana Valverde contends that while it did not exclude women of colour, "the white ribbon ... was a symbol not only of the healthy pure milk they would substitute for alcohol but also of the kind of racial composition they favoured for Canada."[132] Quoting a Mrs (Dr) Wickett, Wentworth County superintendent of heredity and hygiene, she notes a fear of "race suicide" and a denigration of motherhood as practised by other than Anglo-Saxon women. "It is clear that in Mrs Wickett's eyes, not all actual mothers qualify as 'real' mothers."[133]

The women of the Ontario WCTU were a product and deeply reflective of their age. They had no pretensions about seeing the problematic issue of "race" any more clearly than other members of society. But the full record suggests that the organization was more tolerant than many of the contribution to Canada made by other races and ethnic groups , and was sometimes reliant on women in those communities to develop temperate and civic virtues amongst their menfolk. To do justice to the question of racism, and also to the women of the WCTU, it is necessary to consider both the intentions of WCTU policies and the means by which these women attempted to implement those intentions with three distinct groups: native Canadians, blacks, and eastern Europeans who made their presence felt to the Ontario WCTU after the First World War. The organization made a concerted attempt to empower black women as temperance advocates in their homes and communities; it seems not to have actively recruited women from the other two groups. Having considered the record by consulting representative views of the organization, one can safely conclude that the Ontario WCTU aimed to include women and, through them, children and men of different races and ethnic groups in a temperate Ontario.

Canadian native groups had been a primary concern of the organization from the provincial convention's inception in 1877 and its establishment of a single department of foreign work to promote temperance with both native Canadians and German immigrants. Native Canadians continued to be a focus for its mission work because of that group's particular problems with alcohol consumption. To facilitate this work, the WCTU for many years sponsored home "missionaries," the best known of whom was the intrepid Miss Sproule. Consistent with this approach of considering native society as "other," nothing in the records indicates that the WCTU attempted to establish native unions. This policy of "missionizing" native people, including women, reflected current Canadian thinking and especially the approaches taken by Protestant missionary societies with which the Ontario WCTU was in close cooperation throughout this period.[134]

The Ontario WCTU was not alerted to the potential membership in the province's black community until long after it was an issue with the National WCTU in the United States. The organization first began the process of formally soliciting black women members at the provincial level in 1894, when Minnie Phelps established a "department of work among colored people." She had been the provincial organization's first recording secretary, and as a long-time president of the local union in St Catharines, she undoubtedly knew a number of black women. The WCTU's plan under Phelps's leadership seems to have been to establish an independent department and sometimes unions, much as it had done with the young women in the YWCTU, and thereby to help black women control alcohol consumption amongst their husbands and sons. If the YWCTU model had been successful, it would have encouraged black women to take on leadership roles, at least with regards to temperance, in their own families and communities, as the Y women had done across Ontario. At the same time, it would have guarded against segregation. The Y model, as will be discussed in chapter 6, permitted independent projects where they seemed appropriate and a great deal of cooperative effort when the YWCTU and the WCTU joined forces. Hence the WCTU's intention was clearly to incorporate black women into the organization through finding common ground with them.

Sadly, their objective was never reached, although a considerable number of black unions and departments were founded, especially after the turn of the century. Phelps began work in the "department among colored people" with great energy. She remained as superintendent of the department until 1897, when she retired from most work at the provincial level. Thereafter the department was taken up by a series of superintendents, but the hoped-for ground swell never developed. Nevertheless, if 1914 is taken as an example, in that year there were "colored unions" or departments in Guelph, Stratford,

Woodstock, Ingersoll, Windsor, London, Owen Sound, Brantford, St Catharines, Sarnia, and Niagara Falls.[135] The main problem seems to have been the way in which the WCTU attempted to fold black women into its membership, not its desire to do so. The most important work of the organization, as has been noted, occurred at the local level, not at the provincial or the dominion. This suggests that unless strong leadership existed locally, with WCTU women who were sensitive to the particular needs of that locale and who were willing to invest local black women with meaningful duties and offices, the best of intentions would fail. Surviving reports about black departments and unions around the province suggest that the local unions did not sufficiently tap the leadership potential of black women. The 1914 provincial annual report notes that "this department ... requires laborers with love – Christ's love – consecration, wisdom and patience, that the ploughing and sowing may be of the best, and we cry in anguish of spirit to the Lord that He may send laborers forth into this part of his vineyards."[136] Are Christ's labourers black or white in this call to the faithful? It seems conceivable that they could have been either or both. Nevertheless, it appears that the WCTU expected most of these labourers to be Caucasian women. Sprinkled throughout the annual reports are such statements as a 1916 motion that a letter of appreciation be sent "to colored people who had been so kind to our Superintendent."[137] At the very least, relations between the WCTU and the black community seemed to be consistently cordial.

In the pre-war period, the Ontario WCTU concerned itself with groups thought to be especially vulnerable to alcohol abuse, but not specifically with European immigrants. Doubtless, the departments working among lumbermen, sailors, and railway men encountered large numbers of immigrant men, as did the evangelistic and flower mission departments with ethnic women. However, the reports at the provincial conventions rarely highlighted the ethnic perspective. In the postwar years, however, the Ontario WCTU became more concerned with the "Canadianization" issue, that is, with the assimilation of European immigrants into Canadian society. The dangers presented by European men were thought to be many: their supposed tendency to socialize while imbibing hard liquor was a long-held WCTU conviction; immigrants' unfamiliarity with democratic practices and especially the responsibilities of the vote pushed the organization into recommending the teaching of civics; their Roman Catholicism planted worries about the authorities to whom immigrants would answer; and during the 1920s, the "danger of "Red" propaganda poisoning and unsettling their minds" appended additional worries for the WCTU. To teach themselves about the issues at stake, the dominion and provincial conventions presented "conferences" on Canadianization.[138] One result of this refocusing on assimilation of European immigrants was the Ontario WCTU decision in 1923 to replace the department of "work in lumber camps" with a renewed department of Canadianization, which would concentrate on working with foreign urban populations. By way of illustration of local work undertaken in response to this provincial organizational change, in 1924 the London WCTU began home visitations, mother's classes, and gospel story hours, all with new Canadians. Similar programs were begun in that year in Toronto, Hamilton, Ottawa, Fort William, Sarnia, and St Catharines, many of which carried on throughout the 1920s.[139] It would appear from these programs that rather than dismissing immigrant women as inadequate nurturers, they were instead regarded as central to the Canadianization process. Had the WCTU believed that immigrant mothers would best be sidestepped, the organization would likely have offered the new programs through pressuring the schools or making links with other religious groups. There is no evidence from this period that it resorted to such strategies.

In fact, there is very little evidence that the women of the Ontario WCTU distrusted mothers of other races to "civilize" their families. If such were the case, why would the WCTU have created the departments of work among Coloured (women!) or the later Canadianization departments, with their emphasis on motherly support for Canadian ways? On the contrary, there is evidence that the WCTU saw itself as dependent on the skills and moral sense of immigrant mothers to carry out its program of Canadianization, even if it did not create special departments for them as it had done with black women. Nellie McClung observed: "We have no reason to be afraid of the foreign woman's vote. I wish we were as sure of the ladies who live on the Avenue."[140] The superintendent of Canadianization reports in 1927 that "WCTU members are awaking to a new consciousness of the importance of the non-Anglo-Saxon woman as a citizen of Canada, and as a result there is an increased friendliness and helpfulness to the New Canadian neighbour in many small towns."[141] At the same time, it is important not to overstate the point. Anglo-Saxon institutions, society, and modes of interaction were definitely seen as superior to non-Anglo-Saxon conventions. Mrs Staith, superintendent of work among coloured people, puts this case in her report to the 1915 Ontario Annual Convention:

As White Ribboners who have undertaken, through this department, to lift the colored man up to a higher plane of citizenship, I would beseech you, as Britishers, to see to it that Britishers have British privileges and responsibilities. The colored man is past his babyhood, or should be. If not, who is to blame? Give your child a chance to develop and show his loyalty to the flag we love and honor. Our Master, Whom we serve, knows no creed, no race, no color, but all are one in Him ... Only one suggestion I submit, and it is this, that every Union having any colored people residing in their locality stretch out the Samaritan hand of neighborliness.[142]

There is a condescending tone in this statement – of the coloured man's prolonged childhood state, of his requiring "the Samaritan hand of neighborliness" – but there is at the same time, a confidence in the community's ability to contribute to Canadian society if given the opportunity. The essence of this imprecation is to accord blacks, and by implication immigrants as well, "British privileges and responsibilities," to include them within the grand British-Canadian community, not to exclude them. The Ontario WCTU demonstrated an obvious sympathy with the position of new Canadians and the particular mandate of introducing them to temperate habits.[143] The superintendent of Canadianization reported in 1929:

If it is true patriotism to be kind to the foreigner, and try to make him feel at home in Canada, ... there are many who hate all foreigners, and who do not hesitate to show their contempt. Self-centred interest is usually responsible for this state of mind. Whatever the reason, it would be well if all could realize that there is something bigger and finer than the satisfaction of a prejudice, and that is the greater satisfaction of a contented brotherhood of Canadian citizens regardless of race or creed. It has been found that 95% of the evils committed by immigrants is traceable to the apathy and indifference of our people towards their incoming neighbor. If we were all aggressively anxious to show them a good example, there would be less trouble. Comparatively few are criminal in their tendency and many are just the opposite, and are anxious to be taught and helped and moulded into useful Canadian citizens.[144]

Again, the sentiment that is "bigger and finer than the satisfaction of a prejudice" is Canadian nationalism born of Christian charity and civic pride. The WCTU was in no doubt as to the superiority of Canadian traditions over European or Eastern ones, based on our British heritage. Such a view is indeed racism, but one aiming to include all races and ethnicities through the ministrations of temperate women leaders.

Perhaps predictably, the balance-scale of pride in British institutions occasionally dipped towards jingoism. The August 1915 issue of *Canada's White Ribbon Bulletin* carried an article entitled "Your Birthright."

There is one race that is fast dominating the world – the Anglo-Saxon race, represented by Great Britain and the USA, born rulers, exceeding all others in the capacity for governing. The only Empire of the present day which answers to this is the British Empire, a Christian Empire, which includes strong young nations, that are federating into a company – which carries the gospel to all lands, in all languages – and which is growing and growing – and bids to fill the earth. Do you belong to the British Empire? Then you belong to the blessed race, the blessed Empire – God's chosen rulers of the world.[145]

The provincial conventions during the war years were more restrained in their advocacy of the British cause than this atypical outburst. Their fundamental anxiety remained the long-range impact of war on children and young people, conflict resolution, and drinking habits. The Ontario WCTU also pledged its loyalty to the imperial cause at the same time as it requested prohibition.

During this time of our National calamity when the Great Empire which is dear to our hearts is embroiled in a bitter war with a relentless enemy, our thoughts turn to the future, and we earnestly desire some means whereby want and famine may be reduced to a minimum, and believing this can be done by conserving our national resources with which God has so abundantly blessed us, therefore resolved, that we petition the Government to close the bars until after the war.[146]

Moreover, it appears from debate and resolution at the Ontario level that engaging in nationalist or imperialist enthusiasms preoccupied the WCTU less than did the tradition of liquor being freely dispensed in military camps to young soldiers. The most consistent WCTU policy was to protest the existence of "wet canteens" whatever the imperial exercise. The organization wrote fiery letters demanding that the wet canteens be discontinued for every military manoeuvre from the Boer War to the First World War.[147] In addition, it denounced compulsory military training in the schools. "Our duty as women is to train the boys and girls in the highest ideals," noted the dominion convention in 1916.[148] It observed that high ideals were in contradiction to free use of liquor. But other aspects of military drill troubled the women as well. In 1909 the Ontario WCTU resolved that "we discourage the celebration of patriotic occasions with the booming of cannon, the marching of soldiery, and all that represents the diabolical arts of that wholesale butchery known as war, remembering that the WCTU stands for peace."[149] As late as 1913 the Ontario WCTU advocated the holding of "peace days" in public schools to teach the principles of arbitration and peace.[150]

It should not be surprising that the Ontario WCTU with an ideology rooted in the evangelical home and family, retained its concerns for the individual soldier and his moral welfare. Indicative of this individualizing and personalizing of all issues was the patriotic work carried out by the local unions. The department of work for the soldiers occupied much of the members' time as they prepared "comfort bags" for the boys overseas. These contained many of the same materials as the nineteenth-century members had sent to lumbermen, but with the addition of chocolate and soups to dull the appetite for liquor. The nature of the organization's war work is also symptomatic of the Ontario WCTU's emphasis on social service.

In international affairs, the early WCTU at the world level took a firm stand on disputes likely to lead to war. By 1883 the World's WCTU had established a department of peace and international arbitration,[151] and at the dominion conventions there was periodic support for this position throughout the nineteenth and twentieth centuries, as well as for the establishment of a similar department in Canada after the turn of the century.[152] Although no such department existed provincially, the provincial conventions regularly passed resolutions supporting the use of arbitration rather than war to settle disputes.[153] In 1914, for example, it placed on record its belief that

> Whereas, The whole world has been disgraced and saddened by the outbreak of an international war, the most terrible known in the history of mankind, and whereas the preparation for peace in huge armaments has not prevented this awful calamity, therefore be it Resolved, That the Provincial WCTU stand for a development of the Hague idea, international law, International Courts of Justice, International sanctions and International Executive which will prohibit armaments and educate for world peace. And moreover we beseech the homes, the schools and the churches to help educate public opinion toward International understanding without war.[154]

In holding to a peace and arbitration agenda, the WCTU ran the risk of seeming to be unpatriotic in a time of crisis.[155]

IDEAS ON EVANGELICALISM

Most historians viewing the WCTU see it having had evangelical roots, particularly during the tenure of Annie Wittenmyer, but following the organization's expansion into community action, it has been largely accepted that the evangelical vision was outgrown and rejected. For example, Ruth Bordin asserts that the "realm of philanthropy" by the early 1890s had "replaced prayer as woman's answer to distress"[156] in the United States. However, the Ontario records at the provincial and particularly at the local level do not bear out this false division between social action and evangelical zeal. Rather, the two coexisted throughout this period in both the urban and the rural unions and to a lesser degree at the provincial and dominion levels.[157] Gospel temperance meetings and jail, hospital, and refuge prayer meetings continued to figure in the work of many unions, alongside such new projects as the Willard Home in Toronto, where young women new to the city were housed, fed, and counselled.

More important, however, the vision of a reformed society espoused by WCTU women, at least in Ontario between 1874 and 1920, was an evangelical one. Arising from revivalism and the essential experience of conversion, through to the millenarianism of the late nineteenth and early twentieth centuries, theirs was above all an evangelical religious motivation. Society would be reformed through the individual will and salvation of the sinner, as supported by a caring community. But the community's Christian program was grounded in individual initiative. Referring to its position on temperance, the Ontario WCTU noted in 1894 that it reaffirmed its policy as "Moral Suasion for the individual and Prohibition for the State."[158]

As the Canadian evangelical community fractured into conservative and liberal parts, the WCTU watched with horror. The Ontario organization recognized the danger of losing the evangelical vision. In 1901 an article appeared in the *Woman's Journal* in which the author pressed for a renewed and systematic plan of action to promote evangelistic work. "The class we need to reach and help, if they will let us, is one over which the church has no power, and it may be that an earnest consideration of the subject by our local unions may open up some plan by which the message of salvation may be carried to every man and woman in this town, and thereby do a work which shall lift them out of their present evil surroundings, and place them in a position which shall help them, both for time and eternity."[159] In 1902 the Ontario WCTU convention passed a resolution in which it underscored the importance of individual conscience, motivated by evangelical ethics, in overcoming the liquor traffic. "Resolved that in our opinion the one insurmountable obstacle to Prohibition is not the liquor traffic with its money coined from blood, and its unscrupulous methods, nor the politician with his flexible conscience; but the disloyal follower of Christ who is over-awed by the fear of loss, or blinded by party loyalty, and who, with his ballot, strengthens the Kingdom of Satan instead of building the Kingdom of Christ."[160] The essential problem in losing sight of the evangelical mission, then, was a tendency to commit one's loyalty to ephemeral, worldly causes while the basic issues of justice and purity languished.

However, by 1909 the only evidence of religion, much less evangelicalism, at the provincial or dominion level was a vaguely Christian poem and eventide prayer.[161] All that remained of the evangelical impulse by 1922 were perfunctory devotionals.[162] In 1930 one of the Canadian WCTU's star performers and representative thinkers, Nellie McClung, defined her religious position thus: "I have never been much of a theologian. Doctrinal discussions have a mouldy taste and are dusty to the palate. I believe we all know enough to live by. It is not so much spiritual food we need as spiritual exercise."[163] In fact, McClung had not always been so casual about her religious identification, but her earlier views had long since been set aside by 1930. What had happened to the conservative evangelical women who had occupied the upper echelons of the organization? It is probable that by 1910 most of these women had left their positions or been persuaded to a more liberal societal interpretation.

The story is very different in the local unions, however. Particularly in the rural and town unions, the records bear eloquent testimony to the evangelical mission being carefully preserved. For example, all-day prayer meetings to speed the success of local option campaigns were reported through 1916 in Meaford and Peterborough.[164] The Cornwall WCTU filled its meetings with prayer, Bible readings, and stirring hymns. Its recording secretary reported in 1920 that "as we sang this wonderful prayer-hymn, our hearts seemed to go up, in unison, to the throne, with the desire, that we might be led by Jesus in all we said & did, not, perhaps, through the meeting alone, but all the way, throughout our lives."[165] The secretary of the Fairmount WCTU noted drolly of a 1926 meeting that the evangelistic superintendent had chosen as the subject for their weekly devotionals "'The Woman at the Well' – St. Teresa, the Patron Saint of Spain was described as a beautiful and noble woman with a perfect passion for water which played a large part in her life. Only the water of life can satisfy the needs of the soul."[166] In response to the question, Who are our enemies? the women of the Keswick union decided at one meeting in 1926 that "our worst enemies were often spiritual and within ourselves; our own evil inclinations but the wicked were those who were deliberately disobeying God and trying to undermine the good."[167] The women of the Owen Sound WCTU were urged by one of their number "to concreate [consecrate?] our lives more earnestly to Christ and to be more obedient to his will."[168]

At a more official level, the literature emanating from Chicago revealed a progression away from strict individualism towards evangelicalism in a societal context. The earliest tracts, the Signal Lights series, argued the case against alcohol and tobacco addiction entirely from the individual perspective. The evidence presented tended to relate to the victim's quandary, not society's. For example, an early Signal Lights pamphlet, probably dating from the 1880s, enumerated only personal reasons to reject smoking, including the unnatural physiological effects causing a person to feel unwell, smoking's expense, its dirtiness, its tendency to produce disease, its wastefulness of time and energy, its link to alcohol in being a "nervine depressant," and its inevitable results of lower grades for students and loss of personal property and lives.[169] In the Canadian context, Letitia Youmans delivered a speech condemning tobacco to the Ontario WCTU in 1881, in which all her arguments were focused on individual, rather than societal, destruction.[170] A tract produced on the same issue from the National Leaflets of a later period, probably at the turn of the century, also cited the personal factors, but added testimonial about the amount spent by the nation annually on tobacco, with vivid illustrations of how this money might better have been used, perhaps to feed the nation's hungry.[171] In both periods, however, the solution to tobacco addiction was seen to be a personal commitment by the "sinner" to reform and, through this reformation, to encourage friends and associates to do likewise for the general betterment of society.

By the 1890s the National WCTU was beginning to view alcoholism as a disease rather than a sin,[172] yet there remained much Canadian comment, even to 1916, which viewed the drink problem in moral terms. For example, the question of whether alcohol could ever be safely used was the basis of the celebrated argument between Lady Henry Somerset, who claimed that it could, and Dr Amelia Youmans, who insisted that this was nonsense and that drink must be totally suppressed because of its dangerous impact on weak character.[173] It might further be argued that the enthusiastic championing of social purity by the Canadian WCTU, which saw the issue of self-abuse and the seduction of young girls in almost exclusively moral terms, appealed to this still-vibrant evangelical strain in the organization.

How widely were the ideas espoused by the WCTU accepted by society as a whole? Ruth Bordin reveals that the American WCTU claimed larger numbers of women in its membership than any other women's organization of the nineteenth century.[174] Mitchinson has shown the same situation for Canada.[175] The WCTU was the first women's mass movement in both countries. The dominion, provincial, and local records also show, however, that more than charter members sympathized with the ideas of the WCTU. In Ontario, for example, the organization was very successful in working with other temperance and denominational groups; large numbers of women were influenced through "mothers' meetings" and children through the Bands of Hope and Loyal Temperance Legions. WCTU-sponsored demonstrations and entertainments drew sizeable crowds at the local level, demonstrating a generalized acceptance of the organization and its principles.[176] It does not seem extreme to assert that the evangelically inspired reformism of the WCTU, including its prohibition demands, represented mainstream thinking in Ontario between 1875 and 1916, and to a reduced extent, until the end of the 1920s.

CHAPTER FIVE

Strategies: "The Darkness of This World"

From 1875 to 1930 the WCTU employed a variety of strategies to achieve its objectives. Four approaches were used at the dominion, Ontario, and local levels: political channels, such as petitions and resolutions; educational means, including leaflets and school courses; religious techniques, with prayer days and temperance revivals; and social and philanthropic works, such as homes and other services for vulnerable elements in the community. The world and dominion WCTUs maintained their faith in the formal political process far longer than did the provincial or local unions. In the latter, informal methods through educational and philanthropic works were increasingly employed to slowly nurture new attitudes. These strategies for change set the Ontario WCTU apart from its American predecessor and established a distinctive Ontario version of the organization.

DOMINION POLITICAL INITIATIVES

Throughout the period under examination, the dominion executive and conventions spent a good deal of time working with the political process, if in a rather haphazard fashion. Issues were condemned or supported with petitions, delegations, letters, resolutions, and motions. Whenever possible, the WCTU participated with other groups to add pressure for the passage of appropriate legislation.

In 1891, for example, two petitions dealing with international matters were circulated at the convention, one concerning the Siberian exiles and the other in support of the Band of Mercy pledge opposing the use of bird plumage in wearing apparel. National failings were also criticized through delegate petitions. In 1890 the dominion convention expressed concern that the "Grand Trunk Railway provides a Railway Buffet at Richmond Station where intoxicating liquor is sold in contravention of the Dunkin Act." A petition was dispatched to Grand Trunk officials that these "hindrances to the efficient operation of the prohibitory law" be immediately removed.[1]

Petitions were often personally delivered by a delegation to the offending parties, combining personal and written authority. Mrs McKee describes the federal anti-tobacco campaign of 1900 during which "petitions, memorials and deputations besieged the Dominion House of Parliament." On this occasion, the women were defeated by a reputed counter-campaign staged by the "Tobacco Trust of Montreal" with twenty thousand dollars at its disposal. "We had no money to spend, nor did we ever dream that money was needed to secure the passage of a Bill which was for the benefit of children and the saving of the race from this evil. One learns a lot when lobbying,"[2] McKee concluded ruefully.

Letters were dispatched on a wide variety of topics. In 1891 and again in 1909, a letter was directed to the Minister of Justice in defence of Annie Robinson, convicted of murder at the Sudbury assizes. The convention respectfully requested on behalf of its twelve thousand members that her sentence be commuted or that she be pardoned. The 1913 dominion convention forwarded a letter objecting to government action that permitted liquor to be sold along the transcontinental railway.[3]

The dominion convention also used formal resolutions to influence political decisions. These were sometimes drafted to comment on concerns beyond Canada's borders: for instance, to support Madame Dreyfus, to call for the use of arbitration in international disputes, or to back Finland in its struggle with Russia.[4] The International Teachers' Association meeting in Toronto received a resolution in support of scientific temperance courses in the schools, and even Queen Victoria was consoled on the conspicuous failings of her son:

> That in the present sorrowful and grievous crisis in the career of the Heir apparent through which reproach is brought upon a reign, pure with the light of motherly and wifely virtues, our sympathies, loyalties and prayers are with Her Majesty the Queen, and we fervently hope and pray that her reign may be prolonged for many years of purity of peace and honor as the fitting sovereign of an empire in which the Bible and the Home are the mightiest safeguards of the State.[5]

The Dominion WCTU assumed that the Queen would appreciate hearing a supportive word from other mothers.

Resolutions were also directed towards national events. In 1899 the convention passed resolutions in favour of prohibition, Lord's Day observance, equal suffrage, non-liquor groceries, dry military canteens, the banning of cigarettes, and increasing the age of consent for girls.[6] The lists of causes are increasingly eclectic, but the association's faith in the resolution was unshaken. Resolutions served to educate delegates and members, provide direction for executive actions, and place pressure on authorities. Occasionally, the dominion convention passed motions to direct its own membership to a particular end. In 1913, for example, it moved that "this convention urges delegates to impress on all Branches the importance of studying the subjects of food, and without advocating any special system of diet, directing attention to food values, and the nutriment and economic advantages of cereals, fruits, nuts and vegetables."[7]

As the organization aged, the dominion level made fewer political demands on the outside community and more social ones. Graeme Decarie has argued that the ambiguous results of the 1898 federal plebiscite shook the Dominion and Provincial WCTU organizations and other members of the prohibition machine. In this prohibition plebiscite, only 44 per cent of eligible voters cast ballots, of whom only 51.3 per cent voted for prohibition.[8] Mrs McKee too notes that the WCTU's reaction to the prohibition plebiscite was "gloom and depression of spirit."[9] Henceforth the WCTU greatly reduced its political action at the federal level and reset its sights on the provincial realm.

The apex of political action by the WCTU in Ontario was, therefore, during the 1880s and 1890s. During this period the provincial executive and conventions used the same political tools as their sisters in the dominion conventions, with resolutions and letters being the favoured devices. Letitia Youmans set the tone for political involvement when speaking to the London convention in October 1881. "It is sometimes said you cannot make people sober by Act of Parliament; we ask our Government to stop making people drunk."[10] After the disappointments of the 1894 provincial and 1898 federal plebiscites, the organization devoted most of its political energies to local-option campaigns. In the last two decades of the nineteenth century, political campaigns in Ontario were fought mainly on three issues: curricular changes in public education, the liquor licence system, and the tobacco trade. By tracing the progress of the Ontario WCTU with these and other issues, we can clearly see the political strategies of the provincial organization.

THE CAMPAIGN FOR SCIENTIFIC TEMPERANCE INSTRUCTION

By examining the campaign to entrench scientific temperance in the

Ontario public school curriculum, one can learn much about useful tactics employed by women such as the WCTU to promote their middle-class objective of sobriety amongst malleable school children. The campaign of this group of "earnest Christian women" visibly gained public respect through a thirty-thousand-name community petition demanding a course in scientific temperance, soon peaked in its authority with the Department of Education with the formal mandating of the course and text in 1893, and then began the long and painful slide into obscurity after the turn of the century. The rise and fall of the WCTU as a forceful pressure group is not unique. Only rarely, however, does an issue so graphically illustrate the ephemeral hold which pressure groups have on public policy. Finally, the pivotal role played by teachers in the initiative for scientific temperance in the curriculum demonstrates the signal importance of implementation over ministerial fiat.[11]

The nineteenth-century program for scientific temperance instruction combined a conventional moralistic temperance message with the study of anatomy to create a hygiene curriculum that emphasized the individual's responsibility to maintain a healthy and pure body. However, as STI ideas evolved into the twentieth century, concerns of "purity of morals as well as health of bodies"[12] diversified into other health issues: fermented food; school playground supervision; visits by district health officers, nurses, and dentists; school design for increased ventilation, access to natural light, and separate boys' and girls' gathering rooms for inclement weather; and non-alcoholic medicines. At the same time, the justification for scientific temperance altered from one based primarily on individual moral reform to one glorifying the personal benefits – principally clear-headedness, health, and vigour – of those who shunned alcohol and narcotics.

Although a Department of scientific temperance had been established by the WCTU at the Ontario provincial convention by 1884,[13] the organization had been concerned with it earlier. An 1881 meeting of the Ontario executive committee framed a resolution, to be debated later that year at the convention, that "we reiterate our request that [a] Temperance Text Book be introduced into the schools of Ontario, believing that the vast importance of the knowledge to be gained therefrom, is more than a compensation for the time required for its study, and that the result in the better conduct of after life, would richly offset the small loss in any other direction."[14]

Throughout the five decades during which STI was championed, the Ontario WCTU's scientific temperance department had two functions. First, it was to exert pressure on the Department of Education for a curriculum policy change: the introduction of a mandatory course in temperance with a required textbook and final examination. Secondly, the department tried to convince principals, teachers, and their professional associations to support it in this policy change by willingly teaching the materials and underlining their importance to students. Although all levels of the organization subscribed to both objectives to a degree, the Ontario provincial and local WCTU organizations used very different methods to achieve them.

The provincial convention gave primacy to the first objective of gaining official recognition with senior educational bureaucrats for temperance instruction in a compulsory hygiene course. Their efforts with teachers and principals were intended to inform them of Department of Education regulations, to support teaching through providing resources, and to monitor the teaching of scientific temperance, with the threat that any backsliding with regard to government policy would be reported to the authorities. It has been argued in the American context that the WCTU campaign for scientific temperance instruction taught the organization essential skills by convincing them that the increasingly multi-tiered educational bureaucracy supporting "expert hegemony" could only be effectively influenced through a similarly tiered bureaucracy by lobbyists. At the same time, this structure fostered a local "internal democracy" by leaving essential monitoring functions to local women.[15]

Women in local WCTU unions assumed that the setting of government policy was someone else's concern, and while they did not object to the provincial convention's efforts in this direction, they often ignored this program of official pressure, to the provincial executive's frustration. Women of local unions poured their energies into the second objective by presenting materials to teachers in training and their experienced counterparts, visiting local classrooms, buying materials for the school library, and most importantly, sponsoring hundreds of essay and poster contests through which children could practise arguing the case for temperance. This fundamental difference in how women in local unions and provincial executive positions chose to wage the battle for scientific temperance illustrates the divergence in strategies and orientation of women in the various levels of the organization. It also permits a comparison of the relative success of two approaches to curriculum change: official ("top-down") policy as opposed to local ("bottom-up") practice.

The first step in the Ontario campaign to have temperance covered by public school teachers was to use moral suasion to convince trustees and teachers that temperance studies be taught voluntarily. This had also been the approach taken by American temperance groups, including the National WCTU,[16] and was consistent with the early program's emphasis on the individual responsibility of both teacher and learner. It had disappointing results, however. Teachers complained that the subject was difficult to teach without an informative and readable textbook.[17]

Recognizing that most teachers were unlikely to do their duty without specific direction from the Department of Education, the Ontario WCTU mounted a campaign to gather support in the community for a course on scientific temperance. The result was a petition in 1887 with thirty thousand names, which demanded that temperance instruction be formally taught in Ontario's public schools. Such a graphic demonstration of public sentiment would have been dangerous for any government to disregard. The Ontario government introduced a course on scientific temperance that same year, just as the American Congress was passing similar legislation for the District of Columbia and the western federal territories.[18] But this official recognition was hollow, for the new course was a voluntary one in the curriculum, without a textbook or formal examination, and as a result many teachers avoided teaching it.

Investing a great deal of confidence in the power of the central ministry to force teachers to include a course on scientific temperance, the Ontario WCTU began its search for a textbook that would entice teachers into its camp.[19] It wanted one that emphasized the physiological impact of alcohol, traced the moral implications of alcohol usage, and was more attractive to children while satisfying other curriculum requirements set by the Department of Education. In the WCTU's words, it sought a text which could "echo God's textbooks of Revelations and of Science."[20] Early in the 1890s, it finally identified William Nattress's *Public School Physiology and Temperance* as a text which satisfied all of its demanding criteria. The book was strenuously promoted to the Department of Education, and in 1893 it received authorization as the textbook recommended for use in Ontario public schools.[21]

Nattress structured his argument so as to emphasize the medical rules for maintaining a healthy body, with the many frightening medical effects of alcohol discussed in negative counterpoint. For example, in the chapter dealing with digestion, the author addressed the need for food, the mouth, proper chewing, the teeth, the structure of a tooth, care of the teeth, the tongue, saliva, salivary glands, the fauces, the tonsils, the pharynx, the epiglottis, the esophagus, the stomach, absorption, the intestines, the pancreas, kinds of food, the digestive system, stomach digestion, intestinal digestion, and the appetite. Having set the scientific stage, at the end of the chapter Nattress appraised the then-controversial use of alcoholic stimulants and tonics, and natural and "prepared" drinks. Only then did he embark on the danger of alcohol to every organ of the body. For example, the skin "assumes a dull and blotchy appearance,"[22] and the arteries of chronic, if moderate drinkers, instead of being "strong, elastic tubes, like new rubber hose, become hardened and unyielding, and are liable to give way."[23] The coating of small blood vessels "become weakened and diseased. The increased force of the heart may burst the weakened coat and allow the blood to escape into the brain substance, and by pressure render the victim unconscious."[24] The liver can reach an enormous weight: fifteen, even twenty to twenty-five pounds.[25] Muscle strength is so compromised that "as sip after sip or glass after glass is taken, the muscles become more and more helpless, and at last the inebriated man sinks beneath the table."[26] The structure of Nattress's book is not inconsistent with many nineteenth-century evangelical tracts: a holy temple – the healthy human body – is beset by evil in the form of alcohol, and its malignant effects are traced for the fascinated and terrified reader as the hero descends into dissolution and usually a ghastly death. Nattress concluded his grisly survey by assuring his readers that there were a great many more horror stories that could be provided, "but the picture already presented should be sufficient to satisfy anyone of the terrible evils it brings to those who indulge in its use."[27]

Only four chapters in the book were mandated for the entrance examination: those on digestion, circulation, respiration, and the nervous system.[28] However, the Department of Education – and the WCTU – recommended that the other chapters on such topics as bones, muscles, skin, special senses, first aid to the sick and injured, and the prevention of disease should all be taught to children in lower and the higher forms. Admittedly, this recommendation ran counter to the WCTU objective of providing graded materials for different age groups. But obviously its desire to have some information in the hands of all children overcame its pedagogical concerns. The WCTU understood very clearly that by being allowed to control the source of information from which scientific temperance would be taught in Ontario classrooms, it was afforded as direct authority over curriculum as was possible by outside interests.

To the WCTU's delight, adoption of the textbook was accompanied in 1893 by the long-awaited announcement that the "physiology and temperance" course was compulsory, ranking equally with other subjects in the entrance examinations. Its sense of achievement was further bolstered with the provision that at least an hour a week was to be devoted to "familiar conversations with the whole school on the effect of alcoholic stimulants and of narcotics upon the human system."[29] "This certainly leaves nothing more to be desired in the way of legislation," reported the provincial superintendent with satisfaction. In this hour of glory, the Ontario WCTU superintendent did not intend to lose sight of the source of this triumph. "We need not stop to ask what agency has had most to do in bringing about this change," she added coyly, "but everyone who has made an earnest, prayerful effort can rejoice in the thought that she has contributed to this result."[30] "The record ... proves that again true earnest Christian women, bent on saving our Canadian childhood and youth from the destruction wrought by alcohol, have been giving faithful service in this Department."[31] It was well that the WCTU celebrated, since the future for scientific temperance instruction after 1893 was considerably less rosy.

Heartened by its evident authority with the Department of Education, the WCTU next set its sights on wringing from the government a formal examination for public school students in the junior grades. It suggested that the entrance examinations could act as a model for younger students. The *Canadian White Ribbon Tidings* helpfully published a sample of questions which had appeared on entrance examinations:

1 If there are before you two tumblers of colorless liquid and you are told one contains water and the other alcohol, by what four tests can you determine which contains alcohol?
2 Explain how the juices of raspberries, cherries and currants are changed into wine. Why is the use of such home-made wines objectionable?
3 Explain the real cause of the so-called "stimulating" effect of alcohol on the heart.
4 Explain why employers do not wish to employ persons who use alcoholic liquors, tobacco or narcotics.
5 Why is alcohol which quickens action, hurtful, while exercise, which does the same thing, useful?
6 What is sleep? Show the necessity for it, and the evil effects of narcotics upon it.[32]

The WCTU continued its pressure to have graded curricula developed for such students as well. The focus on junior grades arose from the WCTU's fear that the vast majority of students left school without taking the entrance examinations, the only level at which the government mandate applied. The Ontario superintendent for scientific temperance quoted the world superintendent approvingly on this point: "the saloon exists today by the will of the majority of the voters. A majority of the voters of tomorrow are in the first five years of the Public schools of today. Through Scientific Temperance education in the first five school years means in future no saloon majorities."[33] She might well have added that it also would mean the replacement of other working-class values with appropriate middle-class ones.

But the high-water mark had been reached. Try as it might, the WCTU was never able to convince the government to provide examinations, graded textbooks, or even curricula for students in forms one to four. To make matters worse, the government decided to "unmandate" the Nattress textbook after a committee of the male-dominated teachers' organization, the Ontario Educational Association, criticized it in 1900.[34]

Pushed into a rearguard battle, the Ontario WCTU for the next thirty-five years attempted to move the front forward by finding (and suggesting to be remandated) more attractive curriculum materials. When this approach failed, it sought out materials to supplement teachers' knowledge and classroom resources. For example, the WCTU began importing from the United States a *School of Physiology Journal* with monthly graded lessons. This it circulated to teachers across the province,[35] not always a sympathetic audience. One irate teacher from Ottawa wrote to the provincial executive:

> The Public school teachers of this city have all had professional training in a Normal school and do not need to waste their time at Convention in the miserable farces called "model lessons." I know nothing of the opinion of "your" (the WCTU) teachers regarding the authorized text-book on temperance, but my own opinion, and that of every Public school teacher with whom I have discussed the subject, is that the book is beneath contempt.[36]

In 1903 the provincial WCTU purchased 1,866 copies of an updated textbook entitled *The New Century of the Alcohol Question* and donated these to Ontario schools.[37] This volume clearly emphasized the temperance question over that of general physiology, and for a reason. The WCTU was increasingly worried that physiological instruction was crowding out moral temperance. In one set of guidelines published by the organization for local unions to assess potential textbooks in their own schools, it noted that "only enough physiology to make temperance intelligible [is acceptable], especially to younger students. Temperance should be the chief and not the subordinate topic and should occupy at least one-fourth of space in texts at this level."[38] In 1924 the Ontario WCTU bought 7,000 copies of *Alcohol in Experience and Experiment*, distributing them to local unions, schools, and teachers' associations.[39] It also provided a number of helpful pamphlets to teachers to buttress their knowledge and pedagogy, including *How I Teach Temperance, Safe Remedies, Is Alcohol a Stimulant?*, *The Teacher Taught*, *The Teacher Questioned*, and *The Teacher Helped*.[40] Teachers' guides for scientific temperance instruction were serialized in the *Canadian White Ribbon Tidings*.[41] Local unions purchased student materials that put the case for temperance briefly but purposefully. For example, the Ottawa WCTU purchased 2,000 blotters with appropriate temperance messages, to be distributed to the city's students in 1916.[42] As the years rolled on, the WCTU faithfully recommended appropriate books to the Department of Education. The embattled education minister insisted in a 1909 interview with the president of the Ontario WCTU that he continued to search for a suitable textbook for the course.[43] But increasingly, local unions were referred to such books as ideal reference works to be contributed to school libraries. Beyond 1912 there is only rare mention of the faded dream of the mandated textbook at any level.

As the WCTU lost its anchor of a formal text, so went the mandated course and its entrance examination. The same teachers' committee that had criticized the required textbook suggested the elimination of temperance from the entrance examinations. In an effort to lighten an overburdened curriculum, the Ontario Educational Association's committee recommended dropping scientific temperance and substituting hygiene, which might be taught "if the teacher chose."[44] This proposal reflected the American pattern, where by the mid 1890s, opposition amongst teachers to curricular coercion had developed.[45] When it was rumoured that the Department of Education would accept the teachers' recommendations, the provincial WCTU brought in the strongest speaker it could find to work on the teachers. Mary Hunt, national and world superintendent of scientific temperance and the author of the congressional legislation on scientific temperance, did her best to convince the teachers at a heated Toronto meeting in 1901. Unfortunately, Hunt understood neither the Ontario educational context nor her audience, and her best defence was not good enough. "By vote, this distinguished woman was allowed only fifteen minutes [by the Ontario Educational Association], the presiding officers sitting, watch in hand, during the address, which was made amid a good deal of noise and disorder."[46] One wonders if the WCTU would not have been better off stating its own case and exerting influence behind the scenes, as it had so successfully done on many other occasions. The outcome could hardly have been more negative than what the WCTU experienced after Hunt's disastrous address.

Ontario's record paralleled the American. By 1897 only three

American states were without scientific temperance legislation, but by 1907 most of this had been reversed.[47] In Ontario, scientific temperance was finally removed from examinations by the Department of Education in 1903.[48] However, this is not to suggest that the women of the Ontario WCTU let the matter drop. After yet another unsuccessful bid to have the Ontario Educational Association support "uniform promotion examinations in Physiology and Hygiene including the effects of Alcohol and Narcotics" in 1917, the WCTU representatives reported that "the effort was in vain ... Our hope lies in personal inquiry and enthusiasm."[49]

To forestall any further undercutting of its formal provincial authority, the Ontario WCTU tried to mobilize support throughout the community on somewhat the same lines as the thirty-thousand-name petition. Starting in 1896, the provincial executive decided to expand its lobbying group, and it published a letter in all Protestant denominational papers urging Ontario clergy to use their influence in aid of continuing to have the course declared compulsory. But this time, the process had less effect. Supportive letters from various denominations, educational leaders, editors of religious and civic papers, and the general public did not dissuade the government.[50]

The interest group that had almost single-handedly brought down scientific temperance, the province's teachers, had by no means been neglected by the Ontario WCTU. The route to curricular reform through teacher education had long been a prime component of the WCTU strategies to bolster scientific temperance instruction. At the 1882 provincial convention, Letitia Youmans expressed great hope that "if we could induce the teachers to adopt our views, we would at once have a most potent influence at work upon the growing public opinion of our country."[51] One obvious opportunity to shape teachers' attitudes was to influence the course of study in the province's normal schools and to test prospective teachers on their knowledge of temperance.[52] This had also been a tactic used by American temperance women.[53] Since the vast majority of normal and model school candidates were women, the WCTU felt confident that they could work together amicably. Throughout the 1880s and 1890s there is some evidence that temperance instruction was given to normal school students,[54] but there is no indication that certificates were withheld from students unable to demonstrate a sufficient knowledge of the subject.

The Ontario WCTU also targeted experienced female teachers as critical to the success of its campaign. Sadly, the relationship between the Ontario union and many female classroom teachers was never very positive. As disappointments mounted for the WCTU in its struggle to have scientific temperance taken seriously, the relationship moved perilously close to hectoring antagonism. The organization believed that scientific temperance had a strong moral dimension. In 1892 it interpreted the question hopefully enough.

The majority of our teachers are ready to do our bidding. If we say to them, "prepare our children for Entrance Examinations in the shortest possible time or we will dismiss you," we cannot expect them to give much time to subjects that are not required in the examination. When we succeed in convincing them that *character* is the first essential in the *teacher* and that the laws of health and good morals must form the basis of their teaching, whatever else is delayed or omitted, we shall witness the reform we are praying for.[55]

In 1896 the Ontario WCTU was still sanguine about the sympathetic response it anticipated from teachers when it sent a letter to all public school teachers in the province, most of whom were female, "to impress more deeply upon their minds their personal responsibility in the matter of Temperance Instruction."[56] That year also, the WCTU sent out 7,000 copies of "An Open Letter to Teachers," urging them to take an elevated moral position on the question. In the same spirit, an attempt was made to draft more female teachers into the provincial WCTU executive, causing the 1897 provincial convention to consider changing the days for its next convention to a weekend so that teachers could attend.[57] In 1899 the Ontario WCTU convention passed this resolution:

Whereas, We believe that teachers throughout our land wield a powerful and life-long influence over their pupils,
Resolved, That we urge them to endeavor more earnestly to inspire those under their charge with exalted ideals of purity, nobility and integrity of character, and
Further, That in teaching of physiology and hygiene we ask them to lay special stress upon the evil effects of alcohol and tobacco upon the human system, also their debasing power over mind and soul.
And that still further, We would emphasize our belief that no person addicted to the use of any of these narcotics should ever enter the schoolroom as a teacher.

By 1902 the provincial convention was even more preoccupied with "the great need of educating the educators"[58] and more discouraged than ever about the possibility of positive influence. A year later it was directing local members to "cooperate with the teachers, but see to it that they do their duty. Do not be afraid to let them know that you know what the regulations say, and they are expected to observe them."[59] Wearied from the seemingly interminable battle, the provincial superintendent of scientific temperance instruction noted tersely in 1907 that "we hoped, and are still hoping, for something better, but are beginning to feel the efforts of hope deferred."[60]

But more acrimonious by far was the relationship between the WCTU and the male-dominated Ontario Educational Association. This was the group that had openly rejected the Nattress text, had recommended the elimination of the temperance examination, and which had treated Mary Hunt so shabbily. If the unorganized female teachers had been difficult to win to the scientific temperance banner, the Ontario Educational Association seemed implacably opposed to the WCTU program. Yet throughout its battle with the teachers' association, the WCTU continued to view the issue as one of personal moral responsibility.[61] This position was consistent with the organization's evangelical roots and societal critique, as demonstrated by the following statement from 1898:

> Teachers' Associations do not, as a rule, discuss Scientific Temperance as readily and with as much interest and intelligence as they manifest in the treatment of other subjects. Among the 2,726 men who hold positions as teachers in Ontario Public Schools may still be found those whose personal habits preclude the possibility of their giving effective teaching on the evils of the use of alcohol and tobacco. Among the 5,528 women who daily wend their way to the school rooms of this Province, here and there, may yet be seen one who is willing to shuffle off individual responsibility, because some one in authority over her opposes, or because she herself considers this a matter of little moment.[62]

The inability of the Ontario WCTU to work effectively with teachers organized into the Ontario Educational Association resulted almost directly in the WCTU's loss of official Department of Education support. S.G.E. McKee, a long-serving president of the Ontario WCTU, provides its last word on the provincial struggle to have the course on scientific temperance mandated: "the history of Scientific Temperance has been one of continued and persevering combat with the powers that be, whose glaring obtuseness and blind ignorance, where this moral issue is concerned, has [*sic*] always been inexplicable to us."[63]

Yet it is not difficult to appreciate the opposition of both organized and unorganized teachers to this course. First, despite the name, scientific temperance instruction was not "scientific" according to our modern usage of that term; it operated from a clear moral premise, on the model of evangelical temperance tracts earlier in the century, and made use of medical research, sometimes clumsily, to support that position. Not surprisingly, many teachers found the course inappropriate for the era. It was especially difficult to justify including STI in a crowded curriculum. Secondly, teachers found the subject of temperance difficult to enliven in a classroom. This was due in part to the resources, which they considered trite and moralistic. Finally and most importantly, the course required the teacher to be a moral exemplar, leading children to ethical behaviour through precept and example on the old evangelical model but in a new cause: the inculcation of middle-class values. Many teachers resisted this definition of their role, holding instead to a vision of the teacher as a subject specialist. By the 1890s, teachers would not agree to be accessories to the WCTU's version of middle-class formation. WCTU authority had crested in more ways than one.

After 1904 the real work of scientific temperance was carried out at the local level. To achieve their programmatic aims, the provincial superintendent of scientific temperance urged local unions to name superintendents of scientific temperance and to create a prominent place for STI in the unions' programs. Year after year, the provincial superintendent dispatched questionnaires to assess the strength of unions' scientific temperance achievements. These were generally mislaid, judging from the few explanations received from union members. After years of provincial executives badgering the unions to little effect, one provincial superintendent reported wearily, "Mary Harris Armour says: 'The Scientific Temperance Department is the most important Department of the WCTU work.' From my experience ... I scarcely feel assured that any large number of our women are of this mind."[64]

But this assumption by the Ontario WCTU executive that no formal structure to support scientific temperance in local unions constituted a lack of interest or labour was simply unfounded. The local records of the WCTU across Ontario confirm that many unions were active over the full five decades of this study in promoting scientific temperance. However, they waged this campaign, not by setting up formal structures in their own unions or by insisting on particular textbooks, but primarily by using two strategies: first, by promoting their cause with local teachers, and secondly, by instituting essay, poster, elocution, and occasionally, music contests through which students could practise making a case for temperance and pure living.

There are many examples of local unions attempting to influence the opinions of teachers from their own town or county. That the WCTU interpreted scientific temperance as an issue to be promoted by women, both outside and in the classroom, is clear from the consistent targeting of local women teachers, rather than an entire school staff. Receptions were held by unions to fête the women teachers and, incidentally, to educate them in their duties. For instance, the Brantford WCTU held a reception for the city's women public school teachers. "After a delicious repast and social chat they were invited to give their opinion on Scientific Temperance Teaching etc etc. Of course the Ladies had secured those who could throw true light on the subject and a profitable evening was the result."[65] Similarly, the Toronto union held an annual reception for the four hundred female teachers in the city and also invited the students from the Normal School.[66] Occasionally, women teachers could be enticed to join the WCTU. The Ottawa union was markedly successful in this strategy. Miss Shanock, headmistress of the Model School, and several other city teachers agreed to join, with Miss Shanock noting that she believed that the minister of education favoured temperance workers among the young and "will do all in his power to further the cause of Temperance."[67] As the WCTU did in Alberta, temperance women appeared at teachers' and school board meetings and donated books on alcohol and tobacco to classrooms and libraries.[68]

The second regional program to encourage STI in the public schools was the province-wide network of contests sponsored by local unions for prize-winning essays and posters. The contests seem to have had several origins. There was a well-established tradition of written testimonials in many temperance youth groups; this was further reinforced by the essay examination answers; finally, a system of contests and prizes had been inherited from the WCTU medal contests. Temperance youth groups, such as the Band of Hope and juvenile departments of temperance lodges, frequently expected children to provide verbal and written testimonials about the virtues of abstinence.[69] Often, these resulted in youth oratorical contests and essays. An early account of an essay contest is noted by the Ottawa WCTU. The contest, open only to children who intended to remain non-drinkers, was a popular diversion. "This committee during their visit to one of the Schools desired the pupils to stand up who intended in the future to be total abstainers. All the boys and girls present instantly stood up."[70] As early as 1885, prizes were offered in all of Ottawa's public schools and collegiates, the ladies' college, and Miss Harmon's School.[71] In 1888 the Toronto WCTU women combined three prizes costing $13.00 for the best temperance essays, with a complimentary social for the public school teachers and Normal students.[72]

In the period when students had been given the choice of writing an entrance examination in temperance and hygiene, the typical examination structure had been an essay. It had been particularly satisfying for many union women to witness the best products of this exercise in temperance testimonials. WCTU minute books suggest that this was the loss most keenly felt by many local union members when the course was removed from the list of examined subjects. By the First World War, some unions had returned to the old strategy of sponsoring their own essay contests for students and providing cash or book prizes for the winners.[73] To extend the range of adolescents to be enticed into accepting WCTU ideas, many unions expanded the essay contests to include poster, elocution, and musical competitions during the 1920s. The medal contests had been a hallmark of WCTU youth activities since the 1890s. The product of these three legacies, the scientific temperance essay contests combined features of each to create a definitive program.

Essay competitors were usually given a theme or topical sentence from which to work, as had been the case on the examination. Often they were invited to read their essays at a public meeting or concert, as had been common in temperance youth groups. "It [elocution] can develop in the many the great art of expression. Second only to having truth to tell, is the art of telling it with winning power."[74] While some model essays were available in the style of the medal contests, the scientific temperance essays and speeches were entirely student-generated pieces rather than recitations from approved texts. As such, they were designed to appeal to the older student. The essay, and later the poster contests, became one of the most popular WCTU projects across Ontario.

The Meaford WCTU women presented book prizes to student essayists in the public school.[75] The St Catharines WCTU received one thousand essays in its 1925 contest, while Leamington commanded four hundred essays and fifty posters.[76] The London union had a reputation for successful essay and poster contests, and it offered cash prizes.[77] Some unions made use of the prize-winning student work for their youth education projects. Owen Sound, for example, purchased a lantern slide kit and showed slides on alcohol and tobacco made from the poster contest winners,[78] while the Ottawa WCTU had its prize-winning essays published in the newspaper.[79] The Picton YWCTU was able to convince the town's public schools to run a temperance day once a month. In 1904 it offered a gold medal for the best essay on "The Advantages of total abstinence from strong drink and tobacco."[80]

Because the contests were run entirely by the local unions, the prizes varied according to the union's wealth and interests. Most unions provided cash, suitable books, or medals. Sometimes they were strained to provide prizes which they considered an adequate reward for the students' efforts. In 1932 the Mimico WCTU gave book prizes costing about $10; at the time, the union had a grand total of $15.82 in its treasury![81] On other occasions, unions chose to give the winners pins, paints, or pencil-boxes. Often the awards were given at public concerts, at special school functions, or in connection with medal contests.

The scientific temperance essay contests, along with the medal contests, survived far longer as a WCTU-sponsored educational measure in Ontario schools than did scientific temperance instruction. Based on the premise that teachers and children should enjoy temperance materials, as clearly many participants in the essay, elocution, poster, and musical contests did, and that rewards, in the form of pins, money, books, or drawing materials, would attract even more students and teachers to the fold, the medal and essay contests continued to be offered into the 1970s.

The campaign to have scientific temperance made a compulsory, examined subject with a mandated textbook was a logical result of the Ontario WCTU's view of the primary purpose of education: to reinforce the moral authority of the individual and to raise standards in society. It was one important method by which the organization could help mould Ontario's children into a temperate middle class. But in implementing this campaign the provincial executive and local unions of the Ontario WCTU interpreted their mission differently and used varied tactics to achieve that mission. The provincial executive assumed that once the course, its text, and examination were mandated by the minister of education, the main task would be accomplished. Women in the local unions, conversely, largely disregarded this formal, centralized policy making and instead turned their attention to changing attitudes in their immediate communities by influencing teachers and sponsoring contests. To accomplish their common objective the women of the Ontario WCTU at all levels utilized a wide range of effective strategies. The one group which the WCTU courted assiduously but failed to convince of the merit of its program was the province's teachers, both as individuals and eventually as a competing pressure group. The animosity of Ontario teachers was primarily responsible for the premature loss of scientific temperance instruction from the school curriculum.

LOCAL-OPTION CAMPAIGNS

Political endeavours on the part of local unions, such as the support for local option, took quite a different pattern from either the dominion or provincial campaigns. After receiving notice that the dominion or provincial body had taken a stand on an issue, such as support for a referendum or petition campaign, local unions frequently backed that stand by doggedly gathering signatures[82] or dispatching letters to "influential bodies," as was the case with the Richmond Hill union in response to a letter from the dominion superintendent of the legislation department asking that members write to their member of Parliament to protest the Scott Act amendments. "Action was taken, a letter had been written and signed by the officers."[83] Delegations met with the authorities: the Ottawa WCTU reported in 1882 that it planned "to present a petition on the issue of licences [granted to the wives of saloon keepers] after having interviewed the Licence Commissioners & receiving a positive reception."[84] It also sent money to support the major plebiscite campaigns, and sometimes substantial sums from slim treasuries.[85] On polling day, lunch might be provided for the scrutineer, "not wishing our side to suffer even in a good cause."[86] Very often too, the local unions fought their own local-option campaigns and attempted to weld coalitions with other local temperance groups. The women of the Meaford WCTU concentrated their efforts on "getting the girls that earn salaries on the assessment roll" and looking over the voters' list for any names likely to be antagonistic to the local-option campaign,[87] while the London WCTU divided the campaigners amongst the city wards, allocating the largest delegation to London West, which was the weakest area in its view in supporting local option.[88] But even those members who had no vote participated in the political process by vocally supporting certain candidates. The London union moved "that as soon as it is known who are the candidates for alderman that the ward superintendents meet and decide whom to support."[89] Voteless women were also requested to "use influence in papers & with brothers, husbands."[90] Doubtless all of these strategies had an influence on the political process.

MONITORING THE LIQUOR LICENCE SYSTEM

Second only to the battles to win local option was the monitoring of the liquor licence system. Here the women attacked several problems. They petitioned the government-appointed board to reduce the number of licences throughout the province and to permit fewer in their own towns.[91] For example, the Newmarket WCTU drew up six petitions to circulate "for signatures of rate-payers ... to be presented to the Council at next meeting" that the hotel licences be reduced to four from six and that all shop licences be abolished.[92] The London Union reported the splendid success of the "deputation who waited on the council in opposition to the Liquor Party who asked for an increase in Licences. All present formed in Thanksgiving and together sang the Doxology."[93] When the women of the Thorold WCTU learned that a licence was being sought for a prospective bar in their town, they worked with their YWCTU to rent the rooms before the liquor entrepreneurs could act on their plan![94]

Sometimes the women paid to have an organizer collect the names for the petition.[95] When this tactic was unsuccessful, they maintained their complaints to the provincial inspector about the board members themselves[96] and were quick to suggest appropriate names to fill vacancies: "it was decided to send a letter of recommendation to Mr E.J. Davis in favor of Mr J.S. Green who is a strong man in the Temperance Cause."[97]

They also complained about local enforcement. "The men who are appointed to enforce the Liquor Law draw the wages, but do not do the work. If the Liquor Law were enforced a great deal of drunkenness would be done away with," opined the secretary of the Meaford WCTU.[98] The Ottawa union sent a letter to the police commissioner suggesting that a strong "Temperance Man" be named as the new chief of police.[99] And sometimes, as with the London union, they complained about all of these.

> It was brought to our attention that the licence holders in Pottersburg, London West & Hamilton Road are in daily and flagrant violation of the law. Moved that we as a Union protest against the utter disregard of the Law permitted by the Licence Commissioners of the East Riding of Middlesex, and do urge that steps be taken to arouse the attention of the temperance people in this riding, That the Provincial Licence Inspector be communicated with and, that we co-operate with the London and Western Prohibition Association in doing what we can to abate the evil.[100]

While the number of licences to be granted was regularly challenged, the women conscientiously monitored establishments in their own communities to ensure that no other businesses were selling liquor without a licence and that regulations were being strictly observed.[101] "A little discussion on private detection business in regard to drinking after hours and on Sundays around Hotels ...,"[102] remarked the Newmarket union secretary ominously. Sometimes action was suggested on slender evidence: "Herm West who kept a booth in the Fair Grounds is said to have sold drinks that stupefied some young boys; the case should be taken in hand before another year brings trials in the same way."[103] The Dunnville union instructed the corresponding secretary to "write a letter to the inspector informing him of the rumors circulated that one of the Hotel Keepers has been selling liquors in his barn on Saturday nights."[104] At other times, unions such as London's were conscientious in their information gathering: "we have a tally of the number of persons drunk & disorderly on the city rolls, number of fines laid by Inspector & Police & what happened to the charges."[105]

During the war, the Woodstock WCTU got up a petition against a "wet canteen" liquor licence for Canadian soldiers and managed to get twenty-four women to sign it, eleven being visitors. Still wrestling with the soldiers' taste for liquor, the Peterborough union decided some months later to send chocolates with "WCTU" stamped on them, gum, and "Washington Coffee, which helps to destroy the taste for liquor."[106] The Dunnville WCTU wanted a public demonstration of support for sobriety. It petitioned the council "to pass a by-law to have any man found drunk on the streets at any time arrested."[107]

OTHER LOCAL POLITICAL CAMPAIGNS

Public displays of other offensive acts rankled with the WCTU women also. The London union directed the superintendent of narcotics to write to the local MPP asking him to support an amendment to the Tobacco Act "prohibiting boys under 18 yrs of age from smoking on the public streets."[108] The women of another union struck a committee "to wait on the Storekeepers to have them quit selling tobacco."[109] And like well-brought-up women, they remembered to write their thank-you letters: "decided to write to Dr Sproule thanking him for voting right on the question, and to ask the Editor to write an article ... Scores of Electors write letters to thank the Representatives who stood by the abolition of the cigarette."[110] In fact, it was with the tobacco menace that one local union demonstrated its grasp of the political process, effectively putting this knowledge to good use. After having donated thousands of leaflets to teachers informing them of the dangers of cigarettes, the London WCTU circulated a petition among the teachers in the city asking the board of education to take into consideration the increasing power and extent of the cigarette habit among youth. Reportedly every teacher signed. The minutes tell the remainder of the story. "In response to the teachers the Board passed a resolution requiring the teachers to faithfully teach the evil effect of tobacco upon the system, also asking the co-operation of the parents and guardians in this matter and calling the attention to the

Police Com. to the constant violation of the Ontario Tobacco Act." In celebration, the women distributed another thousand copies of the *Deadly Cigarette* leaflet.[111]

The Meaford WCTU circulated a petition in support of woman's franchise.[112] Similarly, the London Union sent a resolution to their local MP asking him to support the issue of woman's suffrage.[113] When the provincial president asked that unions register their concern on the observance of the sabbath, unions wrote to the premier and their MPs as requested, one union reporting happily that a letter in reply was received from Sir Wilfrid Laurier's private secretary.[114] But the monitoring was carried out at home also. The Richmond Hill union noted that "it was decided that Mrs McLean see Mr, Mrs Throop & see if he would on behalf of the WCTU go to Mrs Smail & tell her [crossed out] persuade her to not break the Sabbath."[115] The London union publicly deplored the running of boats on Sunday, "thus desecrating the 'Lord's Day,'" and fought through resolution the proposed opening of the public library on the sabbath. "This Society looks upon a Sabbath Day devoted to the needful rest and worship as a God-given right as old as Creation and not to be interfered with except at peril to the Moral and Spiritual Life of a Community."[116]

Another favourite local WCTU undertaking of the late nineteenth century was the introduction of a curfew bell, to be installed and administered by the town council. Sometimes the adoption of the curfew bell was as simple as visiting the mayor and council, as in Newmarket. "The [WCTU] committee was rec'd very cordially by the Council. The Mayor thought it would be an excellent thing to have and instructed the bye-law committee to prepare bye-law for the same."[117]

Lotteries and gambling establishments were sniffed out and the town council was pressured to eliminate them,[118] the town council petitioned to have stores close at 9:30 on Saturday evenings,[119] and attempts were made to shut down unseemly social events. "A long discussion followed about the evil arising from the Annual Ball held in the Town Hall by the Trolley Employees. It was decided to talk to the Town Council quietly and try to induce them not to lease the Hall again for the same body as it proved a disgrace to our town."[120] Again, this report was made: "Information has been received that the majority of the Council were in favor of another pool room and passed a bye-law to permit a licence. Arrangements were made to try and petition against it ... many frequent it, young boys, old boys and even married men."[121] The Woodstock union named a committee to "gain what information they could regarding children attending picture shows" unattended by friends or parents.[122]

With such a concerted policy of snooping, the local WCTUs were sensitive to being perceived as busybodies. There is evidence that, as the local unions matured, they became more subtle in their pressure tactics. The Newmarket union, which had been unstintingly vigilant in voicing its alarm on a wide assortment of matters, noted after twenty-two years of frontal attacks: "About having the signs removed from the closed Hotels, it was decided to wait and see if they would come down without our seeming to meddle ... Mrs Hill and Mrs Main will please see that a note to that effect be inserted in the local papers – not as a WCTU item but a general [one] as other than WCTU women have mentioned it before."[123] "Say less pray more," it counselled in another context,"that the men will do better if not nagged too much."[124] The Peterborough WCTU expressed the same idea this way: "We band ourselves together not as a political organization but to stand behind our Council for the Temporal & Moral reform of our own town & to clean up some of places where vice & drunkenness are allowed to exist."[125]

Several conclusions can be drawn about the political strategies of the WCTU. First, there is much evidence of unions specializing in particular kinds of activities. For example, the London union was a much more academic group than the Ottawa union and delighted in staging complicated debates. However, all unions for which records exist used some form of political tactics. Some, like the Newmarket union, changed their forms of political expression over the long period during which they kept records. Overt demands for legislative change were replaced by more subtle pressure tactics to have others effect the desired changes. But this shift represented no reduction in political interest.

Secondly, topics for which the women sought political change were not limited to those involving alcohol; a wide range of other issues were confronted over this period. Issues waxed and waned in popularity. In the 1880s many unions were concerned with the sanctity of the sabbath; by 1916 this question was rarely mentioned, but there was much concern over social purity. In all of these areas, however, reform was sought through political channels. It is important to recognize that although the WCTU rooted its ideas in the pre-eminence of the home and family, it saw the political system as a significant vehicle to right society's wrongs.

EDUCATIONAL INITIATIVES

A second broad strategy of the WCTU for achieving change was through educational means. The campaign to have scientific temperance made a compulsory, examined subject has been presented as a study in the use of political channels, but it was at the same time an example of the most enduring technique developed by the WCTU, that is, changing attitudes through new information. The wide-ranging educational program closely corresponded with the organization's interests in work with children, and it spurred the development of materials and methodologies especially intended for children. The formal educational system was only one target in this campaign; medal contests, public lectures, and children's clubs were also sponsored by the women. Other groups to be targeted were working-class mothers and men and middle-class men sympathetic to the temperance cause. Finally, the WCTU developed a "school of methods" to train its own workers, leaders, and supportive followers. The common assumption behind all of these educational initiatives was that knowledge, combined with evangelical energy, would be sufficient to win "converts" to abstinence for the individual and society. This optimism pervades the educational materials and pedagogical strategies: it seems rarely to have occurred to WCTU members that an enlightened person could do otherwise than support them.

Medal Contests

In the United States, as in Canada, the WCTU's unsuccessful efforts to have scientific temperance made a compulsory school subject was succeeded by a still-surviving educational program: the medal contests.[126] As has been noted, W. Jennings Demorest of New York had begun the contests in April 1886. The next year he introduced them into California and thereafter across the United States and into Canada. Demorest agreed to give medals free to anyone who would drill a class for a speech contest, on the condition that no admission fee was charged or collection taken. By 1894, thirty-four thousand medals worth seventy-five thousand dollars had been given away. The medal contests became an official American WCTU activity the following year and a department of work in 1897, with medals redesigned bearing WCTU mottoes. Recitation books listing selections from which children were to choose were printed on the topics of prohibition, total abstinence, scientific temperance, anti-narcotics, women's franchise, and social purity.[127]

In Canada the medal contests first became a department of work at the dominion level in 1905 and in Ontario in 1908. For a number of years, children seem to have simply recited selections from the recitation books, but gradually essay contests were added to the repertoire, encouraging some personal additions to the set piece. The contests provided a forum for intensive education of children that could form the basis of a public entertainment, including the rewarding of handsome prizes. Furthermore, adults who otherwise were not touched by WCTU influence could be reached through the medium of child proselytizers. "The medal contest can overcome indifference and opposition to our principles faster and surer than any other known force. Saloon-keepers' children, wine drinkers' children, white ribboners' children, the fathers and mothers, the sisters and brothers, the aunts and the cousins whom we reckon by the dozens, come out to hear the entertainment – barriers all down – because it is the young people who are to speak."[128] The medal contests assumed that one could find no better foil for an evil age than the purity of children. Even better, adorable children would attract a paying public. Both the Richmond Hill WCTU[129] and the Windsor union[130] sold tickets to their medal contest entertainments.[130]

One effect of the contests, particularly those based on speechmaking, was to further validate the importance of skills of elocution, so promoted in Canada by the temperance lodges. This was also the preferred method by which children demonstrated competence and were evaluated in Ontario's public school system. Echoes of the usefulness of eloquence, particularly for women, ring through several of the organization's National and YWCTU Leaflets. In *Our Social World*, Frances Barnes proposes that women nurture the art of conversation: "By studying the use of words, and by reading the best authors, we learn to use better language and express ourselves more readily in fitting and faultless terms. When we hear the misuse of words and the superfluity of adjectives among young women of the 'perfectly splendid' type, the desire to have the Ys sign 'anti-slang' pledges is increased to wishing them to exemplify more extended wisdom by the study and application of right words." And what purpose can this rhetorical might serve? "A young woman can put a bashful young man entirely at ease by simple, natural conversation."[131]

Medal contests were rarely run as a separate department in the local unions; most often they fell under the YWCTU, the juvenile department, the Little White Ribboners, the Band of Hope, or the Loyal Temperance Legion. Thus, they formed part of the educational and "outreach" program encompassed by one of the union's several youth groups. The WCTU mirrored the public school system by age-grading children and channelling them into the appropriate youth group: the Little White Ribboners served children under seven; the Bands of Hope, and later the Loyal Temperance Legions, served boys and girls to about age fifteen; and the Young Woman's Christian Temperance Union served single women aged about sixteen and older. After the First World War, young men were also invited to attend the YWCTU, and by the 1930s the organization had become the Young People's Branch. The WCTU developed educational literature for each of its target groups in an effort to mould its message to the interests of particular ages and both sexes.

WCTU *Educational Printed Literature*

The Canadian WCTU distributed five American and one Ontario-produced leaflet series to its supporters. Because of its limited market and financial resources, the Ontario WCTU produced only one leaflet series, which dealt with social purity. The large numbers ordered by the Ontario and local unions indicate the sustained support across the province for the messages carried in the leaflets, each of which had a distinct approach, clientele, and area of concern. The Canadian WCTU, and primarily the Ontario organization, also published its own periodical. This distinctively Canadian record permits a comparison with the American model of prescriptive literature.

The first leaflet series adopted by the WCTU was one called Signal Lights, a scion of the official organ of the American WCTU, the *Union Signal*. While the series was certainly sanctioned by the WCTU, with Frances Willard authoring the first number, it was put out by the Women's Publishing Association of Chicago and probably began appearing in the early 1880s. This first pocket-sized, four-page pamphlet is the most democratic of all the leaflet series: it spoke to an audience of middle-class women, men, and boys. Succeeding leaflets would specialize more rigidly as to the group addressed. These leaflets display an individually directed evangelical fervour that never reappears with the same intensity in later pamphlets. Several examples may provide a flavour of the approach taken.

The early numbers spoke directly to men and women of the middle class, and not exclusively about alcohol. The first, Frances Willard's *Individuality of Conscience*, is a spirited defence of the "home protection" vote with the desired end of legislated prohibition. Another leaflet discussed the problem of location in any city of the dreaded "evil houses" frequented by social undesirables.[132] W. Jennings Demorest, the founder of the medal contests, authored several of the Signal Lights. *Definite Political Action Necessary to Antagonize the Liquor Traffic: A Most Atrocious Public Outrage*, like Willard's contribution, is a call to political action by a united temperance force.

> ... the liquor traffic is the great octopus on society, the monumental curse of our country – a curse without one mitigating feature ... These cormorants of society fully understand this question, and also the significant virtue of

combined action. They have accordingly fortified and entrenched their numerous allies. Using their moneyed interests they have largely subsidized the press to silence, and by the use of sophistical arguments as the most effective means to accomplish their nefarious purposes.

In succeeding numbers, Demorest argued that the liquor interests were so effective in influencing weak people that, without a mighty effort to root out the poison, the nation would be destroyed.

Thus gradually and insidiously has this moral cancer of alcoholic poisoning imbedded itself into the nation's life, and its degrading, desolating grasp on society has become such a domineering influence in our political and social economy that it has blighted our moral sense, destroyed our material prosperity, depressed our commercial vitality and brought all the business relations of the country into such a distressed condition that a terrible paralysis now covers the whole nation.[133]

Several of the leaflets savagely ridiculed the working man's demands for a living wage, underscoring the gap between the unionizing working class and the developing middle class. "Men who strike for higher wages can find enough generally for whiskey and tobacco."[134] Frances Willard asserted in her *Temperance and the Labor Question* that "the central question of labor reform is not so much how to get higher wages as to how to turn present wages to better account. Until our friends the 'Knights' study this problem, they will have learned but half their lesson."[135] In her parable of *The Shoemaker and Little White Shoes*, she pictures a temperance crusader visiting the tenement of a young family in which the husband was a hopeless drunk. The reformer confronts the husband and accuses him of loving the saloon-keeper's daughter more than his own sweet little girl, since the saloon-keeper's child is dressed in delicate white shoes and a pretty dress with a sash, purchased with his liquor bills. Meanwhile, his own daughter dresses in rags with no shoes. He must love the saloon-keeper's wife more than his loyal spouse since his money allows the saloon-keeper's wife to take fine carriages while his wife is in want of food. Predictably, the drunk faces the horror of his life, takes the pledge, and pulls himself and his family out of the degradation into which they had sunk.[136] The temperance visitor received a further boost in *Somebody Is Praying for You*. This is a compilation of treacly stories centring on the thought that each person is being spiritually supported in some way by others, even if the support not apparent, and that this could well change a life of evil to one of good.

A young tobacconist came to me for the temperance pledge. A few days later I took a marked copy of the book of Proverbs and called upon him in his cigar-store. After a few inquiries, I handed him the little volume and said, "Read a few verses in this book every day, and remember I pray for you ..." He gave me a quick look, and turning about, began fumbling among the boxes on the shelf behind him as though I had asked for a box of cigars. But after a moment he turned again toward me, and with moist eyes looked me frankly in the face and said, "Excuse me – you took me by surprise; thank you; nobody in the world ever prayed for me before." "Not your mother?" I asked. "My mother never prays." "Then would you like to have me pray for you?" "Indeed I should. I shall not forget it; I will read the book." "Well," I said, "you may know then that I shall pray for you; but when my prayer is answered you will be in a different business and a different man; will you be willing to make the change?" It was a moment before he replied. Then he said: "The change would be for the better: yes, I should be willing to be anything that your praying would make out of me."

It is worth noting that all of the objects of prayer in this issue are male and most of the visitors female. The salvation recipe is also clearly laid out in this example. The object of concern wants to improve his life and be saved; he presents no resistance to the plea. Indeed, only one plea is required to capture this young man's utter devotion. He changes his life almost before the visitor's eyes and vows to follow the goals she has outlined. Finally, it is worth noticing who is to blame for the young man's wayward state: his non-praying mother. There is no suggestion that the visitor should pursue the mother, however. The prize to be gained is young manhood.

As a foreshadowing of the later White Cross Series, which was directed entirely to young men, two final numbers of the Signal Lights series might be discussed because of their concern for middle-class youth. H.H. Seerley's *The Tobacco Habit and Its Effects upon School Work* is representative of the fear-mongering literature that showed the lasting tragic results of a single character flaw, such as smoking. The author asserts that, after he had surveyed several hundred boys, the following conditions were found in those who used the tobacco narcotic. Boys who began the habit at an early age were stunted physically and "never arrive at normal bodily development." Indigestion, impaired taste, defective eyesight, dull hearing, "nervous affections," and heart diseases were all present in the boys under study. But worst of all, smoking destroyed the ability to apply oneself to study, ravaging memory and comprehension. "The faculties of a boy under the influence of the narcotic seem to be in a stupor, and since depraved nerve power stultifies and weakens the will power, there is but little use for the teacher to seek to arouse the dormant, paralyzed energies, or to interest and foster the fagged desire."[137] An anonymous pamphlet entitled *Smoking* concluded with a math problem which parodied the lifestyle of the working class, but was clearly intended for those seeking respectability. "Tom smokes three cigars, and his father smokes five cigars each day, for which they pay sixty cents a dozen. His father drinks three glasses of beer a day at five cents a glass. Tom's mother buys three loaves of bread a day at five cents a loaf, and two rolls of butter a week at fifty cents a roll. At the end of the year how much more do the cigars and the beer cost than the bread and butter?"[138]

The National Leaflets series was produced for the WCTU by the Woman's Temperance Publishing Association, also in Chicago. This collection, dating from about 1885, devotes its attention primarily to the women of the organization, with special focus on the female schoolteacher. Far less emotional and evangelical in tone, the National Leaflets approach a variety of problems with a measured, often scientific pose. Frances Willard's *Scientific Temperance Instruction in Public Schools* is an example of this type. A polemic to prove that temperance education should occupy pride of place in the school curriculum, her leaflet charges the teacher to impart the dangers of this life-threatening substance. "But how shall the young and thoughtless avoid this supreme peril of their youth unless they know about it, and how shall they learn without a teacher, and how shall they teach except they be sent?" In response to teachers' complaints that there was no room in the curriculum for temperance instruction, she quotes a superintendent of schools in Massachusetts who stated that "this subject ought to be taught. If the schedule is too much crowded already, we will take something out and make room for this, because it is entitled to the right of way."[139]

In her *Safety for School Children*, Willard expanded her argument concerning the teacher's essential role in educating the child about other problems, such as self-abuse. Here, the feminization of teaching convinces Willard that the right-thinking female teacher is often preferable to the natural mother, and certainly preferable to the working-class mother

> But all mothers are not what we would wish. The average teacher is greatly superior in character and culture to the average parents whose children are placed under her care. She knows far better what to say and how to say it ... Two-thirds, if not three-fourths, of our public school teachers are women. As I have watched them, my heart has thanked God for their gentle individuality, their gracious strength and their notable good looks! No factor in the

woman question evolution is more significant than that women are teaching the men that are to be. A solid respect for woman's mental powers must be the mental habit of the boys thus trained ... with all my heart I believe there are two motives on which a lady teacher can rely. One is a boy's love for his mother and his sisters; the other a boy's desire to please the lady who teaches him, and it is possible to establish such esprit de corps that boys will not do what they would be ashamed to have her know or what she assures them would be [a] bad example for the smaller pupils.

Despite the general unwillingness of teachers to shoulder the burden of temperance education, much less social purity, other numbers in the National Leaflets series nevertheless also urged the teacher to consider these issues as essential to her task. Alice Guernsey wrote several pamphlets for teachers, showing that "those boys who most needed to hear that Alcohol is a poison, to stomach and heart, to nerve and brain, to muscles and blood, always and everywhere – in cider, home-made wine and beer, as in brandy, whiskey and gin" cannot expect to be reached in the Sunday schools or Loyal Temperance Legions. They could, she stressed, be sought only in the public schools, with teachers alone able to break the intemperance cycle. This otherwise unreachable group included not only working-class children, but also those from "prosperous families where wine is served to guests, where parents smoke as is fashionable."[140]

In addition to pitching the message to teachers, however, many of the titles in the National Leaflet series were devoted to the women of the WCTU. *Is Alcohol a Stimulant?* was answered in the negative by the authors, "A Symposium of Eminent Physicians." To buttress his argument that alcohol was actually a depressant, a Dr Palmer of the University of Michigan produced this baffling explanation: "Paralysis of the splanchnic nerve causes increased peristaltic motion of the intestines, and the paralysis of the inhibitory nerve of the heart increases the frequency of its beat; but in neither of these cases has the real power of the organ been increased, only a restraining, governing influence been removed."[141] It is doubtful that any WCTU member was expected to understand this pompous and impenetrable explanation; rather, the objective was probably to support moral arguments with respected medical opinion. *The Tobacco Toboggan* carefully traced the effects of narcotics such as tobacco, alcohol, and opium on the body: "each of these affect the brain first, the heart second and the stomach third; from the brain, the whole nervous system is affected, from the heart, the entire circulation of the blood, from the stomach, the digestive and assimilation apparatus is influenced." The medical argument is capped, however, with a moral one: "Boys who use tobacco almost invariably begin a practice of deception, which robs them of integrity of character."[142]

The National Leaflets sought to prescribe other aspects of the WCTU woman's life as well. Frances Willard's *Society and Society Women* criticized scanty dress fashions, gambling, card-playing, and dancing: "Banish wine from the dinner, dancing from the 'evening entertainment' and 'society' with its bare arms and exposed busts, its late hours and indigestions, would collapse."[143] Above all else, the dutiful temperance woman must never let the alcohol interests win through her apathy. She must join forces with other women "against the principalities and powers, against the rulers of the darkness of this world, against spiritual wickedness."[144] "We must cling together, moving forward without regard to politics, as we have in the past, doing right as God reveals it to us. We need not be afraid."[145]

The WCTU began producing a separate series of leaflets for the young women, probably in the early 1890s.[146] The YWCTU leaflets are strongly evangelical and even martial in style. Most were published, apparently privately, by Ruby I. Gilbert of Chicago. Three main types of pamphlets were produced in the series. The earliest leaflets justify the separate existence of the YWCTU from the WCTU. *Wherefore a "Y"?* and *Is a YWCTU a Necessity?*[147] both argue this case. A second category of leaflet concerned the establishment of Y unions, the training of the executive, and the retention of members.[148] The third group contained prescriptive codes for the behaviour of the YWCTU woman, including *Why Should a Christian Girl Sign the Total Abstinence Pledge?*, *Our Social World*, *A Girl's Influence*, and *What is Your Value?*[149] These are discussed more fully in the next chapter.

After the turn of the century, two more leaflet series were produced, both for children, especially males. Both were authored primarily by British temperance leaders and represent a different approach from that generally taken by American authors. The rigidity of sex roles is powerfully presented: nowhere is woman's strength apparent, and her manifold weaknesses are noted often.

The Loyal Leaflets promised to be "crisp, telling stories, that will lead the youthful reader to adopt the motto of the series, 'For Truth and the Right, in the King's Name.'" They were intended to be used for supplementary reading in the public schools, for Sunday school classes on temperance Sundays, and in the Loyal Temperance Legions. Even a sample of the titles speak of male interests: *The Life-Saving Station*, *Boxing the Compass*, *St. George and the Dragon*, *At the Station – On the Square*, *How Ralph Stopped Smoking*, and *The Temperance Circus Tent*.[150]

By far the more popular of the two British series, however, were the White Cross leaflets. While similar in appearance to the Loyal Leaflets, each White Cross number contained a brief introduction with two short stories. The American WCTU had cooperated with the British White Cross Army to produce these social purity tracts for boys in public schools, Sunday schools, and youth groups. Imbued with British evangelicalism, the leaflets are different in style and message from any of the other WCTU examples. *The White Cross Manual* had been penned by Frances Willard and was published by the Woman's Temperance Publishing Association in Chicago. Apparently the distinct differences in approach did not disturb Willard or those in charge of WCTU publications.

The White Cross Series, along with the Ontario WCTU-produced White Life Truths series, provided the basic position of the WCTU on the issue of social purity. The organization had always had problems in transmitting the message effectively because of the need to veil each comment in euphemism and generality. Prior to the White Cross and White Life Truths leaflets, the only other means to transmit the social purity dogma was through itinerant speakers, such as the peripatetic Arthur Beall.

It is impossible to know how effective the various educational campaigns were. Minute books of local unions document the regular purchase of the National and YWCTU Leaflet series, while neither the Loyal nor the White Cross Series received much mention. One explanation for the apparent lack of popularity of the youth pamphlets may lie in the turgid writing style used in the British leaflets, particularly in comparison with the breezy approach of the American-produced materials. For example, the following paragraph appears in the Reverend Horsley's leaflet for boys entitled *Bloodguiltiness*: "I would say that at the sight or knowledge of the girl that most willfully and inexcusably embraces a life of sin, of the foulest in language or habit, even of the procuress, or the vendors of obscene literature or art, our first thought should it be, Thou art my sister! and the second, Am I free from thy blood?" Compare this tortured statement with the opening lines of a sample YWCTU leaflet, *Is a YWCTU a Necessity?*: "There is no time in the home life when a girl receives so much thought and care, when a mother's love and a father's arm are so ready to shield and protect, as when she enters the portals of young womanhood, and stands with all life centred in the happy present and the ever-changing future."

The six leaflet series sponsored or adopted by the WCTU appealed to specific interest groups within the organization. But the most effective educational channel for the women and youth groups was the *Woman's Journal*, later called the *Canadian White Ribbon Tidings* and the *Canadian White Ribbon Bulletin*. Begun in 1885 in Ottawa, this regular publication disseminated news from the world, American National, dominion, and provincial unions, as well as local unions when they could be convinced to submit reports. It printed fiction and advice columns, some produced by its own members, to confront problems and suggest appropriate responses befitting women of this organization. Finally, it helped to shape programming and suggested boundaries for new youth groups so that duplication and conflict would be kept to the minimum.

It has been suggested that much of the effective change initiated by the WCTU was accomplished at the local level, where women could exercise both formal and informal political lobbying. The impetus to identify problems in the community came from meetings at the various levels of the organization and a communication of the ideas generated in those forums through the journal. New approaches to deal with urban problems were also reported. In February 1886 the Ottawa WCTU reported the visit of a David Tatum, a Quaker preacher, who, with his wife, had set up a Home for the Friendless in Cleveland, Ohio, in 1872 in order to break the impact of drink on the working-class community. This institution may well have been one of the inspirations for the very successful Home for Friendless Women later established in Ottawa by the YWCTU. In the first issue of the *Woman's Journal*, another problem of ill-prepared working-class girls was addressed when the Ottawa YWCTU provided an extensive report on its kitchen garden program, which was subsequently adopted by the Toronto YWCTU and other groups.[151] As new issues became popular – for example, social purity – local unions reported in the magazine new ways of educating the membership and population. In 1900 the Toronto union announced that it had assembled a purity library containing eighteen numbers of the *New Crusade* and ninety-seven books, all by Dr Wood-Allen.[152] The Brockville YWCTU reported that it had gathered eighty-five interested observers for a "progressive debate," when eight topics, including "Ought the liquor traffic be prohibited?" were discussed by eight experts, each seated at a table ready to outline the issues to the next group. At the end, leaders summed up the points they had gathered from the presentation and discussion, and presented them to the audience. In modern educational circles, this is called a "modified jigsaw" technique, considered to be an effective methodology for group work.[153]

Provincial superintendents regularly reported to the membership through the *Woman's Journal* and, for example, in 1891 urged women to run as public school trustees in order to more easily place temperance literature in the schools.[154] In fact, as the journal aged, it printed less local material and more from the dominion, national, and world organizations, often pointing out where the Canadian or Ontario policy differed from the international, as in the case of woman's suffrage. The magazine's comment on the violent strategies used by the British suffragists was that "the WCTU has never resorted to force, but has always advocated a liberal educational campaign and then looked confidently to the Captain of our salvation to bring the desired issue to pass."[155]

Almost from the beginning, the *Woman's Journal* ran fiction pieces that served to define behaviour and deal with problematic issues. In January 1886 a heavily melodramatic piece was published describing how a home almost destroyed through liquor was on the way to recovery through the ministrations of a determined and pure Band of Hope girl. Later that year, a story appeared with dire warnings that women who strove to keep too tidy and clean a home would drive their sons and husbands from their door.[156] In fact, the *Woman's Journal* bombarded women with the many mistakes they were prone to make, whose evil effects were vividly portrayed.

A favourite theme during the early 1890s was the danger in using liquor to fortify women after childbirth or as a general tonic. Pretty Mrs Carr, for example, was prescribed "plenty of wine and porter" by her doctor to build her strength, but after her third child, she is deep in the "doze of beer." The children are neglected, she cannot keep servants, and she has head-aches and a bad temper. Her poor husband learns the dreadful truth when he invites guests to dinner and discovers that no dinner is ready! Matters further deteriorate, with the increasingly haggard Mrs Carr pawning her jewels to procure strong drink and then indulging "till she was delirious." To drown his sorrow, her husband also overindulges. They decline together, and as wrecked Mrs Carr lies on her deathbed, she extracts a promise from Mr Carr that he turn to temperance. "Alas!" ends the story, "how many blighted homes there are through the doctor's orders."[157]

In 1891 the *Woman's Journal* began a "Household Page" which included recipes ("Dainty Dishes for Invalids"), "Advice to Mothers," and "Comportment," including diagrams of how to sit, stand, and walk.[158] The education of Ontario WCTU women in middle-class ways is apparent from these features in the magazines. By 1907 the *Canadian White Ribbon Tidings* had a "Family Page," a "Quiet Hour" column, a "Children's Corner," "Household Hints," a "Current Events" column, a "Mother's Corner," and didactic prose and poetry sprinkled liberally throughout.[159]

In 1910 the magazine was reorganized again, this time with the following sections: a lead article, which in January 1910, was from the Dominion Alliance; the "President's Message," the WCTU "Missionary's Message," an editorial page, and columns on "How to Make a Good Local President," "Our Workers and Their Work," "Notices, Notes and Personals," "Evangelistic Work," "The Home Circle," "Daddy's Column," and "Household Hints," as well as sundry recipes, poetry, and fiction. The educational function was never lost, although the significant groups identified in this process changed over time.

The emergence of the Loyal Temperance Legions created a need for more youth programs. This was filled periodically by helpful suggestions in the magazine, including a lesson plan which suggested that leaders compare the healthy human body to a house, showing the required foods and the destruction wracked by alcohol.[160]

In the broadest sense, the *Woman's Journal* shaped the WCTU's activities and programs by maintaining a consistent evangelical message. The columns of the *Woman's Journal* and the *Canadian White Ribbon Tidings* demonstrate an ongoing acceptance and proselytizing of the evangelical creed.[161] In addition, the appropriate role for such groups as the YWCTU and the Loyal Temperance Leagues was discussed freely in the *Woman's Journal* columns, often with frank admissions of the fears expressed by WCTU members.[162]

The WCTU sought to bring about change through a wide variety of educational strategies, including the formal educational system, children's groups, leaflets, and its periodical. The result was a program which was regularly put to the membership and actively debated, from the international to the local level. Combined with its political strategies, the educational program effectively reached most sympathetic observers of the WCTU and sought to enlist their active support. The remaining two strategies, those of social and philanthropic work and the religious efforts, enlisted fewer members in the larger urban unions but many in town and rural groups. Both, however, attest to the organization's grounding in the evangelical ethos.

SOCIAL, PHILANTHROPIC, AND RELIGIOUS INITIATIVES

From its founding the WCTU had supported an active program of philanthropic work, which has been described in detail in chapter 3. It included the provision of warm clothing, bedding, and food to families, particularly to mothers and children in distress; visitations and presents to institutions for the aged, especially aged women; the sponsoring of missionaries working with native peoples; the making of "comfort bags" for men separated from their families, such as lumbermen, miners, and soldiers; and the care and attempted reformation of abandoned and fallen women. In all of these cases, relatively small groups of people were helped, but the nature of the work was intensive and demanding, both financially and emotionally. These projects often formed the weekly work of women in the local unions. For example, the Picnic Grove WCTU from Lancaster operated for some years with between eight and ten members. From 1902 to 1908 the union devoted itself to making curtains and paying to have the organ repaired for the public school and providing china cups, saucers, plates, and financial aid to the Cornwall General Hospital, fuel for poor families, boxes of literature for sailors and lumbermen, and eight "comfort bags," including bandages, bottles of Vaseline, adhesive plasters, two cakes of soap, three spools of thread, needles, buttons, "salvecorn," plaster needles, pins, thread or yarn, three marked Testaments, a Bible, hymn books, and printed letters. The women also produced fourteen "temperance" quilts, some of which were sold and the money donated to worthy causes. The quilting became a mainstay of the women's social interaction, which kept the group convivial and united. The union contained several sisters or sisters-in-law, and the executive occupied the same positions year after year. Clearly, this was a group whose members knew each other well, enjoying their companionship. "Mrs John A. McLennan brought a quilt ready to quilt [for which] she furnished all the material. As it took all the time we did not have a lesson but Ethel and Mabel McIntosh read one of the prepared drills while the members quilted. It was interesting and instructive ... tea served after meeting."[163]

The Lancaster WCTU was not unusual: local unions sustained their membership and commitment to change society by nurturing their personal friendships. Illness was recognized with notes of encouragement and communal prayer; death of a loved one brought effusive statements of support and sympathetic grief; personal achievements and acts of kindness were noted carefully and reciprocated. The local sisterhood was nurtured through countless teas, bazaars, garden parties (including something called a "Shredded Wheat Social"![164]), excursions, and, of course, projects. The local union minute books provide a strong sense of women, wellknown to one another, who were comfortable and generous in their individual triumphs and trials. The Lancaster union, and many others across the province have left a legacy of a flourishing middle-class women's culture, similar to what Carroll Smith-Rosenberg suggests existed at the time in the United States. Unlike the American instance, however, the middle-class women's culture of the local WCTU was evangelical in focus and form. Endorsement by the women's community of the evangelical ethos helps to explain the longevity of traditional evangelicalism in local unions.

The WCTU worked through religious channels to achieve change in several ways. At the county or local community level, the women frequently helped organize temperance revivals and regional meetings.[165] These often featured a rousing speaker or a series of testimonials, musical selections, recitations, readings, and prayers. The hope was that individuals attending the entertainment would pledge themselves to abstinence and remain active in the temperance forces. The women of the Newmarket union carried out an elaborate advertising campaign for one of their temperance meetings. They printed three hundred invitation cards "to be given or sent to any whom we think we can reach in that way, may every card be well laden with Prayers as it goes on its faithful mission."[166] The same women commented that "the Gospel Temperance Meetings held in the Temperance Hall are usually well attended, never less than 40 present. Although we do not get many to sign the Pledge it is educating the young along that line of work in which good results must follow in due time for we rely not on the strength of men but God whose promises are sure."[167]

An alliance was struck in most communities between the WCTU and local clergy, with clerical wives often occupying executive positions in the union.[168] This close association benefited the WCTU in a number of ways. Church buildings were placed at its disposal for meetings. Specific church groups, such as the Women's Missionary Associations[169] and Young People's Societies,[170] were made available to sponsor events or to reach particular groups, such as the Sunday School children, more effectively.[171] Ministers lent their considerable public authority in support of the temperance cause by preaching temperance sermons and visiting the unions to participate in prayer days[172] or to hold devotional services. For instance, the Spencerville union called a meeting in 1897 "of the ministers and influential men of each congregation to organise an educational campaign that shall prepare the way for the Plebiscite."[173] In return, supportive clerics and their congregations often had their philanthropic and educational duties lightened because of the WCTU's work. Thus the relationship was often one of productive symbiosis, with religious principles working hand in glove with temperance.

Local unions did not become strong units just because of their social interaction; the fact that each union followed a devotional program strengthened its communal resolve to carry on an often unpopular campaign. For example, the women of the Newmarket WCTU in the 1880s set aside at least half of the time at each meeting for "devotional exercises." In addition, they identified meetings where devotionals alone were carried out, in addition to the gospel temperance meetings they sponsored for the community. But every meeting's business was influenced by the women's religiosity and the solidarity it engendered: "Mrs. Beckett brought up a case of drunkeness [*sic*] and solicited the prayers of the Union, one of the Ladies offered to visit the party."[174] At the Fairmount union's meeting in 1930, as another example, "Our opening hymn was 'Our Bles't Redeemer, ere He breathed His tender last farewell' – Mrs. Dobson read our devotional lesson from Acts 1st Chapt'r, shewing us that we shall receive power thro the Holy Spirit – That our Lord did all His works – thro' the Holy Spirit after the day of Pentecost – when the Holy Spirit came upon Him. Mrs. Dobson then offered prayer."[175] As late as 1946, the Lambton County union meeting on 26 June opened with a hymn,

> after which Mrs. Brunt led in prayer. Mrs. Hazen read as scripture lesson Joshua Chapter 1 and in her comments called attention to God's command to Joshua to "Be strong and of good courage, for the Lord thy God is with thee whether soever thou goest." Joshua was leading the children of Israel into the promised land and we are trying to lead others away from evil so like him we should be strong, stand firm and have faith in God's promise which is ours today as it was Joshua's in those days.[176]

While the degree and extent varied, all the unions carried on some such religious observances at every meeting. It is safe to assume that this participatory religion gave the women a clear purpose and rationale for the work they carried out so faithfully. It also testified to the evangelical, and later the fundamentalist, character of their work, faith, and vision. Historians rather too anxious to trace the secular origins of mid-twentieth-century life tend to overlook such deep and fundamental religiosity. They concentrate instead on the concrete social policies and reforms. In so doing, they miss the essential character of evangelical social reform as practised by the women of this study.

The Ontario WCTU was a distinct organization that differed from its American model: the Ontario organization's principal interests were based on evangelicalism, and it used different tactics to achieve its objectives. Further, its leadership under Letitia Youmans was markedly different from that provided by Frances Willard. All of these factors meant that the Ontario WCTU developed as a separate phenomenon.

The Ontario organization supported Willard's "do everything" policy by branching out early in its existence from narrow temperance concerns. However, because of the smaller size of the Ontario organization and its firm evangelical foundation, the range of activities in which it engaged was necessarily more limited than that of its American counterpart. At the same time, such causes as the Bands of Hope, gospel, prayer, and temperance meetings, and the limiting and monitoring of licences for everything from poolrooms to taverns were pursued more vigorously than in the United States, attesting to the Ontario WCTU's surviving evangelicalism.

The Ontario union also avoided some issues prized by the American National WCTU. The former offered to throw its weight behind whatever political party would support prohibition,[177] but it never formally allied itself with any party, nor did it attempt to form its own party. Also unlike the National WCTU, the Ontario group avoided close identification with labour and, indeed, exhibited a less-than-coherent position with regard to various labouring groups. For example, while the London WCTU firmly supported the petition of the city's milkmen that the sale of milk be prohibitted on the sabbath,[178] the same union found itself almost continually at war with the working classes over the closing time of bars and the number of liquor licences to be granted.[179] Similarly, at the provincial and dominion levels, there was no consistent policy on political or labour union affiliation.

It is apparent that the Ontario WCTU was less inclined to engage in direct political action than was its American cousin. Hence its operating tactics also differed. Although direct political measures such as the petition were used in Ontario, most of the changes achieved by the Ontario group were through indirect pressure. A multitude of examples of modifications to public policy being achieved through a quiet word with an official or offending citizen, a show of strength at a meeting, or a rallying to the cause at a temperance entertainment appear in the local minute books and in the provincial reports. These indirect measures were especially effective in the towns and villages of Ontario, suggesting another apparent difference with the American organization.

Barbara Epstein has argued that the WCTU had its greatest strength in the cities, rather than the small towns or rural districts of America. Where the nineteenth-century rural woman continued to gain status through her economic role in society, Epstein argues, the middle-class urban women was robbed of this primary identity through urban capitalism and the resulting separation of spheres. Ultimately, however, "the confinement of women to a distinct sphere of activities provided a basis for a distinct set of values; their heightened dependence on men brought a greater subordination to them. In a milieu in which independence was highly valued, resentment often lay close to the surface."[180] The Ontario records indicate, however, that the WCTU in that province was far more than an urban phenomenon. Acting as the unofficial moral arbiters of small communities, members of the WCTU across the province used mainly informal strategies to eliminate liquor, tobacco, gambling, and other activities which they considered to be immoral or illegal. Direct political strategies were used at the provincial and dominion levels, but never to the same degree as in the United States.

How could the demography of the Canadian and American movements differ so radically? One factor that may cause the two organizations to appear more different than they actually were results from the choice of records consulted. Until very recently those favoured were the annual reports and minutes of the National and dominion conventions.[181] The local records of the Ontario organization show that, while the stated membership was obviously smaller in towns and villages than in the cities, the accomplishments were often as impressive as those in the larger centres, and sometimes more so. In western Canada, Nancy Sheehan finds that the WCTU was strongest in the small towns.[182] One might also draw the conclusion that the WCTU could not be considered to have prospered in the small town if the standard of success used was the number of members or the extent of legislation passed, rather than the quieter, informal accomplishments. There is the additional issue that political tactics and large-scale urban movements are easier to track than non-legislative strategies in a small town.

But the greatest single difference between the two organizations resulted from leadership. It has been noted that evangelicalism lent itself to being dominated by charismatic leaders who could command intense devotion and loyalty. Operating from an almost unassailable position of power, evangelical leaders are peculiarly free to establish an empire in which the leader's goals become those of the followers. Frances Willard, seriously called "Saint Frances" and the "Queen of Temperance,"[183] had a very different counterpart in Ontario. As has been discussed in chapter 2, Letitia Youmans was a former farm daughter, teacher at the Cobourg Ladies' Seminary and the Picton Ladies' Academy, devoted wife and stepmother of eight, revivalist, Sunday school teacher, and temperance child-worker.[184] She was as conservatively evangelical as Willard was a "strong, independent, sharp-witted rebel."[185] Instead of being a "superb showwoman,"[186] Youmans demonstrated skills which were more apparent in creating a solid, decentralized organizational structure with a clear sense of evangelical purpose and a collegial working climate that encouraged independent action by local unions within the provincial framework. She was a capable woman who worked especially hard at forging the links between the WCTU and other temperance groups in the province. She was in demand as a public speaker across Canada and in the United States, where she campaigned extensively on behalf of the National WCTU.[187] Throughout her career, Youmans received a great many tributes and expressions of gratitude, but she was never the object of the intense loyalty showered on Willard. Perhaps Youmans's invalidism for the last ten years of her life (which forced her into a state of near penury), coupled with her intense evangelicalism and heavier family responsibilities, created a looser hold on, and a different vision for, the Ontario WCTU.

The members of the Ontario WCTU carved out a distinct organization with different causes, roots of power, tactics, and leadership from its American mentor. It sought to achieve its varied reform objectives through the political process – formal and especially informal – education of the membership and clients, philanthropy and social interactions, and an ever-present evangelical religious underpinning and practice.

CHAPTER SIX

The Young Woman's Christian Temperance Union: "The Work of Winning Souls"

The WCTU was the first temperance organization in Canada to develop a comprehensive childhood education program.[1] This was partly as a result of its long-standing commitment to children and partly to secure a future generation of temperance workers. In addition to the Bands of Hope, which had been adopted from the British temperance movement, the WCTU organized several youth groups, including the Little White Ribboners and the Loyal Temperance Legions. However, the Young Woman's Christian Temperance Union was on a much larger scale and had a rather indeterminant, yet definitely older clientele.

COMPOSITION OF THE YWCTU

Originally intended for single young women of about fifteen to thirty, the organization also included in its ranks a number of older single women from the early 1880s. As well, some unions accepted a few married women into the young women's sector. Nevertheless, the YWCTU in Ontario's larger cities developed an identity which separated it from both the other youth groups and the mother organization. This identity was based, not on age or marital status, but on its evangelicalism, empowering the group to undertake a daunting program of social reform during the nineteenth century. Of all the youth groups created by the Ontario WCTU, the YWCTU was, with the Bands of Hope, the most active. In fact, during the late 1880s, several urban Ontario unions were virtually taken over by the YWCTU (see table 3 in the appendix). Such would never be the case again, and it seems not to have been a phenomenon duplicated in other provinces or at the dominion level (see tables 1,2,4, and 5 in the appendix).

An examination of the YWCTU's mandate, strategies, and achievements enriches our understanding of the urban impact of the WCTU and the contribution made by single women in social reform, and it provides a working example of the power of evangelicalism in reformist activities. Its collapse by 1930 illustrates the waning appeal of temperance and evangelical groups in the twentieth century amongst all classes, the decline of voluntarist measures with the growth of professionalism, and the process of marginalization successfully imposed by a threatened parent organization on its own creation.

Ruth Bordin in her account of the American WCTU provides one of the few scholarly assessments of the impact of the YWCTU: "The exciting, innovative Union projects were not the work of the Ys but of older women."[2] Similarly, Nancy Sheehan identifies the YWCTU as one of the three "informal" youth departments, with the YWCTU trailing as "probably the least successful of the three."[3] The history of the Ontario YWCTU reveals that Bordin's conclusions do not hold for the Canadian case and that Sheehan's assessment, at least for Ontario, is incorrect. This is largely because both are based on data postdating 1918.

Yet it is preferable to be discounted by historians than to be ignored, which has been the fate of the YWCTU in the other relevant historiography. For example, Wendy Mitchinson does not mention the YWCTU. In the organization's early years, it was not an embarrassing failure or a group of smug young women which "concerned itself largely with busywork."[4] It was imbued with seemingly unflagging evangelical energy and carried out the most daunting of the WCTU social projects. In 1886 Mary Scott, superintendent of young women's work for the WCTU, asked: "Do you ever think that if we were to stop the work of young women in the world, at the present day, what a blank there would be? Take away the bright, earnest, young teachers out of the Sunday Schools, the teachers from the Day Schools, stop the Mission Bands, Sewing Societies, Church socials, everything in fact in which young women are concerned and just think what the world would be like."[5]

THE SINGLE WOMAN IN THE WCTU

The WCTU and the Women's Crusade had drawn to their ranks single and married, young and middle-aged women who, in Frances Willard's words, learned the "power to transact business, to mould public opinion by public utterance, and opened the eyes of scores and hundreds to the need of the Republic for the suffrage of women, and made them willing to take up for their homes and country's sake the burdens of that citizenship they would never have sought for their own."[6] Crusaders came from the towns' upper ranks. Charles Isletts estimated that crusader families controlled two-thirds of one Crusade town's wealth,[7] with a correspondingly high educational standing. The American WCTU class position was even higher, with many of the early leaders having "considerable formal education. Those WCTU leaders who worked outside the home usually did so as lecturers, authors, editors, teachers, professors, or professional temperance workers."[8]

Single women who had been convinced of the need to assume "the burdens of that citizenship they would never have sought for their own" during the crusade found a home in the WCTU from the start. The organization's early offices in both countries and at all levels were held by single and married women. Thus the important and equal role of the single woman within the WCTU was apparently widely accepted.

Sadly, such early equal status was not retained. By the late 1870s, the American WCTU began noting the importance of self-renewal through training young – and presumably single – women in separate unions. In 1878 a national committee of young women's work was established, and this group was organized into a department of work in 1880 under the secretariat of Frances J. Barnes.[9] In 1890 Barnes organized the world YWCTU. In Canada, the first record at the dominion level of a YWCTU appears in the minutes of the second convention, held in 1889, while provincially a department of young women's work dates from at least 1885. It was headed by the remarkable Mary Scott, who had helped to found the YWCTU in Ottawa and would serve for many years as the editor of the *Woman's Journal* and in other dominion superintendencies.[10]

IDEAS

As a product of the WCTU, the YWCTU shared many common ideas with the mother group. The sanctity of the home was unquestioned. In 1898 one YWCTU spokeswoman described the Y members as "home-loving women and no public work that will make the home of secondary importance should be favored at all by our bright, winsome Ys."[11] Where the Ys could not sustain a separate organization, as in several Toronto unions, the remaining members apparently merged with little difficulty with the mother union.[12]

Yet any separate structure encourages separate ideas, and this too was true for the YWCTU. The chief difference between the WCTU and its daughter organization was the more powerful evangelical motive in the single women's social reform endeavours, particularly during the 1880s and 1890s. Before the turn of the century, the Ys adopted a more pronounced militant evangelicalism as the foundation of their activities than can be ascertained in the WCTU. Many examples of this potent evangelicalism can be found in the YWCTU's efforts to explain its ideas and role differences, especially in contrast with the WCTU. "Who but women have the power," asked a speaker at the 1886 provincial convention,

> the mighty power of sympathy which alone can roll away the stones of prejudice so that the Master's life-giving words may penetrate into dead hearts! Who but women can perform the individual or personal heart to heart work which is so essential to the success of our object. "Go ye into all the world," meant the shop as well as the church, the kitchen as well as the hospital. It is in these neglected parts of our Lord's vineyard that we desire to extend the influence of our Young Woman's Christian Temperance Union.

The mission of acting as a witness to Christ's salvation has frequently been seen by evangelical groups as the particular purview of young people, and especially young women. This has been found to have been true in both the English and American evangelical revivals,[13] as was discussed in chapter 1.

A YWCTU woman considered the mission before her sisters and herself:

> Thinking it was a self-devised scheme [as opposed to a God-inspired one], she hesitated, was about to abandon the idea, but first laid it before the Lord and awaited His answer. A message from His own word came about immediately. 'Arise, stand upon thy feet, for I have appeared unto thee for this purpose, to make thee a minister and a witness ...' This was our commission, here was our plan of work, the work of bringing souls out of darkness into light, from the power of Satan unto God, and all laid out by an unerring hand.[14]

Young women, then, were particularly fitted to "roll away the stones of prejudice" by approaching sinners individually in the home and in the workplace to effect reform. They could proclaim, in Christ's name, an "eloquent ministry of loving deeds."[15] Further, "women have the abandon of enthusiasm which shows an unselfish and love-like spirit, they can give to a cause a love and loyalty and heart-force that is not found in man."[16] Young women had the time to devote to the mission and the confidence arising from God's challenge. Further evidence of the evangelical ethic was the YWCTU proclivity to provide personal testimony of personal conversion long after the WCTU had ceased to entertain the practice.[17]

At the local level too, the evangelical ethic is striking. The Toronto Central Y union explained its program of visiting elderly women and invalids as springing from "love and for Christ's sake ... We have striven to 'do good as we had opportunity,' remembering 'that pure religion and undefiled before God and the Father is this, to visit the fatherless and widows in their affliction.'"[18] It seems, therefore, that while the YWCTU adopted the basic ideas of the mother organization, its members were more influenced by evangelicalism as a primary motive force in their work during the late nineteenth century.

MEMBERSHIP

The period of greatest expansion and most significant work by the YWCTU in Ontario occurred during the 1880s and 1890s in a number of city and town unions. While various city, town, and rural unions also established YWCTU departments in the post–World War I years, there is little evidence that these Y unions operated during that period as anything other than helpmeets to the main WCTU.[19] During the 1880s, however, the numbers of YWCTU departments grew encouragingly quickly, and the range of activities kept pace. In 1886, for example, there were fourteen YWCTU departments in Ontario,[20] and a year later, the number had almost doubled to twenty-five;[21] by 1888 there were thirty-five.[22]

Still, the membership was more mercurial than solid, particularly in the town unions. By 1896 only six YWCTU departments declared themselves to the provincial superintendent.[23] By the following year's convention, the superintendent freely expressed her disappointment at the Ys' sliding popularity. "We are very nearly discouraged altogether with the slow progress of this Department," she allowed.[24] From this period until the war, membership languished in town unions, and never again would the Ys take on such a challenging program as the urban groups had forged for themselves during the 1880s and early 1890s.[25] To explore the nature and scope of young women's work in the Ontario WCTU, two urban Ys – those in Ottawa and Toronto – and one town Y in Brockville, all of which were established in the late 1880s, will be contrasted with the Ys' work in 1910 and 1931.

THE URBAN YWCTU IN THE NINETEENTH CENTURY

The date of the Y's establishment in Ottawa is unclear, but by 1888 the local YWCTU had 119 members on the rolls[26] and vice-presidents representing the Episcopalian, Reformed Episcopalian, Methodist, Presbyterian, Congregational, and Baptist churches.[27] There were, however, far fewer active members. By 1888 only 18 young women's names appear repeatedly in the minute book. This small group of women, all single, ran entirely by themselves the WCTU's evangelical department.

Some of the Y's works were of an educational nature. Between 1888 and 1890, it managed to offer a night school for working girls to improve literacy, which served about ten students each time. A second motive for the night school was to gain converts to evangelicalism. "Lessons were simple, emotional and emphasized the need to have a religious experience by giving oneself up to Christ,"[28] reports the school superintendent. Sewing schools were maintained in both Upper and Lower Town, where between sixty and eighty girls learned to make quilts and pinafores. A well-subscribed kitchen garden program was undertaken, at which "exercises were well performed" and prizes, a tea, and oranges given to the girls at the end of the season, when "an exhibition of sweeping lesson in St. George's Church" was staged.[29] Never described in much detail, the popular kitchen garden program taught domestic science to working-class girls and often involved sweeping and other cleaning exercises set to music, rather like a domestic revue.[30] The program taught housekeeping "by means of catechism, music and miniature toys, such as toothpicks for kindling wood, tiny dishes, tablecloths, dishpans etc. for setting tables and washing dishes ... It takes the drudgery out of the 'daily round, the common task,' and makes it beautiful, and the lessons learned by the little ones are never forgotten."[31] Occasionally, public exhibitions were staged, as when "twenty little girls in dainty caps and aprons" performed for the Dominion WCTU convention in 1891 in Saint John, NB.[32] The kitchen garden program was so popular that the evangelical superintendent, Bertha Wright, regularly bemoaned the lack of enough teachers to satisfy the demand. Callisthenics classes were also taught.

Temperance education was provided through two Bands of Hope, one in Ottawa and the other in Hintonburg, which children attended on Saturday afternoons. Here, the Ys found themselves in competition with youth temperance instruction offered by the local temperance lodges. A note in the minute book of April 1888 complains that many of the children had been "taken away" by the lodge.

But the area where the Ottawa Ys made their greatest efforts was in evangelical proselytizing. A flower mission provided flowers and fruit weekly to the Protestant Hospital. The hope was that after recovery, the recipient of such gifts would remember the kindness and seek out the generous benefactors for religious advice. A Bible study class met regularly and formed itself into a choir that went weekly to the women's corridor of the county jail, on Sundays to the Protestant Hospital, and to the elderly women's Refuge Branch at the Orphans' Home. It seems that the choristers' enthusiasm outstripped their talent, since reports exist that some of the patients covered their heads with blankets to avoid the inspired young women![33] A "training class" was held weekly, presumably to learn to distribute tracts effectively, 724 of which were delivered during the single month of April 1888. In November of the same year, 109 "friendly letters" were penned by the young women and dispatched to the infirm and depressed, with the same hoped-for result as with the flower mission.

The young women in the Y carried out door-to-door visitations and became so keenly evangelical that a series of gospel meetings were run in Anglesia Square, near the Fish Market. A report of the work at the Anglesia Square mission was submitted to the Ontario convention in 1889. The YWCTU, in concert with the WCTU's Bible reader, started the mission

> with a view of reaching fallen men and women, many of whom we had met in the jail, and in house to house visitation. The meetings, which have been well attended, consist of a short open air song service, which generally attracts quite a number, who are afterwards invited to attend the meeting. In this way we have reached a large number of men and women under the influence of liquor, who have staggered out of the bar-rooms and other dens of iniquity to hear the singing. Several women have been brought from this meeting in an intoxicated state to the Home [for Friendless Women].[34]

Even though the WCTU women did not participate in these evangelical gospel meetings, the Ys came to feel so proprietorial about them that they moved at their March 1889 meeting that the project "be under the auspices of the YWCTU."[35] It was the Y decision to extend the gospel mission to the Catholic stronghold of Hull, Quebec, that resulted in the riots described in chapter 1. Clearly, the YWCTU women from Ottawa were both single-minded and courageous in their evangelical zeal! By late 1889 the Ottawa YWCTU was attempting to reach "students, society girls, young women in the Civil Service, girls in business and working girls." It reported proudly that the union supported eleven branches of preventative and only four of rescue work.[36] Here, then, is demonstration of the changing evangelical ethic: social activism was not discovered by evangelicals in the late nineteenth century, but redefined.

As in the case of the YWCA a few years later,[37] individual rescue work amongst confirmed sinners was seen to have a more limited return in the war against corrupt behaviour than preventative social measures. The most ambitious project undertaken by the Ottawa YWCTU clearly demonstrates this gradual change in focus towards social reform, and away from moral rescue work, as the means to effect lasting lifestyle changes. The Home for Friendless Women was a "mission to the masses," but with a difference; this time the object was mothers who had "fallen." The idea for the home seems to have come from Mayor Howland of Toronto, who addressed the Ottawa WCTU in 1885 on the "advisability of having a home or refuge for female prisoners coming out of Jail. Also having a weekly Evangelistic Meeting so that that class and others addicted to drink might be drawn in."[38] In the final plan, the two ideas seem to have been combined. A short time later the question of "providing a Temporary Home for female prisoners having then been discussed it was decided by a vote of 8 to 3 that the Union should take up work on behalf of discharged female prisoners."[39] It was not the WCTU which took on the project in the end, however, but the YWCTU.

The home was founded and managed for eight years by one of the Ottawa Y's most capable and deeply evangelical members, Bertha Wright. Explaining her entry into the mission field in her *Lights and Shades of Mission Work*, Wright describes watching working-class women on the street with their "pale, careworn, unsatisfied faces" and her growing conviction that God was pointing out the mission that she must follow: "He had really chosen such an instrument to be used in the highest, the noblest, the grandest work in which mortal man can engage – the work of winning souls."[40] To this starkly evangelical end, she had organized the Y's visits to female prisoners to offer a new life. The group's limited successes here convinced her of the futility of such work, however, for such women seemed to be inexorably drawn back to the bar-room since they saw themselves as outcasts without any hope of salvation. She concluded that there was need for a place "where a helping hand and shelter could be offered to any sinful, friendless woman without regard to creed, nationality, age or condition, at any time, night or day, the only requisite being a desire to lead a better life."[41] The Home for Friendless Women was to minister to the spiritual and physical needs of "unfortunates," that is, those women with children, some of whom were living by prostitution, who agreed to stay in the home for a full year so that a new way of life could be forged. Close attention to child care was regarded as essential to regeneration of these fallen mothers since their children were a constant reminder to them that sin had been committed, this recognition being the evangelical precondition to the conversion experience and eventual salvation. The home's rules would end with the stern statement that "the board heartily disapproves of any arrangement or institution that provides for relieving the patients of the care of their offspring, thus rendering it easy for them to escape the full penalty of wrong-doing."[42]

The Y's work with friendless women was not undertaken without an expression of hostility from the community. It was argued that the home would become a "hot bed of vice," housing "vicious creatures" who could not be managed by a troupe of delicate young women. The fever that raged during the winter of 1887 was even used as a warning against the proposal.[43] In spite of Ottawa's anxiety about the home, the YWCTU forged ahead, canvassing the community for private donations. Neither the YWCTU nor the WCTU seems to have made formal financial contributions to the home; the Y contribution was in the form of labour.

In late December of 1887 the YWCTU Bible class cleaned a rented house from top to bottom in readiness for the first "inmates." Furnishings were made from inverted flour barrels covered with white marble oilcloth and draped with cretonne. The work was finally finished on Christmas Eve with a view to opening the residence after the new year. Solemnly, the Y women held a prayer service in the new dining-room and departed for their homes. During the night a water-pipe burst in the upper storey, and water flowed throughout the house all night. When they returned the next day, they found six inches of cold water in the basement, whitewash coating everything, rugs soaked, and icicles hanging from the stoves. "It seemed as though all the forces of evil combined had arrayed themselves against us in order to hinder the commencement of a work which had for its chief aim the glory of God in the salvation of the most degraded."[44] This statement demonstrates that the YWCTU saw its noble evangelical work pitted against the forces of evil in an almost physical contest.

Yet the home survived this early trial and soon flourished. It supported itself by operating a laundry: "The Home is not a place for the maintenance of the idle."[45] In September 1888 the following notice appeared in the Ottawa papers: "Washing and ironing done at the shortest possible notice at the Home for Friendless Women. Good satisfaction guaranteed. Terms cash on delivery."[46] The conditions in which the laundry work was accomplished are reminiscent of a Dickens novel. The furnace and boiler were found in the basement, through which the yard water ran so that the foundations of the engine were undermined. The ceiling was so low that a man or tall woman could not stand upright. A horizontal smoke pipe from the furnace ran so close to the beams that care needed constantly to be taken to ensure that they did not ignite. The washing room was so laden with moisture that one could barely see the other figures in the room; the windows were so warped that none closed tightly; the floor was slippery and the machinery soon covered with rust from the condensation. All linen had to be carried from this basement room to the first floor, where the wringer was kept, and from there to the dry closet on the second floor. The ironing room was also the nursery. "From 15 to 20 babies are to be seen every day scattered on ironing tables, in clothes baskets, or creeping on the floor, while unceasing vigilance has to be exercised to keep them from the machinery."[47]

In 1890 the home moved to larger quarters, and a new steam laundry was installed. But even with the improved quarters, the evangelical creed that one must work hard, shun the world, and adopt moral rigour was apparent. That the rehabilitation program was largely punitive was also clear. Judith Walkowitz has observed: "through laundry work, women could do penance for their past sins and purge themselves of their moral contagion. Clear starching, it would seem, cleanses all sin, and an expert ironer can cheerfully put her record behind her."[48] The analogy between laundry work in these circumstances and the cleansing of sin through baptism also cannot be overlooked.

In addition to fallen women, the home accepted the abandoned children of mothers who, through love of hard drink or desertion by their husbands, neglected them. A Mrs Nelson was found recovering from intoxication in a jail cell.

> She was in a sad plight, poor thing, having slept part of the night in a coal bin, and lost her shawl, hat and shoes, and was evidently much concerned about her children, whom she had left alone in a house on Albert Street. As she was sent down for a month, we went in search of the neglected little ones, and found a beautiful curly haired boy of five, asleep on the broad windowsill, his pale, wan cheek resting against the pane, while his little sister had crept into a clothes basket on the floor which was half full of wet linen and she too, was fast asleep. They had evidently been waiting and watching for mother until at length they had cried themselves to sleep. We took them to the Home, which was only a short distance away and where they were kept until their unworthy mother's release.[49]

Finally, destitute old women who were not eligible for the Refuge Branch of the Orphans' Home were also accepted in the home.

> One cold January morning, an aged woman, clad in a thin calico dress,

without a shawl, cloak or warm wrap of any kind, appeared at the gate. She was homeless and friendless, having been arrested the previous August for vagrancy, and so frail and feeble was she that it was with the greatest difficulty that she was led to the street cars, in which she was conveyed to the Home.[50]

The home's register of inmates from 1888 to 1894 indicates the source of the women agreeing to stay in the Home for Friendless Women. From January 1888 until September 1889, the majority of inmates came from the women's corridor of the local jail, from the street, and from the railway station, where "vulnerable" young women were directed to the home. Such sources are not surprising since the home, like the Anglesia Square mission, had originated in jail visits. It was regarded as an extension of work carried out by the Ottawa superintendent of prison and public works for a number of years.[51] A few other women were referred by the police and the local hospitals. The only period when women came in large numbers from the brothels was in late 1888 and 1889, although a few continued to arrive from this source until 1894. As the home became more settled in its operating procedures, it accepted fewer cases from the jails, believing that such women were particularly hardened to the rough circumstances of life on the street and were not immediately or even gradually amenable to rehabilitation. A fairly steady clientele continued to be routed, however, from the street, railway station, and hospitals.[52]

The register of inmates also indicates the destination of women leaving the home. In 1888 and 1889 most women were transferred elsewhere, whether this was to the hospital, back to their families, or into service. From early 1889, however, increasing numbers of women fall into the "removed" and "left" categories, with fewer moving into other institutions or families. This trend appears to suggest a general recognition that some women were beyond help and might be considered part of the Victorian "social residuum."[53] The record shows also that the home's numbers remained high throughout the period, indicating that there was a real need for the services provided. A rough classification for the inmates reveals that while an approximately equal number were "unfortunate" – that is, living by prostitution – and "abandoned," the largest group by far were "intemperates." Mysteriously, after the home became independent from the YWCTU in 1891, the "intemperate" classification declined precipitously, perhaps because of a changed philosophy, although it is not possible to document this. In terms of nationality, Irish women far outnumbered the other groups, including English, Scots, French,

American, German, and Canadian. The Irish preponderance was likely due to the endemic poverty of that community in Ottawa and to the dominant size of the Irish group in the city at the time.

The Home for Friendless Women was one of several bold experiments by the Ottawa YWCTU and one that required courage and entrepreneurial skills. The organization reported ongoing "difficulties and discouragements" and concluded its report in 1890 by lamenting: "God only knows what it has cost us to rise above all these trying circumstances. He only has seen the tears and heard the cries of distress that have gone up as we have waited at his feet, sometimes for whole nights, pleading for funds, for souls, for success."[54]

The whole history of the home is also consistent with the evangelical woman's refuge concept pioneered in the eastern United States of the period.

> Not only as shelters, but also as retaining centers for fallen women, the homes catered to uniquely feminine needs. Through evangelical religion, education, and discipline, the matrons and managers offered courses to restore the womanhood of residents, daily lessons in reading, writing, sewing and other feminine services, thus ensuring both domesticity and piety. Discipline included the banning of profanity, tobacco, alcohol, and coarse behaviour, plus a routine of early rising, regular work (sewing, laundry, cleaning) and habits of neatness and industry at all times.[55]

What was different from the American example was the failure to develop any apparent sense of "sisterhood" between care-worker and inmate. One possible explanation relates to the change in administrative control. The Home for Friendless Women had had its start with a group of dynamic single young women. In 1891, although "all felt that the Home was doing a grand work ... if it were for the advantage of the Home to be independent of our Union it was certainly wiser to relinquish all claims."[56] Once the home became incorporated and established as a charitable institution under the review of the provincial government, it could claim provincial grants to ensure its survival. This change was accomplished in 1891, but as a result, the home lost most of its single women boosters other than Bertha Wright. The board of management came increasingly to reflect the middle-class married woman associated with, not the YWCTU, but the WCTU. Of course, there is no guarantee that had the young single women maintained control of the Home for Friendless Women, a sisterhood concept would have developed.

Regardless of the apparent lack of female solidarity between classes, the YWCTU in Ottawa accomplished a significant amount in a relatively short period of time. A group of about twenty young women taught, evangelized, and attempted to reform a substantial group of troubled women in the Home for Friendless Women. During the same period, the Ottawa WCTU remained active distributing tracts at the railway and fire stations, monitoring the scientific temperance course in the city's public schools, and establishing a temperance coffee-house. But the Ottawa WCTU never displayed the verve and evangelical energy that was the norm for the city's YWCTU during the same period. It took no hand in the energetic evangelism through gospel meetings or female reform. Although the tracking of membership numbers is difficult, the YWCTU in Ottawa seems to have rivalled, and at times exceeded, the mother group, as is demonstrated by table 3 in the appendix. In 1886 and 1894 the figures show that the YWCTU was considerably stronger than the WCTU. Without doubt, the results of the YWCTU's efforts are far more impressive than those of the WCTU in that city during the same period.

The records for the Toronto YWCTU are not nearly as rich as those for Ottawa, but they do permit some insight to single women's work in the urban setting. In the Toronto area, the strongest YWCTU in the late 1880s and 1890s was the Central Y. In 1889–90, it had sixty-nine members, of which eight were married and presumably younger women. Like the Ottawa YWCTU, it took care to find representatives from the Presbyterian, Methodist, Anglican, and Baptist churches. It had equipped itself with both a motto – "Be not weary in well doing; for in due season we shall reap, if we faint not" – and a poem:

> It is not the deed that we do,
> Though the deed be never so fair,
> But the love the dear Lord looketh for
> Hidden with holy care,
> In the heart of the deed so fair.[57]

Both attest to the perceived difficulty of the tasks the women had set for themselves and the evangelical impulse behind those tasks. The deed was not important of itself, but the love impelling the deed was what the "dear Lord looketh for hidden with holy care."

The Toronto Central Y was well established by 1889, when a "group of girls ... made their chief work the Kitchen Gardens, the forerunner to Domestic Science classes. In classes the children of the poor were taught housewifely duties with toy furniture and utensils. These tasks were set to music and many a Toronto housewife secured a well trained maid from these classes, and many a home was made comfortable through the training of these children."[58] The middle-class imperative shines through this statement from a later period. Nevertheless, it may well have represented the ideas of the nineteenth-century Toronto YWCTU, since it too ran a number of working-class educational programs similar to the Ottawa Y's. The scientific temperance instruction department provided temperance classes in the Girls' Home, News Boys' Home, Orphans' Home, and the Mission Avenue School. A cooking school gave practical lessons and a demonstration course to middle-class women, as well as free classes for working women and children. A kindergarten was also made available to working women. Temperance instruction to working-class boys was not neglected: three Bands of Hope operated out of the city missions. Various works of evangelism were also carried out. A flower mission and a separate letter mission were dispatched to the Sick Children's Hospital, the Old Women's Home, the Home for Incurables, the General Hospital, and sick cases in St John's Ward. A boys' gospel temperance meeting was also maintained. While the Central Y attempted no female reform work, it did demonstrate its commitment to evangelical activities. In sum, aside from the monumental work of the Home for Friendless Women, the Central Y seems every bit as serious and energetic as its Ottawa counterpart and developed, as early as 1890, a social program that included parlour meetings and in 1892 a Bicycle Club.[59]

Two other Toronto unions had a YWCTU during this period, North Toronto and the Toronto Gordon union. During the autumn of 1887, the young women of the North Toronto union took over the kitchen garden program and the flagging Band of Hope. With implements provided by the WCTU for the kitchen garden and a subscription to the *Heredity and Hygiene Magazine*, as well as two dollars from the senior women to the Band of Hope, the Ys got along reasonably well.[60] The Y at the Gordon union was so small that it could support only press, evangelistic, and kindergarten departments, with no elaboration of the work in any of them. In all seven of the remaining Toronto unions with no YWCTU, the proportion of single women involved in WCTU activities was much smaller than in those with YWCTUS. For example, the Western union had only one single woman to twenty married, the Parkdale union had three singles to thirty-eight married, and the Willard union had a lone single woman to twenty-six married women.[61] Thus the existence of a YWCTU organization seems to have provided a welcoming environment for single women. Without the separate status, fewer single women joined.

The records for the Brockville Y are even more scanty, but still furnish a glimpse of the work of single women in a smaller Ontario community. In 1886 the Brockville Y reported that its twenty-five active members maintained a Band of Hope, a flower mission, and a relief committee for the poor.[62] Within a year, however, the Y had grown to thirty-seven members. They had secured a headquarters and sponsored two "social reunions," two public entertainments, relief work, an apron sale, a moonlight excursion, and a Band of Hope. They had arranged for an essay to be read on "The Effect of Alcohol on the blood" and supported departments of press, scientific temperance instruction, unfermented wine, flower mission, and district visitation. Like many of the Ys of this period, the Brockville women proudly reported that they used YWCTU stationery.[63]

Two years later the Brockville Y had added another Band of Hope to its roster, as well as cottage meetings, reading circles, a sewing school, and a girls' night school, and it had undertaken the distribution of temperance literature, all in addition to its former activities. The membership was holding fairly steadily at thirty-five.[64] The following year its activities crested when it added a girls' Saturday evening Bible study meeting while maintaining most of its earlier projects.[65] At that point, the resolve of the Brockville Y began to wane. In 1892 it reported only twenty-two members and work with Sunday school classes, as well as "entertainments," as its only program.[66] For some years nothing is heard from the Brockville Y, but in 1898 the group reported a busy year's schedule, including a "geography party," public meetings, badges given to children during the "campaign," Sunday school temperance work, and comfort bags for lumbermen.[67] By the next year the group had begun parlour meetings and medal contests, resuscitated its flower mission, and carried on with comfort-bag construction.[68] Thereafter, until the annual reports cease mentioning individual Y programs in 1910, the Brockville Y devoted most of its energies to the comfort bags and to the "old folks home," the latter becoming the focus for energetic fund-raising. For example in 1901, the Ys raised $215 for the home, and in 1904 they managed to contribute $275.[69]

Judging from the yearly accounts of activities in the WCTU annual reports, the Brockville Y was representative of those in smaller centres across Ontario. Early in the group's history, there was enthusiastic involvement in a wide variety of projects, both frivolous and serious, the latter especially those associated with childhood education and aid to needy women. Eventually, however, the group specialized in two causes, local lumbermen and the indigent aged, both of which were probably removed from the WCTU roster of causes to be supported. Because of the absence of town Y minute books, however, we are unable to draw firm conclusions about the degree of evangelicalism that motivated these single women. If extrapolations from town and rural WCTU unions hold, and it seems safe to assume they would, the single women in YWCTUs across Ontario were part of an evangelical women's culture.

THE YWCTU MANDATE IN THE TWENTIETH CENTURY

By 1910 all of the YWCTUs were a mere shadow of their robust 1880s and 1890s profile. At the World's level, the Ys were reduced to costume pageants.[70] One suggestion was made to have Ys dress in the costume of countries having YWCTUs. Each representative was to be introduced with a report of Y activities in that country while the hostess wound her with "strands of broad white ribbon."[71] Provincially, accounts of Y activities had virtually disappeared from the annual reports. The *Canadian White Ribbon Tidings* could only recommend the following "hints" for surviving unions:

> Always wear the white ribbon. Let at least 15 minutes be given to the devotional part of the program, have a regularly appointed organist if possible, and see that the leader of the devotions is appointed in advance. Begin each meeting on time. Give each member some definite work to do. Write to your provincial Y Secretary. Secure as many subscribers as possible to the National and Provincial Papers. Study carefully how to conduct all public meetings so that those not interested will be pleased and come again. Make it "go" with a "swing," have a good program, good music, "a presiding genius."[72]

In 1898 an ominous note had been struck when Y groups in various parts of the province began admitting men to full membership. Most of these groups soon thereafter called themselves Young Peoples' Groups or Loyal Temperance Legions, with women's special role being forgotten.[73] By 1910 the Ottawa YWCTU had ceased to exist altogether. That city's WCTU, on the other hand, had 245 members and maintained twenty departments of work. Under its tutelage, the juvenile societies had 272 members, as well as two large anti-cigarette leagues.[74]

After a brief rally in 1899–1900, many Toronto region YWCTUs had folded by 1910, including those at Dovercourt, Western, Parkdale, and Bascom, although the decline was apparent to those in the organization by 1896, when the YWCTU provincial superintendent bemoaned a precipitous decline in Y membership. "This was not the result of any laxity on the part of those in charge, but of the numerous new outlets for Christian activity which have come into existence since those days."[75] The banner organization, the Central Y, struggled on with six single women somewhat dispiritedly running programs for the Band of Hope, flower mission, a general educational and evangelistic department, and soap-wrapper collection. (The Surprise Soap manufacturers offered a rebate on wrappers, which would be donated to the Willard Home for Girls.) The power in Toronto appears to have shifted to the Northern YWCTU which boasted thirty-six single and six married women members. Nevertheless, the forty-two women could maintain efforts only in lumber camp, scientific temperance, and refreshment work. The Youmans Y listed sixteen single and three married members engaged in lumber camp work and reports to the *Canadian White Ribbon Tidings* magazine. The Bathurst Y was barely alive, with no membership list recorded or work completed.[76] In the same year, the Toronto WCTU was experiencing a substantial growth in its membership to 1,138, with nineteen departments of work undertaken.[77]

By 1931 the condition of the Toronto YWCTUs was grim, and the Ottawa and Brockville Ys had long since ceased operation. Toronto's nine unions devoted themselves almost exclusively to social meetings and collecting Surprise Soap wrappers for the Willard Home.[78] In 1914 the dominion constitution was changed to reflect the merger of the YWCTU into the Loyal Temperance Legion.[79] The Ottawa WCTU had also lapsed by 1931. In Toronto, however, it seemed still to command a strong following. Twenty-six unions with 3,228 members worked under the WCTU banner. But what did they do? The reports show that most of their time was spent in securing pledges and seeing that days of prayer were observed. It must be admitted that this is a far cry from the dynamic program successfully undertaken in the nineteenth century. But innocuous as these activities were, the WCTU was at least able to survive.

At the dominion and provincial levels, the YWCTU had been converted into the Young People's Branch, which, of course, included both young men and women. This was also true in many local unions, the Y now referring, not to the YWCTU, but to the YPB. What had been an exclusively female organization, then, was diluted into a catch-all youth group. Increasingly, the great hope for the WCTU was no longer its young women, but sympathetic young men.

What had happened to the YWCTU organization in Ontario? How did its work become so trivialized, irrelevant, and out of women's control? To adequately answer these questions, three lines of investigation might be pursued. First, the nature of the role defined for the Ys by the WCTU must be analysed, along with any evidence of the Ys' acceptance, rejection, or modification of this role. Secondly, the relationship between the YWCTU and the WCTU needs to be traced.

Thirdly, the centrality of the evangelical motivation of the YWCTU, so clearly established in the nineteenth century, must also be surveyed in its twentieth-century context.

THE YWCTU ROLE DEFINITION

The story of YWCTU activity in Ottawa, Toronto, and Brockville represents what the local Ys saw as their function in temperance and social reform. The conception of appropriate endeavours from the YWCTU point of view, however, was a somewhat expanded version of the role set out for them by the WCTU, which produced great quantities of prescriptive literature for its membership, both youth and adult. Canadian temperance youth in the late nineteenth century would have been exposed to the National Leaflets emanating from Chicago, to the more didactic Department Leaflets, to the *Woman's Journal,* and to the reports of the world, dominion, and provincial conventions, in which the organization tried to convince the local unions to invest. Although the message of the appropriate role to be played by single women in all this literature altered over time, it was remarkably consistent in the period before 1905.

The primary role for the young single woman was to be trained so that she could one day take over the tasks of the senior generation as a WCTU member: "These Ys are to be the future Ws, and must be preparing for the work, or it will suffer at their hands."[80] "What hope then for the WCTU army if bands of new recruits have not been trained to fill the gaps and continue the warfare."[81]

If the Y would soon do the work of the WCTU, most would also be burdened with the chief responsibility of the mature married member: running a household. Thus the Ys were often asked to take on the kitchen garden program, which the *Woman's Journal* thought "just the work to attract bright, active young ladies to the YWCTU, and its practical bearing upon the vexed question of the day, 'How to secure competent servants,' must commend it to every one who has the care of a house resting upon his or her shoulders."[82] A later issue of the *Woman's Journal* outlined the importance of the kitchen garden program in emphasizing for working-class girls the central role of the home as "cradle of the nation." Members of the YWCTU were charged with the responsibility of teaching this essential role to working-class girls and, in the process, learning their own future roles as leaders of the WCTU.

In many instances, the Ys accepted this definition of their tutorial role. Most Ys carried out their studies of WCTU work faithfully. They ordered information pamphlets and practised their parliamentary drills, public speaking, and organizational skills. They lent a hand in large WCTU projects. But a group kept perpetually "in waiting" will eventually tire of study and performing menial tasks. Where the Ys did not go beyond training and identify their own special mission, they were doomed to failure. And as we have seen, even where the Y carved out a special role for itself, its survival was fragile.

A second prescribed role for the YWCTU was to further the temperance cause through work with children.[83] "Then will these young women ... be our strongest allies and helpers; and with one hand placed in the hands of our parents for guidance, with the other will grasp the hands of the children, and lead them through brighter, broader and purer pathways, and together, the three generations in one, crush out the great destroyer of the home here and the home eternal."[84] While the kitchen garden programs remained the most popular of the Y ventures during the 1880s and 1890s, this work was supplemented, as has been discussed, by work with children in the Bands of Hope, Sunday schools, sewing and reading groups, and children's gospel meetings. Curiously, however, the Ys seem never to have been invited to direct the Little White Ribboners or the Loyal Temperance Legions.[85] Work with children, as with abandoned women, developed young women's skills and sense of evangelical mission. The Ys not only conformed to the prescriptive literature in this case; they bettered it.

Following the middle-class convention of the era, the WCTU romanticized children and their interests and desire for salvation. Little girls, even from the working class, were typically seen as dainty and delicate.[86] Dominion organizers were not above exploiting children's attractiveness to develop even more sympathy among adults. At the dominion conference in 1916, "while the collection was being taken a little twin boy and girl were made Little White Ribboners, the President pinning the white bow on each."[87] One could only maintain this idealized view of children by not dealing extensively with them. It has been noted that the women of the WCTU often found it difficult to control the children in the Bands of Hope.

The YWCTU seems to have been much more realistic in its assessment and handling of children. Through its extensive work with working-class children, the organization developed some highly effective strategies for teaching a potentially hostile population. Gospel meetings especially for children were offered in the context of the revival meetings that were presented periodically in many Ontario communities during the late 1880s and 1890s.[88] Attracting the children the first time presented little problem. But the task of holding their attention throughout a didactic presentation, as well as encouraging them to return, offered enough difficulties that Y readers of the *Woman's Journal* requested advice. This was provided by the intrepid Bertha Wright of the Ottawa YWCTU, whose suggestions are worthy of much admiration for their advanced pedagogy. Her "classroom management" was far ahead of her teaching contemporaries and fits comfortably with late twentieth-century pedagogical views of faculties of education.

Wright suggests that after the children have been gathered for a gospel meeting, they should be immediately fed: food from the Bible, food from the instructor's experience, and food prepared for their stomachs. In today's terminology, this would be called the "lesson hook" or "motivator." Thereafter, a regular course of exercises should be followed, usually in this order: prayer, recitation of scripture texts, roll-call, the lesson, prayer, testimonials, and prayers by the children. The generally unvarying pattern of classroom activity is today recommended for low-achieving students in order to give them a sense of control and order.[89] The order of the exercises is also one that would be commended in the modern education faculty: move from the personal to the impersonal, from the specific to the general, from teacher direction to student involvement.[90] With such students, concrete illustration of ideas, through "advance organizers," teacher instructional aids, and application exercises, is critical. "Let the lesson be simple and pointed, with practical application for both Christians and the unconverted. We earnestly recommend the use of the blackboard, if only for writing outlines," Wright counsels. Lesson process was not ignored either. She urged that all instructions be definite and clear to the children. She understood what today would be called "reinforcement" or "validation" strategies with difficult students. "Never discourage a child's effort to answer correctly by replying 'no' whatever he may say. Find something good in every answer."

Discipline must have been a major chore, as it is today with students unwillingly held in school. Bertha Wright's suggestions here are relevant and cover most sources of discipline that could be imagined.

Remove any possible occasion for disorder. Be wise in seating the children. Sometimes it works admirably to make certain older children officers, with the leader commander-in-chief. Occupy the ground so thoroughly that there will not be foot-hold for the enemy. But if disorder actually breaks out, try first, by all means, the counter-irritant, or divertive treatment. Write a word or make a symbol on the blackboard. Tell a story. Talk with increased animation;

direct your words toward the offenders; ask them a question. These methods usually accomplish their purpose. If not, try the direct method, earnest remonstrance with the offender personally. But this should always be out of meeting, and usually with each one alone. Detain the offender, and tell him that such disorder is a pain and grief to you, and to God. Ask him never to repeat it, and assure him, kindly but firmly, that it *must* not be repeated!

One would be hard-pressed to provide any better pointers to maintaining discipline in any situation. Her column ended with a worthy motto for any teacher, "Keep on teaching; keep on trying new plans; keep on expecting; keep on praying."[91] If followed, such sound advice would have created outstanding teaching skills and a sense of major achievement in the women who used these strategies to teach difficult children.

Even more important for the direction taken by the YWCTUs in the late nineteenth century, however, was the opportunity provided by the education of children in honing a strong evangelical philosophy to underpin their activities: "scientific knowledge must be introduced on dangers of alcoholism and tobacco to boys and girls in public schools and in Sunday Schools, to produce the 'arrest of thought' in those so introduced to new and powerful ideals." A Christian girl must "let her 'light so shine before men, that others seeing her good works may glorify her Father which is in heaven.'"[92] Both sterling example and the opportunity for sinners individually to reflect on their sinfulness was necessary in carrying out God's plan for young women. Imbued with this evangelical understanding of their place in the universe, the Ys of the 1880s and 1890s were emboldened to fortify themselves by developing new skills, and then to spread the gospel to children.

THE YWCTU-LED BANDS OF HOPE

The major vehicle used by the YWCTU for inculcating in children temperance values within an evangelical context were the Bands of Hope. Although most Ontario Bands of Hope were sponsored by local WCTU/YWCTU unions after 1875, there remained a few under the auspices of local temperance lodges. These tended to be less evangelical in orientation. In 1890, 14,945 children were enrolled in the Ontario Bands of Hope under the auspices of the WCTU.

The bands tended to be large; one hundred children in each was typical, and a large Y union might support several of these. For instance, in 1893 the Hamilton Y ran ten Bands of Hope (as well as three sewing schools, a sewing circle, and a newsboys' club).[93] The children met on Friday evenings or Saturday afternoons during the school year to hear lectures and stories, read the Bible, and sing hymns and temperance songs:

Touch not the foaming, tempting glass,
Nor look upon the wine!
A serpent vile is hid within
The liquid of the vine.

Its ruddy gleam invites you all
To taste the sparkling bowl,
And hides beneath the poison fangs
Which smite into your soul.

Touch not nor taste the seething ill,
Flee from the tempting foe;
Let not its hue profane your lips,
'Twill bring you bitter woe.[94]

About once a year many groups busied themselves with preparing a public entertainment of marching, singing, "acrostic [rhyming] prohibition," or the popular "temperance cantatas." The children were encouraged to give recitations and dialogues to develop their oratorical skills. Periodically the children were expected to adopt the pledge that they would reject intoxicating liquors, tobacco in any form, and bad language, the so-called triple pledge.[95] In at least one instance, the signing of the pledge seems to have come as a surprise. When the Prescott YWCTU advertised a new Band of Hope, a hundred children arrived, but only fifty stayed after they learned that they were expected to sign the temperance pledge.[96]

It is in the activities that differences between Y-sponsored and lodge-sponsored bands are clear.[97] A two-hundred-strong Good Templars' Band of Hope met in Ottawa in 1886. The *Woman's Journal* reported that the children marched around the room to the sound of musical instruments, carrying banners and Good Templars' regalia. Thereafter, the children provided recitations, sang temperance songs, and recited some stirring dialogues.[98] By contrast, Letitia Youmans's Picton band was representative of YWCTU/WCTU groups. "Every recitation, dialogue or song rendered, even by the youngest of the crowd, inculcated some strictly moral or temperate sentiment. Nothing merely comic was ever tolerated, so that the entertainments never degenerated, as is sometimes the case, into mere buffoonery,"[99] she reported. Nevertheless, WCTU-sponsored bands had available to them an array of paraphernalia to maintain loyalty to the cause: bright banners decked their meeting rooms, blue scarves with "Band of Hope" in white were worn around the neck, and badges made with red, white, and blue ribbon were looped into buttonholes. Temperance medals were offered for outstanding achievement. Special songbooks, song cards, alphabetical texts, temperance manuals, juvenile catechisms on alcohol, pledge cards, and lesson quarterlies, all laced with the evangelical subtext, were to be had through the literature depository of the Ontario WCTU.[100] The following poem from the *Canadian WCTU Medal Contest Book* (No. 4) would have been the type to have been recited by Band of Hope children:

One night they had a burglar in
At Brown's across the street,
He stole, oh, such a lot of things –
Their money, clothes and meat.

The milkman said they'd left some door
Or window open wide;
That's how the thief got in the house
And stole the things inside.

So now when father goes to bed
He bolts and bars the door,
And sees that every window catch
Is fastened safe and sure.

Our teacher says that's just the way
To keep out Alcohol;
For when we shut our lips quite tight
He can't get in at all.

So if he comes with stealthy tread –
This thief of bad renown,
To steal our money, brains and health,
And turn things upside down;

We'll take the pledge of abstinence
To bolt and bar the door;
And so for every boy and girl,
A barrier safe secure.

In this account of how evil in the personified form of Alcohol might be shut out of one's lips and life, the child is invited to draw analogies with household security – surely an image with which most children could easily identify. There is no doubt as to who is responsible for the theft of "money, brains and health": the child takes responsibility for his or her own security through an abstemious life. Images such as this recall Albert Carman's address to the newly united Methodist Church in 1884 that revivalism had endowed Methodism with "the lively doctrines of practical, personal, experimental and spiritual religion and grace."[101] The YWCTU/WCTU message to children in their Bands of Hope was a fundamentally evangelical one.

There is evidence that the children worked hard at mastering their songs and recitations, particularly when an entertainment for parents and community was to be staged. The band from Lindsay mounted a full concert: "the most exacting could not fail to be charmed with the spirit and almost faultless precision with which the children sang and recited, reflecting the greatest credit upon themselves and those who trained them."[102] In 1900, forty members of the Maganetawan Band of Hope staged a concert featuring four choruses, two dialogues, one motion song, a recitation by ten boys, four single recitations, and two solos.[103]

Where no YWCTU had been formed, the married women often took on the task. The Newmarket union visited each school to announce the founding of a Band of Hope, and as a result, twenty-five children met at the Temperance Hall "with warm hearts and true" to attend classes on temperance. The women arranged to present each child with a red, white, and blue ribbon as a sign of membership.[104] Later a blackboard and a dozen hymn-books were purchased for the band.[105] The Spencerville WCTU arranged for a lecture to be given to the children about cruelty to animals.[106] Clearly, there was a good deal of variety in the kinds of activities engaged in by the Bands of Hope. This worried a correspondent to the *Woman's Journal* in 1885 who served notice that the provincial organization would be asked to regulate lessons so "teaching may be uniform."[107] No such standardization seems to have occurred.

Under YWCTU and WCTU sponsorship the bands themselves sometimes took on the task of providing help in the community wherever it was possible. The children in the Bands of Hope in Newmarket and London formed "Bands of Mercy," with the girls competing against the boys for the number of kind deeds done and recorded at Band of Hope meetings.[108] At the end of six months, the Newmarket WCTU volunteered to present a suitable banner to the winning side.[109] Nine months later, 325 acts of kindness were reported.[110] The YWCTU-operated Central Toronto Band of Hope purchased plants in order to stage a flower show in the autumn and with the flower mission women, managed to distribute 22,188 pages of temperance literature in one year throughout the community.[111] At other times, the bands were entertained at such festivities as a lawn party given by the Richmond Hill WCTU[112] and a reception featuring cake and oranges by the women of the North Toronto union, even though the bands were run by the YWCTU.[113] Unions sometimes set up sewing and literacy night schools for boys and girls in association with the Band of Hope.[114]

The Bands of Hope figured prominently in the inspiring fiction pieces of the *Woman's Journal*. In one maudlin piece in 1886, a graphic description is painted of a household on the verge of being destroyed by alcoholic parents. An adorable, pure, and righteous Band of Hope child leads the family back to temperate bliss.[115] A second story, purportedly a true account by "an esteemed clergyman," tells of a six-year-old Band of Hope child sent by his mother to fetch his father home from the public house.

> He found his parent drinking with some other men; one of them invited the little fellow to take some beer. Firmly and at once the boy replied: "No, I can't take that; I'm in the Band of Hope." The men looked at one another, but no one was found to repeat the temptation. The man then said: "Well, if you won't take the beer, here's a penny for you to buy some candy." The boy took the penny and said: "I thank you, but I had rather not buy candy, I shall put it into the savings bank." The men looked at one another and for some moments were entirely silent. At length one of them rose and gave utterance to his feelings in these words: "Well, I think the sooner we sign the pledge and put our savings in the bank the better." The men immediately left the house.[116]

A child's pure-hearted and right-minded example could have a remarkable impact on hardened adults, thought the WCTU, even effecting an almost immediate conversion!

Of course, even with supportive literature, not all of the Bands of Hope prospered. Particularly vulnerable were those sponsored by unions with no YWCTU. After a number of false starts, the Richmond Hill WCTU rather desperately resolved that "one or two Ladies of the Union be appointed at each meeting ... whose duty it shall be to attend the Band of Hope and do something to make the Band of Hope interesting."[117] The women appeared none too clear as to specifically what would make the children's meetings interesting. And even in cases where the group flourished, the women sometimes felt overwhelmed by their duties. The North Toronto union suggested that with 170 members, "there is a great need of more ladies to keep the children in order."[118] The Ontario WCTU's sense of inadequacy in effectively leading the Bands of Hope was shared by its American cousins. Nancy Garner's study of the Kansas WCTU demonstrates that the fortunes of one of the band's successors, the Loyal Temperance Legion, were consistently ignored by the women of the Kansas union.[119] Kansas seems to have had no YWCTU.

One major difference between the British and Canadian Band of Hope movements was the class and gender of children involved. The British children were preponderantly male working class. The Canadian Bands of Hope under the jurisdiction of the WCTU welcomed both male and female children, but particularly those of the middle class. They often held executive positions and appear regularly in the records of band activities. It might be speculated that the positive role models of YWCTU or WCTU leaders encouraged little girls to develop their own abilities. In this, they were similar to the American groups. A report of the death of a child in the Newmarket band indicates that the "little boy who prized his badge" was the grandson of the union's president.[120] Girls often dominated membership rolls in Bands of Hope. The Thorold Band of Hope had 140 children in 1886, most of whom were girls.[121]

One of the exceptions to this pattern of female middle-class membership, along with working-boys' clubs in Ottawa, Prescott, and Toronto, was the London Band of Hope, with a membership in 1893 of 74 working boys.[122] The London YWCTU's band superintendent reported that they had "taken up the study of Beer and the body, as some of our boys are employed in the Brewerys [*sic*], we thought it well to instruct them as to its dangers, 'forewarned is forearmed.' Last Thursday evening we held an open meeting to which the parents were invited but no one came. But it was a successful meeting as far as the boys were concerned. There were 100 persons present: 87 boys and 13 officers and teachers."[123] Even the activities chosen by the London Band of Hope reflected the male working-class clientele. At a later meeting, "an exhibition of Dumb Bell swinging was given by Mr Heury Westman and 12 or 15 other young men and was thoroughly appreciated."[124] This model for the Band of Hope, then, was very different from the Ontario norm, and it closely replicates the British example.[125]

Thus the YWCTU developed innovative teaching strategies through its work both with children's gospel meetings and the Bands of Hope. The highly competent and productive Ys may well have intimidated the older women in the WCTU since they took charge of challenging groups such as the Bands of Hope and appear in general to have been far more successful in running the bands than were the WCTU. There is little direct evidence that the Ws forced the Ys to abandon their projects; the one example available is of the Newmarket union, where the Y did fail because of lack of support from the WCTU. Did this constitute a subtle "putting in their place" or a more simple policy of permitting independence for the young women? The available records do not say, but perhaps both were true.

A third component of the role for YWCTU members was to convince their peers, as no older person could do, to reject evil. Female friends must be turned to the righteous path: "You stand between your own sister-girls who had not had your advantages and the wisdom of the mother WCTU from which you may draw. You stand between hosts of uncertain ones and the tempting wine, and the deadly cigarette, the card party, the dance, the theatre – everything that may degrade."[126] Of even greater urgency, however, were those most vulnerable to the siren call, young men, who could only "be reached through the influence and companionship of the young women."[127] The second annual meeting of the Ontario WCTU in 1878 urged unions to establish Ys "whose members shall be pledged to use their influence with the gentlemen of their acquaintance to sign the pledge."[128] This enormous task was underlined repeatedly in fictional pieces that ran in the *Woman's Journal*.

One story depicts Edith, a young, beautiful, and brave woman who has been left crippled and bedridden for life after being grievously injured by a horse that threatened to run down a child in its path. She encounters her brother planning to take wine at a Christmas celebration. After having confided her fears to a Sunday school teacher and receiving sage advice, she resolves to start a YWCTU in her community. "With eager, earnest words she told them of the need there was for every young woman to stand firmly on the right side of every question of moral reform and to show her colours, if not for her own sake, for that of her brothers and friends."[129]

Young men's weakness, and young women's tolerance of it, is lampooned in a National Leaflet story in which Dune, the heroine, announces that she will have nothing to do with any man who smokes. And who is mainly to blame for this noxious habit? "I blame the men, but candidly, girls, I blame you more, for it lies with you to check this evil in large measure, if not entirely. How can you have so little spirit, so little womanliness, as to lay aside your own self-respect to win the favor of these men, to lower your own standards of what is true and sweet in character, for a few paltry attentions from men whom you ought to despise."[130] Such self-blame was not just levelled in fictional pieces. A column in the *Woman's Journal* blamed the YWCTU "or our older sisters ... that such a large percentage of young men were found unfit for service in our last war as a result of the use of tobacco. Let us not try to shirk our responsibility."[131] By "saving" a society's young men, one also wins over "the coming leaders of the future in State and philanthropic work."[132] Young women's superiority carries with it a heavy burden. And not only young men will be protected by a young woman's courage.

Her influence can extend even into her own home: "Many a mother has been brought into the work by a consecrated young life in her own household."[133] It would seem, therefore, that nothing less than the protection of society is in the care of righteous young women. "Will there not be an equally terrible responsibility resting upon us if we are not willing to do everything possible to stay the tide of iniquity, to save our weaker brothers, to save ourselves, to save our homes, to save our nation?"[134] It is important to note the connection made here between self-protection and societal protection. There can be no neutral stance in this war against evil. "If she is not for the movement, she is against it! And if she gathers not with it, she scatters abroad! The pledge of total abstinence is the muster-roll of the army"[135]

Whether or not members of the YWCTU took this challenge seriously or, in the event that they did so, how successful they were in convincing others to take the moral path is not known. One way of assessing the attempt to influence others, peers in particular, is by charting the use of "parlour meetings" or "at homes" where uncommitted women, and sometimes men, were invited to attend. The Ys of the early 1880s rarely held social gatherings of any kind. This is consistent with evangelicalism, where all behaviour must be purposeful and have a greater object than mere personal fulfillment. The women in the Ottawa Y did not find the time to arrange a parlour social until 1891, when one was held to raise money for Y projects.[136] In the Toronto Central Y, the social gathering was introduced through a department of parlour meetings in 1889, and the social outing seems to have been introduced with the Bicycle Club, organized in 1892.

By 1901, however, its literature and scientific temperance departments had been replaced by a department of parlour meetings, a convener, literary committee, current events committee, personal work, a librarian, and auditors![137] As early as 1890, the *Woman's Journal* was abetting this approach by suggesting a "Y Peanut Party," a musical pastime in which guests would be presented with such titles as "Piano Piece Played Per Prominent Person," being a piano solo, and "Paper 'Peanuts' Per Prosaic Penman," which translated as an essay on peanuts.[138] In 1902 the Windsor Y held a social to which fifty members and their guests came, each representing a book. This was followed by a guessing contest lasting over two hours. The evening ended with a vocal and instrumental music show and candy refreshments.[139]

Doubtless, Y unions that devoted themselves to socials succeeded in adding more names to the membership rolls. But these new members were a different sort of woman than had been attracted during the 1880s and 1890s. The minute books of local unions demonstrate that with the higher incidence of socials to attract outsiders, fewer evangelically inspired good works were attempted. It is not clear how often men were included in these festivities, or the nature of the informal conversation in promoting "right thinking," but undoubtedly it would be difficult in such settings to exert sustained and effective peer pressure on male and female friends without becoming a social outcast.

A second way by which the Ys' influence on others, particularly men, might be investigated is to follow a single issue, such as the anti-tobacco campaign, noting the YWCTU efforts in this regard. Until the 1920s, the tobacco habit was associated in WCTU literature almost exclusively with men. Frances Willard had adopted early temperance societies' condemnation of tobacco as a drug and had published a National Leaflet in which she classified nicotine with alcohol as poison.[140] A later leaflet, dating from around 1887, groups tobacco with alcohol and opium as a narcotic which "first excites, then depresses, then deranges" the victim. But the gravest danger was the appetite created in the tobacco addict for other, stronger narcotics. "The tobacco road, though reeking with smoke and the filthiest kind of filth, is the broadest, and by all means the shortest and most direct route to that river of death, Alcohol."[141]

To what extent, then, did the YWCTU take on the battle of the cigarette? Only to a limited degree, it seems. Wherever the Y encouraged boys to sign the pledge, of course, tobacco was one of the banned substances. But rarely did Ys organize separate anti-cigarette leagues. The Toronto Y appears to stand alone in Ontario by having two such leagues for a short time. Very possibly, YWCTU women informally discouraged their male friends and family members from using tobacco, but this cannot be established from the available sources.

At the same time, rural WCTU members in Ontario characteristically fought a pitched battle with the vendors of tobacco to young men. For example, after the Spencerville union had discussed the possibility of petitioning for a curfew bell in its town to reduce the neglect of children, three women were named a committee "to wait on the Storekeepers to have them quit selling tobacco."[142] Again, the Newmarket WCTU reported that "Mrs. Penrose saw the Inspector and asked him if he knew the young boys were using tobacco etc. Of course he does but felt unable to stop it yet. The kind [of pressure] given him by Mrs. Penrose may show him the WCTU means business. it [*sic*] was suggested that other members follow Mrs. Penrose fairly besieging the inspector until he does his duty in order to get peace."[143] There are no indications that the YWCTU besieged storekeepers or inspectors. Thus a social evil that affected many young men and could have been a rallying point for the organization was missed. The inescapable conclusion to be drawn is that women of the YWCTU had relatively little influence on their unaffiliated peers.

In the event that young women were able to forge a righteous alliance with young men, the hope was expressed over and over again by the WCTU that its often-unpopular goals could be made more acceptable to a wider society through the evident support of such cultured young men and women. This can be seen as the fourth component of the YWCTU role, and it was one with the most potential for internal conflict. While priding itself on the fundamental truth promoted by a select women's organization and on the strength of character required of the small band prepared to broadcast this truth, the WCTU fretted that its was "not a popular institution" because it acted "on the principle that prevention is better than cure, and therein lies the root of the trouble ... It is far easier for the mankind of to-day to assist in ameliorating the poverty and degradation growing out of intemperance than it is to countenance and aid any work which aims at the abolishment of intoxicating drink."[144] Although the WCTU recognized the difficulty of the young women's position, the YWCTU members were encouraged nevertheless to have courage and wear the white ribbon, even though they might not be able to preach actively against alcohol.[145]

At times, the description of young women's temperance work took on an embattled tone. A fictional piece written especially for the *Woman's Journal* by Mrs Reede of Teeswater, Ontario, has the heroine, Flora, exclaiming: "Oh, no, it is not a popular society, and all the girls do not belong to the Y. It requires more courage to belong to the Y than it does to go to South Africa and fight the Boers or to go and nurse the boys who are wounded while fighting on behalf of our beloved Empire."[146] This is not the only instance when it is suggested that the rebuffs experienced by temperance workers dispirited them. The hope was that the optimism of sunny young women would reinvigorate all temperance warriors: "Now the greatest obstacle in the way of our young ladies doing just this work is a feeling of prejudice, conscious or unconscious, that enters into our estimate of temperance work and temperance workers; and more than any other reason why we need a YWCTU is to take off the disagreeable edge from an unpopular subject, and to prove that the very best class of young ladies and gentlemen, socially and intellectually, are in this work; to make the principle of total abstinence a fashionable one"[147] The Toronto Ys even wrote a recruiting song for the organization:

The evening hours are fleeting fast,
As down the long church aisles there pass
Bright maidens with their ribbons white,
Who say, "pray join us in our fight –
Oh do be Ys?"

"What makes us Ys?" you'd like to ask –
To tell you that will be no task:
"If you this better part will choose,
To sign the pledge – and pay your dues,
You will be Ys."

"What do we do?" We work for right,
For "God and Home" we wage our fight.
Our unrelenting hate we'd prove
For wrongs that blight the land we love.
Will you be Ys?

Our young men also have their part,
In wisdom's ways they've made a start –
'Tis not the Ys' way to be funny –
We'll just say that what they ask is money;
Now do be wise.

King Solomon, in days of old,
A choice did make, we have been told,
'Twixt gold and wisdom, and his name
Is to us synonym of fame
For being wise.

His choice was good, we all confess,
For "wisdom's ways are pleasantness,"
But in the story we are told
That Solomon received much gold
Through his good choice.

That we are Ys there is no question,
To you, dear friends, we make suggestion:
We're not yet rich. Before you go
We hope your great good-will you'll show –
In our collection.[148]

The Toronto Y's song plainly describes the various approaches taken to increasing support for the YWCTU and thus for the WCTU cause. "Bright maidens" implore their friends to join battle with them against "wrongs that blight the land we love." What is wanted, in addition to new Y members who will sign the pledge and pay their dues, is visible financial support from young men and other "dear friends." There is a good deal of evidence to suggest that women in the YWCTU worked very hard at recruiting new members, particularly from the late 1890s until about 1910. In fact, the Northern Toronto Y was first in Ontario to incorporate young men into its meetings in 1901 to broaden its membership. One result of this extended membership was programming of a very different type than most Ys had developed before, including a model parliament in which countries debated the wisdom of invoking prohibition.[149] A further effect may have been a hastening of the YWCTU's demise, since its female-oriented and controlled mandate was lost. By 1904 the union was left with no departments of work and only a skeletal executive.[150] There can be no doubt either that, as the nineteenth century drew to a close, it was increasingly unpopular to be a member of a young women's temperance association such as the YWCTU. All the bluster of brave songs and membership drives could not dispel the fact that the Y was designed to attract a particular type of serious young woman. By its very nature, it would not appeal to a mass audience in a narcissistic era characterized by a "culture of abundance."[151] This is likely one of the strongest explanations for the organization's demise.

The final element in the prescribed YWCTU role was individual self-improvement. "The fact seems overlooked that any movement for improving the race, to be successful, must primarily be directed toward the betterment of the individual in the first person, singular number ... So our Y union offers to girls the opportunity to become something better and worthier than they at present are. Yet primarily for our union, we seek the girls of strength and principle."[152] Betterment of one's knowledge and parliamentary skills was demanded in much of the literature of the period: "'I haven't the ability,' is a poor excuse; make an effort to *cultivate* ability, and rather be *ashamed* of your lack of it."[153] One authority was quoted admiringly, encouraging girls to gain "true nobility of character through study, effort and self-restraint."[154] Self-improvement meant that strong leaders would be nurtured within the organization. "Select well the leader ... she should be as near perfect as it is possible to be; she should likewise be judicial and have a knowledge of parliamentary practice. Do not select a quiet, meek, humble woman. I do not underestimate those qualities, and they are charming in their place, but such an one is not fitted to be a Napoleon."[155] Nevertheless, Napoleonic qualities must be tempered with a sense of humility and self-restraint. "God Himself gave to woman an invisible armor, imperfectly described by that good, old-fashioned word, *modesty*. Wearing this, she may still do her best, physically, intellectually and spiritually, without harm. ... No matter what you lack in wealth, culture or beauty, you can be self-controlled, dignified, *modest*."[156]

With this modest, but forceful comportment, the young woman must be mindful of her domestic duties so that a healthy balance could be maintained. To remind its readers that self-help involves selfishness, which must be subdued, the *Woman's Journal* offered a profile of Marion, who was so busy improving herself that she neglected her overworked mother. "Those eyes grew dim sewing for the girls, to give them time to study ancient history and modern languages; those wrinkles came because the girls had not time to share the cares and worries of every day life. That sigh comes because the mother feels neglected and lonely, while the girls are working for the women in India; that tired look comes from getting up so early, while the poor, exhausted girls are trying to sleep back the late hours they gave to study or spent at the concert." So Marion dutifully decides to stay away, gives up presenting her "bright essays," loses her ambition to be highly educated, and creates her own Society for the Prevention of Cruelty to Mothers.[157] Self-improvement, then, would be tempered by self-denial.

How successful were the Y women in holding to this portion of the prescription? A careful reading of the nineteenth- as opposed to the twentieth-century records suggests that evangelicalism permitted the YWCTU of the 1880s and 1890s to combine self-help with helping others. All of the strong Y unions assumed that in order to right society's wrongs, one must study the conditions and determine a course of action carefully. Discussion of issues was at the very root of both YWCTU and WCTU meetings. When considering the leaders of the Ottawa and Toronto YWCTUs, one finds women who adhered closely to the model defined in the literature: the most complete surviving profile of any YWCTU leader is that of Ottawa's Bertha Wright.

Relentlessly self-improving while devoted to a myriad of causes, Wright was a model Victorian single woman.[158] She had been born in Aylmer, Quebec, of a prominent family: as has been noted, her great-grandfather, Philemon Wright, had founded Hull. After graduating from the Ottawa Ladies College, she lived for a time with her aunt and uncle, the Curriers, at 24 Sussex Drive. Joseph Currier was a wealthy lumber baron and member of Parliament for Ottawa in the 1870s and 1880s. As part of Ottawa's social and political élite, Bertha Wright worked with determination and zeal in a variety of activities in addition to her YWCTU work, including evangelical reform, temperance work, literacy instruction, maternal care, and education, but always with a suitably modest demeanour. "After hearing Miss Wright," an observer noted, "one does not wonder at her success. One element of that success, we should imagine, is her 'womanliness,' there is nothing of the 'new woman' about this charming speaker."[159] Yet modesty did not keep Wright from undertaking the most challenging of projects. She was the major force behind the Home for Friendless Women and the campaign that resulted in the Hull riots of 1890. In the course of her life, she authored six books, including an evangelical autobiography, a historical novel of Hull's founding by her ancestor and several religious defences.[160] All of her efforts were supported by her own family living in Aylmer, and by her adopted family, the Curriers. In turn, she lavished affection on her kin. "But what will I ever do without you for five long months," writes Bertha to her aunt on holiday in Bermuda in 1883. "I often wish that I could fly to the first flat of the Hamilton Hotel – steal one good kiss from each of you, and fly back again."[161] This warm relationship remained as long as her aunt and uncle lived.

In 1896, at age thirty-three, Bertha Wright left Ottawa to marry Robert Carr-Harris, a professor of engineering at the Royal Military College in Kingston. He was twenty years her senior and a widower with six children. The taking on of a widower's family was not unusual in Victorian Canada. The Carr-Harrises would have another six children of their own. Here was a dutiful, self-denying woman indeed. But she was also an accomplished and serious woman who had exerted her leadership through the YWCTU. Does this aspect of the YWCTU help to explain the organization's decline? One fact strikes the observer immediately: being a Y woman involved a great deal of work, most of which was self-denying and unexciting.

After the Y's heyday had passed, a revealing "Declaration of Principles of the YWCTU" was published. It codified the role that has been outlined and emphasized the importance of evangelicalism as the foundation of all behaviour:

We believe in the coming of His Kingdom whose service is perfect freedom, because His laws, written in our members, as well as in nature and in grace, are perfect, converting the soul. We believe in the gospel of the Golden Rule, and that each man's habits in life should be an example safe and beneficent in every other man to follow. We believe that God created both man and woman in His own image, and, therefore, we believe in one standard of purity for both men and women, and in the equal right of all to hold opinions and to express the same with equal freedom. We believe in a living wage; in an eight-hour day; in the course of conciliation and arbitration; in justice as opposed to greed and gain; in "peace on earth and good will to men." We therefore formulate, and for ourselves adopt the following pledge, asking our sisters and brothers of a common danger and a common hope, to make common cause with us, in working its reasonable and hopeful precepts into the practice of every day life. I hereby solemnly promise, God helping me, to abstain from all distilled, fermented and malt liquors, including Wine, Beer and Cider, and to employ all proper means to discourage the use and traffic in the same. To confirm and enforce the rationale of this pledge, we declare our purpose to educate the young; to form a better public sentiment; to reform, so far as possible, by religious, ethical and scientific means, the drinking classes; to seek the transforming power of divine grace for ourselves and all for whom we work, that they and we may willfully transcend no law of pure and wholesome living; and finally we pledge ourselves to labor and to pray that all these principles, founded upon the Gospel of Christ, may be worked out into the customs of society and the laws of the land.[162]

Originally limited to a role encompassing only public relations, self-training, and work with children, the YWCTU obviously had expanded its range far beyond those limits. By 1905 the Ys were on record as supporting equal suffrage for men and women, social purity, a shorter work day, higher wages, and enlightened resolution of labour disputes. That their ideas and actions were "founded upon the Gospel of Christ" and the belief in "the coming of His Kingdom" gave these women the needed justification to "seek the transforming power of divine grace for ourselves and all for whom we work." Thus not only would illegitimate decisions relating to alcohol *per se* or the training of children draw their righteous fire, but also any threat that challenged their wider role to uphold the "law of pure and wholesome living." However, the order of their stated concerns is most revealing. The abstinence pledge is placed last, almost as an afterthought, following an extended statement outlining their broad social program. And the objects of this program are vividly defined as "the drinking classes." This was indeed a far-flung net, and

Christian labour in defence of all the social injustices encompassed by it would require service in many just causes.

THE YWCTU VERSUS THE WCTU

If one were to compare the role mandated for the YWCTU and its large expansion of that role, at times so energetically as to eclipse the senior WCTU, the danger posed by this organization in the nineteenth century to the WCTU can be sensed. While freely admitting the many advantages of organizing a young woman's sector, the WCTU was anxious almost from the beginning about having such a separate body. In 1886 the provincial president attempted to soothe the older women's concerns in her address to the annual convention: "Do not think that a Y in any place of considerable size will interfere with the work of the senior Union. The records all point the other way. Young ladies naturally feel more at home with a president and officers of their own, arranging and planning for their own work. Then their influence will be greater and more widespread when banded together as societies than as individuals, and they can reach and influence for good those whom the older ones among us cannot touch."[163] "I know there is a feeling of opposition in some quarters from a fear of a division of interest in the work of the WCTU,"[164] admitted another speaker in 1886. And the opposition did not evaporate with the years. In 1892 a debate ensued in the *Woman's Journal* over whether or not the Y should remain separate from the WCTU. One writer ("an old president") declared herself very much in favour of a continuing special sector for the young women, since "there was always too much work for too few in the days before the Ys."[165] In 1897 the provincial YWCTU superintendent suggested "that local presidents of the WCTU lay aside all personal objections to Y work and be willing to allow and assist the Superintendent to organize in her territory."[166]

Yet the fact that the issue was considered so often over the years suggests that many WCTU members never reconciled themselves to a YWCTU. That at least some of the criticism levelled at the Ys was rooted in unkind comparisons is suggested by one writer in the *Woman's Journal*: "I would be ashamed of any member of our Union, who would look upon this success [of the YWCTU] with any feeling of jealousy, or consider them rivals in any way ... Jealousies and rivalries are the death of many good societies and poison at the fountain head, the very waters of healing which we are trying to carry to the suffering."[167] Did the Ys threaten the WCTU women with their passion and competence? The situation may well have varied from region to region in Ontario, but it seems clear that at least some of the older women were ungrateful and perhaps afraid of their young and single associates.

Yet in those unions where the YWCTU prospered, and particularly in the early years, relations seem to have been very good between the two sectors. In 1884, for example, members of the Ottawa YWCTU presented a basket of flowers to Mrs Tilton, "as a token of their appreciation of the President of the Union and the kindness she had shown to them during the year."[168] The Ys regularly invited the married women to their lectures, reading groups, and Bible meetings.[169] The London union considered the Y work so important that it established a management committee comprised of the presidents of the YWCTU and the WCTU, with a past-president as advisory member.[170] Perhaps distance from the YWCTU increased the WCTU's fear? Nevertheless, there were many more unions without a Y than those with one, and the hostility towards the Ys with which so many of the records bristle makes one amazed that they survived as long as they did.

The definition of Y membership was another issue to create acrimony with the mother union. In theory, beyond the early years when the YWCTU was a department of work, the Ys were considered to be full unions on a par with the Ws. However, in practice, Ys often operated more like a department within the mother union. While most Ys from their inception had sought single women under the age of thirty, some married women had also held membership in the Ontario YWCTU from the early 1880s. Similarly, age restrictions were relaxed so that some mature single women with firm friendships in their Y unions could maintain their membership.[171] In some cases, such as in Ottawa, the WCTU voted to make the YWCTU fully fledged members of its union, creating a kind of double membership.[172] Frequently also, the executive Y members were married women. An 1890 issue of the *Woman's Journal* asked again, "Should married women remain Y members?" and concluded that no answer was yet available.[173] In 1896 a WCTU benefactor, Mr J. Hale Ramsay, offered a commemorative banner to the province showing the greatest increase of members in Y unions. However, he restricted it to the unions that had no married women. The Ontario delegation to the dominion convention in that year petitioned the assembly to send an official communication to Mr Ramsay imploring him to remove the restriction.

In 1912 the fees required from Ys were lowered to encourage a membership drive. However, this precipitated a furious argument in the convention, ending with an agreement that married women in Y unions would pay the same dues as married women in W unions: "If married women are eligible to membership in the Ys at a lower fee than that prevailing in the Ws, this would be liable to do serious injury to the Ws – diverting from their ranks many who, while not active members, desire to wear the white ribbon and be counted amongst the feminine contingent of the Temperance Workers."[174] At the same time, where no Y unions existed, single women were welcomed into W unions. Occasionally, Y unions in the general proximity corresponded with young women in the WCTU, encouraging them to establish a separate Y union.[175] The confusion in membership standards, and the obvious anxiety reflected by the WCTU, suggests that even as the YWCTU declined in strength and purpose, the WCTU continued to fear its presence.

CLASS IDENTIFICATION

But surely the issue of YWCTU membership was not related only to age and marital status. The question of class identification must also be assessed. In the 1880s there seems to have been some support within the YWCTU to expand its membership into the respectable working classes. The establishment of the Willard Home in Toronto and a similar residence in London for working girls undoubtedly had the potential to incorporate these women into the framework of the Y. A hopeful statement was also issued by the London YWCTU in 1886: "Do not let us be content with looking forward to the reunion of our own family circles, much as we love them, but let us think of the many who have no homes and nothing to brighten their lives ... Some young women with just as refined tastes, and social natures as their more fortunate sisters are living in boarding houses."[176] But the challenge was ignored and the YWCTU remained determinedly middle class.

The Canadian Y's position on membership was questioned by the Glasgow YWCTU in 1911. The latter welcomed working-class women and had a stronger organization than its Canadian counterpart. "We just go for everyone," said the Scottish Y organizer.[177] By this date in Canada, however, the Y position on the young working-class woman had hardened to revulsion. One report of a British Factory Girls' Drinking Club portrayed the women as participating in "wanton orgies" with their hard-earned salaries. It concluded, "Drunkenness saps a woman's moral fibre more quickly than it does a man's, yet these misguided factory girls are the potential mothers of a future generation."[178]

If they were not prepared to be identified with even the respectable working classes, the Ys could not hope to be considered part of the "smart" upper middle classes either. In a lament on the WCTU's class position, a correspondent to the *Woman's Journal* begs the YWCTU not to separate from the main organization since it is so badly needed. Though the WCTU expected to achieve prohibition in five or ten years, it is still beyond the organization's grasp, she says in 1892. "So we learned more than we accomplished ... we learned that not many rich or influential women will join, that we cannot expect to be popular or numerous ... most of us keeping no servants."[179] The Ys must have assumed the same class profile as the Ws; by rejecting the possibility of expanding their organization into the working classes, they may have further assured their demise.

One of the major tasks of the Ys was to lead the Bands of Hope. Tables 1, 2, and 3 in the appendix demonstrate that as the Ys lost membership, so did the Bands of Hope. Or perhaps the causality ran in the other direction: as the Bands of Hope declined, so did the YWCTU. It is difficult now to know which group was the prime agent, but clearly their fates were intertwined. Picton County reported in 1902 that while a Band of Hope had operated for years there, it became discouraged and disbanded when it could find no one who could command the attention of a large group of children. It reported also that in its later years of operation, only younger children attended, and of these, mainly girls. So the "very boys, who need the help the most, will not attend," the women lamented.[180] By the 1890s in the United States, the Bands of Hope faced competition from the United Boys' Brigade, a quasi-militaristic, uniformed, and church-sponsored marching and drilling organization.[181] While this group did not affect the Canadian bands, it is possible that the newly formed Boy Scouts might have provided a similar outdoor/militaristic rival.

In Ontario the apex for Band of Hope unions was reached in the early 1890s, with the movement remaining healthy until the turn of the century. The gradual sapping of strength can be detected by the mid 1890s, however, by comparing numbers of children enrolled in the unions (see table 1 in the appendix). The reported figures indicate that while unions proliferated, they included smaller groups of children. The Ontario experience was duplicated at the dominion level (see tables 4 and 5 in the appendix). With occasional periods of recovery, as between 1910 and 1914, when temperance forces of all kinds revived across Canada, the bands became progressively weaker after the mid 1890s. The membership figures tell a more accurate story than the numbers of unions, which also appear to have decreased.

By 1910 the Bands of Hope in Ontario had been absorbed into the Loyal Temperance Legions, an organization established by the

National WCTU in 1890 as an exclusive WCTU temperance group catering to boys and girls over the age of seven.[182] Information about the LTL in Ontario is limited, but it is safe to assume that the organization was modelled on the American LTL. The latter had borrowed the idea of temperance banners, music, and marching from a popular American youth temperance band called the Cold Water Army; its constitution, rituals, and weekly meeting plan were lifted from various juvenile temperance orders; and from the Band of Hope, it had taken its "platoon system" for maintaining order. To this heritage was added juvenile officer positions to encourage leadership amongst the children, public entertainments, and encouragement to affiliate with other youth groups.[183]

A minute book of the LTL in Salford, Ontario, from 1902 has survived. Generalizations based on a single minute book must be made cautiously, of course, but if the Salford LTL was representative of other Canadian operations, several tentative conclusions might be drawn. The meetings have an even more didactic tone than that cultivated by the Bands of Hope. The children met in the schoolhouse and were examined weekly on memorization of passages and elocution. The minute book contains twenty-seven examination marks for the twenty-eight active and seventeen associate members. The children presented public readings, recitations, dialogues, and musical choruses. They recited prayers, their motto, and their pledge:

God Helping Me,
I promise not to buy drink, sell or give
Alcoholic liquors while I live
From all tobacco I'll abstain
And never take God's name in vain.

As prizes, the children received blue ribbons.[184] Therefore the LTL appears to have been much like the Band of Hope in Ontario. However, the main difference between it and the Bands of Hope was that the new organization had no connection with the YWCTU. Was this an instance of the WCTU further delimiting the Y mandate?

A final factor in explaining the YWCTU decline involves the ideas held by the organization in the twentieth century. The YWCTU experienced an apparent lessening of the sense of evangelical mission that had been so obvious in the earlier period. Here again the records do not pinpoint the exact date when the vision began to slip. As the Y unions' activities by 1910 suggested a religious social club lost in self-absorption, the erosion was probably well under way by that time. By 1931 the official ideas of the YWCTU were contained in the *Manual of the Young People's Branch*. The prospective member is told that, although she can expect to study "Christian Citizenship" and "Social Welfare," there also awaits her a veritable "University of Reforms," "delightful entertainment," and a "community of pleasure and interest." Y organizers were directed in the manual to run meetings with lots of Y songs and to provide some temperance information: "bright, pithy news items from latest Press reports ... All meetings should bristle with brightness and song and good cheer."[185] The evangelical nightmare of self-indulgence to the exclusion of societal needs seems to have become reality for the Ys sometime prior to the First World War. Before long, all YWCTUS were absorbed into the omnibus Young People's Branch, with young men welcomed into full membership.

In summary, the YWCTU disappeared for a number of reasons: as a "farm team" for the WCTU, it lacked authority in the wider organization and eventually suffered from too prescriptive a mandate. As long as it could combine its evangelicalism and work with children, it prospered, particularly where the Y women extended the range of children under instruction. But as the Band of Hope, kitchen gardens, and gospel bands waned in popularity internationally, the targets for instruction disappeared. YWCTU women needed to find another cause, but because of the marginalization of temperance organizations of all types, their own ambiguous position within the women's temperance organization, and their weakening evangelical vision, they failed to do so. The result was a gradual slide into a new role as rather pathetic cheer-leaders for an increasingly unpopular cause. Their decline into social gadflies seems to have been mourned by none of the WCTU members. They too were forgetting the evangelical mission.

CHAPTER SEVEN

Epilogue – 1916–30: "For Though It Be Frayed and Dingy and Worn on a Shabby Dress ..."

Between the passage of the Ontario Temperance Act in 1916 and the end of the province's experiment with prohibition in 1927, the path taken by the Ontario WCTU was "uncertain and obscure," as the women of the Fairmount union observed.[1] During the decade best remembered in Canadian history for its optimism and promise, for the Jazz Age and the triumph of Hollywood,[2] all manner of societal taboos were compromised, including traditional views of female modesty, limited consumerism, restrained public entertainment, and restricted social drinking. Yet it is interesting that during the 1920s, membership in the WCTU did not decline; in fact, it enjoyed modest increases through to the end of the decade. Even the WCTU was surprised at how minimally its membership rolls seem to have been affected by the new mores. The explanation for the maintenance of membership numbers is likely the ongoing sense of crisis of the period, shared alike by members of the WCTU and those who feared that the province was sliding inexorably into hedonism, secularism, and moral decline. It should be stressed too that these records were gathered at the provincial and dominion levels through yearly tallies provided by the local unions. This is an important point, because in the 1920s quite a different picture of the membership emerges from the provincial and dominion records on the one hand and local records on the other. While the official provincial and dominion figures would lead one to believe that the WCTU remained a powerful force with a strong following, local records show that this strength was more apparent than real. Moreover, there is no sense in the records beyond 1922 that the WCTU saw itself as winning the battle before it at all easily. Inflated membership figures were perhaps one of the last gasps of a dying organization.

Provincially, there was some increase in membership after the First

World War and again during the Second. In 1917 the Ontario WCTU annual report recorded a total provincial membership of 6,974,[3] while the reported total for 1927 was almost double at 12,518.[4] Realizing that this still represented a slow membership growth and fearing the worst, the provincial convention recommended that wherever possible, the WCTU should work cooperatively with other women's organizations, "in order that greater unity and acquaintanceship may be fostered."[5] Canadian membership totals for these years suggest generally the same pattern: in 1917 there were 12,885 registered WCTU women,[6] including YWCTU members, while ten years later, the total had increased to 21,743.[7] However, in contrast to the optimistic pattern revealed by these bare figures, the speeches and reports of the provincial and dominion conferences, rally songs and poetry, and the ever-illuminating local union minutes betray a sense of dread that the organization was losing ground in public esteem and authority. The last supremely confident statement to be issued by the Dominion WCTU on the state of its membership totals and the quality of the forces arrayed against it appears in 1922. In that year, the president summoned almost-convincing bravado in her assessment of the WCTU position:

While accounting for the past, we face the future undismayed, because while the past two years record a saturnalia of lawless excess on the part of the outlawed remnant of the liquor traffic everywhere in our fair land, yet we are two years nearer victory, final and complete. Much of the effrontery has disappeared from the traffic, and it has deteriorated to a skulking, defiant, outlaw without any claim to legitimacy, or lawful protection ... The rest, while aristocracy of the traffic[,] are today at best only outlaws, bootleggers and illicit operators, whose ranks are getting thinner with each change of the moon ... The last and only real hope of the traffic left it to trade upon is the apathy of the non-resistant citizen, the jellyfish type, slippery as an eel and spineless as an oyster.[8]

Still, it is clear that the WCTU knew, even in 1922, that it was often considered by others to be a "spent force." The Dominion WCTU reciter for medal contests painfully shows that the organization was not blind to increasingly sceptical assessments of its power in the community. One of the selections is entitled "Comrades! Carry On!":

Who claims that the work of our White Ribbon host
Is a thing of the past – a spent force?
A possible need of a former regime,
But a need which has finished it's [*sic*] course.

Do the deeds of the Crusaders – noble and true –
Count for naught? Does their memory fade?
Are their prayers, faith and tears but a dream? can it be
'Twas a valueless thing which they paid?
Nay! Nay! while the dark-pinioned demons of vice
Overshadows and curses its prey,
While the Drink-Foe – insidious, wary and bold
As a thief lies in wait by the way;
While a sorrowing mother-heart bleeds in our land,
O'er the victims of arrogant pride,
While a child may be led by sweet counsel to walk
In the steps of the Heavenly Guide;
May the White Ribbon host tread its mission of cheer,
In the spirit the Master shall own,
Yea, with zeal born of sacrifice, hope born of faith,
And a love born of Heaven alone,
Yea; the years speak the message in clarion-tones,
For the sake of the toilers [*sic*] agony,
For the sake of humanity's need of the hour,
Carry on! Carry on! Carry on![9]

The phrases that must have alarmed at least some of the WCTU sisterhood asked them to find zeal "born of sacrifice" for the sake of the toilers, that is *their* "agony." In their hearts, WCTU members knew that the chapter on their proudest achievements was closing; perhaps like the crusaders to whom they were compared, they realized that their best, most noble deeds now belonged to history.

But it was at the local level that the plight of the WCTU was much more visible and the assessment of WCTU support much more bleak. Many Ontario unions collapsed during the 1920s, and of those which hung on, most stumbled through the decade with an aging and dispirited membership.[10] The Newmarket WCTU, long one of Ontario's most active unions, was forced to sell its temperance hall in late 1923, and two years later was still worriedly discussing "how to interest the people in our WCTU."[11] The Mimico union considered disbanding when the membership sank to five members in 1922, but it limped along until 1926, when the few remaining women gave up. Bravely, they resuscitated the union in 1927 in order to establish a Band of Hope, and this plan seems to have given the Mimico women enough focus to run a minimal children's education program until the end of the 1920s.[12] The Peterborough WCTU marked the death of two more of its members at its September meeting in 1921 and decided that its resources were too slim to pay the $2.00 affiliation fee to the Local Council of Women.[13] Months passed between meetings, until in 1924 the union finally began the redefinition of its role in emphasizing childhood education. Poster and medal contests were held, scientific temperance urged in the public schools, and pledge cards distributed to the Sunday schools. But these were all old issues, fought most strenuously and to good effect in the 1890s and first decade of the new century. By the 1920s, they must have seemed frayed, even to the conscientious women of the Peterborough WCTU.

Despite this revival, the Peterborough union was heavily dependent on other women's organizations. By 1922 it worked closely with the Local Council of Women, several women's missionary societies, the Salvation Army, various young peoples' church organizations, and local ministers.[14] Yet the clearest evidence that the Peterborough WCTU's hour had passed and that if had lost most of its moral command in the town exists in an offhand comment in the union's minute book concerning the "Women's Prohibition Committee." One would have thought that the presence of the Peterborough WCTU would have made a Women's Prohibition Committee superfluous. Apparently not. In November 1926 the recording secretary noted: "The [local WCTU] president urged all to attend the public meeting on Friday night in the Grand Opera to hear Mrs Gordon Wright [of the Canadian WCTU]. Mrs C.H. Edwards who is chairman of the Women's Prohibition Committee invited the WCTU Executive members to sit on the platform."[15] If the Peterborough union had taken any hand in helping to stage the public meeting, it obviously would not have been pleased to be invited to its own event. Here was one of the Canadian WCTU luminaries addressing an assembly that ignored the local union. But just in case there were any hard feelings, the local union executive was offered platform seats. It would be difficult to imagine a better example of the patronizing of a marginalized group![16] Lest it should be thought that this marginalization was limited to the Peterborough union, the 1929 convention of the Canadian WCTU expressed appreciation for "the action taken by the General Board of the Women's Missionary Society of the United Church of Canada in appointing a Temperance Secretary and providing for the appointment of secretaries in Conference Branches, Presbyteries and local Auxiliaries. We commend this model to other denominations."[17] If this model had been adopted, of course, there would have been no further need for the local WCTUs to exist.

At the county level, too, much of the discussion centred on sagging membership. The Oxford County WCTU resolved at its 1923 meeting to have a crusade or rally meeting in each union in the coming year, "preferably in September for the purpose of enthusing, and building up our membership."[18] Six years later, the same group resolved to "double our county membership by new unions and out-post workers."[19] The observer is left wondering at the contrast between the apparently healthy membership figures at the provincial and dominion levels and the evident distress at sagging hopes reflected in the dominion and provincial speeches, in the poetry, and, even more graphically, in the minute books of the local unions. It seems very possible that many women kept up their membership through registering each year, but failed to take an active part in union activities. Hence the more accurate reflection of WCTU status at all levels is the general decline contained in the local minute books.

While the women of the Ontario WCTU had taken little time from their program of social activism to bother commenting on the passage of the Ontario Temperance Act in 1916, in the following decade they devoted much worried discussion and action to the obvious erosion of public support for prohibition. For a few years, the temperance forces had been well satisfied with the evidence that their main ideas concerning alcohol were enshrined in legislation. The temporary wartime prohibition law had been replaced in 1919 with a permanent one. That same year, an amendment to the Dominion Temperance Act permitted provincial referenda on the question of importing liquor into provinces. Accordingly, Ontario held such a referendum in 1921 and voted to ban the importation of liquor and spirits.[20] But the consensus for temperance was beginning to fracture in the community and amongst pressure groups, with internal battles fought between forces favouring government controls and those, like the WCTU, which demanded a continuation and extension of prohibition. One group against which the WCTU focused a verbal assault in 1923 was the Moderation League of Ontario. It favoured a system of government control rather than prohibition.[21] In its defence of the Ontario Temperance Act, the WCTU noted that

> in 1914 ... there were 14,247 cases of drunkenness [in Toronto]; in 1921, under Prohibition, there were only 4,727; in 1914 "disorderly conduct": 2,734 cases; in 1921 "disorderly conduct": 1,084 cases; in 1914 "vagrancy": 18,996 cases; in 1921 "vagrancy": 6,864 cases. Not even the Moderation League will pretend that the reduction of 64 per cent in the number of cases of drunkenness, disorderliness and vagrancy, as against an 1 per cent increase in the population, is not directly related to the operation of the Ontario Temperance Act.[22]

It is notable that here the Ontario WCTU chooses to justify the prohibition legislation as any socially concerned secular liberal would: by recourse to factual statistics, rather than to God's will. Prohibition, as opposed to government-licensed sale, was put to another referendum in October 1924, with the prohibition forces winning by a narrow majority.[23] To the WCTU's immense relief, its position continued to be endorsed by popular will, but the margin was narrowing dangerously. Early in 1925, unions were amazed and angered to hear that Premier Howard Ferguson intended to amend the OTA by permitting the sale of 4.4% beer.[24] "Unlike the western provinces," gasped the Toronto District Union, "we did not lose [the referendum], but gained 36,682 ... What caused Premier Ferguson to change his mind so quickly? What would the Moderationists have done if they had secured 36,682 majority?"[25] The Ontario WCTU maintained a stream of literature opposing the new policies. A 1926 brochure, for example, fumes, "For two dollars of the hard-earned money of the toiler he can buy a 'permit' to purchase and take to his home a supply of liquors to steal his manhood, and sodden and degrade his best instincts and befoul his fireside in the presence of, and to the detriment of his wife and children."[26]

The Mimico union reported that its 23 February 1926 meeting opened "by the singing of 'Tell Me the Old, Old Story' and a Bible reading from Joshua 24:13–27 by Mrs Dowdall. She spoke particularly of the peoples' decision [to revoke prohibition]. 'As for us we will serve the Lord.' In order to serve the Lord well, there must be salvation, separation, singleness of aim and the Joy of Service."[27] In spite of the WCTU's best efforts, government sale of alcohol began in June 1927. Of the repeal of prohibition that year, the Ontario annual report observed stoically:

> There has been on the pages of the years successes and reverses, but through sunshine and shadow ever a growing power of public opinion and an enlarging field of endeavor. Political propaganda has for the time being brought a reversal, for the enemy has sowed tares. His tactics never change. He does his work when men sleep. He stands for vested interests and knows no politics except personal protection.[28]

Increasingly, the anti-alcohol message was presented by groups other than the WCTU, and typically, no mention was made by these partisans of the important WCTU legacy and position. An example of this is a pamphlet produced by the literature department of the Women's Missionary Society of the United Church of Canada in the early 1930s. The pamphlet offers conventional criticism of the liquor traffic, using arguments that the WCTU had honed for more than fifty years. But in suggestions of ways that members of the WMS could fight the liquor menace, no mention is made of joining the WCTU or of making common cause with WCTU women. Obviously, its star had set.[29]

The erosion of prohibition support caused a profound upheaval in the Ontario WCTU. This study has traced the process whereby women of the Ontario organization made an early and conscious choice to diversify their mandate beyond temperance *per se* into a broad program of social reform, evangelism, and childhood education. While they threw their support behind the battle for prohibition, they were never key players in that male-dominated movement. With prohibition's failure, WCTU women began to question whether they had taken the best course. Some blamed themselves for having directed only sporadic interest to the many prohibition battles and for having diverted their attention into other endeavours, and they expressed doubt about the wisdom of their early decision to expand their program far beyond the temperance issue. At the 1924 convention, a speaker used the metaphor of gardening as a preamble to one of the convention's major resolutions:

> There are amateur gardeners who diligently and joyfully tend their flower beds when the seedlings first appear. Then they lose interest. Soon the little plants are choked out by a rank growth of useless and noxious weeds. We deride much foolishness – but how much better have we done? Whenever the labors of years were about to come to fruitage through some Provincial campaign, we and the other temperance organizations, and the churches, have flung ourselves headlong into the contest. When the day was over, we let the law we had secured run itself, while we dropped back into charitable and philanthropic work. The folly of such a course was never more self-evident than in this, our sixth great prohibition battle, when we face a foe that has money without stint, and that has not ceased labor since 1921. Therefore Resolved, That we cut down to a minimum such work as can be done by other societies and that was never intended to be for us, other than a side line to the great Prohibition question – for the settlement of which we came into being. Let us hark to that magnificent vision, "A Dry Canada," and do our utmost to bring it to pass.[30]

The resolution passed, but succeeding annual reports reveal that the Ontario WCTU did not abandon its social program in favour of the political. Nor should the speaker's message be taken at face value. She castigates the assembly for having "let the law we had secured run itself," for having dropped "back into charitable and philanthropic work." The records would dispute that the Ontario WCTU was ever content to let anything run itself, much less the Ontario Temperance Act. Again, the WCTU program always amounted to much more than simple charity or philanthropy, as has been shown. This statement does reveal two important points, however: first, that the Ontario WCTU knowingly expanded its authority beyond temperance issues early in its history, and secondly, that the organization was deeply shaken by 1927, when prohibition's collapse called into question its most fundamental ideals, leadership, and operating principles. But the speaker was not correct in her assessment that the WCTU had made a wrong choice, for there had been and always would be poor neighbour women to tide over, men to remind of their responsibilities, broken spirits to help mend, and children to organize into extracurricular temperance, purity, and other anti-abuse programs. And although many of the problems addressed by the nineteenth-century evangelical social program had been resolved or taken up by the new professional social workers and an increasingly interventionist state, individual women of the Ontario WCTU continued well past the 1920s to devote themselves to spiritual and social change. Nevertheless, the organization was fast losing confidence that it had made the right decisions in the past or that it could effectively wage the battle for temperance or social change in the future.

Throughout the 1920s the provincial organization maintained active socially and spiritually directed departments in Canadianization, citizenship, prison reform, and police; in evangelistic endeavours, including missionary work, systematic giving, and travellers' aid; in childhood education, such as the Little White Ribboners, Loyal Temperance Legions, temperance in Sunday schools, medal contests, scientific temperance, the essay bureau, prize essay and poster contests, moral education, and slides; and in adult education encompassing mothers' meetings, parlour meetings, and the *Tidings* department. Even when disillusioned by the vagaries in the political sphere, the Ontario WCTU kept steadily to the path of social and moral regeneration. By 1927 the president of the Toronto District union termed the year "a time of crisis," characterized by "a letdown of moral forces," but also one in which much progress in social matters was discernible. The president ended her ringing address by rationalizing WCTU goals this way: "Our cause is the cause of home and purity and virtue and Heaven. We shall fight on until it prevails ... The cross will conquer!"[31]

This study of the Ontario WCTU has argued that after 1905 there was a clear difference between provincial executive and local WCTU motivations and actions. By that date, the provincial executive (and many women in large urban unions) had moved away from the conservative evangelical vision towards a more liberal interpretation. Only rarely did these women offer evangelical principles as explanations for their programs. In contrast, the minute books of most local unions demonstrate that these groups held to an evangelical analysis well into the 1920s. As the WCTU felt itself increasingly marginalized after the First World War, the old evangelical notions were gradually replaced by a negative, backward-turned, and even repressive variant of Protestant fundamentalism. This was a natural and short progression for women in local unions, but there is considerable evidence that both the provincial and Canadian conventions also adopted portions of fundamentalism during the 1920s. No longer in the vanguard, the WCTU found the new fundamentalism comforting and supportive of fragments at least of their conservative evangelicalism. One historian of the era has observed that "the mood of Protestant evangelicals changed in response to the tensions of industrialization and immigration from one of cocky optimism to chastened uncertainty."[32]

Betty DeBerg's analysis of the roots of American fundamentalism in the 1920s is especially suggestive to explain this last, sad decade of the Ontario WCTU.[33] She finds that in addition to operating as an intellectual and theological backlash to modernism and to troubling social change created by industrialism, urbanization, immigration, the new consumer economy, and open hedonism of postwar America, fundamentalism was also caused by deep and enduring changes in gender roles.[34] Many of these had been the product of nineteenth-century evangelical women's campaigns, such as those of the WCTU. Changing gender prescriptions so threatened the fragile fundamentalist identity, DeBerg argues, that in pronouncements relating to women's appropriate activities, first-wave fundamentalists called for a reversion to women's role based on the Victorian "cult of true womanhood." This had demanded that women devote themselves to the glorification of motherhood within the "divinized" home, to dutiful domestic labour, and to uncomplaining self-sacrifice. Fundamentalists feared the effects of community work, suffrage, higher education, social-reform activism, and paid employment on women and the family. They were alarmed by the increasing divorce rate and sought to tighten divorce laws and ostracize from the Christian community those who had divorced.

Beyond women's sphere of activity, fundamentalists of the 1920s were troubled by the corruption of societal morals. The debased theatre and motion pictures, immoral literature in the form of novels and popular fiction, dancing, immodest dress ("flapperism"), and birth control were all held up by fundamentalists as evidence of declining morality. Within this construct, then, the importance of the family as the site for "domestic religion"[35] took on special qualities, producing the notion of a reconstituted "divinized home."[36] "So complete was the translation of the domestic into the sacred that the home replaced the church in fundamentalist literature as the primary location of religious meaning and as the cornerstone of Christian civilization."[37] Just as the reconstituted family had been one of the primary concerns of nineteenth-century evangelicals, the divinized home became the focus for twentieth-century fundamentalists, although with important differences. Fundamentalists averred that, as the home's moral exemplar, the mother occupied as central a role in the 1920s as she had in the Victorian era, generating a powerful prop in sustaining Victorian gender ideology well into the twentieth century.

A great many of the issues worrying fundamentalists during the 1920s resonate from the Canadian, Ontario, and local records of the WCTU. Clearly, the fundamentalist critique attracted many in the Ontario WCTU, particularly those at the local union level who continued to hold to a conservative evangelical vision of society. The difference between conservative evangelicalism and twentieth-century fundamentalism, however, was monumental where the position of women was concerned. Evangelicalism's heritage had been a liberating one for women: it had provided a rationale for powerful, agential action in the defence of society's victims; it had developed skills essential in the successful carrying out of this mission; and it had proven to these conservative women and their many admirers that moral authority had a legitimate place in the political and social process. Not surprisingly, this outlook resulted in women generally (and WCTU women in particular) viewing themselves and their potential very positively as intelligent and active participants in their communities. The new fundamentalism prescribed quite a different role for women. Essentially backward-looking, it sought to reconfine women to the domestic sphere, to convince them of their inferiority and of their frailty. By the 1920s many Ontario WCTU women had also assumed this pessimistic view of their own abilities and proper range of activities, for they blamed themselves for prohibition's failure and thus saw their collective confidence as able, energetic women deeply shaken.

An analysis of the Ontario WCTU poetry, temperance literature, convention discussions, resolutions, and minute books of the post-1917 decade demonstrates the passage traced by DeBerg. While many women in the WCTU held to the principles of conservative evangelicalism as long as possible, others gradually accepted the tenets of premillennialist fundamentalism. Mainstream nineteenth-century Protestant evangelicalism had been postmillenialist, that is, characterized by a belief that its era was one of consistent advancement toward the Kingdom of God and the return of Christ. However, the more pessimistic premillenialist view held that the present age, far from being one of progress, was distinguished by debauchery and violence, apostasy and cruelty, which the true Christian was forced to endure while waiting for the second coming of Christ. Ultimately, the Kingdom of Heaven would be held by those who kept the faith in a faithless age. "Truly," one fundamentalist leader mourned, "society is evoluting backwards."[38]

To contrast their momentary temporal defeats with the eternal truths represented by the organization's increasingly fundamentalist orientation, the Toronto District women recited this poem:

I seek it, the white, white ribbon,
In parlor and street and cars,
I watch for its flashing message
As those who watch for the stars.
For though it be frayed and dingy
And worn on a shabby dress,
It lends to its faithful wearer
A charm you can never guess.
So wear it with pride, dear women,
Morning and noon and night,
Glad to show, wherever you go,
You're standing for God and right.[39]

The symbolism of the "frayed and dingy" ribbon worn on a "shabby dress" illustrates also that the Toronto WCTU, one of the most progressive and powerful unions in Ontario, felt exhausted by the long, and apparently futile, war against evil in its many forms.

The WCTU had always held to the signal importance of the family as the source of spiritual renewal, but in the nineteenth century, the WCTU woman's moral guidance in the domestic realm was the touchstone for an active life outside the home. By the 1920s the organization had absorbed the new imagery associated with the family by emphasizing the sanctity of "home," rather than family, as a justification for a more limited identity; indeed, for some writers, the home represented a garrison within which they – but not necessarily their families – could hide. In a "clip sheet"[40] produced as a resource by the Canadian WCTU for local unions, the program leader was instructed to read aloud this statement of the home's significance: " A home is an opportunity for service given to a woman by the same Master who rested in the home of Mary and Martha and blessed it.

We are personally responsible for the stewardship of our homes, and for the contribution they make to the increase of the Kingdom of Heaven on earth."[41] It is worth noting that woman's role is here delimited to the "stewardship of our homes," not anyone else's home and certainly not outside homes in the wider society. In a curiously passive phrasing, the contribution "to the increase of the Kingdom of Heaven on earth" is to be made not by a person, but by "our homes." Woman, as keeper of the home and identified almost exclusively by it, is reflected also in an anonymous Canadian WCTU pamphlet produced during the 1920s entitled *The Woman's Christian Temperance Union, Why You Should Join*. The chief reason for becoming a member was "because the WCTU gives every woman in Canada a chance to help in the work of making our country 'a land of happy homes.'" Another pamphlet dating from this period expresses the same message: "I wish that every boy and girl could realize the heart anguish of parents over 'missing girls' or 'missing boys' who leave the old home fireside to have a 'good time' in the gay city. HOME IS THE GOD-GIVEN SHELTER FROM THE TEMPTATIONS AND SINS THAT WRECK AND RUIN LIVES."[42]

The powerful image of a home defiled is woven into many of the WCTU arguments of the era. A temperance tract dating from 1919 tallies the destructive results of alcohol use: "It wrecks homes, blights lives, separates husband and wife, sends the drunken son forth a wanderer and a reproach upon the earth."[43] The destruction of the sanctified home is given pride of place at the beginning of the list, and when the author essays the impact on the family son, it is the son's "wandering" from home which captures the writer's attention, so that his rootlessness is seen to be "a reproach upon the earth" as it would be a reproach on the mother who was somehow unable or unwilling to save her home from this curse.

In all of these statements, then, woman's passivity is almost total: her societal mission has been superseded by the structure of which she is the steward, her home. Somehow, the keeper of the "home" has replaced the keeper of the "family," with all of its human possibilities. This compliant creature, the WCTU member of the 1920s, would not have been recognizable to Bertha Wright and her "brave little band," fearlessly, if incautiously, inciting riots in Hull in 1890.

In retrospect, what was the Ontario WCTU contribution to society? There were many collective achievements to celebrate: a compulsory course on scientific temperance in Ontario's public schools, important for itself and a precedent for more recent "values" curricula that address drug abuse, drunk driving, and safe sex; hundreds of thousands of children reached through Bands of Hope and Loyal

Temperance Legions, as well as Sunday schools with similar messages not only against intemperance, but also in support of healthy, compassionate, spiritual living and communities; mothers directly educated and supported in their capacity as defenders of the family and home; men convinced to act more responsibly and less violently to their wives and families; scores of social programs implemented, from boys' and girls' night schools to homes for abandoned and "fallen" women and to care for the aged; significant social legislation passed, and not just the prohibition acts; validation over five decades for evangelical women to take on public roles and to exercise moral and community authority; and the creation of a structure where women in small communities and large could reach out to one another in true Christian charity and friendship, welding bonds that lasted a lifetime for many of these women.

The WCTU effectively passed from the scene in the 1920s, and these and many other accomplishments soon faded into the mists of the forgotten past. Replacing this important historical record was the stereotypical view of the WCTU as a group of aging women rather irrelevantly railing against mainstream society and its mores. This inaccurate and demeaning interpretation trivializes the historical significance of the Ontario WCTU and the many causes it fought. Whether by coincidence or intention, for example, the WCTU white ribbon campaign has in the 1990s been appropriated by *men* as a public symbol condemning male violence against women – an ironic, but not unwelcome, gesture to those who remember the original meaning of the white ribbon.

The most accurate record of this remarkable women's culture is found in the local minute books, such as this final excerpt:

> The WCTU met at the home of Mrs Wm Marritt in April [1921]. The President opened the meeting by singing "Onward Christian Soldiers." After which the President led in prayer. Mrs Connell read the scripture lesson 16th Chapter of Ruth & gave a little talk on it. Showing the influence of one good woman. I wonder how far each of us realize how far our influence goes ... After which we had a discussion about the lesson.[44]

The history of the Ontario Woman's Christian Temperance Union is ultimately the story of many principled and energetic women pushing the limits of the "influence of one good woman."

APPENDIX
Membership and Union Totals

Table 1
Ontario Membership Totals

Date	YWCTU *Members*	WCTU *Members*	*Band of Hope/*LTL *Members*
1890	638	4,733	14,945
1891		4,318	10,613
1892	321	3,287	9,040
1893	600	4,614	6,840
1894	498	4,992	10,028
1895	351	4,311	6,005
1896		5,110	6,285
1897	474		
1898	671	5,597	4,978
1899	585	5,469	3,847
1900	414	5,521	4,140
1901	333	5,505	4,737
1902	568	5,235	
1909	264	6,022	4,500
1910	413	7,103	8,000
1911		7,128	5,969
1912	588	7,700	4,948
1913		8,179	3,443
1914	1,046	9,500	3,712
1917		6,974	2,883

Source: AO, Minutes and Annual Reports of the Ontario WCTU Conventions.
Note: Certain years of the Ontario records do not provide membership totals.

Table 2
Ontario Union Totals

Date	YWCTU *Unions*	WCTU *Unions*	*Band of Hope/*LTL *Unions*
1886	12	150	6
1887	25	137	18
1888	35	188	14
1889	33	193	14
1890	25	219	13
1891	19	175	80
1892	19	179	109
1893	16	229	89
1894	12	202	88
1895	11	205	84
1896	12	220	95
1897	20	228	43
1898	25	244	89
1899	26	223	74
1900	26	222	69
1901	20	224	83
1902	23	192	59
1903	23	217	
1904		216	
1905	11	187	
1906	18	201	
1907	9	178	
1908	7	181	
1909	13	209	62
1910	21	230	91
1911	21	215	80
1912	25	240	64
1913	25	479	60
1914	40	548	67
1915	40	234	67
1916	49	230	58
1917	41	205	59
1918	32	237	14

Source: AO, Minutes and Annual Reports of the Ontario WCTU Conventions.
Note: Certain years of the Ontario records do not provide membership totals.

Table 3
Selected Examples of Ontario WCTU, YWCTU, and Band of Hope Membership

Year	*Location*	WCTU *Members*	YWCTU *Members*	*Band of Hope Members*
1886	Toronto	100	42	4 (250)
	Ottawa	66	119	2
	Hamilton	100	130	1 (100)
	Brockville	24	25	1 (50)
	Brantford	80	45	1
	Picton	50		1 (300)
1888	Toronto	502	121	10 (1,164)
	Ottawa	105	67	2(221)
	Hamilton	275	164	10 (1,955)
	Brockville	145	42	2 (100+)
	Brantford	100	40	2 (202)
	Picton	33		2 (220)
1890	Toronto	225	60	7
	Ottawa		50	1
	Hamilton	222	83	10 (2,000)
	Brockville	50	32	1 (100)
	Brantford	40	23	1 (95)
	Picton	8	34	1 (100)
1892	Toronto	281	39	5 (474)
	Ottawa	50		1 (89)
	Hamilton	149	107	8 (1,819)
	Brockville		22	1 (80)
	Brantford	46		1 (78)
	Picton	11	17	1 (100)
1894	Toronto	339	41	4 (378)
	Ottawa	100	200	1
	Hamilton	200	180	11 (3,600)
	Brockville			
	Brantford	40		1 (70)
	Picton	18	15	1

Source: AO, Minutes and Annual Reports of the Ontario WCTU Conventions.
Note: Certain years of the Ontario records do not provide membership totals.

Table 4
Dominion Membership Totals

Date	YWCTU *Members*	WCTU *Members*	*Band of Hope/*LTL *Members*
1890		9,040	19,184
1891		9,343	19,557
1892		6,982	15,107
1893	1,265	9,310	10,869
1894		9,676	10,028
1895		8,449	9,959
1896		9,959	9,839
1897			
1898		10,886	8,531
1899	896	10,628	6,757
1900	860	10,319	6,795
1901	1,051	9,849	7,448
1902	1,469	9,488	2,684
1909	758	11,428	7,667
1910	947	14,283	10,702
1911			9,688
1912	1,152	15,948	8,586
1913			8,802
1914	1,596	16,838	11,535
1917		13,825	7,731

Source: AO, Minutes and Annual Reports of the Dominion WCTU Conventions.
Note: Certain years of the Ontario records do not provide membership totals.

Table 5
Dominion Union Totals

Date	YWCTU *Unions*	WCTU *Unions*	*Band of Hope/*LTL *Unions*
1890	46	368	192
1891	38	335	206
1892	40	363	202
1893	35	442	117
1894	35	422	185
1895		404	189
1896		450	185
1897			
1898		505	189
1899	52	483	153
1900	47	446	150
1901	45	435	150
1902	41	404	114
1909	29	421	148
1910	49	538	164
1911			181
1912	57	539	177
1913			179
1914	56	939	222
1917		578	160

Source: AO, Minutes and Annual Reports of the Dominion WCTU Conventions.
Note: Certain years of the Ontario records do not provide membership totals.

Notes

ABBREVIATIONS

AO Archives of Ontario (WCTU Collection)
NAC National Archives of Canada
UWO University of Western Ontario Archives (Regional Collection)

CHAPTER ONE

1 *Ottawa Daily Citizen*, 5 February 1890.
2 Ibid., 8 February 1890.
3 Ibid.
4 *Evening Journal*, 10 February 1890.
5 Ibid.
6 *Le Spectateur*, 7 February 1890.
7 Ibid., 11 February 1890.
8 *Daily Citizen*, 13 February 1890.
9 *Evening Journal*, 12 February 1890.
10 Ibid.
11 *Daily Citizen*, 13 February 1890.
12 Ibid.
13 *Le Spectateur*, 14 February 1890. In no time *Le Spectateur* found itself fighting a media war with a number of English papers. For example, on 18 February it attempted to answer charges recently made in the *Daily Citizen*, the *Evening Journal*, the *Free Press*, the *Aylmer Times*, and the *Weekly Dispatch*. Although the editor argued convincingly on several points, the challenge of inadequate police support was not answered.
14 *Daily Citizen*, 12 February 1890.
15 *Evening Journal*, 13 February 1890.
16 Ibid., 25 February 1890.

17 Although the Ontario WCTU was interdenominational, the majority of members appear to have been adherents of the Methodist Church, judging from the references in local records and religious affiliation given in annual reports.
18 McKillop, *Matters of Mind*, 96.
19 Ibid., 99–100.
20 For example, see Mitchinson, "Aspects of Reform," and Sheehan, "Temperance, the WCTU and Education in Alberta, 1905–1930," 1980.
21 The minute books of the local Ontario unions indicate some of the occupations of members' husbands. On the basis of this admittedly scattered evidence, it appears that most members of the Ontario WCTU could safely be identified as middle class. Lynne Marks's detailed examination of three Ontario small towns, Ingersoll, Campbellford, and Thorold, supports this view (Marks, "Ladies, Loafers, Knights and 'Lasses,'" 210–222). Typical occupations in urban and small-town unions included merchants, clergy, doctors, journalists, and contractors. In rural districts, most WCTU members were farmers' wives. There is some evidence, for example, in Ottawa during the 1890s that the WCTU had less cachet than newer, non-evangelical groups, such as the National Council of Women. See, for instance, AO, Minute Book of the Ottawa WCTU, and Mitchinson, "The Woman's Christian Temperance Union," 153. Similarly, one can discern a pattern in several small towns where the WCTU successfully siphoned off female members from working-class-oriented temperance lodges. As an instance of this, the Newbury village report to the district council of the Royal Templars of Temperance noted that there were "too many other meetings in the village, a WCTU had been started there and some of the Sisters had joined it" (UWO, Minute Book of the West Middlesex District Council, Royal Templars of Temperance, n.d.). For a discussion of the class position of the Royal Templars of Temperance and other Ontario temperance lodges, see S. A. Cook, "'Continued and Persevering Combat.'"
22 This process seems to have had a close parallel with the experiences of small-town and rural American women involved during the nineteenth century with women's foreign missionary societies, especially as the interests of women at the local level became increasingly in conflict with those of the societies' leadership in the regional and national headquarters. See Hill, *The World Their Household*.
23 See Bebbington, *Evangelicalism in Modern Britain*, Marsden, *Fundamentalism and American Culture*, Westfall, *Two Worlds*, and McKillop, *Matters of Mind*.
24 Westfall, *Two Worlds*, 12.
25 DeBerg, *Ungodly Women*, 9–10.
26 Grant, *A Profusion of Spires*, 103–5.

27 Marshall, *Secularizing the Faith*, 30.

28 See Westfall, *Two Worlds*, and Grant, *A Profusion of Spires*.

29 It is important to distinguish evangelicalism, whatever the denominational context, from evangelism. The latter, derived from the Greek word for "gospel" (euanggelion), generally refers to the enthusiastic spreading of the "good news." However, it ignores the system of thought being transmitted to others. Thus, while most evangelicals were also evangelists of their faith, by no means were all evangelists evangelicals. See Hardesty, Women Called to Witness, 9–10, on this issue.

30 See, for example, Sweet, "The Evangelical Tradition in America"; Moberg, *The Great Reversal*; McKillop, *A Disciplined Intelligence*; and Airhart, *Serving the Present Age*. This view as applied to Canada is disputed by Gauvreau in his closely argued and insightful *The Evangelical Century*. He contends that English-Canadian evangelicalism lacked a tradition of philosophical or speculative theology, making it less vulnerable to the divisive effects of scientific evolutionary thought. Evangelicalism was further protected by the very nature of its theology, which "was not so much a fixed philosophical system of doctrine as a much looser, and consequently more pervasive, body of beliefs and assumptions concerning God, the individual, and society" (7–8). Rather than fearing the challenge posed by Darwinism or inflexible theology, Canadian evangelicals, Gauvreau suggests, worried about the implications of higher criticism, historical scholarship, and the insights of the social sciences. He grants that evangelical theology proved unable to cope successfully with these difficulties after the turn of the century and most particularly after the First World War, when the authority of evangelicalism, historical theology, and Baconian induction were abandoned by the theological colleges. Gauvreau's persuasive thesis centres on the thought and teachings of the clergymen-professors of the Canadian Methodist and Presbyterian church colleges. He assumes that the religiosity of Methodist and Presbyterian adherents in rural districts, towns, and cities across English-speaking Canada was developed on the same model as their ministers' and that there was no real distinction between liberal and conservative factions. He argues that the clergymen-professors of both denominations, through their dual roles as ministers and teachers, set the standard for Canadian evangelical beliefs. The records of the women of the WCTU do not show this to be true. While some urban women may well have been influenced by the intellectual debates of the clergymen-professors, introducing unease about such matters as historical theology, the same level of inquiry does not seem to have affected the women of small-town Ontario. Of course, very few of Gauvreau's subjects were women. Women's evangelicalism was built more on a nineteenth-century understanding – grounded in the

processes of the awakening, sin, and salvation, and supported by evangelical family life – than was that of their sisters at the provincial and national levels.

31 Hardesty, *Women Called to Witness*.
32 DeBerg, *Ungodly Women*, esp. chap. 1.
33 Sizer, *Gospel Hymns and Social Religion*, 87.
34 Hardesty, *Women Called to Witness*, 9.
35 Cott, *The Bonds of Womanhood*.
36 Boylan, *Sunday School*.
37 Sizer, *Gospel Hymns and Social Religion*, esp. 86–7.
38 Sklar, *Catharine Beecher*.
39 First identified by Barbara Welter, the term has been widely applied to the idealization of the Victorian middle-class woman. The qualities of the quintessential "true woman" were purity, heightened spirituality, innocence – especially in sexual matters – submissiveness, gentleness, and self-effacement.
40 Welter, "The Feminization of American Religion." Also see her "She Hath Done What She Could."
41 Blauvelt, "Women and Revivalism," 2.
42 Brouwer, "Transcending the 'Unacknowledged quarantine,'" 47.
43 Brouwer, *New Women for God*, 4.
44 Gagan, *A Sensitive Independence*.
45 Airhart, *Serving the Present Age*, 26.
46 See, for example, Rawlyk, *Ravished by the Spirit*, *Wrapped Up in God*, and *Champions of the Truth*.
47 Pedersen, "The Young Woman's Christian Association in Canada."
48 Van Die, *An Evangelical Mind*. She presented a stimulating paper entitled "A Woman's Awakening: Evangelical Belief and Female Spirituality in Mid Nineteenth Century Canada" at the Canadian Historical Association meeting, Queen's University, 1991.
49 McKenna, "'The Union between Faith and Good Works.'"
50 Valverde, *The Age of Light, Soap, and Water*.
51 Grant, *A Profusion of Spires*.
52 Westfall, *Two Worlds*.
53 In an early article on the Dominion WCTU, Wendy Mitchinson raises the issue of its social conservatism, but only hints at the organization's religious conservatism. See Mitchinson, "The Woman's Christian Temperance Union," esp. 145.
54 Houghton, *The Victorian Frame of Mind*, 229.
55 Ibid., 343.
56 Bradley, *The Call to Seriousness*, 22. For a comparable statement on American evangelicalism, see Winthrop Hudson, who described evangelicalism as less a "theological system" than a spirit or temperament that captures

both strands of Calvinism as part of an international movement of experiential religion (Hudson, *Religion in America.*) Similarly, Bruce Shelley describes evangelicalism as a "mood" (Shelley, *Evangelicalism in America*).

57 McKillop, *Matters of Mind*, 96.

58 For example, see Bordin, *Women and Temperance.*

59 Sizer, *Gospel Hymns and Social Religion*, 88. See also Pedersen, "The Young Woman's Christian Association in Canada."

60 AO, Minute Book of the Grey and Dufferin County Council WCTU, 21 June 1928.

CHAPTER TWO

1 Youmans, *Campaign Echoes*, 51–52.

2 Ibid., 42.

3 Ibid., 89–90.

4 A common Canadian example of this genre is Rev. James C. Seymour's *The Temperance Battle-Field*. Seymour's compendium provides several short anecdotes on a given theme of intemperance in each "chapter." Although he directs the work to "the young of all ages," most of the anecdotes apply to young men. A comparable British example is Rev. T. de Witt Talmage's *The Abominations of Modern Society* (even though Talmage was American.) Like Seymour, Talmage provides a series of stirring tales, most of which are based on his lectures, to underscore many evils of late-nineteenth-century society, including intemperance.

5 Grant, *A Profusion of Spires*, esp. chap. 4. See also Marsden, *Fundamentalism and American Culture.*

6 Youmans, *Campaign Echoes*, 53.

7 Sizer, *Gospel Hymns and Social Religion*, 89.

8 Tyrrell, *Woman's World, Woman's Empire*, p. 18–19.

9 The first meeting of the Dominion WCTU was held in Ottawa in 1885, when the constitution was adopted (AO, 8396, notes on history of the Ontario WCTU by Miss Duff, Toronto).

10 McKee, *Jubilee History*, 22.

11 Ibid.

12 S.A. Cook, "Letitia Youmans."

13 Mitchinson, "Aspects of Reform," 177.

14 Ibid., 176–77.

15 See, for example, AO, Convention of the Dominion WCTU, 1916.

16 Tyrrell, *Woman's World, Woman's Empire*, 47.

17 Ibid., 2.

18 See, for example, AO, Conventions of the World's WCTU, and Tyrrell, *Woman's World, Woman's Empire*, chap. 9, esp. 200–12.

19 Cherrington, *Standard Encyclopedia of the Alcohol Problem*, 2021.

20 Peck, *A Short History of the Liquor Traffic*, 5.
21 Decarie, "The Prohibition Movement in Ontario," 5.
22 Spence, *Prohibition in Canada*, 38–40, and Campbell, *Demon Rum or Easy Money*, chap. 1.
23 Clemens, "Taste Not; Touch Not; Handle Not." See also Airhart, "Sobriety, Sentimentality and Science."
24 Tyrrell, *Sobering Up*, 54–55.
25 Spence, *Prohibition in Canada*, 39.
26 Decarie, "The Prohibition Movement in Ontario," 4.
27 Bailey, *Leisure and Class in Victorian England*, chap. 1.
28 The Sons of Temperance were first located in Canada in 1848, and their literature suggests that they were the first temperance "order" to enter Canada (Sons of Temperance of North America, Centennial Sept. 29th, 1942). Tyrrell notes that the Sons of Temperance arrived in 1847 (Tyrrell, *Woman's World, Woman's Empire*, 17).
29 Tyrrell, *Woman's World, Woman's Empire*, 17.
30 Blocker, *American Temperance Movements*, 48.
31 Decarie, "The Prohibition Movement in Ontario," 161.
32 AO, Minute Book of Orono Division Sons of Temperance, 3 April 1878.
33 Ibid., 9 March 1881.
34 Ibid., 24 May 1854, UWO, Minute Book of the West Middlesex District Council, Royal Templars of Temperance, 4 February 1897.
35 Ibid., 29 April 1897.
36 Blocker, *American Temperance Movements*, 48.
37 AO, Minute Book of the Orono Division Sons of Temperance, 15 March 1876.
38 Minute Book of the Orono Division Sons of Temperance, 8 November 1853.
39 Ibid.
40 Ibid., 2 December 1874.
41 Ibid., 15 March 1876.
42 Grant, *A Profusion of Spires*, 59.
43 AO, Minute Book of the Orono Division Sons of Temperance, 3 April 1878.
44 Ibid., 24 May 1854.
45 See, for example, ibid.
46 Ibid., 15 March 1876.
47 Ibid., 3 April 1878.
48 Ibid.
49 Ibid., 18 September 1878.
50 Ibid., 29 October 1879.
51 Blocker, *American Temperance Movements*, 48.
52 AO, Minute Book of the Newmarket WCTU, 3 November 1896.

53 Interestingly, in his study of male voluntary societies in Halifax during the 1840s, David Sutherland finds little evidence of ritual, but much of such "rational recreations" as speaking competitions, lectures and debates, outings, and philanthropic and Christian enterprise (D. Sutherland, "Fraternalism and the Process of Middle Class Formation").
54 For the importance of ritual in fraternal or vocational organizations, see Kealey and Palmer, *Dreaming of What Might Be*, and for its female counterpart, Parr, *The Gender of Breadwinners*.
55 UWO, Minute Book of the West Middlesex District Council, Royal Templars of Temperance, 4 February 1897.
56 UWO, Membership Book of the Wardsville Council No. 419, Royal Templars of Temperance, 1898.
57 Blocker, *American Temperance Movements*, 48.
58 Houston and Smyth, *The Sash Canada Wore*.
59 Marks, "Ladies, Loafers, Knights and 'Lasses,'" 207–14.
60 Blocker, *American Temperance Movements*, 50.
61 The American Sons of Temperance created a category for women called "lady visitors" through a constitutional change in 1854. In 1867 women were admitted to full membership but without much encouragement to take leadership. By the 1870s, a few women occupied high positions in the main organization (Sons of Temperance of North America, Centennial Sept. 29th, 1942, 43–5).
62 See Epstein, *The Politics of Domesticity*, 93ff.
63 UWO, Membership Book of the Wardsville Council no. 419, Royal Templars of Temperance, 1899.
64 For example, see UWO, Minute Book of the West Middlesex District Council, Royal Templars of Temperance, 4 February 1897.
65 Marks, "Ladies, Loafers, Knights and 'Lasses,'" 211. In Thorold, Marks finds that most of the men in lodge executive positions were older and married; in contrast: only 15 per cent of the men as opposed to 90 per cent of the women officers were single.
66 Tyrrell, *Woman's World, Woman's Empire*, 18–19.
67 See UWO, Minute Book of the West Middlesex District Council, Royal Templars of Temperance, 29 April 1897.
68 Ibid., 27 January 1898.
69 Marks, "Ladies, Loafers, Knights and 'Lasses,'" 210–21.
70 This characteristic style of women's conversation and comportment has been analysed at length by Belenky, Clinchy, Goldberger, and Tarule in *Women's Ways of Knowing*. See especially their discussion of "connected knowing," 112–23.
71 A representative statement was made by the Fairmount WCTU on the occasion of recording secretary Miss Mary J. MacLennan's retirement from her post with the Glengarry, Stormont, and Dundas WCTU: "dur-

ing your years as our recording secretary your sterling worth has become more and more apparent; your abounding enthusiasm and untiring energy has made itself felt in our society. It has not only been a pleasure to us to associate with you at these our joint meetings where you were very faithful in attendance, but also your ready help in all difficulties, the ideal to which you lived up and the example which you set before us, have been an inspiration and an incentive to go forth, when the path seemed somewhat uncertain and obscure" (AO, Letter transcribed in minute book of the Fairmount WCTU, 1924.

72 UWO, Minute Book of the West Middlesex District Council, Royal Templars of Temperance, 4 February 1897.

73 Blocker, *American Temperance Movements*, 48.

74 UWO, Minute Book of the West Middlesex District Council, Royal Templars of Temperance, 26 October 1899.

75 See, for example, annual reports of the Ontario WCTU for 1897 and 1907: "There are several ways of killing a cause, but none so easy as indifference and duty carelessly performed."

76 UWO, Minute Book of the West Middlesex District Council, Royal Templars of Temperance, 6 March 1897.

77 Ibid., 29 April 1897.

78 Ibid., 6 March 1897.

79 AO, Minute Book of the Orono Division, Sons of Temperance, 18 September 1878.

80 See also the women's auxiliaries of such groups as the Washington Society and the American Sons of Temperance (Epstein, *The Politics of Domesticity*, 91ff.).

81 See Hardesty, *Women Called to Witness*; Hewitt, "The Perimeters of Women's Power in American Religion"; Reynolds, "The Feminization Controversy"; Ryan, "A Women's Awakening"; Sweet, "The Evangelical Tradition in America"; and Welter, "The Feminization of American Religion."

82 Epstein, *The Politics of Domesticity*, 100.

83 Blocker, *"Give to Thy Winds Thy Fears,"* 222.

84 Epstein, *The Politics of Domesticity*, 114.

85 Bordin, *Woman and Temperance*, 32.

86 Willard, *Glimpses of Fifty Years*, 336.

87 Warsh, "'John Barleycorn Must Die,'" 5.

88 Blocker, *"Give to The Winds Thy Fears,"* 227.

89 Rorabaugh, *The Alcoholic Republic*, 8.

90 Ibid.

91 By 1894 consumption had dropped to .742 gallons a year (Decarie, "The Prohibition Movement in Ontario," 35).

92 Blocker, *American Temperance Movements*, 65.

93 Rorabaugh, *The Alcoholic Republic*, 189.
94 Epstein, *The Politics of Domesticity*, 107. See also Warsh, "'John Barleycorn Must Die,'" 6.
95 Boylan, "Evangelical Womanhood," 74–5.
96 Blocker, *"Give to The Winds Thy Fears,"* 232.
97 Strachey, *Frances Willard*, 210–11.
98 Hardesty, *Women Called to Witness*, 14.
99 Ibid., 18.
100 Epstein, *The Politics of Domesticity*, 136.
101 Ibid., 119–20.
102 Hardesty, *Women Called to Witness*, 21.
103 Blocker Jr., Retreat from Reform, 29.
104 Epstein, *The Politics of Domesticity*, 116.
105 Hardesty, *Women Called to Witness*, 154. See also Randi Warne, who argues that Willard (and Nellie McClung) carried out a maternal feminist critique of the structural inequities perpetuated by an "androcentric, competitive economic system." "Frances Willard's dictum, to 'make the whole world home-like,' takes on a completely different meaning when understood as a demand that the public sphere become accountable to women and women's lives, as defined by women themselves" (Warne, *Literature as Pulpit*, 150–1).
106 See Rorabaugh, *The Alcoholic Republic*, 189–96, Bordin, *Frances Willard*, 11; and Blocker, *American Temperance Movements*, 64.
107 See, for example, Conrad, Laidlaw, and Smyth, *No Place Like Home*.
108 Bordin, *Frances Willard*, 10.
109 Tyrrell, *Woman's World, Woman's Empire*, 45.
110 Earhart, *Frances Willard*, 79–80.
111 Bordin, *Frances Willard*, 37.
112 Willard, *Glimpses of Fifty Years*, 638–45.
113 AO, Minute Book of the Ottawa WCTU, 1881.
114 AO, Minutes of the Dominion WCTU, 1890.
115 See, for example, ibid., 1891.
116 McKee, *Jubilee History*, 28.
117 UWO, London District WCTU Records, 28 February, 1893.
118 McKee, *Jubilee History*, 86.
119 Youmans, *Campaign Echoes*, 96.
120 Ibid., 100–1.
121 Jennie Fowler Wiling was a college professor, writer, suffragist, and co-founder of the Women's Foreign Missionary Society of the Methodist Episcopal Church.
122 Youmans, *Campaign Echoes*, 101.
123 Bailey, *Leisure and Class in Victorian England*, 6. See also Bailey, "A Mingled Mass of Perfectly Legitimate Pleasures," 7–28, and

Cunningham, *Leisure in the Industrial Revolution.*
124 Laqueur, *Religion and Respectability*, 189.
125 Simon, *Studies in the History of Education.*
126 Laqueur, *Religion and Respectability*, 37. See also Laqueur, "Working-Class Demand."
127 Lynn and Wright, *The Big Little School*. For a much more incisive analysis of the importance of evangelicalism in socializing children and in moulding the American Sunday school, see Boylan, "Sunday Schools and Changing Evangelical Views."
128 Grant, *A Profusion of Spires*, 107, and Boylan, *Sunday School.*
129 Grant, *A Profusion of Spires*, 105.
130 Ibid., 107.
131 Houston and Prentice, *Schooling and Scholars*, 40.
132 Greer, "The Sunday Schools of Upper Canada," 170–3.
133 Gidney and Millar, *Inventing Secondary Education*, 50, 78.
134 Houston and Prentice, *Schooling and Scholars*, 306.
135 Welter, "The Feminization of American Religion," 139.
136 Headen, "The Origins of Canadian Methodist Involvement in the Social Gospel Movement, 1890–1914," 110.
137 Lynn and Wright, *The Big Little School*, 67.
138 Boylan, "Sunday Schools and Changing Evangelical Views," 326.
139 Ibid., 331.
140 Sizer, *Gospel Hymns and Social Religion*, 5.
141 Lynn and Wright, *The Big Little School*, 64.
142 Shiman, "The Band of Hope Movement," 50.
143 Ibid.
144 Ibid., 63.
145 Ibid.
146 Youmans, *Campaign Echoes*, 90.
147 Ruth Bordin says otherwise – that no work was undertaken with youth (Bordin, *Women and Temperance*, 101).
148 Sons of Temperance of North America, *Centennial Sept. 29, 1942*, 45–7.
149 Garner, "Molding and Making the Next Generation of Men," 3.
150 Ibid.
151 Ibid.
152 Shiman, "The Band of Hope Movement," 50.
153 AO, Minute Book of the Ottawa WCTU, 19 October 1881. In fact, when faced with the choice between work with mothers or with children, local unions typically chose the children. For example, in November 1895 the women of the Newmarket union were considering a new project: "Mrs. C.E. Cern then asked permission of the President to explain what the Mothers Meetings are like [*sic*] after full explanations were given the union was asked about taking up the work but it was

decided to try the B of Hope first, not liking to get too many irons in the fire at one time" (AO, Minute Book of the Newmarket WCTU, 5 November 1895).

154 Youmans, *Campaign Echoes*, 92.

155 AO, Minute Book of the Ottawa WCTU, 2 April 1883.

156 Ibid., 7 May 1883.

157 AO, Minute Book of the Dunnville WCTU, 27 November 1888.

158 AO, Minute Book of the Newmarket WCTU, 15 September 1896.

159 AO, Treasurer's Book of the Richmond Hill WCTU, 2 August 1887; AO, Minute Book of the Ottawa WCTU, 7 April 1884.

160 S.A. Cook, "Educating for Temperance."

CHAPTER THREE

1 Decarie, "The Prohibition Movement in Ontario," 41.

2 AO, Treasurer's Book of the Richmond Hill Treasurer's Book of the WCTU, 14 May 1884.

3 Even at the provincial level, the licensing system was criticized regularly at the annual conventions. For example, this resolution was passed at the 1894 Ontario convention: "That we ask immediate relief from some of the more burdensome features of the present license [*sic*] system, such as the misnumbering of offences – long the source of flagrant abuse; the lack of legal provision for relief in cases where licensed bars exist in sections where public sentiment does not sustain them; and the continuance in office of men out of sympathy with the laws they were appointed to enforce" (AO, Annual Meeting of the Ontario WCTU, 1894).

4 The Scott Act was silent on the issue of the manufacture of liquor, "perhaps in deference to the interests of capital and labour involved" (Decarie, "The Prohibition Movement in Ontario," 42).

5 Ibid., 44.

6 AO, Annual Report of the Ontario WCTU, 1887.

7 Decarie, "The Prohibition Movement in Ontario," 86.

8 Ibid., 83.

9 McKee, *Jubilee History*, 42.

10 Ibid.

11 Ibid., 44.

12 Ibid., 49.

13 UWO, London District WCTU Records, 9 October 1900.

14 AO, Minute Book of the Dunnville WCTU, 17 October and 21 November 1900.

15 Decarie, "The Prohibition Movement in Ontario," 272.

16 Schull, *Ontario Since 1867*, 220.

17 See Decarie, "The Prohibition Movement in Ontario," chap. 7, and McKee, *Jubilee History*, 104–5.
18 Mitchinson, "The Woman's Christian Temperance Union: a Study in Organization," 150.
19 Kerr, *Organized for Prohibition*, 48–50.
20 Clark, *Deliver Us from Evil*, 84–8.
21 The life history of Addie Chisholm is unusual for the WCTU because of her marital status, but utterly consistent with that of her sisters in her devotion to evangelicalism during the nineteenth century. "We stand today where two roads meet," she observed during her 1887 presidential address. "One lies behind us over which we can yet see the sunshine and the dark shadows that lie here and there across its path, while tender memories linger round the track of feet that eagerly rushed to do the bidding of the Master, or grew tired and heavy as the darkness came on." Addie Davis had married Daniel Black Chisholm, a barrister and mayor of Hamilton, Ontario, and a member of Parliament from 1872 to 1874. Both had been prominent in temperance reform through their Methodist church, where they seem to have met as Sunday school teachers. Chisholm helped found the provincial WCTU, succeeding Letitia Youmans as president. In 1884 she was president of the Ontario County union. Through 1885 she remained active in the organization as a single parent, having a son in tow. From that year she appears in the Ottawa directory as living at 127 Bank Street and apparently renting out rooms. One of her tenants was George E. Foster, then minister of fisheries in the Macdonald government. Foster was a thirty-eight-year-old bachelor in 1885, having spent most of his working life as a travelling temperance lecturer and professor of classics at the University of New Brunswick. Foster and Chisholm became engaged in 1888 and married in 1889, after which she seems to have had nothing further to do with the WCTU. She went on to become Lady Foster, busying herself with a number of cultural clubs in the Ottawa area, and died in 1919. See AO, Annual Report of the Ontario WCTU, 1887; Ottawa Directories, 1882–89; NAC, Sir George E. Foster Papers, 1885–1919; W.S. Wallace, *The Memoirs of the Rt. Hon. Sir George Foster; Ottawa Journal*, 20 Sept. 1919.
22 AO, Minutes of the Ontario WCTU Annual Meeting, 1887.
23 Ibid.
24 AO, Minute Book of the Lancaster WCTU, 5 March 1902.
25 AO, Minute Book of the Ottawa WCTU, 1 October 1881.
26 Ibid., 3 January 1882.
27 AO, MU 8406, assorted "methods booklets."
28 AO, Annual Report of the Ontario WCTU, 1887.
29 AO, Minutes of the Second Convention of the Dominion WCTU,

Toronto, 1889.

30 AO, Minute Book of the North Toronto WCTU, 1887.

31 AO, Minute Book of the Dunnville WCTU, 7 January 1888.

32 AO, Minute Book of the North Toronto WCTU, 19 September 1887.

33 AO, MU 8432, *The Progress of Half a Century.*

34 AO, Toronto Directory and Report, 1905.

35 Those dominion-level departments concerned directly with education in 1909 were scientific temperance instruction, health and heredity, medical temperance, moral education, mother's meetings, Sunday schools, anti-narcotics, press, railway employees, school of methods, school saving banks, literature depository, work among young peoples' societies, and medal contests. Departments in which education was a secondary, but important, issue include foreign work, raftsmen and lumbermen, soldiers and militia, and work among coloured people.

36 Nattress, *Public School Physiology and Temperance*, 78.

37 See, for example, Giles, "'I Like Water Better.'"

38 AO, Minutes of the Convention of the Dominion WCTU, 1909.

39 Among the unsuccessful political causes championed in this period were halfway houses for female former prisoners, prohibition of cigarettes and alcohol, a ban on the sale of liquor on the transcontinental railways, and female suffrage.

40 AO, Report of the Annual Convention of the Ontario WCTU, 1909.

41 AO, Minutes of the Ontario WCTU Annual Meeting, 1910.

42 AO, Minute Book of the Newmarket WCTU, 1 February 1910. The Newmarket recording secretary's erratic capitalization has been reproduced as it appears in the minute book.

43 Ibid., 2 February 1909.

44 Ibid., 2 March 1909.

45 Ibid., 7 December 1909.

46 Ibid., 4 January 1910.

47 Ibid., 5 January 1909.

48 Ibid., 11 October 1910.

49 Ibid., 3 May 1910.

50 Ibid., 6 April 1909.

51 Mitchinson, "Aspects of Reform," 176.

52 Ibid.

53 Daniel Malleck in his analysis of four Ontario WCTU unions – Ottawa, London, Newmarket, and Dunnville – contends that the more successful unions were those, such as London's, that sought out community problems on which to focus their energies, while the less successful, such as Dunnville's, seemed unaware of community issues (Malleck, "Women and Children First"). My reading of these unions' records does not confirm his interpretation. All unions, including Dunnville's,

analysed their local communities and identified projects in light of this information. The failure of some unions where others prospered had much more to do with internal leadership and the existence of other competing women's groups, in my view. It would also be fair to note that the Dunnville WCTU survived for a total of thirty-five years (1888–1909 and 1923–37) while London's records show it to have persisted for only twenty-seven years (1879–1906)!

54 AO, Minutes of the Convention of the Dominion WCTU, 1891.

55 Ibid., 1909.

56 Ibid., 1914.

57 Mitchinson, "Aspects of Reform," 171, asserts that it was the largest Canadian non-denominational organization. Recent work carried out by Margaret Kechnie shows that the Women's Institute in Ontario was larger than the Ontario branch of the WCTU in the post-1900 period. For example, in 1906, the Women's Institute registered 10,479 members; in 1909, 13,841; and in 1917, 30,335. See Kechnie, "Keeping Things Clean."

58 AO, Minutes of the Convention of the Dominion WCTU, 1889–1916.

59 McKee, *Jubilee History*, 15.

60 Ibid., 28.

61 Ibid., 38.

62 Ibid., 50.

63 Ibid., 85.

64 Ibid., 94.

65 Ibid., 104–5.

66 AO, Minute Book of the Meaford WCTU, 29 August 1902 to 7 November 1902.

67 See, for example, the 1898 annual meeting of the Ontario WCTU and the 1890 and 1909 Annual Meetings of the Dominion WCTU.

68 Youmans, *Campaign Echoes*, 125.

69 AO, Annual Meeting of the Executive Committee of the Dominion WCTU, 28 May 1890.

70 AO, Minute Book of the Woodstock WCTU, 22 May 1913.

71 AO, Toronto WCTU Directory and Summary of Work, 1888.

72 Ibid., 13 July 1899.

73 AO, Minute Book of the Newmarket WCTU, 23 February 1885 and 6 September 1892; AO, Treasurer's Book of the Richmond Hill WCTU, 23 March 1886.

74 UWO, London District WCTU Records, 29 June 1897.

75 AO, Minute Book of the Newmarket WCTU, 30 April 1886; UWO, London District WCTU Records, 29 May 1905.

76 AO, Minute Book of the Ottawa WCTU, 7 June 1884.

77 UWO, Minute Book of the West Middlesex District Council, Royal Templars of Temperance, 29 April, 1897.

78 Decarie, "The Prohibition Movement in Ontario," 8–10.
79 Ibid., 11.
80 Ibid., 103.
81 Ibid., 12.
82 Masters, *The Rise of Toronto*, 31.
83 Decarie, "The Prohibition Movement in Ontario," 12.
84 UWO, Minute Book of the West Middlesex District Council, Royal Templars of Temperance, 26 October 1899. The minutes indicate that in Glencoe there was "not much interest taken with just a medium attendance" and in Appin "but very little interest taken in attending the regular meeting," while in Ekfrid it is reported that "they have no place of meeting and not much interest". At the same time in nearby London, the WCTU had fifty-five at a meeting and reports of work completed at the local jail, with the Band of Hope, in the Industrial School, with the franchise, and in other areas of work (UWO, London District WCTU Records, 26 September 1899).
85 Blocker, *American Temperance Movements*, 98.
86 Decarie, "The Prohibition Movement in Ontario," 24.
87 See, for example, AO, Annual Report of the Dominion WCTU, 1889; AO, Annual Report of the Provincial WCTU, 1887.
88 AO, Minute Book of the Ottawa WCTU, 18 February 1884.
89 Ibid., 3 January 1882.
90 *Woman's Journal*, August 1899.
91 Ibid., 3 March 1884.
92 AO, Minute Book of the Dunnville WCTU, 2 November 1901.
93 See AO, Treasurer's Book of the Richmond Hill WCTU, 14 January 1885; AO, Minute Book of the Newmarket WCTU, 28 June 1892 and 5 January 1915; AO, Minute Book of the Meaford WCTU, 2 September 1898; AO, Minute Book of the Peterborough WCTU, October 1914.
94 AO, Minute Book of the Dunnville WCTU, 31 September 1902 and 17 December 1902.
95 AO, Minute Book of the Meaford WCTU, 6 January 1899.
96 See AO, Minutes of the Convention of the Dominion WCTU, 16 June 1892; AO, Minute Book of the Ottawa WCTU, 21 September 1881; UWO, London District WCTU Records, 25 August 1896 and 22 September 1896.
97 AO, Minute Book of the Woodstock WCTU, 28 January 1915.
98 AO, Minutes of the Annual Meeting of the Ontario WCTU, 1887.
99 See UWO, London District WCTU Records, 28 March 1893; AO, Treasurer's Book of Richmond Hill WCTU, 3 January 1895; AO, Minute Book of the Meaford WCTU, 3 March 1899; AO, Minute Book of the Dunnville WCTU, 5 November 1888.
100 AO, Minute Book of the Newmarket WCTU, 15 November 1887; UWO, London District WCTU Records, 23 May 1893.

101 Graeme Decarie suggests that this occurred with Methodist Church Union in 1883–84 (Decarie, "The Prohibition Movement in Ontario," 25). However, Phyllis Airhart indicates that the Methodist General Conference did not add the footnote prohibiting the drinking of alcoholic beverages (as well as card-playing, dancing, circus going, and theatre attendance) to its *Discipline* until 1886 (Airhart, *Serving the Present Age*, 24).

102 Grant, *A Profusion of Spires*, 190.

103 Mitchinson, "Aspects of Reform," 200–2.

104 AO, Minute Book of the Dunnville WCTU, 16 October 1888; AO, Minute Book of the Ottawa WCTU, 6 November 1882.

105 See, for example, AO, Minute Book of the Meaford WCTU, 3 May 1901.

106 UWO, London District WCTU Records, 25 April 1893.

107 Ibid., 13 June 1893.

108 For example, ibid., 26 September 1899. See also Griffiths, *The Splendid Vision*, chap. 1.

109 NAC, MG 28 III, vol. 719, Bronson Family Papers, Local Council of Women file.

110 Saywell, *The Canadian Journal of Lady Aberdeen*, 74.

111 Roberts, "'Rocking the Cradle for the World,'" 25.

112 Pedersen, "The Young Woman's Christian Association in Canada," 82.

113 AO, Report of the Convention of the Dominion WCTU, 1893.

114 AO, Report of the Convention of the Ontario WCTU, 1901.

115 AO, Minutes of the Convention of the Dominion WCTU, 1913.

116 Pedersen, "The Young Woman's Christian Association in Canada," 88.

117 AO, MU 8471, *World's Y Hand-Book*, 1906.

118 AO, Annual Report of the Ontario WCTU, 1918.

119 Mitchinson, "Aspects of Reform," 184.

120 UWO, London District WCTU Records, 23 January 1894.

121 S.A. Cook, "'A Helping Hand and Shelter,'" app. I.

122 AO, Minute Book of the Peterborough WCTU, 26 March 1928 and 25 September 1929.

123 This is corroborated by Naomi Griffith's recent work on the National Council of Women. "in one sense the local councils had a more disparate group of affiliates than did the National Council, for bodies such as the Women's [*sic*] Christian Temperance Union, which would not join the latter, were frequently members of the local organization" (Griffiths, *The Splendid Vision*, 80.)

124 AO, Annual Meeting of the Ontario WCTU, 1922.

125 An International Woman's Christian Temperance Union under the leadership of Margaret Parker was established in 1876 with the firm backing of Frances Willard. Although Annie Wittenmyer claimed it to have been "the first ... international convention ... for women the

world has ever known," it was largely a moribund organization (Tyrrell, *Woman's World, Woman's Empire*, 20).

126 AO, Treasurer's Book of the Richmond Hill WCTU, 27 August 1884 and 8 February 1886.
127 AO, Minutes of the Ontario Provincial Executive Meeting, April, 1899.
128 AO, Proceedings of the Conference of the Dominion WCTU, 1911.
129 AO, Annual Convention of the Ontario WCTU, October 1896.
130 *Canadian White Ribbon Tidings*, January 1904.
131 McKee, *Jubilee History*, 70.
132 *Canada's White Ribbon Bulletin*, August 1915.
133 I am grateful to Carolyn Heald at the Archives of Ontario for her help in clarifying publication dates for the various WCTU journals.
134 AO, Minutes of the Dominion WCTU Convention, June 1916.
135 Tyrrell, *Woman's World, Woman's Empire*, 3.
136 Ibid., 33.
137 Ibid., 194.
138 Ibid., 201–8.
139 Epstein, *The Politics of Domesticity*, 145.
140 AO, Executive Meeting of the Ontario WCTU, May 1898.
141 *Woman's Journal*, December 1898.
142 *Toronto Globe*, 27 October 1897.
143 Tyrrell, *Woman's World, Woman's Empire*, 207.
144 *Woman's Journal*, December 1898.
145 Tyrrell, *Woman's World, Woman's Empire*, 10.
146 Wendy Mitchinson notes that at least some of the WCTU strength resided in this policy of fierce independence (Mitchinson, "The Woman's Christian Temperance Union," 152).

CHAPTER FOUR

1 Semple, "'The Nurture and Admonition of the Lord.'" See also N. Sutherland, *Children in English-Canadian Society*, esp. parts I and II.
2 Rooke and Schnell, "Childhood and Charity in Nineteenth- Century British North America," 157.
3 Willard, *Glimpses of Fifty Years*, 637–8.
4 *Why Should a Christian Girl Sign the Total Abstinence Pledge?* YWCTU National Leaflet No. 109.
5 See fiction pieces supporting children's purifying influence in *Canadian White Ribbon Tidings*, March 1913.
6 AO, Minutes of the Annual Report of the Ontario WCTU Convention, 1890. See also AO, Minutes of the Convention of the Dominion WCTU, 1916.
7 AO, Minute Book of the Newmarket WCTU, 2 November 1915.

8 Dr James R. Nichols, *Spirituous Liquors Not Needed in Medicine or the Arts*, National Leaflet No. 40. See also a condemnation of Lydia Pinkham's Vegetable Compound for its high percentage of alcohol in *Canadian White Ribbon Tidings*, August 1910.

9 Frances Willard, *Society and Society Women*, National Leaflet No. 27.

10 AO, Minute Book of the Meaford WCTU, 3 January 1908.

11 Mrs. Lucy A. Scott, *Busy Women and the WCTU*, National Leaflet No. 41.

12 While the Toronto WCTU noted that one of the many advantages of the working-class kitchen garden program was the training of competent servants, it did not underscore the need for these servants in WCTU members' homes. Some may have found employment there, but the expectation seems to have been that graduates of the program would be better equipped to find work in any middle-class home or to improve their own homes.

13 See, for example, Mitchinson, "Aspects of Reform."

14 See, for example, Strong-Boag, "The Parliament of Women."

15 A December 1891 article in the *Woman's Journal* told the story of a young man who blames his too tidy mother for driving him into the streets, bad company, and taverns. "The over-neat and fussy mother is working against temperance and good order every day of her life."

16 *Canadian White Ribbon Tidings*, August 1910.

17 *Woman's Journal*, December 1886.

18 See the *Canadian White Ribbon Tidings*, March–October 1913.

19 *Woman's Journal*, July/August 1893.

20 Davidoff and Hall, *Family Fortunes*, 335.

21 *Canadian White Ribbon Tidings*, October 1910.

22 Ibid., March 1910.

23 Ibid., February 1910.

24 AO, Minutes of the Annual Meeting of the Ontario WCTU, 1887.

25 Ibid.

26 Anna M. Vail, *A Girl's Influence*, National YWCTU Leaflet No. 102.

27 Ellice Hopkins, *What Can We Do?* The White Cross Series No. 7.

28 Frances Willard, *Safety for School Children*, National Leaflet No. 48.

29 Mrs S.M.O. Henry, *Somebody Is Praying for You*, Signal Lights No. 22.

30 Mrs Lucy A. Scott, *Personal Purity*, The White Cross Series No. 11.

31 *Canadian White Ribbon Tidings*, April 1910.

32 Willard, *Safety for School Children*.

33 *Woman's Journal*, 1 January 1901.

34 Ibid., October 1890.

35 Lucy A. Scott, *Real Chivalry*, The White Cross Series No. 12.

36 *Canadian White Ribbon Tidings*, September 1915.

37 Rotundo, "Boy Culture".

38 Marks, "Ladies, Loafers, Knights and 'Lasses,'" iv–v, 237–40.

39 *Woman's Journal*, January 1893.
40 Mitchinson, *The Nature of Their Bodies*, esp. chap. 1.
41 *Canadian White Ribbon Tidings*, February 1910.
42 AO, Annual Report of the Ontario WCTU, 1926.
43 Nancy Garner argues that this contradiction in American WCTU thought ultimately hobbled its social agenda. "The existence of the LTL and its emphasis on the training of boys was an expression of the WCTU members' disappointment in and frustration with the men around them. The Loyal Temperance Legion was part of their attempt to reform men into more acceptable companions, fathers, colleagues, and citizens, without openly confronting the patriarchy inherent in the structures of the 19th and early 20th century American Victorian society that had led to their disappointment and frustration" (Garner, "Molding and Making the Next Generation of Men," 7–8).
44 Esther Pugh, *The Spirit of the Crusade*, National Leaflet No. 64, and Mrs S.M.O. Henry, *Somebody Is Praying for You*, Signal Lights No. 22.
45 *Woman's Journal*, 1 January 1901.
46 *Smoking*, Signal Lights No. 7.
47 Frances Willard, *Temperance and the Labor Question*, Signal Lights No. 18, and Willard, *The Shoemaker and Little White Shoes*, Signal Lights No. 9.
48 Anna M. Vail, *A Girl's Influence*, YWCTU National Leaflet No. 102.
49 AO, Minute Book of the Mizpah WCTU, 4 April 1916.
50 Bordin, *Women and Temperance*, 117.
51 Ibid.
52 See, for example, Epstein, *The Politics of Domesticity*, where the motive is seen to be female anger directed against a male-dominated family and society, or Bordin's *Women and Temperance*, in which women's empowerment is located in the nineteenth-century temperance campaigns, during which women discovered their communal strength. The present author does not mean to suggest that evangelicalism did not persist in American local unions as long as it did in Ontario's. This may well be true, particularly in small-town America as opposed to metropolitan areas. However, no major study has yet been made available to show such to be the case. This study is grounded in Ontario evidence and argues that the tenacity of evangelicalism is clear in this region. There is always the possibility that similar patterns emerged elsewhere, but this study could make no such claim.
53 Tyrrell, *Woman's World, Woman's Empire*.
54 Mrs Helen I. Bullock, *The Tobacco Toboggan*, National Leaflet No. 32.
55 Frances Willard, *Scientific Temperance Instruction in Public Schools*, National Leaflet No. 9.
56 A Symposium of Eminent Physicians, *Is Alcohol a Stimulant?* National Leaflet No. 23.

57 Willard, *Scientific Temperance Instruction in Public Schools.*
58 Dr James R. Nichols, *Spirituous Liquors Not Needed in Medicine or the Arts*, National Leaflet No. 40.
59 N. Clark, *Deliver Us from Evil*, 51–3. See also Gusfield, *Symbolic Crusade*, 79–80, and Blocker, Retreat from Reform, 8–10.
60 Epstein, *The Politics of Domesticity.*
61 Willard, *Glimpses of Fifty Years*, 418.
62 Tyrrell, *Woman's World, Woman's Empire*, 191.
63 Valverde, *The Age of Light, Soap, and Water*, 17.
64 Ibid., 18.
65 Pivar, *Purity Crusade*, 10.
66 Ibid.
67 Willard, *Glimpses of Fifty Years*, 418.
68 AO, Annual Report of the Dominion WCTU, 1890.
69 AO, Annual Report of the Ontario WCTU, 1886. Valverde, *The Age of Light, Soap, and Water*, 59, notes that "it is significant that the Purity departments were renamed 'Moral Education and Mother's Meetings,'" presumably at both the dominion and provincial levels. This is true for neither group. Provincially, the social purity department was created separately, but later merged with mothers' meetings into a common department. At the dominion level, the department of health and heredity was reconstituted as the purity department and mothers' meetings. Moral education always stood apart from purity.
70 AO, Report and Directory of the WCTU of York and Peel Counties, 1909–10.
71 Pivar, *Purity Crusade*, esp. chap. 3.
72 *Canadian White Ribbon Tidings*, February 1910. See also Gorham, "The 'Maiden Tribute of Modern Babylon' Re-examined," 354.
73 MacLaren, *Our Own Master Race*, 69 and 71.
74 AO, Minute Book of the Richmond Hill WCTU, 4 October 1927.
75 Beall, *The Living Temple*, 53.
76 Ibid., 33.
77 Pivar, *Purity Crusade*, 159.
78 Ibid., 108–10.
79 Frances E. Willard, *Society and Society Women*, National Leaflets No. 27 (n.d., but about 1883). In the same vein and directed especially to young women, see Mrs Frances J. Barnes, *Our Social World*, YWCTU National Leaflet No. 110.
80 AO, Minutes of the Convention of the Dominion WCTU, 1890.
81 AO, Annual Report of the Ontario WCTU, 1913.
82 *Woman's Journal*, 15 March 1901.
83 UWO, London District WCTU Records, Minute Book of the London WCTU, 9 May 1893.

84 In her useful study of Canadian social purity in the late nineteenth and early twentieth centuries, Mariana Valverde does not consider gender to be particularly significant in shaping the content of social purity's message (Valverde, *The Age of Light, Soap, and Water*). The present study of the WCTU suggests that the gender of the sponsors and clients is an important determinant in the nature of the content.
85 Pivar, *Purity Crusade*, 111.
86 Willard, *Glimpses of Fifty Years*, 429.
87 Pivar, *Purity Crusade*, 104.
88 Ellice Hopkins, *My Little Sister*, The White Cross Series.
89 Ibid.
90 Rev. A.G. Butler, *An Evil Tradition*, The White Cross Series No. 6.
91 Nellie McClung attacked the "new chivalry" as unworkable and demeaning to women (Warne, *Literature as Pulpit*, 159ff.).
92 Butler, *An Evil Tradition*.
93 Ellice Hopkins, *What Can We Do?* Such statements demonstrate the limitations of Mariana Valverde's study of English-Canadian social purity in *The Age of Light, Soap, and Water*. The author argues that purity was not presented simply as "the absence of lust; it was an active, aggressive process of self-mastery that could be likened to a military campaign" (31). Clearly, this was true for males, but certainly not females in this heavily used purity series.
94 Bliss, "'Pure Books on Avoided Subjects.'"
95 Mrs Lucy A. Scott, *Personal Purity*, The White Cross Series No. 11. Emphasis appears in the original text. See also Scott, *Real Chivalry*, The White Cross Series No. 12.
96 Scott, *Personal Purity*.
97 "We do not by any means advocate the free circulation of 'doctor books' among young people: we have too many inheritances of impure thought and prejudice to contend with for that to be wise, but we would advocate that such matters be delicately and tactfully taught to the growing child by every parent ... One thing should deeply impress itself upon our minds – HOMES are of the greatest importance in any country" (AO, MU 8288, F.A. Danard, *A Schoolroom Story*, White Life Truths Social Purity Series [Toronto: Henderson & Co & Samuel Farmer, n.d.], 5).
98 Ibid.
99 See, for example, the Kingsville WCTU mother's meetings as reported in the *Canadian White Ribbon Tidings*, January 1910.
100 Pivar, *Purity Crusade*, 111.
101 See AO, Annual Report of Dominion WCTU, 1891, 1903, 1905.
102 Tyrrell, *Woman's World, Woman's Empire*, 195.
103 Willard, *Glimpses of Fifty Years*, 419.

104 Pivar, *Purity Crusade*, 137–41.
105 Tyrrell, *Woman's World, Woman's Empire*, 195.
106 Gorham, "The 'Maiden Tribute of Modern Babylon' Re-examined," 353.
107 Bordin, *Women and Temperance*, 110.
108 R.C. Macleod, "The Shaping of Canadian Criminal Law, 1892 to 1902," as cited in Snell, "'The White Life for Two,'" 117.
109 Snell, "'The White Life for Two,'" 121.
110 Parker, "The Origins of the Canadian Criminal Code," 268.
111 Snell, "'The White Life for Two,'" 121.
112 AO, Annual Report of the Ontario WCTU, 1894.
113 Snell, "'The White Life for Two,'" 119–20.
114 AO, Annual Report of the Ontario WCTU, 1909.
115 The Ontario WCTU took some time to arrive at this position. In 1883 the official stance of the organization was that Parliament be asked to completely suppress the liquor traffic, but through a free liquor trade system. The local-option method was endorsed, while any licensed system was rejected on the grounds that this would provide an official stamp of propriety that it did not deserve. See summary of 1883 provincial convention in AO, Minute Book of the Ottawa WCTU, 15 October 1883. In 1889 the provincial convention opposed licensing because "a revenue taken from the liquor traffic has a tendency to blind the eyes of the taxpayers to the evils of the trade and demoralize the conscience of the public generally" (AO, Annual Report of the Ontario WCTU, 1889). By 1894, however, the Ontario convention indicated its support for licensing in principle when it passed a resolution deploring the insufficiencies of the license system and requesting that it be reformed (McKee, *Jubilee History*, 37).
116 Willard, *Glimpses of Fifty Years*, 351.
117 Bordin, *Women and Temperance*, 57–8.
118 Ibid.
119 Bacchi, "Divided Allegiances," 89–94.
120 Malleck, "Women and Children First."
121 UWO, Minute Book of the London WCTU, 14 February, 1893.
122 AO, Minute Book of the Dunnville WCTU, 19 February 1903.
123 AO, Treasurer's Book of the Richmond Hill WCTU, 26 April 1887.
124 AO, Annual Report of the Ontario WCTU, 1888.
125 See, for example, AO, Minutes of the Ontario WCTU Convention, 1887.
126 AO, Annual Report of the Dominion WCTU, 1896.
127 AO, Annual Report of the Ontario WCTU, 1899.
128 *Canadian White Ribbon Tidings*, February 1910.
129 AO, Annual Report of the Dominion WCTU Convention, June 1916.
130 McKillop, *Matters of Mind*, 224–5.

131 Valverde, "'When the Mother of the Race Is Free,'" esp. 15–21.

132 Ibid., 15.

133 Ibid., 17.

134 The Ontario WCTU's consistent worry concerning native Canadians was the ease with which liquor could be obtained and transmitted to other vulnerable groups. For example, in 1926 the annual convention passed this resolution: "Since there is no other restraint on the purchase of native wine except that it must be bought by the keg or dozen bottles, its use, especially amongst foreigners, is on the increase, and it is a serious detriment to the enforcement of prohibition. Resolved that this source of drinking and drunkenness and of many acts amongst our foreign population, should suffer the same prohibition placed upon other intoxicants" (AO, Annual Report of the Ontario WCTU, 1926).

135 Ibid.

136 Ibid.

137 AO, Annual Report of the Dominion WCTU, 1916.

138 See, for example, ibid., 1922.

139 AO, Annual Report of the Ontario WCTU, 1929.

140 Warne, *Literature as Pulpit*, 162.

141 AO, Annual Report of the Ontario WCTU, 1927.

142 Ibid., 1915.

143 Warne presents a good deal of evidence that Nellie McClung, long a member and representative of WCTU views, believed in "the fundamental equality of all persons, regardless of race, religion, or gender" (Warne, *Literature as Pulpit*, 188).

144 AO, Annual report of the Ontario WCTU, 1929. See also 1928 report, where the superintendent of Canadianization notes that "almost all nationalities have made good in Canada in their respective lines of work and in the shouldering of Canadian burdens and the carrying on of Canadian industries."

145 *Canada's White Ribbon Bulletin*, August 1915.

146 Ibid.

147 See AO, Annual Report of the Ontario WCTU, 1899 and 1914; AO, Minute Book of the Spencerville WCTU, 3 August 1899; and AO, Annual Report of the Dominion WCTU, June 1916.

148 AO, Annual Report of the Dominion WCTU, June 1916.

149 AO, Annual Report of the Ontario WCTU, 1909.

150 Ibid., 1913.

151 AO, Convention of the World's WCTU, 1883.

152 See, for example, AO, Annual Reports of the Dominion WCTU, 1909, 1920, and 1929.

153 AO, Annual Report of the Ontario WCTU, 1899.

154 Ibid., 1914.

155 Tyrrell, *Woman's World, Woman's Empire*, 170ff.
156 Bordin, *Women and Temperance*, 95.
157 See, for example, AO, Minute Book of the Dunnville WCTU, 22 January 1907, where the secretary notes a clear connection made in the conversation between intemperance and sin.
158 AO, Annual Report of the Ontario WCTU, 1894.
159 *Woman's Journal*, 1 April 1901.
160 AO, Annual Report of the Ontario WCTU, 1902.
161 Ibid. and AO, Minute Books of the Executive Committee of the Dominion WCTU, November 1909.
162 AO, Annual Report of the Dominion WCTU, November 1922.
163 Warne, *Literature as Pulpit*, 185.
164 See, for example, AO, Minute Book of the Meaford WCTU, 1912–14, and AO, Minute Book of the Peterborough WCTU, 1914–16.
165 AO, Minute Book of the Cornwall WCTU, 20 September 1920.
166 AO, Minute Book of the Fairmount WCTU, 21 January 1926.
167 AO, Minute Book of the Keswick WCTU, 13 January 1926.
168 AO, Minute Book of the Owen Sound WCTU, 4 September 1923.
169 *Smoking*, Signal Lights No. 7.
170 AO, Minute Book of the Ottawa WCTU, October 1881.
171 Mrs Helen I. Bullock, *The Tobacco Toboggan*, National Leaflet No. 32.
172 Willard, for example, argued that "a purpose to drink liquors is a sin" but that the "appetite thus formed and forced is a disease" (Bordin, *Women and Temperance*, 99).
173 See Fitzpatrick, *Lady Henry Somerset*, 120. Dr Youmans professed to back the "time honoured principles of absolute abolition and prohibition of all and every kind of licenced sin" (*Woman's Journal*, December 1898.
174 Bordin, *Women and Temperance*, 3.
175 Mitchinson, "Aspects of Reform," 185.
176 Lynne Marks draws a distinction between the general societal acceptance of such policies as prohibition and suffrage within the WCTU program of reform. While she accepts that the prohibition platform did reflect the dominant ideology of the era, other components, such as the WCTU position on sexuality and suffrage, were "neither dominant nor mainstream." Even where prohibition is concerned, she documents violent reactions from sectors of the community in, for example, Ingersoll. See Marks, "Ladies, Loafers, Knights and 'Lasses,'" 246–7.

CHAPTER FIVE

1 AO, Convention of the Dominion WCTU, 1890.
2 McKee, *Jubilee History*, 50.
3 AO, Annual Report of the Dominion WCTU, 1891, 1909, 1913.

4 Ibid., 1899.
5 AO, Minutes of the Dominion Convention of the WCTU, 1891.
6 AO, Annual Report of the Dominion WCTU, 1899.
7 Ibid., 1913.
8 Decarie, "The Prohibition Movement in Ontario," 108.
9 McKee, *Jubilee History*, 49.
10 AO, Minute Book of the Ottawa WCTU, 19 October 1881.
11 For a fuller analysis of the campaign for scientific temperance instruction, see S.A. Cook, "Earnest Christian Women."
12 AO, Annual Report of the Ontario WCTU, 1920.
13 This is the latest date by which the department had been set up; it is the first year for which provincial records exist.
14 AO, Recording Secretary's Book of the Provincial WCTU, 1881 executive committee meeting.
15 Zimmerman, "'The Queen of the Lobby,'" 11–14.
16 Bordin, *Women and Temperance*, 135.
17 See, for example, AO, Annual Report of the Ontario WCTU, 1890: "The objection most frequently met is the unsuitability of the text-book, but the fact that it is successfully taught by some proves that it can be by all who give sufficient attention to the subject. The same complaint is made in reference to the text-book on history, it is altogether beyond the children, yet it is successfully taught because *it must* be taught."
18 AO, Annual Report of the Ontario WCTU, 1887, *Women and Temperance*, and Bordin, 136.
19 This was one of many respects in which the Ontario WCTU followed the direction of Mary Hunt of the National WCTU. By 1892 her committee had identified twenty-three acceptable textbooks for use in American schools (Sheehan, "Temperance, the WCTU and Education in Alberta", 47).
20 AO, Annual Report of the Ontario WCTU, 1905.
21 Nancy Sheehan argues that in obtaining mandated status for a temperance textbook, the Ontario WCTU was working against important Ontario precedents. Unlike the McGuffey Readers, with their strong temperance message, which were used in many American states, the Ontario standardized textbooks included the Irish National Readers, followed by the Ryerson and Ontario Readers. The latter stressed the virtues of courage, obedience, humility, thrift, and industry, but not temperance (Sheehan, "Temperance, the WCTU and Education in Alberta," 80–1). See also B. Curtis, *Building the Educational State*, chap. 7.
22 Nattress, *Public School Physiology and Temperance*, 57.
23 Ibid., 90.
24 Ibid., 120.
25 Ibid., 79.

26 Ibid., 46.
27 Ibid., 124.
28 Ibid., 194.
29 "Regulations of the Education Department Respecting the Study of Physiology and Temperance," ibid., 194.
30 AO, Annual Report of the Ontario WCTU, 1893.
31 Ibid., 1895.
32 *Canadian White Ribbon Tidings*, May 1911.
33 AO, Annual Report of the Ontario WCTU, 1905.
34 Ibid., 1900.
35 Ibid., 1896.
36 Ibid., 1891.
37 Ibid., 1903.
38 Ibid., 1905.
39 Ibid., 1924.
40 For example, see the list published in ibid., 1904.
41 *Canadian White Ribbon Tidings*, June 1928.
42 AO, Annual Report of the Ontario WCTU, 1916.
43 Ibid., 1909.
44 McKee, *Jubilee History*, 51.
45 Bordin, *Women and Temperance*, 137. Nevertheless, by 1901 every state and territory in the United States had a course in scientific temperance instruction as a result of the unflagging efforts of the National WCTU's superintendent for scientific temperance, Mary Hunt (Zimmerman, "'The Queen of the Lobby,'" 2).
46 McKee, *Jubilee History*, 54.
47 Bordin, *Women and Temperance*, 136–8.
48 AO, Minute Book of Ontario and Durham Counties WCTU, 1904.
49 Annual Report of the Ontario WCTU, 1917.
50 Ibid., 1900, 1904, 1905, 1907.
51 AO, Minute Book of the Ottawa WCTU, 4 November 1882.
52 For example, see AO, Annual Reports of the Ontario WCTU, 1894, 1915, and Zimmerman, "'The Queen of the Lobby.'"
53 Bordin, *Women and Temperance*, 136. In 1885 Pennsylvania required all new teachers to pass an examination on scientific temperance instruction (Zimmerman, "'The Queen of the Lobby,'" 1–2).
54 AO, Minute Book of the Ottawa WCTU, 19 October 1881, and AO, Annual Reports of the Ontario WCTU, 1890, 1893, 1901.
55 AO, Annual Report of the Ontario WCTU, 1892.
56 AO, Ontario WCTU Executive Meeting, Toronto, March 1896.
57 Ibid., 1897.
58 AO, Annual Report of the Ontario WCTU, 1902.
59 Ibid., 1903.

60 Ibid., 1907.
61 In his analysis of the American scientific temperance instruction movement, Jonathan Zimmerman contends that one of the many appealing components of STI for American lobbyists was that it made use of "legal suasion" to "institutionalize moral suasion of the young" (Zimmerman, "'The Queen of the Lobby,'" 5–6).
62 AO, Annual Report of the Ontario WCTU, 1898.
63 McKee, *Jubilee History*, 51.
64 AO, Annual Report of the Ontario WCTU, 1922.
65 AO, Minute Book of the Newmarket WCTU, 13 June 1893.
66 AO, Annual Report of the Ontario WCTU, 1890.
67 AO, Minute Book of the Ottawa WCTU, 4 November 1882.
68 See Sheehan, "The WCTU on the Prairies."
69 S.A. Cook, "Educating for Temperance."
70 AO, Minute Book of the Ottawa WCTU, 4 May 1885.
71 Ibid., 18 October 1885.
72 AO, Directory and Summary of Work of the Toronto WCTU, 1888.
73 AO, Minute Book of the Owen Sound WCTU, 1914; and AO, Minute Book of the Ottawa WCTU, 1914. See also AO, Annual Reports of the Ontario WCTU, 1913, 1915, 1918, 1924.
74 AO, MU 8450, untitled pamphlet on the medal contests, 11.
75 AO, Minute Book of the Meaford WCTU, 6 February 1903.
76 AO, Annual Report of the Ontario WCTU, 1925.
77 UWO, London District WCTU Records, Minute Book of the London WCTU, 24 May 1894.
78 AO, Minute Book of the Owen Sound WCTU, 1924.
79 AO, Annual Report of the Ontario WCTU, 1925.
80 *Canadian White Ribbon Tidings*, 1 April 1904.
81 AO, Minute Book of the Mimico WCTU, 1931.
82 See UWO, Minute Book of the London WCTU, 14 February 1893, and AO, Minute Book of the Newmarket WCTU, 27 January 1891.
83 AO, Treasurer's Book for the Richmond Hill WCTU, 10 June 1885. See also AO, Minute Book of the Newmarket WCTU, 30 November 1886.
84 AO, Minute Book of the Ottawa WCTU, 3 and 17 April 1882.
85 AO, Minute Book of the Newmarket WCTU, 5 December 1893.
86 Ibid., 26 December 1893.
87 AO, Minute Book of the Meaford WCTU, 30 November 1906, September 1911, 1 March 1912, and December 1912.
88 UWO, Minute Book of the London WCTU, 14 November 1893.
89 Ibid., 26 December 1893.
90 AO, Minute Book of the Ottawa WCTU, 2 January 1885.
91 AO, Treasurer's Book of the Richmond Hill WCTU, 14 February 1895.
92 AO, Minute Book of the Newmarket WCTU, 5 February 1895 and 1 May

1906. See also strategies used by the Ingersoll WCTU (Marks, "Ladies, Loafers, Knights and 'Lasses,'" 226–7).

93 UWO, Minute Book of the London WCTU, 28 February 1893.

94 Marks, "Ladies, Loafers, Knights and 'Lasses', 226.

95 AO, Treasurer's Book of the Richmond Hill WCTU, 6 March 1899.

96 Ibid., 14 May 1884, and AO, Minute Book of the Newmarket WCTU, 6 September 1886.

97 AO, Treasurer's Book of the Richmond Hill WCTU, 21 August 1894.

98 AO, Minute Book of the Meaford WCTU, 6 December 1901.

99 AO, Minute Book of the Ottawa WCTU, 20 April 1885.

100 UWO, Minute Book of the London WCTU, 23 January 1894.

101 AO, Treasurer's Book of the Richmond Hill WCTU, 8 December 1885.

102 Minute Book of the Newmarket WCTU, 3 April 1900.

103 Ibid., 3 October 1905.

104 AO, Minute Book of the Dunnville WCTU, 19 October 1905.

105 UWO, Minute Book of the London WCTU, 11 October 1893 and 12 December 1893.

106 AO, Minute Book of the Peterborough WCTU, 29 October 1915, and AO, Minute Book of the Woodstock WCTU, 24 June 1915.

107 AO, Minute Book of the Dunnville WCTU, 16 January 1901, and this note from 23 July 1903: "A letter read by Secy from the License Inspector in ans to the one sent him last month in which he states he is in communication with the Government in regard to the License Law enforcement and one fine of $50. has been imposed for selling illegally since and we intend more shall follow. From his letter we find that there is a Bye Law of the town that it is an offence for a man to be seen on the streets any day under the influence of liquor and it was suggested that we call the notice of the officers to the fact."

108 UWO, Minute Book of the London WCTU, 11 April 1893.

109 AO, Treasurer's Book of the Richmond Hill WCTU, 31 January 1895.

110 AO, Minute Book of the Meaford WCTU, 1 May 1903.

111 UWO, Minute Book of the London WCTU, 9 October 1900.

112 AO, Minute Book of the Meaford WCTU, 3 June 1899.

113 UWO, Minute Book of the London WCTU, 11 April 1893.

114 AO, Minute Book of the Meaford WCTU, 6 May 1906.

115 AO, Treasurer's Book of the Richmond Hill WCTU, 21 April 1898.

116 UWO, Minute Book of the London WCTU, 27 June 1893; see also 26 September 1899.

117 AO, Minute Book of the Newmarket WCTU, 24 April 1894.

118 Ibid., 5 June 1894.

119 Ibid., 7 November 1900.

120 Ibid., 8 May 1901.

121 Ibid., 2 October and 6 November 1906. See also AO, Minute Book of the

Peterborough WCTU, 19 April 1917.
122 AO, Minute Book of the Woodstock WCTU, 26 June 1913.
123 AO, Minute Book of the Newmarket WCTU, 5 February 1907.
124 Ibid., 4 April 1911.
125 AO, Minute Book of the Peterborough WCTU, 15 March 1917.
126 Bordin, *Women and Temperance*, 138.
127 AO, MU 8450, untitled leaflet on the medal contests.
128 Ibid., 10.
129 AO, Treasurer's Book of the Richmond Hill WCTU, 8 August 1895.
130 AO, Minute Book of the Windsor WCTU, 25 April 1913.
131 Frances J. Barnes, *Our Social World*, YWCTU National Leaflet No. 110, 9–10.
132 V.A. Lewis, *Where?* Signal Lights No. 5.
133 W. Jennings Demorest, *Our National Dilemma*, Signal Lights No. 6.
134 Mrs Augusta C. Bristol, *Words for Wage-Workers*, Signal Lights No. 8.
135 Frances E. Willard, *Temperance and the Labor Question*, Signal Lights No. 18.
136 Frances E. Willard, *The Shoemaker and Little White Shoes*, Signal Lights No. 9.
137 H.H. Seerley, *The Tobacco Habit and Its Effects upon School Work*, Signal Lights [no number].
138 *Smoking*, Signal Lights No. 7.
139 Frances E. Willard, *Scientific Temperance Instruction in Public Schools*, National Leaflets No. 9.
140 Alice M. Guernsey, *The Teacher Questioned*, National Leaflet No. 37. See also Guernsey, *The Teacher Helped*, National Leaflet No. 38.
141 A Symposium of Eminent Physicians, *Is Alcohol a Stimulant?* National Leaflet No. 23.
142 Mrs Helen I. Bullock, *The Tobacco Toboggan*, National Leaflet No. 32. See also Dr James R. Nichols, *Spirituous Liquors Not Needed in Medicine or the Arts*, National Leaflet No. 40.
143 Frances E. Willard, *Society and Society Women*, National Leaflet No. 27. See also Maud Rittenhouse, *A New Regime*, National Leaflet No. 104.
144 Margaret B. Platt, *The Hour and Its Needs*, National Leaflet No. 45.
145 Mrs Lucy A. Scott, *Busy Women and the WCTU*, National Leaflet No. 41. See also Mrs E.C. Read, *Why?* National Leaflet No. 46; Esther Pugh, *The Spirit of the Crusade*, National Leaflet No. 64; and Alice M. Guernsey, *The Child of the Crusade*, National Leaflet No. 66.
146 It is difficult to know if the collection of pamphlets deposited in the Archives of Ontario is a representative sample. The earliest sample is YWCTU Departmental Leaflet No. 52, and its strong evangelical tone and the issues raised suggests that it was produced in about the middle of the last decade of the nineteenth century. Nevertheless, the collection is

sizeable, running to number 115.

147 Anna Pearl McVay, *Wherefore a "Y"?* YWCTU Departmental Leaflet No. 52, and Ida C. Clothier, *Is a YWCTU a Necessity?* YWCTU Department Leaflet No. 58.

148 See the following YWCTU National Leaflets in AO, MU 8449, none with authors: *Why and How, To Hold and to Gain, Hints and Helps, What a Superintendent Should Know,* and *A Problem Solved: How to Maintain Interest in Our Meetings*. See also Ida C. Clothier, *Inasmuch*, YWCTU National Leaflet No. 112; Mary G. Fernald, *A Field of Practical Y Work*, YWCTU National Leaflet No. 113; and Mrs Ella A Boole, *A 'Y' Catechism*, YWCTU National Leaflet No. 115.

149 *Why Should a Christian Girl Sign the Total Abstinence Pledge?* YWCTU National Leaflet No. 109; Mrs Frances A. Barnes, *Our Social World*, YWCTU National Leaflet No. 110; Anna M. Vail, *A Girl's Influence*, YWCTU National Leaflet No. 102; and Mrs L.A. Scott, *What Is Your Value?* YWCTU National Leaflet No. 111. See also Margaret Wintringer, *One Summer's Flower Mission Work*, YWCTU National Leaflet No. 103, and Eva Kinney Griffith, *Counting One*, YWCTU National Leaflet No. 105.

150 AO, MU 8449, Loyal Leaflets Series.

151 *Woman's Journal*, January 1885 and periodically thereafter; for example, 1 February 1900.

152 *Woman's Journal*, 15 March 1900.

153 *Canadian White Ribbon Tidings*, 1 December 1905.

154 *Woman's Journal*, December 1891.

155 *Canadian White Ribbon Tidings*, March 1910.

156 Ibid., December 1886.

157 Ibid., October 1890.

158 Ibid., January 1891.

159 *Canadian White Ribbon Tidings*, June 1907.

160 Ibid., October 1911.

161 Many examples could be suggested to support this contention. One might consider a column from the *Canadian White Ribbon Tidings*: the annual week of prayer was announced for February 1910, "in which all other work is laid aside and God is implored to overthrow the Liquor Traffic and kindred evils, upbuilding righteousness in the White Ribbon membership and for the salvation of souls" (*Canadian White Ribbon Tidings*, 1 January 1910). Miss Mary Jameson counsels Y girls that "knowing that truest joy comes by surrender, I urge you to 'surrender all' to His clear will" (ibid. November 1910). In March 1912 the journal printed its answer to "the Ideal Y": "a consecrated girl who is not afraid under any circumstances to show she is endeavouring to follow the Master. She studies her Bible to know her Master's Will and uses the compass of prayer to guide and has great faith" (ibid., March 1912).

162 For example, see *Woman's Journal*, June 1890.
163 AO, Minute Book of the Lancaster WCTU, 21 December 1904 and March 1906.
164 AO, Minute Book of the Meaford WCTU, 7 June 1912.
165 See AO, Minute Book of the Spencerville WCTU, 14 November 14 1894.
166 AO, Minute Book of the Newmarket WCTU, 5 March 1895.
167 Ibid., 1 September 1896.
168 See AO, Minute Book of the Ottawa WCTU, 21 September 1881.
169 See AO, Minute Book of the Meaford WCTU, 3 February 1905.
170 For example, see UWO, Minute Book of the London WCTU, 24 January 1893.
171 For example, see AO, Minute Book of the Dunnville WCTU, 10 February 1888, and AO, Minute Book of the Woodstock WCTU, 21 September 1916.
172 AO, Minute Book of the Woodstock WCTU, 25 February 1916.
173 AO, Minute Book of the Spencerville WCTU, 1 February 1897.
174 AO, Minute Books of the Newmarket WCTU, 9 April 1886.
175 AO, Minute Book of the Fairmount WCTU, 20 March, 1926.
176 AO, Minute Book of the Lambton County WCTU, 26 June 1946.
177 For instance, in 1904 the provincial convention passed this motion: "that we, the Ontario WCTU, do hereby affirm that should either party declare, in clear and unmistakable terms, that they, if elected, will enact such prohibitive legislation as will reduce the liquor traffic to a minimum, it will be not only our duty, but our pleasure, to promote, by every means within our power, the election of such party" (McKee, *Jubilee History*, 63–4).
178 UWO, London District WCTU Records, 13 October 1896.
179 Ibid., 27 March 1894, for example.
180 Epstein, *The Politics of Domesticity*, 2.
181 See Decarie, "The Prohibition Movement in Ontario"; Epstein, *The Politics of Domesticity*; Mitchinson, "Aspects of Reform"; and Strong-Boag, "The Parliament of Women."
182 Sheehan, "The WCTU and Educational Strategies on the Canadian Prairie."
183 Bordin, *Frances Willard*, 5.
184 Youmans, *Campaign Echoes*.
185 Bordin, *Frances Willard*, 38.
186 Ibid., 3.
187 Mitchinson, "Aspects of Reform," 189.

CHAPTER SIX

1 Jack Blocker contends that the WCTU was the first temperance organization to proselytize among children (Blocker, *American Temperance Movements*, 82). Considering the Juvenile Societies and Bands of Hope

sponsored by many temperance lodges from the 1850s to the 1880s, this seems to be an overstatement.. Nevertheless, youth temperance education was not the central concern of any temperance society other than the WCTU. Thus it does seem fair to credit the WCTU with providing the first fully defined youth temperance education program.

2 Bordin, *Women and Temperance*, 151.

3 Sheehan, "The WCTU and Educational Strategies on the Canadian Prairie," 112.

4 Bordin, *Women and Temperance*, 150.

5 AO, Annual Report of the Ontario WCTU, 1886.

6 Frances Willard, "Introduction" to Annie Wittenmyer, *History of the Woman's Temperance Crusade*, 15–21.

7 Isletts, "A Social Profile," 104–7.

8 Blocker, *American Temperance Movements*, 81.

9 AO, MU 8288, *Manual: Young People's Branch of the Canadian Woman's Christian Temperance Union*, 4–5.

10 Surviving documents make it difficult to specify exact dates. The first available report for a dominion convention dates from 1889, the second to be held, and by this time a YWCTU had been organized. The first provincial records in the Archives of Ontario date from 1886, by which time figures were being collected for YWCTU groups around the province.

11 *Woman's Journal*, October 1898.

12 For example, the Newmarket YWCTU seems to have existed from at least December 1887 until it amalgamated with the WCTU in October 1888. During that brief period it organized a flower mission and supported the WCTU in its many endeavours. A second Y was organized sometime in early 1906, when its main activity seems to have been a social in April that year staged by the members in the Temperance Hall, followed by refreshments. By 1909 the YWCTU was running working-class mothers' meetings (AO, Minute Book of the Newmarket WCTU, 1885–1913).

13 See Hardesty, *Women Called to Witness*; Blauvelt, "Women and Revivalism"; Bebbington, *Evangelicalism in Modern Britain*; and Heeney, *The Women's Movement in the Church of England*.

14 AO, Annual Report of the Ontario WCTU, 1886.

15 Austin, "What Christ Has Done for Woman."

16 AO, MU 8471, *World's Y Hand-Book*, 1906.

17 *Woman's Journal*, June 1892.

18 AO, Records of the Toronto Union WCTU, 1904–05.

19 See note 12. The Mizpah union was unable to sustain its own YWCTU, but a Coloured WCTU and YWCTU operated for a time in 1917 under its direction (AO, Minute Book of the Mizpah WCTU, 1916–18). The Peterborough union established a Y in November 1915 which survived

until May 1916. It was resuscitated in the 1920s and concerned itself primarily with travellers' aid work (AO, Minute Book of the Peterborough WCTU, 1914–30).

20 AO, Annual Report of the Ontario WCTU, 1886. Departments were reported in Smith Falls, Brockville, Parkdale, Toronto (2), Cornwall, Ottawa, Oshawa, Galt, Owen Sound, Brantford, Prescott, Hamilton, and Guelph.

21 Ibid., 1887. Reports were received from each of the following: Almonte, Brantford, Brockville, Galt, Goderich, Hamilton, Napanee, Ottawa, Owen Sound, Parkdale, Peterborough, Pembroke, Smiths Falls, Toronto, Trenton, and Thorold.

22 Ibid., 1888. Reports were received from the following: Brantford, Thamesford, Kingston, Guelph, Owen Sound, Pembroke, Belleville, Goderich, Ottawa, Toronto, and Galt.

23 Ibid., 1896. The report is ambiguous on numbers. While the provincial Y superintendent indicated that only 6 Y departments survived, reports exist for thirteen, including Toronto Central, Hamilton, Teeswater, Ottawa, Picton, St Catharines, London, Chatham, New Edinburgh, Amherstburg, Barrie, Thamesville, and Rockaway. Because the local records for several of these unions are not available, cross-referencing is not possible. Nevertheless, it is clear that more Ys existed than can now be traced. Lynne Marks notes that both Campbellford and Thorold had strong Ys during the 1890s, of which only Thorold was reported to the provincial Y superintendent (Marks, "Ladies, Loafers, Knights and 'Lasses,'" 226–30).

24 AO, Annual Report of the Ontario WCTU, 1897.

25 The annual reports indicate that by 1914 there were thirty-three Y unions, and by 1920, twenty-eight.

26 City of Ottawa YWCA Records, Minute Book of the Ottawa YWCTU, 1888.

27 Ibid., 20 September 1889.

28 Carr-Harris, *Lights and Shades of Mission Work*, 36.

29 Carr-Harris Collection, untitled newspaper clipping, 14 February 1890.

30 One cannot help but be reminded of Marks' description of the hallelujah lasses' "knee drills" and parades with banners, tambourines, and other instruments in the attempt to appeal to young people of the working class (Marks, "The 'Hallelujah Lasses,'" 71–6). The WCTU records are silent on whether any of the kitchen garden manouevers were modelled on Salvation Army tactics, consciously or not. An alternative or additional inspiration for the kitchen garden program arises from Judith Erickson's research into American juvenile temperance groups. She discusses militarist exercises which became popular around the time of the Civil War. Although Willard strongly supported military drills for youth groups, strict evangelicals were understandably

strongly opposed. Moving underground for a time, the drills were reintroduced with the LTL in 1886. These included two special drills for girls. "Their 'arms' were not to be the masculine implements of war, but broom and fan. After an illustrated introduction to the 'Parts of the Broom' (including the Point, Upper Band, Stick, Lower Band, Handle, Monogram)," they proceeded "through the intricacies of 'the Broom Drill' that exactly paralleled the boys' 'Manual of Arms' ... girls looking like The Little Colonel go through their paces, dressed in white cheese cloth skirts (which must hang evenly and be five inches from the floor), caps and waists of Turkey red calico, and bearing monogrammed dust-pans on their backs" (Erickson, "Making King Alcohol Tremble," 345).

31 *Woman's Journal*, 1 February 1900.
32 AO, Annual Report of the Dominion WCTU Convention, 1891.
33 Carr-Harris, *Lights and Shades of Mission Work*, 24.
34 AO, Annual Report of the Ontario WCTU, 1889.
35 City of Ottawa YWCA Records, Minute Book of the Ottawa YWCTU, 8 March 1889.
36 AO, Annual Report of the Ontario WCTU, 1889.
37 Pedersen, "The Young Woman's Christian Association in Canada," 3.
38 AO, Minute Book of the Ottawa WCTU, 17 February 1885.
39 Ibid., 20 April 1885.
40 Carr-Harris, *Lights and Shades of Mission Work*, 11.
41 Ibid., 38.
42 Ibid., 55–6.
43 Ibid., 39.
44 Ibid,, 41.
45 Ibid., 36.
46 Carr-Harris Collection, untitled newspaper clipping, September 1888.
47 City of Ottawa YWCA Records, Home for Friendless Women, Annual Report, 1931–32.
48 Walkowitz, *Prostitution and Victorian Society*, 221.
49 Carr-Harris, *Lights and Shades of Mission Work*, 52.
50 Ibid., 53.
51 AO, Annual Report of the Ontario WCTU, 1888.
52 City of Ottawa YWCA Records, Register of Inmates for Home for Friendless Women, 1888–94. A fuller analysis can be found in S.A. Cook, "'A Helping Hand and Shelter,'" chap. 4, app. 2 to 6.
53 G.S. Jones, *Outcast London*.
54 AO, Annual Report of the Ontario WCTU, 1890.
55 Freedman, *Their Sisters' Keepers*, 55.
56 AO, Minute Book of the Ottawa YWCTU, 9 February 1891.
57 AO, Annual Report for the Toronto Central YWCTU, 1889–90.

58 AO, MU 8432, *The Progress of Half a Century* (pamphlet).
59 AO, Directory and Summary of Work of Toronto WCTU, 1888. See also 1889–90, 1890–91, 1891–92, and 1892–93.
60 AO, Minute Book of the North Toronto WCTU, 1885–89.
61 AO, Directory and Report of Toronto, 1889–90.
62 AO, Annual Report of the Ontario WCTU, 1886.
63 Ibid., 1887.
64 Ibid., 1889.
65 Ibid., 1890–91.
66 Ibid., 1892.
67 Ibid., 1898.
68 Ibid., 1899.
69 Ibid., 1900–10.
70 It is interesting that in an otherwise thorough survey of the work of the World's WCTU, Ian Tyrrell makes no mention of the YWCTU. See Tyrrell, *Woman's World, Woman's Empire.*
71 "A World's Y Demonstration," in AO, MU 8471, *World's Y Hand-Book*, 1906.
72 *Canadian White Ribbon Tidings*, March 1910.
73 AO, Annual Reports for the Ontario WCTU, 1886–1907.
74 AO, Minutes of the Ontario WCTU Convention, 1910.
75 AO, Annual Report of the Ontario WCTU, 1896.
76 AO, Records of the Toronto Union, 1910.
77 Ibid., and AO, Minutes of the Ontario WCTU Convention, 1910.
78 AO, Minutes of the Ontario WCTU Convention, 1931.
79 AO, Report of the Dominion WCTU, 11 October 1913.
80 Ida C. Clothier, *"Is a YWCTU a Necessity?"* YWCTU Department Leaflet No. 58.
81 AO, Annual Report of the Ontario WCTU, 1887.
82 *Woman's Journal*, January 1885.
83 Ibid., June 1890.
84 Clothier, *"Is a YWCTU a Necessity?"*
85 See, for example, AO, Minute Book for the Woodstock WCTU, 28 January 1915, and AO, Minute Book of the Newmarket WCTU, 2 March 1915.
86 AO, Report of the Dominion WCTU Convention, June 1891.
87 Ibid., 1916.
88 See, for example, AO, Minute Book of the Newmarket WCTU, 8 January 1889. For a discussion of Methodism's search for a "new evangelism" in the late nineteenth century, often expressed through revivals, see Airhart, *Serving the Present Age*, esp. chap. 4.
89 Ontario Secondary School Teachers' Federation, *The General Store.*
90 Henson, *Methods and Strategies for Teaching in Secondary and Middle Schools*, 91–107. See also Ontario Ministry of Education *Resource Guide: Behaviour.*

91 *Woman's Journal*, March 1890.
92 Gilbert, *Why Should a Christian Girl Sign the Total Abstinence Pledge?* YWCTU National Leaflets No. 109.
93 AO, Annual Report of the Ontario WCTU, 1893.
94 AO, MU 8396, "Temperance Hymn."
95 UWO, London District WCTU Records, 28 September 1897.
96 *Woman's Journal*, July 1885.
97 In some Ontario communities where the lodges remained powerful, the WCTU co-sponsored Bands of Hope. For example, the Whitby Sons of Temperance and the WCTU formed a band in 1886 (*Woman's Journal*, January 1886).
98 Ibid., February 1886.
99 Youmans, *Campaign Echoes*, 94.
100 *Woman's Journal*, July 1885.
101 Airhart, *Serving the Present Age*, 28.
102 *Woman's Journal*, July 1885.
103 Ibid., June 1900.
104 AO, Minute Book of the Newmarket WCTU, 19 November 1895.
105 Ibid., 3 December 1895.
106 AO, Spencerville WCTU Minute Book, 17 January 1895.
107 *Woman's Journal*, July 1885.
108 UWO, London District WCTU Records, 11 October 1893.
109 AO, Minute Book of the Newmarket WCTU, 17 December 1895.
110 Ibid., 15 September 1896.
111 AO, Directory and Summary of Work of the Toronto WCTU, 1888.
112 AO, Treasurer's Book of the Richmond Hill WCTU, 10 May 1887.
113 AO, Minute Book of the North Toronto WCTU, 12 March 1888.
114 The Stratford WCTU reported establishing a girls' sewing school (*Woman's Journal*, November 1885) and the Prescott YWCTU ran a night school for boys (ibid., December 1885).
115 Ibid., January 1886.
116 Ibid., February 1886.
117 AO, Treasurer's Book of the Richmond Hill WCTU, 29 March 1886.
118 AO, Minute Book of the North Toronto WCTU, 15 April 1885.
119 Garner, "Molding and Making the Next Generation of Men."
120 AO, Minute Book of the Newmarket WCTU, 7 April 1896.
121 Marks, "Ladies, Loafers, Knights and 'Lasses,'" 227.
122 The London WCTU also opened a newsboys' home over the winter of 1881–82. As in so many other instances across the province, the older women seem to have had difficulty maintaining order. *London Advertiser* ran an article in 1882 entitled "Unruly Boys Who Trouble the WCTU." It noted that "the boys were in a chronic state of insubordination. The rules were being constantly broken." The project appears

to have been abandoned after one season (*London Advertiser*, 12 April 1882. Malleck, "Women and Children First").

123 UWO, London District WCTU Records, 12 December 1893.

124 Ibid., 13 February 1894.

125 Youmans, *Campaign Echoes*, 92.

126 *Woman's Journal*, July 1900.

127 Ida C. Clothier, *Is a YWCTU a Necessity?* YWCTU Department Leaflets No. 58.

128 AO, Minute Book of the Annual Meeting of the Ontario WCTU, 1878.

129 *Woman's Journal*, November 1893.

130 Maud Rittenhouse, *A New Regime*, National Leaflet No. 104.

131 *Woman's Journal*, 15 November 1899.

132 Ibid., 1 January 1901.

133 Clothier, *Is a YWCTU a Necessity?*

134 Ruby I. Gilbert, *Why Should a Christian Girl Sign the Total Abstinence Pledge?* YWCTU National Leaflets No. 109.

135 Ibid.

136 City of Ottawa YWCA Records, Minute Book of the Ottawa YWCTU, 1888–91.

137 AO, Toronto District Report and Directory of the WCTU, 1889–1901.

138 *Woman's Journal*, October 1890.

139 Ibid,, February 1902.

140 Frances E. Willard, *Scientific Temperance Instruction in Public Schools*, National Leaflet No. 9.

141 Helen I. Bullock, *The Tobacco Toboggan*, National Leaflet No. 32.

142 AO, Minute Book of the Spencerville WCTU, 31 January 1895.

143 AO, Minute Book of the Newmarket WCTU, 4 February 1896.

144 *Woman's Journal*, 1 April 1901.

145 Ibid.

146 Ibid., 15 February 1900.

147 Clothier, *Is a YWCTU a Necessity?*

148 *Woman's Journal*, 15 March 1900.

149 Ibid., February 1901.

150 AO, Toronto District Report and Directory of the WCTU, 1889–1918.

151 Airhart, *Serving the Present Age*, 24.

152 Anna Pearl McVay, *Wherefore A 'Y'?*, YWCTU Departmental Leaflet No. 52.

153 *A Problem Solved: How to Maintain Interest in Our Meetings*, YWCTU National Leaflets No. 101. Emphasis is in original document.

154 L.A. Scott, *What is Your Value?*, YWCTU National Leaflet No. 111.

155 *A Problem Solved.*

156 Scott, *What is Your Value?* Emphasis is in original document.

157 *Woman's Journal*, December 1891.

158 Wright did eventually marry (in 1896), but throughout the 1880s and 1890s she championed projects for and by single women, and lived the life of a single woman.

159 Carr-Harris Collection, untitled newspaper clipping, 14 June 1895.

160 Bertha Wright (Carr-Harris)'s books include *Lights and Shades of Mission Work ... , The White Chief of the Ottawa, Love's Immensity, Stranger Than Fiction, Joy Unspeakable,* and *The Five A's vs. The Four A's, or A Fight to a Finish.*

161 Carr-Harris Collection, Bertha Wright to Hannah Currier, 27 November 1883.

162 *Canadian White Ribbon Tidings,* 1 April 1905.

163 AO, Minutes of the Ontario WCTU Convention, 1886.

164 Ibid.

165 *Woman's Journal,* June 1892.

166 AO, Annual Report of the Ontario WCTU, 1897.

167 *Woman's Journal,* June 1892.

168 AO, Minute Book of the Ottawa WCTU, 17 September 1884.

169 Ibid., 5 November 1883 and 8 June 1885.

170 UWO, Minute Book of the London WCTU, 27 March 1894.

171 For example, in 1902 there were fifty-eight married women and twenty single women in the Toronto Central YWCTU, but in the Parkdale Y there were twenty-four single and only one married woman, and the Northern Toronto Y had only single women. By 1913 the Central Toronto Y had fifteen single women and one married, the Parkdale Y had all single members, and the Northern Toronto Y had eight married and thirty single women members (AO, Records of the Toronto WCTU, 1902–14).

172 AO, Minute Book of the Ottawa WCTU, 7 October 1884.

173 *Woman's Journal,* June 1890.

174 AO, Annual Report of the Ontario WCTU, 1912.

175 For example, see AO, Minute Book of the North Toronto WCTU, 1886–89.

176 *Woman's Journal,* December 1886.

177 *Canadian White Ribbon Tidings,* December 1911.

178 Ibid., August 1910.

179 *Woman's Journal,* June 1892.

180 Ibid., June 1902.

181 Bordin, *Women and Temperance,* 101. Judith Erickson notes, however, that the Band of Hope never attained much success in the United States (Erickson, "Making King Alcohol Tremble," 336).

182 E.P. Gordon, *Women Torch Bearers,* 298. Erickson indicates that the LTL was organized in 1887, with Anna Gordon's manual of operations appearing in 1888. Its motto was "Tremble, King Alcohol." See Erickson, "Making King Alcohol Tremble," 339.

183 Erickson, "Making King Alcohol Tremble," 340.
184 AO, Minute Book of the Loyal Temperance Legion for Salford, 1902.
185 AO, MU 8288, *Manual* of the Young People's Branch of the Canadian WCTU.

CHAPTER SEVEN

1 AO, Minute Book of the Fairmount WCTU, copy of "letter of appreciation" to Miss Mary J. MacLennan, Lancaster, recording secretary for the Glengarry, Stormont, and Dundas County WCTU.
2 R. Cook, "The Triumph and Trials of Materialism," 424.
3 AO, Annual Report of the Ontario WCTU, 1917.
4 Ibid., 1927.
5 Ibid., 1923.
6 AO, Annual Report of the Dominion WCTU, 1917.
7 The Dominion WCTU changed its name to the Canadian WCTU in June 1925 (AO, MU 8397, announcement brochure). Membership totals are found in AO, Canadian WCTU Convention Report, 1928.
8 AO, Canadian WCTU Convention Report, 1922.
9 AO, MU 8285, Lottie Moore, *Comrades! Carry On!*, Canadian WCTU Medal Contest Book, No. 4.
10 The following Ontario unions disbanded during the 1920s, but later re-established a WCTU (where known, date is noted in parentheses): Glengarry, Stormont, and Dundas counties (1934), Howard Park (1936), Huron County (1933), Ingersoll (1944), Lakeshore (1944), Lindsay (1929), Lockiel (1947), Lincoln County (1948), Leeds and Frontenac (1947), Leamington (1944), Lambton County (1932), Madison (1945), Norwich (1942), Picnic Grove (1941), Plainville (1930), Rutherford (1947), Salford (1943), Spencerville (1941), Stouffville (1936), Summerlea (1941), Tillsonburg (1936), Wynchwood, Woodstock, Windsor, Waterloo County, York and Peel counties.
11 AO, Minute Book of the Newmarket WCTU, December 1923 and 1 December 1925.
12 AO, Minute Book of the Mimico WCTU, 24 May 1922, May 1926, 1 March 1927.
13 AO, Minute Book of the Peterborough WCTU, 28 September 1921.
14 Ibid., 25 October 1922 to 30 April 1930.
15 Ibid., 24 November 1926.
16 It should be noted that the Peterborough WCTU rose to fight again. It was reconstituted in 1945 and until 1970 carried an active program roster, including medal contests, Sunday school temperance work, and community activism (AO, Minute Books of the Peterborough WCTU).
17 AO, Annual Report of the Canadian WCTU, 1929.

18 AO, Minute Book of the Oxford County WCTU, 14 June 1923.
19 Ibid., 14 June 1928.
20 Campbell, *Demon Rum or Easy Money*, 32.
21 See, for example, Moderation League of Ontario, *Sobriety and the Ontario Temperance Act* (1923).
22 AO, MU 8396, WCTU handbill, 1923.
23 For prohibition: 585,676; for government sale: 551,645 (AO, MU 8397, W.W. Peck, *A Short History of the Liquor Traffic in Canada* (pamphlet published by the Canadian Temperance Federation).
24 See, for example, AO, Minute Books of the Mimico WCTU, 24 February 1925.
25 AO, Toronto District WCTU Directory, 1924–25.
26 Mrs Gordon Wright, *Is Government Control in Canada a Success or Failure?* 1926.
27 AO, Minute Book of the Mimico WCTU, 23 February 1926.
28 AO, Annual Report of the Ontario WCTU, 1927.
29 Mrs R.W. Craw, *The Challenge of the Liquor Traffic to the Home* (Literature Department of the Women's Missionary Society, United Church of Canada).
30 AO, Annual Report of the Ontario WCTU, 1924.
31 AO, Annual Meeting of the Toronto District WCTU, 1926–27.
32 Sandeen, *The Roots of Fundamentalism*, xvi.
33 The author does not mean to suggest that the Ontario WCTU ceased to exist after 1930; it continues today in a much reduced state. The end of this study is 1930, however.
34 DeBerg, *Ungodly Women*, esp. chap. 1.
35 McDannell, *The Christian Home in Victorian America*, 19.
36 DeBerg, *Ungodly Women*, esp. chap. 3.
37 Ibid., 62.
38 J.L. Brooks, "Civilization and Crime," *Truth, or, Testimony for Christ* 18 (1892): 363–4; as quoted in DeBerg, *Ungodly Women*, 121.
39 AO, Toronto District WCTU Directory, 1922–23.
40 First produced during the 1920s, the WCTU clip sheets were among the most important sources of information for local union programs. The minute books indicate that for many unions after 1920, clip sheets were the only resource used, other than the Bible.
41 AO, MU 8432, Clip Sheet, April 1932.
42 Stella Blanchard Irvine, *Wish Bones*.
43 AO, MU 8396, Samuel Groves, *Principles of Temperance*, with forward by Sara Rowell, Dominion WCTU President.
44 AO, Minute Book of the Keswick WCTU, n.d.

Bibliography

ARCHIVAL SOURCES

ARCHIVES OF ONTARIO, WCTU COLLECTION (AO)

St. Catharines YWCTU, Minute Book, 1913

Cornwall WCTU, Minute Books, 1920–9

Dunnville WCTU, Minute Books, 1888–1909, 1923–37

Fairmount WCTU, Minute Book, 1924–32

Grey and Dufferin Counties WCTU, Minute Books, 1922–30

Keswick WCTU, Minute Book, 1921–28

Lambton County WCTU, Minute Book, 1946–49

Lanark County WCTU, Minute Book, 1897

Lancaster, (Picnic Grove) WCTU, Minute Book, 1902–08

Meaford WCTU, Minute Books, 1898–1917, 1923–36

Mimico WCTU, Minute Book, 1915–16, 1919–39

Mizpah WCTU, Minute Book, 1916–23

Newmarket WCTU, Minute Books, 1885–1918

North Toronto WCTU, Minute Books, 1885–90

Ontario and Durham Counties WCTU, Minute Books, 1895–1909

Ottawa WCTU, Minute Books, 1881–86.

Owen Sound WCTU, Minute Books, 1923–30

Peterborough WCTU, Minute Books, 1885, 1914–22, 1945–70

Richmond Hill WCTU, Minute Books (called Treasurer's Books), 1884–87

St Catharines WCTU, Minute Book, 1913

Spencerville WCTU, Minute Book, 1897–1900

Toronto District WCTU, Annual Reports, 1885–1917, 1922–27 (including Annex, Barbara, Bascom, Bathurst, Beaches, Central, College, Connaught, Conton, Cynthia, Deer Park, Dovercourt, Eastern, Gordon, Hezzlewood, Howard Park, Kew Beach, Lytle, North, Northern, Parkdale, Riverdale, Sherbourne, Silvery, Stevens, Thornley, West India, Western, Westwood,

Willard, Wilshire, Wynchwood, Youmans, Youmans Paull)
Toronto District YWCTU, Annual Reports, 1889–1927 (including Barbara, Bascom, Bathurst, Beaches, Central, College, Connaught, Cynthia, Dovercourt, Gordon, Hezzlewood, India, Kew Beach, North, Northern, Parkdale, Riverdale, Silvery, Thornley, Westwood, Wilshire, Western, Youmans).
Windsor WCTU, Minute Book, 1913
Woodstock WCTU, Minute Books, 1912–19
York and Peel Counties WCTU, Minute Book, 1909–10
Ontario WCTU, Annual Reports, 1886–1930
Ontario WCTU Conventions, Minutes, 1884–1930
Ontario WCTU Activities, Records, 1886–1967
Canadian WCTU, Medal Contest Books (many undated, but about 1900–81)
Dominion WCTU, Annual Reports and Minutes, Conventions, 1889–1930
Dominion WCTU, Records of Activities, 1889–1969
World's WCTU, Records, 1883–97
Sons of Temperance, Minute Books, Orono Division 1853–81, 1892–94
Loyal Temperance Legion, Salford, Minute Book, 1902

GRANT CARR-HARRIS PRIVATE COLLECTION, OAKVILLE
Bertha Wright (Carr-Harris), Papers

CITY OF OTTAWA YWCA RECORDS
Home for Friendless Women, Annual Report, 1931–32
Home for Friendless Women, Register of Inmates, 1888–94
Ottawa YWCTU, Minute Book, 1888–91

NATIONAL ARCHIVES OF CANADA (NAC)
Bronson Family Papers, MG 27 III, vol. 719
Sir George E. Foster Papers, MG 27 II D7, vol. 109

UNIVERSITY OF WESTERN ONTARIO ARCHIVES, REGIONAL COLLECTION (UWO)
Royal Templars of Temperance, West Middlesex District Council, Minute Book, 1897–1901
Royal Templars of Temperance, Wardsville Council No. 419, (a subsidiary of West Middlesex District Council, Royal Templars of Temperance, Membership Book, 1898–1902
London District WCTU, Records, 1879–1906
Oxford County WCTU, Minute Book, 1915–18

PRINTED SOURCES

Note: Pamphlets in the following series are located in the WCTU Collection at the Archives of Ontario: Loyal Leaflets, Signal Lights, WCTU National Leaflets, White Cross Series, White Life Truths Social Purity Series, and YWCTU National Leaflets. Individual titles in these series are not separately listed in the bibliography.

The collection at the Archives of Ontario also includes files of the WCTU's journals, *Canada's White Ribbon Bulletin,* the *Canadian White Ribbon Tidings,* and the *Woman's Journal.* Because these publications are irregularly numbered and individual issues are generally short, they have been cited by date, rather than volume number and page.

Airhart, Phyllis D. "The Eclipse of Revivalist Spirituality: The Transformation of Canadian Methodist Piety, 1884–1925." Ph.D. thesis, University of Chicago, 1985.

– *Serving the Present Age: Revivalism, Progressivism, and the Methodist Tradition in Canada.* Montreal & Kingston: McGill-Queen's University Press, 1992.

– "Sobriety, Sentimentality and Science: The WCTU and the Reconstruction of Christian Womanhood." *Papers of the Canadian Methodist Historical Society,* 1988 & 1990: 117–36.

Allen, Richard. *The Social Passion: Religion and Social Reform in Canada, 1914–28.* Toronto: University of Toronto Press, 1971.

Anderson, James D. "The Municipal Government Reform Movement in Western Canada, 1880–1920." In *The Usable Urban Past,* ed. Alan Artibise and Gilbert Stelter, 73–111. Toronto: Macmillan of Canada 1979.

Archibald, Edith J. "The Dominion Woman's Christian Temperance Union." *Dominion Illustrated Monthly* 2 (February 1893): 251–9.

Armstrong, Christopher, and Nelles, H.V. *The Revenge of the Methodist Bicycle Company: Sunday Streetcars and Municipal Reform in Toronto, 1888–1897.* Toronto: P. Martin Associates, 1977.

Austin, Principal. "What Christ Has Done for Woman." *Friend of the Friendless,* October 1892. (Copy in City of Ottawa YWCA Records.)

– *Woman, Her Character, Culture and Calling: A Full Discussion of Women's Work in the Home, the School, the Church and the Social Circle, with an account of her Successful Labors in Moral and Social Reform.* By a galaxy of distinguished authors in the United States and Canada. Brantford: Book & Bible House, 1890.

Bacchi, Carol. "Divided Allegiances: The Response of Farm and Labour Women to Suffrage." In *A Not Unreasonable Claim,* ed. Linda Kealey, 89–108. Toronto: Canadian Women's Educational Press, 1979.

– "Race Regeneration and Social Purity: A Study of the Social Attitudes of

Canada's English-Speaking Suffragettes." *Social History* 11 (November 1978): 460–74.

Baehre, Rainer. "Paupers and Poor Relief in Upper Canada." Canadian Historical Association, *Historical Papers*, November 1981: 339–68.

Bailey, Peter. *Leisure and Class in Victorian England: Rational Recreation and the Contest for Control, 1830–1885*. Toronto: Routledge & Kegan Paul, University of Toronto Press, 1978.

– "A Mingled Mass of Perfectly Legitimate Pleasures: The Victorian Middle Class and the Problem of Leisure." *Victorian Studies* 21 (1977): 7–28.

Bassett, Isabel. *The Parlour Rebellion*. Toronto: McClelland & Stewart, 1975.

Beall, Arthur W. *The Living Temple: A Manual on Eugenics for Parents and Teachers*. Whitby: A.B. Penhale Publishing Co., 1933.

Bebbington, D.W. *Evangelicalism in Modern Britain: A History from the 1730's to the 1980's*. London, 1989.

Belenky, Mary Field, et al. *Women's Ways of Knowing: The Development of Self, Voice and Mind*. New York: HarperCollins, 1986.

Berger, Carl. *Science, God and Nature in Victorian Canada: The 1982 Joanne Goodman Lectures*. Toronto: University of Toronto Press, 1983.

– *A Sense of Power: Studies in the Ideas of Canadian Imperialism, 1867–1914*. Toronto: University of Toronto Press, 1970.

Best, G.F.A. *Shaftesbury*. New York: Arco Publishing Co., 1964.

Birrell, A.J. "D.I.K. Rine and the Gospel Temperance Movement in Canada." *Canadian Historical Review* 58 (1977): 23–43.

Blauvelt, Martha Tomhave. "Women and Revivalism." In *Women and Religion in America*, 1, ed. Rosemary Radford Ruether and Rosemary Skinner Keller, 1–45. San Francisco: Harper & Row, 1981.

Bliss, Michael. *Northern Enterprise: Five Centuries of Canadian Business*. Toronto: McClelland & Stewart, 1987.

– "'Pure Books on Avoided Subjects': Pre Freudian Sexual Ideas in Canada," In *Historical Papers*, Canadian Historical Association, ed. J. Atherton, J.P. Heisler, and J. Monet, 1970: 89–108.

Blocker, Jack S., Jr. *American Temperance Movements: Cycles of Reform*. Boston: Twayne Publishers, 1989.

– *"Give to Thy Winds Thy Fears": The Women's Temperance Crusade, 1873–1874*. Westport, Conn.: Greenwood Press, 1985.

– *Retreat from Reform: The Prohibition Movement in the United States, 1890–1913*. Westport, Conn.: Greenwood Press, 1976.

Bordin, Ruth. *Frances Willard: A Biography*. Chapel Hill: University of North Carolina Press, 1986.

– *Women and Temperance: The Quest for Power and Liberty, 1873–1900*. Philadelphia: Temple University Press, 1981.

Boutilier, Beverly. "Gender, Organized Women, and the Politics of Institution Building: Founding the Victorian Order of Nurses for Canada, 1893–1900."

Ph.D. thesis, Carleton University, 1993.

Boyer, Paul. *Urban Masses and Moral Order in America, 1820–1920*. Cambridge: Harvard University Press, 1978.

Boylan, Anne M. "Evangelical Womanhood in the Nineteenth Century: The Role of Women in Sunday Schools." *Feminist Studies* 4 (October 1978): 62–80.

– *Sunday School: The Formation of an American Institution, 1790–1880*. New Haven: Yale University Press, 1988.

– "Sunday Schools and Changing Evangelical Views of Children in the 1820's." *Church History* 48 (September 1979): 320–33.

Bradbury, Bettina. "The Fragmented Family: Family Strategies in the Face of Death, Illness, and Poverty, Montreal, 1860–1885." In *Childhood and Family in Canadian History*, ed. Joy Parr, 109–28. Toronto: McClelland & Stewart, 1982.

Bradley, Ian. *The Call to Seriousness*. London: J. Cape, 1976.

Branca, Patricia. *Silent Sisterhood*. London: Croom Helm, 1975.

Brouwer, Ruth Compton. *New Women for God: Canadian Presbyterian Women and India Missions, 1876–1914*. Toronto: University of Toronto Press, 1989.

– "Transcending the 'Unacknowledged Quarantine': Putting Religion into English-Canadian Women's History." *Journal of Canadian Studies/Revue d'études canadiennes* 27 (Fall 1992): 47–61.

Brown, Thomas E. "Dr. Ernest Jones, Psychoanalysis, and the Canadian Medical Profession, 1908–1913." In *Medicine in Canadian Society: Historical Perspectives*, ed. S.E.D. Shortt, 315–60. Montreal & Kingston: McGill-Queen's University Press, 1981.

Buckley, Suzanne. "Ladies or Midwives?: Efforts to Reduce Infant and Maternal Mortality." In *A Not Unreasonable Claim*, ed. Linda Kealey, 131–50. Toronto: Canadian Women's Educational Press, 1979.

Campbell, Robert A. *Demon Rum or Easy Money: Government Control of Liquor in British Columbia from Prohibition to Privatization*. Ottawa: Carleton University Press, 1991.

Canada's White Ribbon Bulletin, 1910–19.

Canadian White Ribbon Tidings, 1904–28.

Carnes, Mark C. "Middle-Class Men and the Solace of Fraternal Ritual." *Meanings for Manhood: Constructions of Masculinity in Victorian America*, ed. Mark C. Carnes and Clyde Griffen, 37–52. Chicago: University of Chicago Press, 1900.

Carr-Harris, Bertha. *Lights and Shades of Mission Work, or Leaves from a Worker's Note Book. Being Reminiscences of Seven Years Service at the Capital, 1885–1892*. Ottawa: Free Press, 1892.

Cherrington, E.H., ed. *Standard Encyclopedia of the Alcohol Problem*. Vol. 5, Ohio, 1929.

Clark, Alice. *Working Life of Women in the Seventeenth Century*. New York: A.M. Kelley, 1919.

Clark, Norman. *Deliver Us from Evil: An Interpretation of American Prohibition.* New York: Norton, 1976.

Clemens, James M. "Taste Not; Handle Not: A Study of the Social Assumptions of the Temperance Literature and Temperance Supporters in Canada West between 1839 and 1859." *Ontario History* 64 (September 1972): 142–60.

Cleverdon, Catherine L. *The Woman Suffrage Movement in Canada: The Start of Liberation, 1900–1920.* Toronto: University of Toronto Press, 1950.

Conrad, Margaret, Toni Laidlaw, and Donna Smyth, eds. *No Place Like Home: Diaries and Letters of Nova Scotia Women, 1771–1938.* Halifax: Formac, 1988.

Cook, Ramsay. *The Regenerators: Social Criticism in Late Victorian English Canada.* Toronto: University of Toronto Press, 1985.

– "The Triumph and Trials of Materialism, 1900–1945." In *The Illustrated History of Canada,* ed. Craig Brown, 375–466. Toronto: Lester & Orpen Dennys, 1987.

– and Wendy Mitchinson, eds. *The Proper Sphere: Woman's Place in Canadian Society.* Toronto: Oxford University Press, 1976.

Cook, Sharon Anne. "'Continued and Persevering Combat': The Ontario Woman's Christian Temperance Union, Evangelicalism and Social Reform, 1874–1916." Ph.D. thesis, Carleton University, 1990.

– "'Earnest Christian Women, Bent on Saving our Canadian Youth': The Ontario Woman's Christian Temperance Union and Scientific Temperance Instruction, 1881–1930." *Ontario History* (in press).

– "Educating for Temperance: The Woman's Christian Temperance Union and Ontario Children, 1880–1916." *Historical Studies in Education/Revue d'histoire de l'education* 5 (Fall 1993): 251–77.

– "'A Helping Hand and Shelter': Anglo-Protestant Social Service Agencies in Ottawa, 1880–1910." MA thesis, Carleton University, 1987.

– "Letitia Youmans: Ontario's Nineteenth-Century Temperance Educator." *Ontario History* 84 (December 1992): 329–42.

– "The Ontario Young Woman's Christian Temperance Union: A Study in Female Evangelicalism, 1874–1930." In *Changing Roles of Women Within the Christian Church in Canada,* ed. Marilyn Fardig Whitely and Elizabeth Muir, 502–39. Toronto: University of Toronto Press, 1994.

– "A Quiet Place ... To Die: Ottawa's First Protestant Old Age Homes for Women and Men." *Ontario History* 81, (March 1989): 25–40.

Cook, Terry. "Nailing Jelly to a Wall: Possibilities in Intellectual History." *Archivaria* 11 (Winter 1980): 205–18.

Cott, Nancy. *The Bonds of Womanhood: Woman's Sphere in New England, 1780–1835.* New Haven: Yale University Press, 1978.

– "Young Women in the Second Great Awakening in New England." *Feminist Studies* 3 (Fall 1975): 15–29.

Cox, Jeffrey. *The English Churches in a Secular Society: Lambeth, 1870–1930.* Oxford: Oxford University Press, 1982.

Crossley, H.T. *Practical Talks on Important Themes.* Toronto: Wm Briggs, 1895.

Crowley, Terry. "Madonnas before Magdalenes: Adelaide Hoodless and the Making of the Canadian Gibson Girl." *Canadian Historical Review* 67 (December 1986): 520–47.

Crysdale, Stewart. "Social Awakening among Protestants, 1872–1918." In *Religion in Canadian Society,* ed. Stewart Crysdale and Les Wheatcroft, 191–206. Toronto: Macmillan of Canada, 1976.

Cunningham, Hugh. *Leisure in the Industrial Revolution.* London: Croom Helm, 1980.

Curtis, Bruce. *Building the Educational State: Canada West, 1836–1871.* London: The Falmer Press, 1988.

Curtis, Susan. "The Son of Man and God the Father: The Social Gospel and Victorian Masculinity." In *Meanings for Manhood: Constructions of Masculinity in Victorian America,* ed. Mark C. Carnes and Clyde Griffen, 67–78. Chicago: University of Chicago Press, 1990.

Daily Citizen (Ottawa), February–July 1890.

Davidoff, Leonore, and Catherine Hall. *Family Fortunes.* Chicago: University of Chicago Press, 1987.

Dayton, Donald. *Discovering an Evangelical Heritage.* New York: 1976.

de Beavoir, Simone. "The Date of Biology," In *The Second Sex,* Part 1, Destiny, New York: Knopf, 1952.

DeBerg, Betty A. *Ungodly Women: Gender and the First Wave of American Fundamentalism.* Minneapolis: Fortress Press, 1990.

Decarie, Malcolm Graeme. "The Prohibition Movement in Ontario: 1894–1916." Ph.D thesis, Queen's University, 1972.

Douglas, Ann. *The Feminization of American Culture.* New York: Knopf, 1977.

Dublin, Thomas. *Women at Work: The Transformation of Work and Community in Lowell, Massachusetts, 1826–1860.* New York: Columbia University Press, 1979.

Earhart, Mary. *Frances Willard: From Prayers to Politics.* Chicago: Women's Publishing House, 1944.

Emery, George N. "The Origins of Canadian Methodist Involvement in the Social Gospel Movement, 1890–1914." *Journal of the Canadian Church Historical Society* 19 (March–June 1977): 104–19.

Epstein, Barbara Leslie. *The Politics of Domesticity: Women, Evangelism, and Temperance in Nineteenth–Century America.* Middletown, Conn.: Wesleyan University Press, 1981.

Erickson, Judith B. "Making King Alcohol Tremble: The Juvenile Work of the Woman's Christian Temperance Union, 1874–1900." *Journal of Drug Education* 18 (1988): 333–57.

Evans, Richard. *The Feminists: Women's Emancipation Movements in Europe, America and Australasia, 1840–1920.* London: Croom Helm, 1977.

Evening Journal (Ottawa), February–July 1890.

Filshie, Margaret A. "Sacred Harmonies: The Congregational Voice in Canadian Protestant Worship, 1750–1850." In *Religion and Culture: Comparative Canadian Studies*, ed. William Westfall, Louis Rousseau, Fernand Harvey, and John Simpson, 287–309, Waterloo: Wilfrid Laurier University Press, 1984.

Finnegan, Frances. *Poverty and Prostitution: A Study of Victorian Prostitutes in York.* Cambridge: Cambridge University Press, 1979.

Fitzpatrick, Kathleen. *Lady Henry Somerset.* London: J. Cape, 1923.

Freedman, Estelle. "Separatism as Strategy: Female Institution Building and American Feminism, 1870–1930." *Feminist Studies* 5 (Fall 1979): 512–29.

– *Their Sisters' Keepers: Women's Prison Reform in America, 1830–1930.* Ann Arbor: University of Michigan Press, 1981.

French, Goldwin. "The Evangelical Creed in Canada." In *The Shield of Achilles: Aspects of Canada in the Victorian Age*, ed. W.L. Morton, 15–35, Toronto: Ontario Historical Society, 1968.

Gagan, Rosemary R. "More than 'A Lure to the Gilded Bower of Matrimony': The Education of Methodist Women Missionaries, 1881–1925." *Historical Studies in Education/Revue d'histoire de l'education* 1 (Fall 1989): 239–60.

– *A Sensitive Independence: Canadian Methodist Women in Canada and the Orient, 1881–1914.* Kingston & Montreal: McGill-Queen's University Press, 1992.

Garner, Nancy C. "Molding and Making the Next Generation of Men: the Kansas Woman's Christian Temperance Union and the Loyal Temperance Union, 1890–1935." Paper presented to the International Congress on the Social History of Alcohol, London, Ontario, 1993.

Gauvreau, Michael. *The Evangelical Century: College and Creed in English Canada from the Great Revival to the Great Depression.* Montreal & Kingston: McGill-Queen's University Press, 1991.

Gelman, Susan. "'The "Feminization" of the High Schools'? Women Secondary School Teachers in Toronto: 1871–1930." *Historical Studies in Education/Revue d'histoire de l'education* 2, (Spring 1990): 119–48.

Gidney, R.D. and W.P.J. Millar. *Inventing Secondary Education: The Rise of the High School in Nineteenth-Century Ontario.* Kingston & Montreal: McGill-Queen's University Press, 1990.

Giles, Geoffrey J. "'I Like Water Better': A Comparative Study of Temperance Materials for Children in Britain, France and Germany." Paper presented to the International Congress on the Social History of Alcohol, London, Ontario, 1993.

Goheen, Peter G. "Currents of Change in Toronto, 1850–1900." In *The Canadian City: Essays in Urban History*, ed. Gilbert Stelter and Alan Artibise, 54–93, Ottawa: Carleton University Press, 1984.

Gordon, Elizabeth Putnam. *Women Torch Bearers: The Story of the Woman's Christian Temperance Union.* Evanston: Women's Publishing House, 1924.

Gordon, Linda. *Heroes of Their Own Lives: The Politics and History of Female*

Violence. New York: Viking, 1988.

Gorham, Deborah. "The 'Maiden Tribute of Modern Babylon' Re-examined: Child Prostitution and the Idea of Childhood in Late-Victorian England." *Victorian Studies* 21 (Spring 1978): 353–79.

– "Singing Up the Hill." *Canadian Dimension* 10 (1975): 26–38.

– *The Victorian Girl and the Feminine Ideal.*

Bloomington: Indiana University Press, 1982.

Grant, John Webster. "Burning Bushes: Flames of Revival in Nineteenth Century Canadian Presbyterianism." *Canadian Society of Church History Papers,* 1991: 97–112.

– *A Profusion of Spires: Religion in Nineteenth-Century Ontario.* Toronto: University of Toronto Press, 1988.

Greer, Allan. "The Sunday Schools of Upper Canada." *Ontario History* 67 (September 1975): 169–84.

Griffin, Clyde. "Reconstructing Masculinity from the Evangelical Revival to the Waning of Progressivism: A Speculative Synthesis." In *Meanings for Manhood: Constructions of Masculinity in Victorian America,* ed. Mark C. Carnes and Clyde Griffen, 183–204. Chicago: University of Chicago Press, 1990.

Griffiths, N.E.S. *The Splendid Vision: Centennial History of the National Council of Women of Canada, 1893–1993.* Ottawa: Carleton University Press, 1993.

Gusfield, Joseph. *Symbolic Crusade: Status Politics and the American Temperance Movement.* Urbana: University of Illinois Press, 1963.

Hall, Winfield Scott. *Sexual Knowledge: Knowledge Concerning Self and Sex.* Toronto: McClelland, Goodchild & Stewart, 1916.

Handy, Robert T. "Dominant Patterns of Christian Life in Canada and the United States: Similarities and Differences." In *Religion and Culture: Comparative Canadian Studies,* ed. William Westfall, Louis Rousseau, Fernand Harvey, and John Simpson, 344–55. Waterloo: Wilfrid Laurier University Press, 1984.

Hardesty, Nancy. *Women Called to Witness: Evangelical Feminism in the 19th Century.* Nashville: Abingdon Press, 1984.

Headen, Christopher. "The Origins of Canadian Methodist Involvement in the Social Gospel Movement 1890–1914." *Journal of the Canadian Church Historical Society,* 19 (March–June 1977): 104–11.

– "Women and Organized Religion in Mid and Late Nineteenth Century Canada." *Journal of the Canadian Church Historical Society* 20 (March–June, 1978): 3–18.

Heeney, Brian. "The Beginnings of Church Feminism: Women and the Councils of the Church of England, 1897–1919." *Journal of Ecclesiastical History* 33 (1982): 89–109.

– *The Women's Movement in the Church of England, 1850–1930.* Oxford: Clarendon Press, 1988.

Henson, Kenneth T. *Methods and Strategies for Teaching in Secondary and Middle Schools.* New York: Longmans, 1988.

Hewitt, Nancy. "The Perimeters of Women's Power in American Religion." In *The Evangelical Tradition in America*, ed. Leonard Sweet, 233–56. Macon, Ga: Mercer University Press, 1984.

Higgs, Edward. "Domestic Service and Household Production." In *Unequal Opportunities: Women's Employment in England, 1800–1918*, ed. Angela V. John, 125–152. Oxford: B. Blackwell, 1988.

Hiley, Michael. *Victorian Working Women: Portraits from Life.* Boston: D.R. Godine, 1979.

Hill, Patricia R. *The World Their Household: The American Woman's Foreign Mission Movement and Cultural Transformation, 1870–1920.* Ann Arbor: University of Michigan Press, 1985.

Hofstadter, Richard. *Anti-Intellectualism in American Life.* New York: Knopf, 1963.

Holbrook, M.L. "Parturition without Pain." In *The Physical Life of Woman*, ed. George Napheys. Toronto: Maclear, 1875.

Holcombe, Lee. *Victorian Ladies at Work.* Hamden, Conn.: Archon Books, 1975.

Houghton, Walter E. *The Victorian Frame of Mind.* New Haven: Yale University Press, 1957.

Houston, Cecil, and William Smyth. *The Sash Canada Wore: A Historical Geography of the Orange Order in Canada.* Toronto: University of Toronto Press, 1980.

Houston, Susan E. "The 'Waifs and Strays' of a Late Victorian City: Juvenile Delinquents in Toronto." In *Childhood and Family in Canadian History*, ed. Joy Parr, 129–42. Toronto: McClelland & Stewart, 1982.

– and Alison Prentice. *Schooling and Scholars in Nineteenth-Century Ontario.* Toronto: University of Toronto Press, 1988.

Hubbard, Ruth, Mary Sue Henifin, and Barbara Fried. *Women Look at Biology Looking at Women.* Boston: G.K. Hall, 1979.

Hudson, Winthrop S. *Religion in America.* New York: Scribner, 1965.

Hunter, Jane. *The Gospel of Gentility: American Women Missionaries in Turn-of-the-Century China.* New Haven: Yale University Press, 1984.

Iacovetta, Franca. "Making 'New Canadians': Social Workers, Women and the Reshaping of Immigrant Families." *Gender Conflicts: New Essays in Women's History*, Franca Iacovetta and Mariana Valverde, ed., 261–303. Toronto: University of Toronto Press, 1992.

Innis, Mary Quayle, ed. *The Clear Spirit: Twenty Canadian Women and Their Times.* Toronto: University of Toronto Press, 1966.

Isletts, Charles A. "A Social Profile of the Woman's Temperance Crusade: Hillsboro, Ohio." In *Alcohol, Reform and Society: The Liquor Question in Social Context*, ed. Jack S. Blocker, 101–10. Westport, Conn.: Greenwood Press, 1979.

Jones, Andrew, and Leonard Rutman. *In the Children's Aid: J.J. Kelso and Child Welfare in Ontario.* Toronto: University of Toronto Press, 1981.

Jones, Gareth Stedman. *Outcast London: A Study in the Relationship between Classes in Victorian Society.* London: Clarendon Press, 1971.

Katz, Michael. *The People of Hamilton, Canada West.* Cambridge: Harvard University Press, 1975.

Kealey, Gregory S., and Palmer, Bryan D. *Dreaming of What Might Be: The Knights of Labor in Ontario, 1880–1900.* New York: Cambridge University Press, 1982.

Kealey, Linda. "Introduction." In *A Not Unreasonable Claim*, ed. Linda Kealey, 1–14. Toronto: Canadian Women's Education Press, 1979.

Kechnie, Margaret. "Keeping Things Clean 'For Home and Country': The Federated Women's Institute of Ontario, 1897–1919." Ph.D. thesis, Ontario Institute for Studies in Education, (in progress).

Kerr, K. Austin. *Organized for Prohibition: A New History of the Anti-Saloon League.* New Haven: Yale University Press, 1985.

Kessler-Harris, Alice. *Out to Work.* Oxford: Oxford University Press, 1982.

Kingsley Kent, Susan. *Sex and Suffrage in Britain, 1860–1914.* Princeton: Princeton University Press, 1987.

Kraditor, Aileen. *The Ideas of the Woman Suffrage Movement, 1890–1920.* New York: Columbia University Press, 1971.

– *Up from the Pedestal.* Chicago: Quadrangle Books, 1970.

Kress, Daniel H. *The Cigarette as a Physician Sees It.* [n.p.]: Pacific Press Publishing Company, 1931.

Laqueur, Thomas W. "Working-Class Demand and the Growth of English Elementary Education, 1750–1850." In *Schooling and Society*, ed. L. Stone, Baltimore: Johns Hopkins University Press, 1976: 192–205.

– *Religion and Respectability: Sunday Schools and Working Class Culture 1780–1850.* New Haven: Yale University Press, 1976.

Lebsock, Suzanne. *The Free Women of Petersburg: Status and Culture in a Southern Town, 1784–1860.* New York: Norton, 1984.

Lenskyj, Helen. "A 'Servant Problem' or a 'Servant-Mistress Problem'?" *Atlantis* 7 (Fall 1981): 3–11.

– "Training for 'True Womanhood': Physical Education for Girls in Ontario Schools, 1890–1920." *Historical Studies in Education/Revue d'histoire de l'education* 2 (Fall 1990): 205–24.

Lowe, Graham. "Women, Work and the Office: The Feminization of Clerical Occupations in Canada, 1901–1931." In *Rethinking Canada: The Promise of Women's History*, ed. Veronica Strong-Boag and Anita Clair Fellman, 107–22. Toronto: Copp Clark Pitman, 1986.

Luker, Ralph E. "Religion and Social Control in the Nineteenth-Century American City." *Journal of Urban History* 2 (May 1976): 363–9.

Lynn, Robert W., and Elliott Wright. *The Big Little School: Sunday Child of*

American Protestantism. New York: Harper & Row, 1971.

McDannell, Colleen. *The Christian Home in Victorian America, 1840–1900*. Bloomington: Indiana University Press, 1986.

McKee, S.G.E. *Jubilee History of the Ontario Woman's Christian Temperance Union, 1877–1927*. Whitby: G.A. Goodfellow, 1927.

McKenna, Katherine M.J. *A Life of Propriety: Anne Murray Powell and Her Family, 1755–1849*. Montreal & Kingston: McGill-Queen's University Press, 1994.

– "'The Union between Faith and Good Works': The Life of Harriet Dobbs Cartwright, 1808–1887." Paper presented at the Canadian Historical Association meeting, Queen's University, 1991.

McKillop, A.B. *A Disciplined Intelligence: Critical Inquiry and Canadian Thought in the Victorian Era*. Montreal & Kingston: McGill-Queen's University Press, 1979.

– *Matters of Mind: The University in Ontario, 1791–1951*. Toronto: University of Toronto Press, 1994.

McLaren, Angus. *Our Own Master Race: Eugenics in Canada, 1885–1945*. Toronto: McClelland & Stewart, 1990.

McLoughlin, William G., ed. *The American Evangelicals, 1800–1900: An Anthology*. New York: Ronald Press Co., 1968.

Malleck, Daniel J. "'Sisters, Conduct Yourselves Appropriately': The Early Development of the Woman's Christian Temperance Union in Ontario, 1877–1895." Paper presented to the International Congress on the Social History of Alcohol, London, Ontario, 1993.

– "Women and Children First: The Woman's Christian Temperance Union in Four Ontario Communities, 1878–1899." MA thesis, University of Western Ontario, 1992.

Marks, Lynne. "The 'Hallelujah Lasses': Working-Class Women in the Salvation Army in English Canada, 1882–92." Iacovetta and Valverde, *Gender Conflicts*, 67–117.

– "Ladies, Loafers, Knights and 'Lasses': The Social Dimension of Religion and Leisure in Late Nineteenth-Century Small Town Ontario." Ph.D. thesis, York University, 1992.

Marr, Lucille M. "Church Teen Clubs, Feminized Organization? Tuxis Boys, Trail Rangers, and Canadian Girls in Training, 1919–1939." *Historical Studies in Education/Revue d'histoire de l'education* 3 (1991): 249–67.

– "Hierarchy, Gender and Goals of the Religious Educators in the Canadian Presbyterian, Methodist and United Churches, 1919–1939." Canadian Society of Church History, *Historical Papers*, 1990: 1–28.

Marsden, George M. *The Evangelical Mind and the New School Presbyterian Experience: A Case Study of Thought and Theology in Nineteenth-Century America*. New Haven: Yale University Press, 1970.

– *Fundamentalism and American Culture: The Shaping of Twentieth Century*

Evangelicalism, 1870–1925. Oxford: Oxford University Press, 1980.
Marshall, David B. *Secularizing the Faith: Canadian Protestant Clergy and the Crisis of Belief, 1850–1940*. Toronto: University of Toronto Press, 1992.
Masters, D.C. *The Rise of Toronto*. Toronto: University of Toronto Press, 1947.
Mezvinsky, Norton. "Scientific Temperance Instruction in the Schools." *History of Education Quarterly* 1 (March 1961): 48–56.
Mitchinson, Wendy. "Aspects of Reform: Four Women's Organizations in Nineteenth-Century Canada." Ph.D. thesis, York University, 1977.
– "Causes of Disease in Women: The Case of Late 19th Century English Canada." In *Health, Disease and Medicine: Essays in Canadian History*, ed. Charles G. Roland, 381–97. Hamilton: Hannah Institute for the History of Medicine, 1983.
– "Early Women's Organizations and Social Reform: Prelude to the Welfare State." In *The Benevolent State: The Growth of Welfare in Canada*, ed. Allan Moscovitch and Jim Albert, 77–94. Toronto: Garamond Press, 1987.
– "Gynecological Operations on Insane Women, London, Ontario, 1895–1901." *Journal of Social History* 15 (Spring 1982): 467–84.
– *The Nature of Their Bodies: Women and Their Doctors in Victorian Canada*. Toronto: University of Toronto Press, 1991.
– "The WCTU: 'For God, Home and Native Land': A Study in Nineteenth-Century Feminism." In *A Not Unreasonable Claim*, ed. Linda Kealey, 151–68. Toronto: Canadian Women's Educational Press, 1979.
– "The Woman's Christian Temperance Union: a Study in Organization." *International Journal of Women's Studies* 4 (1981): 143–56.
Moberg, David. *The Great Reversal: Evangelism Versus Social Concern*. Philadelphia: Lippincott, 1972.
Montagu, Ashley. *The Natural Superiority of Women*. New York: Collier Books, 1974.
Morris, Jenny. "The Characteristics of Sweating: The Late Nineteenth-Century London and Leeds Tailoring Trade." In *Unequal Opportunities: Women's Employment in England, 1800–1918*, ed. Angela V. John, 95–121. Oxford: B. Blackwell, 1988.
Morrison, T.R. "'Their Proper Sphere': Feminism, the Family, and Child-Centred Social Reform in Ontario, 1875–1900." *Ontario History* 68 (March 1976): 45–64.
Nattress, William. *Public School Physiology and Temperance*. Toronto: Wm Briggs, 1893.
Nelles, H.V. *The Politics of Development: Forests, Mines and Hydro-Electric Power in Ontario, 1849–1941*. Toronto: Macmillan of Canada, 1974.
Nesmith, Tom. "The Philosophy of Agriculture: The Promise of the Intellect in Ontario Farming, 1835–1914." Ph.D. thesis, Carleton University, 1988.
Oldfield, Sybil. *Spinsters of This Parish: The Life and Times of F.M. Mayor and Mary Sheepshanks*. London: Virago, 1984.

O'Neill, William L. *Everyone Was Brave.* Chicago: Quadrangle Books, 1969.

Ontario Ministry of Education. *Resource Guide: Behaviour.* Toronto, 1986.

Ontario Secondary School Teachers' Federation. *The General Store: Meeting the Needs of the General Level Student.* Toronto, 1980.

Ottawa Citizen. September 1919.

Ottawa directories, 1882–89.

Parker, G. "The Origins of the Canadian Criminal Code." In *Essays in the History of Canadian Law,* ed. D.H. Flaherty, 249–80. Toronto: University of Toronto Press, 1981.

Parr, Joy. *The Gender of Breadwinners: Women, Men and Change in Two Industrial Towns, 1880–1950.* Toronto: University of Toronto Press, 1990.

– "The Skilled Emigrant and Her Kin: Gender, Culture, and Labour Recruitment." *Canadian Historical Review* 68 (December 1987): 529–51.

Peck, W.W. *A Short History of the Liquor Traffic.* [n.p.] Canadian Temperance Federation, [n.d.].

Pedersen, Diana. "'A Building for Her': The YWCA, Evangelical Religion, and Public Space in Canadian Cities, 1870–1930." Paper presented to the Ninth Berkshire Conference on the History of Women, Vassar College, 1993.

– "The Young Woman's Christian Association in Canada, 1870–1920: A Movement to Meet a Spiritual, Civic and National Need." Ph.D. thesis, Carleton University, 1987.

Pinchbeck, Ivy. *Women Workers and the Industrial Revolution.* London: Cass, 1969 (reprint).

The Pioneer: A Weekly Journal of Social Progress and Moral Reform Brantford: Ontario Branch of the Dominion Alliance for the Suppression of the Liquor Traffic, 1923.

Piva, Michael J. *The Condition of the Working Class in Toronto, 1900–1921.* Ottawa: University of Ottawa Press, 1979.

Pivar, David J. *Purity Crusade, Sexual Morality and Social Control, 1868–1900.* Westport, Conn.: Greenwood Press, 1973.

Pleck, Elizabeth. *Domestic Tyranny: The Making of American Social Policy against Family Violence from Colonial Times to the Present.* New York: Oxford University Press, 1987.

Prentice, Alison, et al. *Canadian Women: A History.* Toronto: Harcourt, Brace, Jovanovich, 1988.

– "The Feminization of Teaching in British North America and Canada, 1845–1875." *Social History* 8 (May 1975): 5–20.

– "Writing Women into History: The History of Women's Work in Canada." *Atlantis* 3 (Spring 1978): 72–84.

Rawlyk, George A. *The Canadian Protestant Experience, 1760–1990.* Burlington: Welch Publishing, 1990.

– *Champions of the Truth: Fundamentalism, Modernism, and the Maritime Baptists.* Montreal & Kingston: McGill-Queen's University Press, 1990.

– *Ravished by the Spirit: Religious Revivals, Baptists, and Henry Alline.* Montreal & Kingston: McGill-Queen's University Press, 1984.

– *Wrapped Up in God: A Study of Several Canadian Revivals and Revivalists.* Burlington: Welch Publishing, 1988.

– and Mark A. Noll, eds. *Amazing Grace: Evangelicalism in Australia, Britain, Canada and the United States.* Montreal & Kingston: McGill-Queen's University Press, 1994.

Reynolds, David S. "The Feminization Controversy: Sexual Stereotypes and the Paradoxes of Piety in Nineteenth-Century America." *New England Quarterly* 53 (1980): 96–106.

Roberts, Barbara. "'A Work of Empire': Canadian Reformers and British Female Immigration." In *A Not Unreasonable Claim*, ed. Linda Kealey, 185–201. Toronto: Canadian Women's Educational Press, 1979.

Roberts, Wayne. "'Rocking the Cradle for the World': The New Woman and Maternal Feminism, Toronto, 1877–1914." In *A Not Unreasonable Claim*, ed. Linda Kealey, 15–46. Toronto: Canadian Women's Educational Press, 1979.

Rooke, Patricia T., and R.L. Schnell. "Childhood and Charity in Nineteenth-Century British North America." *Social History* 15 (May 1982): 157–179.

– "The Rise and Decline of British North American Protestant Orphans' Homes as Woman's Domaine, 1850–1930." *Atlantis* 7 (Spring 1982): 21–36.

Rorabaugh, W.J. *The Alcoholic Republic: An American Tradition.* New York: Oxford University Press, 1979.

Rosen, Ruth. *The Lost Sisterhood: Prostitution in America, 1900–1918.* Baltimore: Johns Hopkins University Press, 1982.

Rosenberg, Rosalind. *Beyond Separate Spheres: Intellectual Roots of Modern Feminism.* New Haven: Yale University Press, 1982.

Rotundo, E. Anthony. "Boy Culture: Middle-Class Boyhood in Nineteenth-Century America." In *Meanings for Manhood: Constructions of Masculinity in Victorian America*, ed. Mark C. Carnes and Clyde Griffen, 15–36. Chicago: University of Chicago Press, 1990.

Rudy, Norma. *For Such a Time as This: L. Earl Ludlow and a History of Homes for the Aged in Ontario, 1837–1961.* Toronto: Ontario Association of Homes for the Aged, 1987.

Rutherford, Paul, ed. *Saving the Canadian City: The First Phase, 1880–1929.* Toronto: University of Toronto Press, 1974.

Ryan, Mary. *Womanhood in America from Colonial Times to the Present.* New York: F. Walts, 1983.

Ryan, Mary P. "A Women's Awakening: Evangelical Religion and the Families of Utica, New York, 1800–1840." *American Quarterly* 30 (1978): 602–23.

Sandeen, Ernest R. *The Roots of Fundamentalism: British and American Millenarianism, 1800–1930.* Chicago: University of Chicago Press, 1970.

Savage, Leslie. "Perspectives on Illegitimacy: The Changing Role of the Sisters of Misericordia in Edmonton, 1900–1906." In *Studies in Childhood*

History: A Canadian Perspective, ed. Patricia T. Rooke and R.L. Schnell, 105–34. Calgary: Detseig Enterprises, 1982.

Saywell, J.T., ed. *The Canadian Journal of Lady Aberdeen, 1893–1898.* Toronto: Champlain Society, 1960.

Schull, Joseph. *Ontario Since 1867.* Toronto: McClelland & Stewart, 1978.

Selles-Roney, Johanna. "A Canadian Girl at Cheltenham: The Diary as an Historical Source." *Historical Studies in Education/Revue d'histoire de l'education* 3 (Spring 1991): 93–103.

Semple, Neil. "'The Nurture and Admonition of the Lord': Nineteenth-Century Canadian Methodism's Response to 'Childhood.'" *Histoire sociale/Social History* 14 (May 1981): 157–75.

Seymour, James C. *The Temperance Battle-Field and How to Gain the Day: A Book for the Young of All Ages,, Full of Humourous and Pathetic Stories.* Toronto: Wm Briggs, 1882.

Sheehan, Nancy M. "Philosophy, Pedagogy, and Practice: The IODE and the Schools in Canada, 1900–1945." *Historical Studies in Education/Revue d'histoire de l'education* 2 (Fall 1990): 307–22.

– "Temperance, the WCTU and Education in Alberta, 1905–1930," Ph.D. thesis, University of Calgary, 1980.

– "The WCTU on the Prairies, 1886–1930: An Alberta-Saskatchewan Comparison." *Prairie Forum* 6 (Spring 1981): 17–35.

– "The WCTU and Educational Strategies on the Canadian Prairie." *History of Education Quarterly* 24 (1984): 101–19.

– "Women Helping Women: The WCTU and the Foreign Population of the West, 1905–1930." *International Journal of Women's Studies* 6 (1983): 395–411.

Shelley, Bruce. *Evangelicalism in America.* Grand Rapids: Eerdmans, 1967.

Shiman, Lilian Lewis. "The Band of Hope Movement: Respectable Recreation for Working-Class Children." *Victorian Studies* 17 (September 1973): 49–74.

Simon, Brian. *Studies in the History of Education, 1780–1870.* London: Lawrence & Wishart, 1960.

Sizer, Sandra. *Gospel Hymns and Social Religion: The Rhetoric of Nineteenth-Century Revivalism.* Philadelphia: Temple University Press, 1978.

– "Politics and Apolitical Religion: The Great Urban Revivals of the Late Nineteenth Century." *Church History* 48 (March 1979): 81–98.

Sklar, Kathryn Kish. *Catharine Beecher: A Study in American Domesticity.* New Haven: Yale University Press, 1973.

Smith, Daniel Scott. "Family Limitation, Sexual Control, and Domestic Feminism in Victorian America." In *Clio's Consciousness Raised: New Perspectives on the History of Women,* ed. Mary Hartman and Lois Banner, 119–36. New York: Harper & Row, 1974.

Smith, Timothy L. *Revivalism and Social Reform in Mid Nineteenth-Century America.* New York: Abingdon Press, 1957.

Smith-Rosenberg, Carroll. "Beauty, the Beast, and the Militant Woman: A

Case Study in Sex Roles and Social Stress in Jacksonian America." In *Disorderly Conduct: Visions of Gender in Victorian America,* 109–28. New York: Knopf, 1985.

– "The Cross and the Pedestal: Women, Anti-Ritualism, and the Emergence of the Nineteenth-Century America." In *Disorderly Conduct: Visions of Gender in Victorian America,* 129–64. New York: Knopf, 1985.

– "The Female World of Love and Ritual: Relations between Women in Nineteenth-Century America." In *Disorderly Conduct: Visions of Gender in Victorian America,* 53–76. New York: Knopf, 1985.

– "The New Woman as Androgyne: Social Disorder and Gender Crisis, 1870–1936." In *Disorderly Conduct: Visions of Gender in Victorian America,* 245–96. New York: Knopf, 1985.

– "Puberty to Menopause: The Cycle of Femininity in Nineteenth-Century America." In *Disorderly Conduct: Visions of Gender in Victorian America,* 182–96. New York: Knopf, 1985.

– *Religion and the Rise of the American City: The New York City Mission Movement, 1812–1870.* Ithaca: Cornell University Press, 1971.

Snell, James G. "'The White Life for Two': The Defense of Marriage and Sexual Morality in Canada, 1890–1914." *Social History* 16 (May 1983): 111–28.

Sons of Temperance of North America. *Centennial, Sept. 29th, 1942. The Pioneer Abstinence Order of North America, 1842–1942.* [Halifax, 1942].

Southcott, Jane. "Tonic Sol-fa, Temperance, Sunday Schools and Empire." Paper presented at the combined conference of the Australian and New Zealand History of Education Society and the Canadian History of Education Society/Association canadienne d'histoire de l'education, Melbourne, Australia, 1993.

Le Spectateur (Hull, Quebec). February–July 1890.

Spence, R.E. *Prohibition in Canada.* Toronto: Ontario Branch of the Dominion Alliance, 1919.

Splane, Richard B. *Social Welfare in Ontario, 1791–1893: A Study in Public Welfare Legislation.* Toronto: University of Toronto Press, 1965.

Stansell, Christine. *City of Women: Sex and Class in New York, 1789–1860.* Urbana: University of Illinois Press, 1987.

Stelter, Gilbert A. "The City-Building Process in Canada." In *Shaping the Urban Landscape: Aspects of the Canadian City-Building Process, ed.* Gilbert A. Stelter and Alan F. J. Artibise, 1–29. Ottawa: Carleton University Press, 1982.

Strachey, Ray. *Frances Willard: Her Life and Work.* London, 1912.

Strong-Boag, Veronica. "Canada's Women Doctors: Feminism Constrained." In *A Not Unreasonable Claim,* ed. Linda Kealey, 109–130. Toronto: Canadian Women's Educational Press, 1979.

– "The Parliament of Women: The National Council of Women of Canada, 1893–1929." Ph.D. thesis, University of Toronto, 1975.

– "Pulling in Double Harness or Hauling a Double Load: Women, Work and

Feminism on the Canadian Prairie." *Journal of Canadian Studies* 21 (Autumn 1986): 32–52.

– "'Setting the Stage': National Organization and the Women's Movement in the Late 19th Century." In *The Neglected Majority: Essays in Canadian Women's History*, ed. Susan Mann Trofimenkoff and Alison Prentice, 87–103. Toronto: McClelland & Stewart, 1977.

Sutherland, David. "Fraternalism and the Process of Middle Class Formation: A Case Study of Halifax during the 1840s." Paper presented at the Canadian Historical Association meetings, Calgary, 1994.

Sutherland, Neil. *Children in English-Canadian Society: Framing the Twentieth Century Consensus*. Toronto: University of Toronto Press, 1976.

Sweet, Leonard. "The Evangelical Tradition in America." *The Evangelical Tradition in America*, ed. Leonard Sweet, 1–86. Macon, Ga: Mercer University Press, 1984.

Talmage, T. De Witt. *The Abominations of Modern Society*. London: W. Nicholson & Sons, 1872.

Taylor, John H. *The History of Canadian Cities: Ottawa, An Illustrated History*. Toronto: Lorimer, 1986.

Templar Quarterly. Hamilton: The Templar Publishing House, 1897.

Thompson, E.P. *The Making of the English Working Class*. London: Gollancz, 1963.

Tilly, Louise A., and Joan W. Scott. *Women, Work and Family*. New York: Holt, Rinehart and Winston, 1978.

Tyrrell, Ian R. *Sobering Up: From Temperance to Prohibition in Antebellum America, 1800–1860*. Westport, Conn.: Greenwood Press, 1979.

– *Woman's World, Woman's Empire: The Woman's Christian Temperance Union in International Perspective*. Chapel Hill: University of North Carolina Press, 1991.

Urquhart, M.E., ed.; K.A.H. Buckley, ass. ed. *Historical Statistics of Canada*. Toronto: University of Toronto Press, 1965.

Valverde, Mariana. *The Age of Light, Soap, and Water: Moral Reform in English Canada, 1885–1925*. Toronto: McClelland & Stewart, 1991.

– "'When the Mother of the Race Is Free': Race, Reproduction and Sexuality in First-Wave Feminism." In *Gender Conflicts: New Essays in Women's History*, ed. Franca Iacovetta and Mariana Valverde, 3–26. Toronto: University of Toronto Press, 1922.

Van Die, Marguerite. *An Evangelical Mind: Nathanael Burwash and the Methodist Tradition in Canada, 1839–1918*. Montreal & Kingston: McGill-Queen's University Press, 1989.

Vicinus, Martha. "Introduction." In *Independent Women: Work and Community for Single Women, 1850–1920*, ed. Martha Vicinus, 1–9.

– "The Reformed Boarding Schools: Personal Life and Public Duty." In *Independent Women: Work and Community for Single Women, 1850–1920*, ed.

Martha Vicinus, 163–210. Chicago: University of Chicago Press, 1985.

– Women's Colleges: An Independent Intellectual Life." In *Independent Women: Work and Community for Single Women, 1850–1920,* ed. Martha Vicinus, 121–162. Chicago: University of Chicago Press, 1985.

Walkowitz, Judith. *Prostitution and Victorian Society*. Cambridge: Cambridge University Press, 1980.

Wallace, Elizabeth. "The Origin of the Welfare State in Canada, 1867–1900." *Canadian Journal of Economics and Political Science* 16 (August 1950): 383–93.

Wallace, W. Stewart. *The Memoirs of the Rt. Hon. Sir George Foster*. Toronto: Macmillan, 1933.

Walters, Ronald G. *American Reformers, 1815–1860.* New York: Hill and Wang, 1978.

Ware, Vron. *Beyond the Pale: Women, Racism and History*. London: Verso, 1992.

Warne, Randi R. *Literature as Pulpit: The Christian Social Activism of Nellie L. McClung*. Waterloo: Wilfrid Laurier University Press, 1993.

Warsh, Cheryll Krasnick. "'John Barleycorn Must Die': An Introduction to the Social History of Alcohol." In *Drink in Canada: Historical Essays*, ed. Cheryl Krasnick Warsh, 1–26. Montreal & Kingston: McGill-Queen's University Press, 1993.

– "'Oh, Lord, Pour a Cordial in her Wounded Heart': The Drinking Woman in Victorian and Edwardian Canada." In *Drink in Canada: Historical Essays*, ed. Cheryl Krasnick Warsh, 70–91. Montreal & Kingston: McGill-Queen's University Press, 1993.

Welter, Barbara. "The Feminization of American Religion, 1800–1860." In *Clio's Consciousness Raised: New Perspectives on the History of Women*, ed. Mary Hartman and Lois W. Banner, 137–57. New York: Harper & Row, 1974.

– "She Hath Done What She Could: Protestant Women's Missionary Careers in Nineteenth-Century America." *American Quarterly* 30 (1978): 624–38.

Westfall, William. "The End of the World: An Aspect of Time and Culture in Nineteenth-Century Protestant Culture." *Religion and Culture: Comparative Canadian Studies*, ed. William Westfall, Louis Rousseau, Fernand Harvey, and John Simpson, 72–85. Waterloo: Wilfrid Laurier University Press, 1984.

– *Two Worlds: The Protestant Culture of Nineteenth-Century Ontario.* Montreal & Kingston: McGill-Queen's University Press, 1989.

White, Ronald C., Jr, and Howard C. Hopkins. *The Social Gospel: Religion and Reform in Changing America*. Philadelphia: Temple University Press, 1976.

Willard, Frances E. *Glimpses of Fifty Years.* Chicago: Women's Temperance Publishing Association, 1889.

Wittenmyer, Annie. *History of the Woman's Temperance Crusade*. Chicago: Women's Publishing House, 1882.

Woman's Journal. 1885–1903.

Youmans, Letitia. *Campaign Echoes.* Toronto: Wm Briggs, 1893.

Young, G.M. *Portrait of an Age.* London: Oxford University Press, 1953.

Zimmeck, Meta. "Jobs for the Girls: The Expansion of Clerical Work For Women, 1850–1914." In *Unequal Opportunities: Women's Employment in England, 1800–1918*, ed. Angela V. John, 153–78. Oxford: B. Blackwell, 1988.

Zimmerman, Jonathan. "'The Queen of the Lobby': Mary Hunt, Scientific Temperance, and the Dilemma of Democratic Education in America, 1879–1906." *History of Education Quarterly* 32 (1992): 1–30.

Index